Letter of Transmittal

July 30, 1998

Dear Mr. Chairman:

I have the honor to present to the Board of Governors the Annual Report of the Executive Board for the financial year ended April 30, 1998, in accordance with Article XII, Section 7(a) of the Articles of Agreement of the International Monetary Fund and Section 10 of the IMF's By-Laws. In accordance with Section 20 of the By-Laws, the administrative and capital budgets of the IMF approved by the Executive Board for the financial year ending April 30, 1999 are presented in Chapter XIII. The audited financial statements for the year ended April 30, 1998 of the General Department, the SDR Department, accounts administered by the IMF, and the Staff Retirement Plan and the Supplemental Retirement Benefit Plan, together with reports of the External Audit Committee thereon, are presented in Appendix IX.

Yours sincerely,

Michel Camdessus
Chairman of the Executive Board

Left to right: Shigemitsu Sugisaki, Deputy Managing Director; Stanley Fischer, First Deputy Managing Director; Michel Camdessus, Managing Director; and Alassane D. Ouattara, Deputy Managing Director.

Managing Director and Chairman of the Executive Board
Michel Camdessus

First Deputy Managing Director
Stanley Fischer

Deputy Managing Directors
Alassane D. Ouattara   Shigemitsu Sugisaki

Executive Directors[1]

Karin Lissakers
Barry S. Newman

Bernd Esdar
Wolf-Dieter Donecker

Yukio Yoshimura
Hideaki Ono

Jean-Claude Milleron
Ramon Fernandez

Gus O'Donnell[2]
Jon Shields

Enzo R. Grilli
John Spraos

Thomas A. Bernes
Charles X. O'Loghlin

Kai Aaen Hansen
Olli-Pekka Lehmussaari

Abdulrahman A. Al-Tuwaijri
Sulaiman M. Al-Turki

Dinah Z. Guti
José Pedro de Morais, Jr.

Aleksei V. Mozhin
Andrei Vernikov

Roberto F. Cippa
Wieslaw Szczuka

Abbas Mirakhor
Mohammed Daïri

Alexandre Kafka
Hamid O'Brien

M. R. Sivaraman
A.G. Karunasena

[1]Alternate Executive Directors are indicated in italics.
[2]Effective August 1, 1998, Stephen Pickford replaced Gus O'Donnell.
[3]Effective July 1, 1998, ZHANG Fengming replaced HAN Mingzhi.

EXECUTIVE BOARD AND SENIOR OFFICERS

Senior Officers

Michael Mussa
Economic Counsellor

K. Burke Dillon
Director, Administration Department

Evangelos A. Calamitsis
Director, African Department

Hubert Neiss
Director, Asia and Pacific Department

Michael C. Deppler
Director, European I Department

John Odling-Smee
Director, European II Department

Shailendra J. Anjaria
Director, External Relations Department

Vito Tanzi
Director, Fiscal Affairs Department

Mohsin S. Khan
Director, IMF Institute

François P. Gianviti
General Counsel, Legal Department

Paul Chabrier
Director, Middle Eastern Department

Manuel Guitián
*Director, Monetary and
Exchange Affairs Department*

Jack Boorman
Director, Policy Development and Review Department

Michael Mussa
Director, Research Department

Reinhard Munzberg
Secretary, Secretary's Department

Carol S. Carson
Director, Statistics Department

David Williams
Treasurer, Treasurer's Department

Claudio M. Loser
Director, Western Hemisphere Department

Massimo Russo
Special Advisor to the Managing Director

Warren N. Minami
Director, Bureau of Computing Services

Patrice Guilmard
Acting Director, Bureau of Language Services

Lindsay A. Wolfe
Director, Office of Budget and Planning

Eduard Brau
Director, Office of Internal Audit and Inspection

Kunio Saito
Director, Regional Office for Asia and the Pacific

Christian Brachet
Director, Office in Europe (Paris)

Alan A. Tait
*Director and Special Trade Representative,
Office in Geneva*

J.B. Zulu
*Director and Special Representative to the UN,
Office at the United Nations*

David M. Cheney
Chief, Editorial Division

Willy Kiekens
Johann Prader

J. de Beaufort
Wijnholds
Yuriy G. Yakusha

Juan José Toribio
Javier Guzmán-Calafell

Gregory F. Taylor
Okyu Kwon

A. Shakour Shaalan
*Mohamad Hassan
Elhage*

ZAMANI Abdul
Ghani
Cyrillus Harinowo

ZHANG Zhixiang
HAN Mingzhi[3]

A. Guillermo Zoccali
Nicolás Eyzaguirre

Koffi Yao
*Alexandre Barro
Chambrier*

ANNUAL REPORT 1998   *iii*

Board of Governors, Executive Board, Interim Committee, and Development Committee

The *Board of Governors*, the highest decision-making body of the IMF, consists of one governor and one alternate governor for each member country. The governor is appointed by the member country and is usually the minister of finance or the governor of the central bank. All powers of the IMF are vested in the Board of Governors. The Board of Governors may delegate to the Executive Board all except certain reserved powers. The Board of Governors normally meets once a year.

The *Executive Board* (the Board) is responsible for conducting the day-to-day business of the IMF. It is composed of 24 Directors, who are appointed or elected by member countries or by groups of countries, and the Managing Director, who serves as its Chairman. The Board usually meets several times each week. The Executive Board carries out its work largely on the basis of papers prepared by IMF management and staff. In 1997/98, the Board spent more than half of its time on member country matters (Article IV consultations and reviews and approvals of arrangements) and most of its remaining time on policy issues (such as the world economic outlook exercise, developments in international capital markets, the IMF's financial resources, surveillance, data issues, the debt situation, and issues related to IMF facilities and program design).

The *Interim Committee* of the Board of Governors on the International Monetary System is an advisory body made up of 24 IMF governors, ministers, or other officials of comparable rank, representing the same constituencies as in the IMF's Executive Board. The Interim Committee normally meets twice a year, in April or May, and at the time of the Annual Meeting of the Board of Governors in September or October. Among its responsibilities are to advise and report to the Board of Governors on issues regarding the management and adaptation of the international monetary system, including sudden disturbances that might threaten the international monetary system, and on proposals to amend the Articles of Agreement.

The *Development Committee* (the Joint Ministerial Committee of the Boards of Governors of the Bank and the Fund on the Transfer of Real Resources to Developing Countries) is composed of 24 members—finance ministers or other officials of comparable rank—and generally meets at the same time as the Interim Committee. It advises and reports to the Boards of Governors of the World Bank and the IMF on all aspects of the transfer of real resources to developing countries.

Contents

The following conventions have been used in this Report:

n.a.   to indicate not applicable;

. . .   to indicate that data are not available;

—   to indicate that the figure is zero or less than half the final digit shown or that the item does not exist;

–   between years or months (for example, 1997–98 or January–June) to indicate the years or months covered, including the beginning and ending years or months;

/   between years or months (for example, 1997/98) to indicate a fiscal or financial year.

"Billion" means a thousand million; "trillion" means a thousand billion.

"Basis points" refer to hundredths of 1 percentage point (for example, 25 basis points are equivalent to ¼ of 1 percentage point).

Minor discrepancies between constituent figures and totals are due to rounding.

The 1997/98 financial year began May 1, 1997, and ended April 30, 1998.

All references to dollars are to U.S. dollars unless otherwise noted; as of April 30, 1998, the SDR/U.S. dollar exchange rate was US$1 = SDR 0.742580, and the U.S. dollar/SDR exchange rate was SDR 1 = US$1.34666.

As used in this Report, the term "country" does not in all cases refer to a territorial entity that is a state as understood by international law and practice. As used here, the term also covers some territorial entities that are not states but for which statistical data are maintained on a separate and independent basis.

Asian Financial Crisis Propels IMF Activity to New Levels in 1997/98

The Asian financial crisis that broke out in July 1997 in Thailand, and its subsequent global reverberations, dominated the IMF's work in 1997/98, absorbing an unprecedented amount of time of the Executive Board, management, and staff. The crisis—whose global consequences continued after the end of the financial year—also prompted a record level of IMF lending in 1997/98, adding immediacy to the need to strengthen the financial resources of the institution to enable it to continue playing a fully effective role in the globalized world economy. The crisis also led to the creation of a new lending facility (the Supplemental Reserve Facility); stepped-up work on strengthening the conduct of IMF surveillance; and, more generally, led to the elaboration of a framework for strengthening the architecture of the international monetary system. Separately, the Executive Board undertook an extensive review—drawing on both internal and external assessments—of the IMF's concessional lending facility for low-income countries (the Enhanced Structural Adjustment Facility) and continued its work aimed at ensuring the uninterrupted availability of financial resources for the ESAF. Together with the World Bank and other creditors, the IMF made important headway in implementing the initiative to reduce the external debt burden of a number of heavily indebted poor countries (the HIPC Initiative).

* * *

The Asian financial crisis had a major impact on the scale of *IMF financial assistance* in 1997/98. During the year, member countries drew SDR 19.0 billion (\$25.6 billion)[1] from the IMF's General Resources Account in the credit tranches—nearly four times the level of the previous year. The IMF approved nine new Stand-By Arrangements, with total commitments of SDR 27.3 billion, and four new Extended Arrangements, with total commitments of SDR 2.8 billion. The largest Stand-By Arrangements were for Korea (which also made use of the new Supplemental Reserve Facility), Indonesia, and Thailand; the largest Extended Arrangement was for Argentina. In addition, the IMF approved eight new ESAF Arrangements with commitments totaling SDR 1.7 billion. As of

---

[1]As of April 30, 1998, SDR 1 = \$1.34666.

April 30, 1998, 14 Stand-By Arrangements, 13 Extended Arrangements, and 33 ESAF Arrangements were in effect with member countries. Net of repayments of previous drawings, total IMF credit outstanding rose to a record SDR 56 billion ($75.4 billion) as of April 30, 1998, compared with SDR 40.5 billion ($55.3 billion)[2] a year earlier.

In December 1997, the Executive Board established the Supplemental Reserve Facility to provide additional financial assistance to members facing exceptional balance of payments difficulties attributable to a large short-term financing need resulting from a sudden and disruptive loss of market confidence.

As a result of the large new demands on the IMF's resources in 1997/98, its net uncommitted usable resources (adjusted to meet the requirement to maintain adequate working balances of currencies) declined to SDR 22.6 billion at the end of April 1998 from SDR 43.5 billion a year earlier. Over the same period, the IMF's liquid liabilities rose sharply—reflecting an increase in members' reserve tranche positions—and its liquidity ratio fell to 44.8 percent as of April 30, 1998, from 120.5 percent a year earlier.

In January 1998, the IMF's Board of Governors adopted the Executive Board's recommendation that total IMF quotas be increased by 45 percent (to SDR 212 billion from SDR 146 billion) under the Eleventh General Review of Quotas. The increase will take effect after members having not less than 85 percent of total quotas as of December 28, 1997, have consented to their quota increases.

* * *

The IMF's work on *surveillance issues* intensified following the outbreak and spread of the financial crisis to other Asian economies and the subsequent pressures on other emerging market economies. Surveillance was also intensified in recognition that promoting good governance, making budgets more transparent, improving data collection and disclosure, and strengthening financial sectors are increasingly important if countries are to establish and maintain private sector confidence and lay the groundwork for sustained growth.

In a preliminary review in March 1998 of the *implications for IMF surveillance of the Asian financial crisis,* the Executive Board drew five lessons:

- effective surveillance depends critically on the timely availability of accurate information;
- the focus of surveillance has to extend even further beyond short-term macroeconomic issues, yet remain appropriately selective;
- surveillance at the country level should pay more explicit attention to policy interdependence and the risks of contagion;
- the crucial role of credibility in restoring market confidence underscores the importance of transparency; and

---

[2]As of April 30, 1997, SDR 1 = $1.36553.

- effective surveillance depends fundamentally on the willingness of members to take the IMF's advice.

In July 1997, the Executive Board adopted *guidelines clarifying the IMF's role in governance issues.* The guidelines call for a more comprehensive treatment, in the context of both bilateral consultations with members under Article IV and IMF-supported programs, of governance issues within the IMF's purview and expertise; for evenhanded treatment of member countries; and for enhanced collaboration with other institutions—notably the World Bank—to make better use of complementary areas of expertise. The guidelines identify two areas in which the IMF can make a particular contribution: improving the management of public resources and supporting the development and maintenance of a transparent and stable regulatory environment conducive to efficient private sector activities.

Similarly, in an effort to enhance the accountability and credibility of members' fiscal policies, the Interim Committee, at its April 1998 meeting, adopted a *Code of Good Practices on Fiscal Transparency: Declaration on Principles.*

In December 1997, the Executive Board reviewed members' progress in *providing data to the IMF for surveillance* and saw scope for improvement. Recent experience also suggested the need to complement traditional "core" indicators with data on reserve-related liabilities, central bank derivative transactions, private sector external debt, and prudential banking system indicators.

To guide members in *disseminating data to the public,* the Executive Board endorsed a two-tier approach: the Special Data Dissemination Standard, established in March 1996 for countries that have or might seek access to international financial markets, and a less ambitious General Data Dissemination System, approved in December 1997, for all member countries.

The importance of *strengthening members' financial sectors* was a recurring theme of Board discussions in 1997/98—including the importance of enhancing IMF and World Bank collaboration so that emerging financial sector problems are promptly identified, each institution takes the lead in its own areas of responsibility, and the IMF's macroeconomic analysis and the Bank's sectoral policy recommendations are fully coordinated.

* * *

To enhance the transparency of its surveillance, the IMF in May 1997 introduced Press/Public Information Notices—following the conclusion of Article IV consultations. PINs summarize the Executive Board's assessment of member countries' economic policies and prospects. Of the 136 Article IV consultations in 1997/98, 77 resulted in the issuance of PINs. PINs appear on the IMF's website, http://www.imf.org, and are published three times a year as *IMF Economic Reviews.*

* * *

At the Annual Meetings in Hong Kong SAR in September 1997, the Interim Committee issued a *Statement on the Liberalization of Capital Movements Under*

an Amendment of the IMF's Articles of Agreement. The statement invited the
Executive Board to complete its work on a proposed amendment to make the liberalization of capital movements one of the purposes of the IMF and extend, as
needed, the IMF's jurisdiction in this area. In 1997/98, the Board considered various aspects of such an amendment and, to help inform its work, sponsored a
high-level seminar in March 1998 to elicit views from a wide range of private and
official observers outside the IMF. At its April 1998 meeting, the Interim Committee noted the progress made thus far and the provisional agreement reached
by the Executive Board on that part of the amendment dealing with the IMF's
purposes. The Committee asked the Board to pursue with determination its work
on other aspects, including policy issues, with the aim of submitting an appropriate amendment of the Articles for the Committee's consideration as soon as
possible.

* * *

Since the Mexican financial crisis of 1994–95, the IMF has taken a number of
steps to enhance the functioning of the international monetary system. The
heightened challenges posed by the ongoing globalization of financial markets—
as exemplified by the Asian financial crisis—highlighted the need for further
efforts in this direction. In its continuing discussions of additional initiatives to
strengthen the architecture of the international monetary system, the Executive
Board in 1997/98 identified the following imperatives:

- improving international and domestic financial systems;
- strengthening IMF surveillance further;
- promoting the wider availability and greater transparency of information
  regarding economic data and policies;
- reinforcing the central role of the IMF in crisis management; and
- introducing more effective procedures for involving the private sector in
  forestalling or resolving financial crises.

The Interim Committee, at its April 1998 meeting, endorsed these objectives
and asked the Executive Board to report on its work in these areas at the Committee's next meeting in October 1998.

* * *

Since the mid-1980s, the IMF has provided concessional financing through the
Enhanced Structural Adjustment Facility (ESAF) and its predecessor, the Structural Adjustment Facility (SAF), to respond to the balance of payments difficulties
confronting many of the world's poorest developing countries. As of April 30,
1998, SDR 6.4 billion ($8.6 billion) had been disbursed under 71 ESAF
Arrangements to 48 countries, and SDR 1.8 billion ($2.4 billion) disbursed
under SAF arrangements. For the *continuation of the ESAF*—and to finance the
IMF's contribution to the HIPC Initiative—the Executive Board took steps in
1997/98 to mobilize financing from bilateral contributions and from the IMF's

own resources. In April 1998, Uganda became the first country to reach its completion point under the HIPC Initiative. Uganda will receive from its creditors the equivalent of about $350 million in net present value terms, which is estimated to reduce its nominal debt service by nearly $650 million; the IMF's assistance will reduce the present value of its claims on Uganda by about $70 million. Five additional countries (Bolivia, Burkina Faso, Côte d'Ivoire, Guyana, and Mozambique) also became eligible for assistance that would reduce their nominal debt service by about $5 billion.

Two in-depth evaluations of the ESAF were undertaken in 1997/98 (both of which have been published): an internal review by IMF staff of the record of 10 years of ESAF-supported programs, and an evaluation under the guidance of the Executive Board by outside experts—the first of its kind—of certain aspects of ESAF-supported programs. Both assessments confirmed the value of the ESAF in assisting low-income countries, while identifying areas for improvement and further consideration.

* * *

Member countries' demand for *IMF technical assistance and training* remained strong in 1997/98. Assistance provided by IMF staff and external advisors averaged about 300 person-years and accounted for about 17 percent of total IMF administrative expenses.

* * *

In December 1997, the IMF opened a Regional Office for Asia and the Pacific in Tokyo.

* * *

In December 1997, the Republic of Palau became the IMF's 182nd member.

Main Developments in the World Economy in 1997/98

The dominant developments in the world economy and for the IMF in 1997/98 were the Asian financial crisis and its repercussions. The crisis broke out in July 1997 in Thailand when, following several episodes of exchange market pressure and reserve losses, the authorities abandoned the peg of the baht to the U.S. dollar. The forced exit from the U.S. dollar peg, in turn, raised doubts about the viability of exchange rate arrangements elsewhere. Spillover effects were soon felt in other countries in the region, especially Indonesia, Malaysia, and the Philippines, exposing underlying structural weaknesses in these economies. Measures to tighten liquidity conditions in Indonesia failed to stem the growing exchange market pressures, and the Indonesian authorities allowed the rupiah to float in mid-August. The situation worsened markedly over the next two months and spillover effects spread to other countries. In Hong Kong SAR, strong pressures on the Hong Kong dollar in October led to a surge in interest rates, followed by a substantial equity market decline. In Korea, downward pressures on the won intensified in late October, following the attack on the Hong Kong dollar, and equity prices fell sharply, reflecting diminished confidence about economic prospects and the growing difficulties encountered by the financial sector in rolling over external loans. After making efforts to defend the won, the Korean authorities widened the daily fluctuation band from 4½ percent to 20 percent in late November, and subsequently requested financial support from the IMF (see Chapter V).

The unfolding crisis, which saw exchange rates and equity prices plunge dramatically (Figure 1), was one of the worst in the postwar period. It was centered in countries that had long pursued prudent fiscal policies and enjoyed high saving rates. What went wrong? The key elements, especially in Thailand, were a buildup of inflationary pressures, manifested in large external deficits and inflated property and stock markets; maintenance for too long of pegged exchange rate regimes, which came to be viewed as implicit guarantees of exchange value, encouraging unhedged external borrowing—often at short maturities; lack of timely and relevant data and information; lax enforcement of prudential rules, as well as weaknesses in the institutional structures of supervision in financial systems; government-directed lending practices that led to a sharp deterioration in the quality of banks' loan portfolios, in turn reducing the scope for raising interest rates; and problems of governance that, together with political uncertainties, worsened the crisis of confidence. External elements also played a role: foreign investors underestimated the risks associated with their search for higher yields during a period of sluggish economic growth in Japan and Europe and low international interest rates, and contagion effects of the crisis led to an excessive devaluation of the affected currencies.

Global Overview

The financial turmoil that erupted in southeast Asia in mid-1997 quickly began to take its toll on demand and activity in the affected countries. It also began to have a dampening impact on global growth late in the year and in early 1998. In 1997 as a whole, however, world output growth continued at about 4 percent (Figure 2), with slower growth in Africa, Asia, and the Middle East offset by faster expansion in the industrial countries, the developing countries of the Western Hemisphere, and the countries in transition (Table 1). Growth in the volume of world trade rebounded in 1997 to 9½ percent, matching the expansion of 1995—the most rapid rate for two decades. The acceleration was widely shared between the advanced and developing country groups, but the growth in trade of the transition economies slowed somewhat.

Associated with the Asian crisis was a dramatic drop in net private capital flows to emerging market economies (Table 2). Such flows had reached a record $240 billion in 1996, with Asia attracting more than 40 percent of the total. After rising further in the first half of 1997, net flows fell steeply, as the crisis in Asia deepened, and for the year as a whole were about $70 billion less than in 1996. Net flows to the developing countries of Asia fell by more than $60 billion to about $40 billion—the lowest inflow since 1992. The devel-

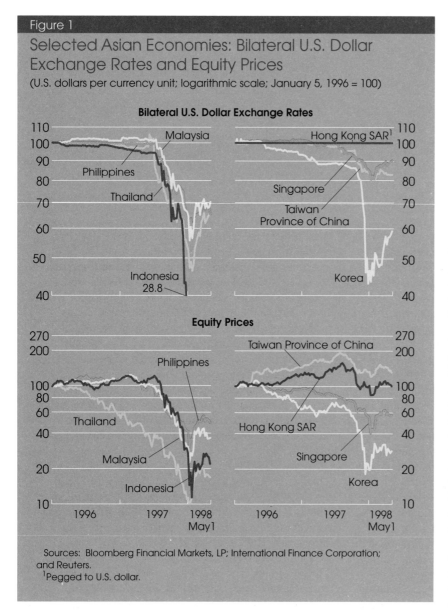

Figure 1

Selected Asian Economies: Bilateral U.S. Dollar Exchange Rates and Equity Prices

(U.S. dollars per currency unit; logarithmic scale; January 5, 1996 = 100)

Bilateral U.S. Dollar Exchange Rates

Malaysia
Philippines
Thailand
Indonesia 28.8

Hong Kong SAR[1]
Singapore
Taiwan Province of China
Korea

Equity Prices

Philippines
Thailand
Malaysia
Indonesia

Taiwan Province of China
Hong Kong SAR
Singapore
Korea

1996   1997   1998 May1

Sources: Bloomberg Financial Markets, LP; International Finance Corporation; and Reuters.
[1]Pegged to U.S. dollar.

pluses. In 1997 as a whole, a widening of current account deficits among a number of Latin American countries, reflecting the increase in foreign direct investment in the region, was the main counterpart to the narrowing of deficits in the Asian emerging markets (Table 3). In late 1997 and early 1998, however, a number of advanced economies—most notably the United States—and the oil-exporting countries began to show signs of deteriorating current account balances.

Consumer price inflation declined further in each of the main country groups in 1997 (see Figure 2). The decline was helped by the weakness of primary commodity prices, including those for oil. In early 1998, oil prices fell further; indeed, by April 1998, in SDR terms, oil prices were about 31 percent lower than a year earlier, while non-oil commodity prices had fallen by 20 percent over the same period. To some extent, the declines reflected the reduced demand for commodities in the countries embroiled in the Asian crisis; the sharp depreciation of these countries' currencies may also have led to reductions in the foreign currency prices of their commodity exports.

The redirection of financial flows toward the mature markets following the onset of the crisis, together with prospects for lower inflation, contributed to significant declines in medium- and long-term interest rates in the industrial countries in late 1997 and early 1998—in some cases to 50-year lows. This easing of financial conditions, particularly in North America and in western Europe, contributed, in turn, to further gains in equity markets, with many indices reaching new peaks. These developments helped support the growth of domestic demand in industrial countries at the same time that net exports began to be adversely affected by the Asian crisis.

In foreign exchange markets, after considerable initial strengthening during 1997/98, the yen experienced strong selling pressures for most of the period, reflecting market concerns about progress in Japan's economic recovery. After falling to ¥127 per dollar at the end of April 1997, the yen rebounded sharply in May and early June to reach a high of ¥110. With the recov-

oping countries of the Middle East and Europe saw a smaller decline in inflows, while flows to the Western Hemisphere, Africa, and the countries in transition actually increased. In the first quarter of 1998, net capital inflows to emerging market countries remained close to their already reduced levels of late 1997.

The sharp declines in private capital flows to emerging market economies in Asia, although cushioned to some extent by an increase in official financing flows, required substantial adjustments in these countries' external positions. For the Asian developing countries, taken together, the current account deficit narrowed by almost $30 billion in 1997. And by early 1998, the countries most affected by the crisis—Indonesia, Korea, and Thailand—were each running current account surery losing momentum by midyear and with concerns about the domestic financial sector, the yen subsequently weakened anew; by the end of April 1998, it had depreciated to ¥132 per dollar. Although the deutsche mark depreciated further against the dollar during 1997 and in early 1998, the depreciation in nominal effective terms was moderate. The pound sterling rose steeply in 1997 and in early 1998, owing mainly to short-term cyclical factors.

Advanced Economies

Cyclical divergences remained sizable among the advanced economies in 1997. Economic activity was strong in the United States and the United Kingdom, with both economies operating close to capacity and unemployment rates at their lowest in many years. The major economies of continental Europe saw a strengthening of growth in the second half of 1997 and in early 1998, but significant margins of slack remained in most of these countries. The Japanese economy faltered after the first quarter of 1997, then slipped into recession in the fourth quarter of the year, with output contracting in the first quarter of 1998 by 5.3 percent at an annual rate. The impact of the Asian crisis on the advanced economies varied depending on two main factors. The first was the importance of trade and financial links with the crisis economies; these links were generally closest in the Asia-Pacific region.[3] The second was the economy's starting position. The dampening effects of the crisis had a relatively large adverse impact on Japan, where activity and confidence were already weak; by contrast, these effects most likely helped contain inflationary pressures in countries facing the risk of overheating.

After a strengthening of growth in 1996 following four years of weak recovery, self-sustaining growth seemed to be taking hold in Japan in the early part of 1997. But activity declined sharply in the second quarter and picked up only weakly during the remainder of the year. The loss of growth before the middle of the year was attributable primarily to domestic factors, including an increase in the consumption tax in April 1997, cuts in public spending, and financial sector fragility. In the latter part of the year, concerns about the Asian crisis and about the domestic financial sector, together with a renewed softening of equity prices, contributed to continued weakness in domestic spending. For the year as a whole, GDP grew by ¾ of 1 percent. The Japanese authorities responded to these developments by announcing a large fiscal stimulus package in April 1998 and by taking steps to address

[3]For example, in 1996, trade with the Asian newly industrialized and developing economies represented 5 percent of GDP in Japan, compared with 1½ percent to 3 percent in the major industrial economies of Europe and North America.

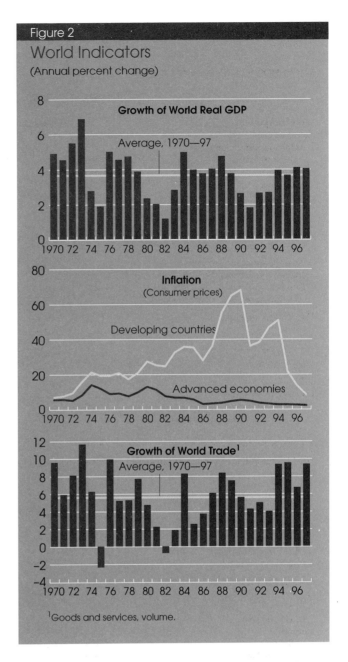

Figure 2

World Indicators
(Annual percent change)

Growth of World Real GDP

Average, 1970—97

Inflation
(Consumer prices)

Developing countries

Advanced economies

Growth of World Trade[1]

Average, 1970—97

[1]Goods and services, volume.

banking problems, including making public money available to strengthen deposit insurance and boost bank capital. Nevertheless, uncertainties remained about how the banking sector measures would be implemented. In July 1998, the Japanese authorities announced a series of further banking sector initiatives in a Comprehensive Plan for Financial Revitalization, including a "bridge bank" facility intended to facilitate the resolution of failed institutions and measures to strengthen bank supervision and increase transparency.

In the other advanced economies in the Asia-Pacific region, cyclical positions were generally stronger than in Japan when the Asian crisis erupted. In Australia,

Table 1
Overview of the World Economy
(Annual percent change unless otherwise noted)

	1994	1995	1996	1997
World output	**3.9**	**3.6**	**4.1**	**4.1**
Advanced economies	3.1	2.5	2.7	3.0
Major industrial countries	2.8	2.0	2.5	2.8
United States	3.5	2.0	2.8	3.8
Japan	0.6	1.5	3.9	0.9
Germany	2.7	1.8	1.4	2.2
France	2.8	2.1	1.5	2.4
Italy	2.2	2.9	0.7	1.5
United Kingdom	4.3	2.7	2.2	3.3
Canada	3.9	2.2	1.2	3.8
Other advanced economies	4.5	4.3	3.8	4.0
Memorandum				
Industrial countries	2.9	2.1	2.5	2.9
European Union	2.9	2.5	1.7	2.6
Newly industrialized Asian economies	7.6	7.3	6.4	6.1
Developing countries	6.8	6.0	6.6	5.8
Africa	2.5	3.0	5.5	3.2
Asia	9.6	9.0	8.3	6.7
ASEAN-4[1]	7.7	8.1	7.1	3.9
Middle East and Europe	0.7	3.6	4.9	4.4
Western Hemisphere	5.1	1.2	3.5	5.0
Countries in transition	−7.6	−1.3	−0.1	1.7
Central and eastern Europe	−3.0	1.4	1.5	2.7
Excluding Belarus and Ukraine	3.0	5.3	3.6	3.1
Russia	−12.6	−4.0	−2.8	0.4
Transcaucasus and central Asia	−10.2	−4.3	1.5	2.2
World trade volume (goods and services)	**9.3**	**9.5**	**6.6**	**9.4**
Imports				
Advanced economies	9.7	8.9	6.4	8.6
Developing countries	7.1	11.9	9.3	12.1
Countries in transition	7.8	18.3	7.6	5.4
Exports				
Advanced economies	8.8	8.8	5.9	9.8
Developing countries	13.2	10.6	8.7	10.8
Countries in transition	8.3	12.3	4.9	3.5
Commodity prices				
Oil[2]				
In SDRs	−7.8	1.9	24.3	−0.9
In U.S. dollars	−5.5	8.0	18.9	−6.0
Nonfuel[3]				
In SDRs	10.8	2.1	3.1	1.6
In U.S. dollars	13.6	8.2	−1.3	−3.7
Consumer prices				
Advanced economies	2.6	2.5	2.4	2.1
Developing countries	50.7	21.7	13.7	8.5
Countries in transition	268.4	124.1	41.4	27.8
Six-month LIBOR (in percent)[4]				
On U.S. dollar deposits	5.1	6.1	5.6	5.9
On Japanese yen deposits	2.4	1.3	0.7	0.7
On deutsche mark deposits	5.3	4.6	3.3	3.4

[1]Indonesia, Malaysia, the Philippines, and Thailand.
[2]Simple average of spot prices of U.K. Brent, Dubai, and West Texas Intermediate crude oil. The average price of oil in U.S. dollars a barrel was $19.18 in 1997; the assumed price is $14.59 in 1998 and $15.94 in 1999.
[3]Average, based on world commodity export weights.
[4]London interbank offered rate.

growth strengthened during 1997 against a background of subdued inflation, a budget near balance, and a reduced current account deficit. Partly as a result of the Asian crisis, however, the Australian dollar depreciated substantially against the currencies of other industrial countries late in the year. In Hong Kong SAR, by contrast, competitiveness deteriorated as a result of regional currency depreciations, and interest rates rose sporadically to relatively high levels in the face of intermittent pressures on the currency. These developments, together with the effects of the regional crisis on trade and confidence, rapidly reduced the overheating pressure that had emerged in early 1997 and led to a sharp contraction of activity in early 1998. As in Hong Kong SAR, a strong financial sector helped limit the contagion of the regional crisis in Singapore and Taiwan Province of China, although in both significant currency depreciation and marked increases in domestic interest rates occurred.

The advanced economies of North America and Europe were less adversely affected by the Asian crisis. U.S. economic performance in 1997 was exceptionally strong, with GDP growing at 3¾ percent, the fastest growth in nine years. Furthermore, inflation in terms of the GDP deflator was the lowest in 32 years, unemployment fell to its lowest level in 24 years, and the federal budget was virtually in balance for the first time since the early 1970s. The strength of the U.S. economy provided essential support for global growth in the face of the Asian crisis. The weakening of external demand associated with the Asian crisis, and the strength of the U.S. dollar, dampened potential inflationary pressures in the U.S. economy and shifted the balance of arguments against monetary tightening in late 1997 and early 1998. Canada also experienced strong growth in 1997, but with significant slack remaining, inflation eased further. A considerable widening of the current account

Table 2
Net Capital Flows to Developing Countries, Countries in Transition, and Newly Industrialized Economies[1]
(Billions of U.S. dollars)

	1984–89[2]	1990–96[2]	1994	1995	1996	1997
Total						
Net private capital flows[3]	15.2	148.1	160.5	192.0	240.8	173.7
Net direct investment	12.9	63.1	84.3	96.0	114.9	138.2
Net portfolio investment	4.7	54.1	87.8	23.5	49.7	42.9
Other net investment	−2.5	30.9	−11.7	72.5	76.2	−7.3
Net official flows	23.9	15.3	−2.5	34.9	−9.7	27.3
Change in reserves[4]	−13.8	−81.2	−77.2	−120.5	−115.9	−54.7
Developing countries						
Net private capital flows[3]	18.2	131.2	136.6	156.1	207.9	154.7
Net direct investment	12.1	56.8	75.4	84.3	105.0	119.4
Net portfolio investment	4.2	49.3	85.0	20.6	42.9	40.6
Other net investment	1.9	25.1	−23.8	51.2	60.0	−5.3
Net official flows	25.8	15.6	9.1	27.4	−3.4	15.8
Change in reserves[4]	5.8	−55.7	−42.4	−65.6	−103.4	−55.2
Africa						
Net private capital flows[3]	3.6	4.4	10.6	13.8	4.5	8.9
Net direct investment	1.1	2.9	3.6	4.2	5.3	7.7
Net portfolio investment	−0.8	−0.2	0.5	1.4	−0.3	2.6
Other net investment	3.3	1.6	6.5	8.1	−0.6	−1.3
Net official flows	5.1	7.1	8.1	5.2	6.5	6.7
Change in reserves[4]	0.2	−1.9	−4.4	−1.4	−6.4	−11.3
Asia						
Net private capital flows[3]	13.0	55.9	63.1	91.8	102.2	38.5
Net direct investment	4.5	32.2	43.4	49.7	58.5	55.4
Net portfolio investment	1.5	6.8	11.3	10.8	10.2	−2.2
Other net investment	7.0	16.9	8.3	31.3	33.5	−14.7
Net official flows	7.7	8.4	6.2	5.1	9.3	17.7
Change in reserves[4]	−2.1	−29.0	−39.7	−29.0	−48.9	−17.2
Middle East and Europe						
Net private capital flows[3]	1.7	25.2	15.5	14.8	20.7	16.1
Net direct investment	1.1	3.0	4.2	5.1	4.3	5.1
Net portfolio investment	4.4	12.8	12.5	8.4	7.9	6.8
Other net investment	−3.8	9.4	−1.2	1.3	8.6	4.2
Net official flows	4.8	−1.8	−1.2	−4.8	−5.8	−1.3
Change in reserves[4]	7.2	−6.4	−3.1	−9.4	−21.2	−14.3
Western Hemisphere						
Net private capital flows[3]	−0.2	45.7	47.4	35.7	80.5	91.1
Net direct investment	5.3	18.7	24.3	25.3	36.9	51.2
Net portfolio investment	−0.9	29.9	60.6	−0.1	25.2	33.5
Other net investment	−4.6	−2.8	−37.5	10.5	18.5	6.5
Net official flows	8.2	1.8	−4.0	22.0	−13.4	−7.3
Change in reserves[4]	0.5	−18.4	4.7	−25.9	−27.0	−12.3
Countries in transition						
Net private capital flows[3]	−1.0	12.8	18.4	29.8	21.3	34.5
Net direct investment	−0.2	6.3	5.4	13.2	13.1	18.2
Net portfolio investment	—	2.0	4.1	2.9	2.2	7.3
Other net investment	−0.8	4.6	8.9	13.6	5.9	9.0
Net official flows	0.2	0.5	−11.0	8.4	−5.5	0.8
Change in reserves[4]	−3.6	−7.8	−8.5	−35.9	0.4	−6.2
Newly industrialized economies[5]						
Net private capital flows[3]	−2.0	4.1	5.5	6.1	11.7	−15.4
Net direct investment	1.0	0.1	3.5	−1.5	−3.2	0.6
Net portfolio investment	0.5	2.8	−1.2	0.0	4.6	−5.0
Other net investment	−3.6	1.2	3.2	7.6	10.3	−11.1
Net official flows	−2.0	−0.8	−0.6	−0.9	−0.8	10.7
Change in reserves[4]	−16.0	−17.7	−26.3	−19.0	−12.9	6.7

[1]Net capital flows comprise net direct investment, net portfolio investment, and other long- and short-term net investment flows, including official and private borrowing.

[2]Annual averages.

[3]Because of data limitations, "other net investment" may include some official flows.

[4]A minus sign indicates an increase.

[5]Hong Kong SAR, Korea, Singapore, Taiwan Province of China, and Israel.

Table 3
Selected Economies: Current Account Positions
(Percent of GDP)

	1995	1996	1997
Advanced economies			
Major industrial countries			
United States	–1.8	–1.9	–2.1
Japan	2.2	1.4	2.2
Germany	–1.0	–0.6	–0.3
France	0.7	1.3	2.7
Italy	2.3	3.2	2.9
United Kingdom	–0.5	–0.1	0.3
Canada	–1.0	0.4	–2.0
Other advanced economies			
Australia	–5.6	–4.0	–3.4
Austria	–2.0	–1.8	–1.8
Finland	4.1	3.8	5.3
Greece	–2.1	–2.6	–2.9
Hong Kong SAR[1]	–3.9	–1.3	–1.5
Ireland	2.8	2.0	1.8
Israel	–5.6	–5.6	–3.4
Korea	–2.0	–4.9	–2.0
New Zealand	–3.7	–4.0	–7.0
Norway	3.3	7.1	5.5
Singapore	16.8	15.7	15.2
Spain	0.2	0.3	0.5
Sweden	2.1	2.5	3.1
Switzerland	6.9	7.3	8.3
Taiwan Province of China	2.1	4.0	2.6
Memorandum			
European Union	0.6	1.1	1.4
Developing countries			
Algeria	–5.3	2.7	6.7
Argentina	–1.5	–1.9	–3.8
Brazil	–2.5	–3.1	–4.1
Cameroon	–0.4	–2.4	–1.3
Chile	–2.1	–5.4	–5.3
China	0.2	0.9	2.4
Côte d'Ivoire	–6.0	–4.8	–4.5
Egypt	2.3	–0.3	0.3
India	–1.6	–1.2	–1.5
Indonesia	–3.3	–3.3	–2.6
Malaysia	–10.0	–4.9	–4.8
Mexico	–0.5	–0.6	–1.8
Nigeria	–3.7	2.4	0.4
Pakistan	–3.4	–6.5	–6.0
Philippines	–4.4	–4.7	–5.2
Saudi Arabia	–4.2	0.2	0.2
South Africa	–2.0	–1.3	–1.5
Thailand	–8.0	–7.9	–2.0
Turkey	–0.6	–1.5	–1.7
Uganda	–2.5	–1.8	–0.9
Countries in transition			
Czech Republic	–2.7	–7.6	–6.3
Hungary	–5.7	–3.8	–2.2
Poland[2]	3.3	–1.0	–3.2
Russia	1.3	0.5	–0.3

[1]Includes only goods and nonfactor services.
[2]Based on data for the current balance, including a surplus on unrecorded trade transactions, as estimated by IMF staff.

deficit, in part owing to weak global commodity markets, contributed to downward pressures on the Canadian dollar. Official interest rates were raised in late 1997 and in January 1998, mainly to offset the consequences of the currency depreciation for monetary conditions.

European countries' cyclical positions continued to diverge notably in 1997 and early 1998. In the United Kingdom, output grew by 3¼ percent in 1997, and unemployment fell by year-end to 5 percent—a 17-year low. In Germany, France, and Italy, growth strengthened moderately in 1997 after faltering in the two preceding years. Unemployment rates remained high in all three countries but declined somewhat in France beginning in mid-1997 and in Germany in early 1998. In Germany, growth was driven mainly by continued buoyancy in exports; however, machinery and equipment investment and, subsequently, demand for consumer products picked up. The recovery in France, which also relied heavily on exports, became better balanced, with a pickup in domestic demand emerging in the second half of 1997. Despite a large fiscal correction, growth in Italy also firmed in 1997, with the pickup sustained by a recovery of private consumption, a strengthening of export growth, and a replenishment of inventories. Inflation was less than 2 percent in Germany, France, and Italy in 1997.

Elsewhere in continental Europe—Denmark, Finland, Ireland, Luxembourg, the Netherlands, Norway, Portugal, and Spain—economic growth continued strong in 1997 after periods of sluggishness; more convincing expansions emerged in Austria, Belgium, and Sweden. In some of these cases, important structural reforms adopted in earlier years underpinned growth, especially with respect to promoting greater flexibility of labor markets. Subdued growth in Switzerland continued a period of stagnation that has spanned almost five years, but activity picked up in the first quarter of 1998. Inflation in these countries remained fairly uniformly low.

In March 1998, the European Commission determined that 11 of the 15 EU member states had qualified to participate in European Economic and Monetary Union (EMU) in 1999. The Commission based its recommendation (which included as input the European Monetary Institute's convergence report) on its assessment of the countries having met the convergence criteria for 1997 as outlined in the Maastricht Treaty for inflation, public finances, interest rates, and exchange rates. Of the other four EU countries, Denmark, Sweden, and the United Kingdom had indicated that they did not wish to participate immediately in EMU; the Greek government aimed to join EMU in 2001. In March 1998, the drachma joined the exchange rate mechanism (ERM) of the EU, with an announced central parity against the European currency unit (ecu) that implied a depreciation of 12½ percent; at the same time, the Irish pound was revalued by 3 percent in terms of its central parity.

Developing Countries

A number of developing countries experienced contagion in their financial markets from the Asian crisis during 1997, and many others began to feel other economic effects from the crisis around the turn of the year, including generally higher risk premiums on foreign credits. These influences aggravated a number of other problems limiting growth, such as loss of competitiveness, lower commodity prices, and domestic and external imbalances. In the developing countries as a group, economic growth slowed to 5¾ percent in 1997 from about 6½ percent in 1996. The slowdown was significant in Asia, but most marked in Africa (Figure 3). In the developing countries of the Western Hemisphere, in contrast, growth in 1997 was actually stronger than in the previous two years but weakened in the first quarter of 1998. The slower growth was the result of spillovers from the Asian crisis and policy measures to reduce vulnerability to adverse shifts in investor sentiment and to widening current account deficits.

In the Asian region, financial markets in China remained relatively immune to the contagion effects of the crisis, reflecting the country's appropriate macroeconomic policies undertaken since 1993, the fact that its capital inflows consisted mainly of direct investment with limited vehicles for financial speculation, and its large foreign exchange reserves. While China's real exchange rate appreciated somewhat as a result of the currency depreciations of its Asian trading partners, its trade position remained strong and the current account continued in surplus. The authorities remained committed to not devaluing the renminbi, a policy critical to restoring stability in the region. Also, inflation remained low following the sharp drop in 1997. In India, output growth declined to about 6 percent in 1997 from about 7½ percent in 1996. The rupee weakened against the dollar in late 1997, partly because of spillovers from the regional crisis, but its exchange value was little changed on a real multilateral basis. In Pakistan, the government adopted a program to strengthen macroeconomic policies and implemented structural reforms following the widening of macroeconomic imbalances and the threat of a foreign exchange crisis in late 1996 and early 1997.

In Latin America, consumer price inflation declined in Brazil to 4¼ percent in 1997, while output growth at 3 percent remained much the same as in the previous year. In response to spillovers from Asia, the authorities tightened monetary and fiscal policies significantly in October and November 1997, and thereby restored confidence and halted the drain of foreign exchange reserves. In Argentina, output grew by a robust 8½

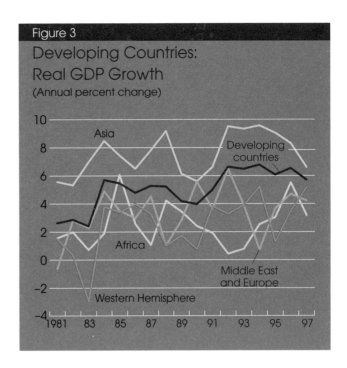

Figure 3

Developing Countries: Real GDP Growth
(Annual percent change)

percent, while prices remained broadly stable; as in Brazil, financial market pressures emerged in October, with a significant stock market correction and widening spreads on sovereign debt. In Mexico, the Asian crisis led to a marked increase in exchange market and interest rate volatility. A substantial temporary increase in interest rates helped stabilize the exchange rate, but the peso fell against the dollar in February 1998. In Chile, the peso came under pressure in December but stabilized by late January after moderate foreign exchange market intervention and a sizable increase in interest rates.

For the Middle East and Europe region, the direct spillovers from the Asian crisis were limited, with temporary declines in equity prices in some countries and a widening of interest spreads on internationally traded debt. In the Islamic Republic of Iran, real GDP growth slowed to 3¼ percent in 1997 from 4¾ percent in 1996, reflecting stagnant non-oil exports, cutbacks in government capital expenditure associated with a decline in oil revenue, and delays in structural reforms. In Turkey, growth continued close to 7 percent in 1997, while in Egypt successful efforts at macroeconomic stabilization and structural reform in recent years helped growth pick up to 5 percent. Jordan continued to reap the benefits of successful implementation of stabilization and reform policies, with continued robust growth in output, further declines in inflation, and a narrowing current account deficit.

Economic growth in Africa in 1997 was just 3¼ percent. The disappointing outcome mainly reflected the impact on a number of countries of poor weather, declines in commodity prices, and, in a few cases, armed conflicts. Among the largest countries in the region, growth in South Africa slowed to 1¾ percent in 1997, owing to weaknesses in domestic and external demand. Nigeria was also affected by weak domestic demand, worsened by a lack of foreign investor confidence. In Algeria, growth slowed significantly, owing mainly to the impact of drought on agriculture and further delays in the recovery of industrial activity. In Kenya, growth weakened partly as a result of financial market pressures related to political uncertainties. Inflation remained under control in most of the region.

Transition Economies

In 1997, both Russia and the transition countries recorded positive growth for the first time in eight years. For the countries as a group, output grew by 1¾ percent and inflation was reduced to about 27 percent—testimony to the progress since early in the decade with stabilization and reform policies in most countries.

Spillovers from the Asian crisis were most apparent in Russia, Ukraine, and, among the Baltic countries, in Estonia. In Russia, where the ruble came under attack in late October and November, and again in late January 1998, the authorities defended the exchange rate by raising interest rates sharply. There were associated steep declines in the stock market. The pressures arose despite an external current account close to balance; they reflected a persistently weak fiscal position characterized by poor revenue collection, concerns about how the external position might evolve if the fiscal imbalance were not dealt with, and the decline in oil prices. In Ukraine, although 1997 appeared to have brought single-digit inflation and positive growth within reach, inadequate fiscal adjustment led to increased reliance on official short-term foreign borrowing. Coupled with slow progress on structural reforms, this heightened Ukraine's vulnerability to adverse developments; thus, when the Asian crisis

intensified in late 1997, exchange market pressures forced the authorities to tighten monetary conditions sharply. In Estonia, domestic pressures on financial markets, associated with a burgeoning current account deficit, were aggravated by contagion from the Asian crisis. Interest rates rose substantially in October and November 1997, and equity prices, which had earlier risen steeply, dropped sharply.

A number of other transition countries experienced little impact from the Asian crisis in their financial markets or in their access to external finance, despite their openness to international capital markets. While the Czech Republic suffered a currency crisis in May 1997, in part triggered by the events in Thailand, it responded by tightening fiscal and monetary policies. The result was a significant narrowing of the Czech current account deficit, albeit at the expense of slower growth, and the subsequent deepening of the Asian crisis brought only limited further turbulence. Hungary also experienced little exchange market pressure from the Asian crisis, owing in no small measure to the country's markedly improved fiscal, growth, and trade performance following the implementation of strong adjustment measures since 1995. In Poland, output grew by about 7 percent in 1997, maintaining the solid expansion of almost six years.

The critical importance of adjustment and reform was highlighted particularly sharply in Albania and Bulgaria. The financial crisis in Bulgaria that had begun in 1996 extended into 1997, and output declined for a second consecutive year. In Albania, the crisis that flared up in March 1997 with the collapse of financial pyramid schemes also led to a drop in output during the year. But in both cases, following significant policy improvements, macroeconomic imbalances narrowed and growth resumed toward the end of 1997 and in early 1998. Bulgaria also recorded a dramatic decline in inflation in 1997, with the currency board arrangement introduced as part of the IMF-supported program playing a central role.

CHAPTER II

World Economic Outlook

The Executive Board regularly reviews global economic developments and policies, based on World Economic Outlook reports prepared by the staff. The reports, which are usually published twice a year, contain comprehensive analyses both of prospects for the world economy and for individual countries and regions, and of topical issues.

In 1997/98, the Board held three discussions on the World Economic Outlook: in August 1997, December 1997 (on the basis of an "Interim Assessment" by the staff), and March 1998.[4] The central focus was the Asian financial crisis.[5] In August 1997, a number of Directors had already cautioned that, while there were many reasons to believe the world expansion could be sustained, there was no room for complacency about the risks and fragilities confronting individual countries that could affect regional and global economic and financial conditions. Especially in the developing world, large external imbalances and fragile banking systems, several Directors noted, had adversely affected investor confidence and heightened the risks associated with volatile capital movements. These difficulties were not expected to affect the generally positive long-term prospects of those countries, provided that disciplined macroeconomic policies and the necessary structural reforms were implemented on a timely basis to ensure the elimination of unsustainable economic imbalances. Directors stressed, however, that those policy efforts would have to be supported by a broader range of institutional reforms aimed at increasing the efficiency of public administration, developing human capital, strengthening financial sector management, setting up transparent regulatory and legal systems, and improving governance. Such reforms would help establish and maintain private sector and investor confidence, which are critical for sustained, high-quality growth.

In their March 1998 discussion, Executive Directors agreed that, while the financial market turmoil in Asia would have a significant negative impact on short-term growth prospects for the world economy, the slowdown was likely to be less pronounced than in earlier episodes of global economic weakness (in 1974–75, 1980–83, and 1990–91). Corrective actions by most countries at or near the center of the turmoil, the robust economic performance of most industrial countries, and policy reforms in many developing and transition economies over the past decade were seen as critical in containing the crisis and its global repercussions. Although growth projections for countries at the center of the crisis had been lowered considerably since the August 1997 discussion of the World Economic Outlook, Directors in March 1998 felt that prospects for other developing and transition economies remained generally encouraging.

This said, Directors noted that uncertainty still remained regarding the resolution of the crisis; resolute implementation of reforms by the crisis countries was therefore essential. Recent declines in oil and other commodity prices, moreover, could lengthen the adjustment process in some crisis countries and pose considerable challenges for commodity and oil-exporting countries in all regions. Also, a reevaluation of risks by international lenders as a result of the crisis, while welcomed, could limit financial flows to developing and transition economies to levels below those justified by the fundamentals. More generally, Directors were concerned that some emerging market economies had relied too heavily on foreign borrowing and short-term instruments to finance public deficits, thus increasing their risk of future financing difficulties.

Advanced Economies

In their March 1998 review of the outlook for the advanced economies, Directors observed that the spillovers from the Asian crisis for Japan were particularly unwelcome, given that its nascent recovery had already stalled in the first half of 1997; this stalling was due both to a fiscal policy that, in hindsight, was overly

---

[4]The three reports were published as IMF, *World Economic Outlook,* issues dated October and December 1997 (the latter subtitled *Interim Assessment*) and May 1998.

[5]Chapter V reviews the Board's discussion of the causes and appropriate policy responses to the crisis.

tight and to continuing fragilities in the financial system. Directors stressed that boosting confidence and fostering stronger sustainable growth in Japan—through a combination of macroeconomic, financial sector, and structural policies—was critical, given the economy's importance for the region and for the world. Economic recovery should be supported by a more expansionary fiscal stance in the near term, while maintaining the objective of medium-term consolidation. Some Directors noted that a permanent tax cut would boost the prospects for an increase in private consumption but cautioned against overreliance on increased public works spending since it would have only a temporary impact and had not proven very effective in the past. In contrast, some other Directors expressed reservations about the effectiveness of tax cuts, fearing that the increase in disposable income might be added to household savings with little or no effect on consumption and growth. Pointing to the government debt accumulated in recent years and the prospective fiscal pressures associated with an aging population, some Directors argued that any backsliding with fiscal consolidation would pose risks while having little positive effect on activity.

Directors noted indications from the Japanese authorities that a substantial fiscal stimulus package would soon be announced. They emphasized that, to have significant and durable effects, the measures needed to be accompanied by serious regulatory and financial sector reforms. Most Directors welcomed recently announced measures committing public funds to protect depositors of failed institutions and to recapitalize viable ones. These measures promised to restore public confidence and strengthen banks' willingness to lend. Directors cautioned, however, against indiscriminate support to banks where closures or consolidation were more appropriate. They suggested that any further allocation of public funds be accompanied by clear measures to facilitate the write-off of bad bank loans to ensure a fair sharing of the burden of restructuring costs and to limit moral hazard. At its April 1998 meeting, the Interim Committee welcomed the Japanese economic policy package, as well as Japan's steps to strengthen its financial system.

Directors agreed that the U.S. economy, in contrast to the Japanese economy, was likely to suffer relatively little from adverse developments in Asia, owing largely to the strength of its cyclical position prior to the crisis and to the positive developments in bond markets, which, in the view of many Directors, reflected a "flight to quality" of international investment flows. They judged the current stance of monetary policy as appropriate, noting that the moderating effects of the Asian crisis—together with the appreciation of the U.S. dollar and the decline in world commodity prices—had alleviated the need for an increase in official interest rates. In view of the tightening labor market conditions, however, the authorities would need to monitor the situation closely, looking for signs that would tip the balance of monetary policy assessment in either direction.

The risks posed by the Asian crisis for the advanced economies in Europe were also likely to be relatively small, Directors agreed. Among the economies operating near full capacity, Directors believed that the previous year's monetary tightening and continued fiscal consolidation in the United Kingdom were likely to keep demand close to productive capacity limits and hold inflation near to target. But further action would be warranted if inflation prospects worsened. In the same vein, the Interim Committee in its April 1998 meeting emphasized the need for the U.K. authorities to remain vigilant as always to inflation risks. In Germany, France, and Italy, where output—while remaining below potential—had recovered quite well since the beginning of 1997, Directors expected the overall impact of the Asian crisis also to be small. Some Directors, however, cautioned against overoptimism, noting that exports had been the main source of demand growth in some of these countries. A weakening of export markets could slow, and possibly stall, the recovery if domestic demand did not pick up. In continental Europe generally, with monetary union among a large number of countries scheduled to begin in nine months, attention had to be given to labor and product market reforms, to continuing fiscal consolidation, and to monetary policy in the transition period.

Developing and Transition Countries

Directors noted that the Asian crisis was affecting most developing and transition economies, albeit to varying degrees. The effects were being felt through, for example, increases in risk premiums in borrowing costs, lower commodity prices, losses in competitiveness to countries at or near the center of the turmoil, or the slowdown in demand in those countries. Several countries—including Brazil, Chile, the Czech Republic, and Mexico—that had suffered exchange market pressures in connection with the Asian crisis had been able to avoid full contagion through appropriate policy adjustments. Although these countries had generally weathered the crisis well, Directors felt it prudent for them to continue strengthening policies to avoid further challenges down the road. In this connection, it was particularly important to contain external imbalances, avoid overheating, and enhance the quality and timeliness of economic and financial information generally. Also critical was a strong financial sector infrastructure, including prudential regulation, internationally accepted accounting standards, and, for some, preestablished exit rules regarding shifting from a fixed exchange regime to a flexible one (see Chapter VI). Several

Directors welcomed China's commitment not to devalue its currency and its efforts to strengthen its banking system.

Many Directors expressed concern about recent trends in commodity prices and the potentially adverse implications for commodity-exporting developing countries of both a deterioration in the terms of trade and increased price volatility. For Africa, the impact of these forces, combined with poor weather and the continuing heavy debt burden, was of particular concern. Nevertheless, Directors remained cautiously optimistic about Africa's growth prospects, based on the expectation of continued implementation of macroeconomic adjustment and structural reforms and of an appropriate flow of foreign assistance. Directors underscored the need to create a favorable environment for foreign direct investment, including through a further opening up of their economies.

Regarding the economies in transition, Directors expressed satisfaction that both Russia and the transition countries as a group had recorded positive growth in 1997 for the first time since the transition began. They noted, however, that although considerable progress was being made in macroeconomic stabilization in virtually all countries, differences in the pace of reform and progress in transformation appeared to have grown larger. Most countries had made substantial progress toward reasonable fiscal balance, but sizable deficits continued to be registered in a number of countries, including Russia and Ukraine. Financing these deficits through foreign currency and short-term borrowing, Directors observed, put the sustainability of fiscal policies in question, indirectly threatened to undermine the soundness of banking sectors, and endangered hard-earned economic stabilization achievements. Severe revenue collection problems in a number of transition countries, moreover, were preventing governments from carrying out their proper functions. Further tax policy reform and improvements in tax administration were unlikely to show their full effect, Directors recognized, unless the political will to collect taxes was also strengthened. Directors also advised central and eastern European transition countries to improve the cost-effectiveness of their social security and welfare systems, and thereby reduce the overall level of government spending.

CHAPTER III

International Capital Markets

In their annual review of developments in international capital markets, conducted in July 1997 shortly after the eruption of the financial crisis in Thailand, Executive Directors engaged in a wide-ranging discussion of mature and emerging capital markets and banking systems. They also assessed the implications of European Economic and Monetary Union for international capital markets. Directors discussed at length developments in emerging markets, strategies for dealing with speculative attacks, and approaches to more effective management of sovereign external liabilities. Later in the fiscal year, in March 1998, the Board examined the role of hedge funds and institutional investors both in connection with the Asian crisis and, more generally, in a world of increasingly integrated capital markets.[6]

Mature Capital Markets

Directors noted the narrowing of interest rate differentials among the mature economies and attributed this to several causes, including fiscal consolidation, reductions in inflation rates, and increased competition in international banking markets. Directors also saw the continued convergence of interest rates as a sign that markets expected a broad EMU to begin on January 1, 1999. As to a second major trend in the mature markets—the continued sharp advances in equity prices, particularly in the United States—many Directors felt that the relatively high valuations of stocks rested on investor expectations of continued strong growth in corporate earnings and relatively low inflation rates. Although diverse views were expressed about the implications of conventional market indicators, many Directors were concerned about the potential for corrections in some equity markets and the possible negative impact of such corrections, especially in emerging equity markets. Directors urged careful monitoring of

stock markets in the United States and other economies.

Banking in Mature Markets

Directors noted that the banking systems in some mature markets had been highly profitable during the preceding 12 months, while others continued to be affected by high levels of nonperforming loans. They discussed the difficulties in ensuring effective financial supervision created by financial deregulation and globalization and noted that, as distinctions between banks and other financial institutions had blurred, a growing number of countries had moved toward consolidating supervision over a broad range of financial institutions into one agency.

Structural Aspects of EMU

Directors viewed the creation of EMU as an important international financial event that was likely to foster the creation of EMU-wide financial markets, benefit European banking systems, and lead to a more efficient European payments system. Although some consolidation and restructuring of banking systems was generally seen as inevitable, several Directors cited the diverse situations of banking systems among European countries. Some stressed the importance of taking into account the performance of all types of financial institutions, such as savings, post office, and cooperative banks, in assessing the efficiency of the European banking system. Market-based solutions were seen as desirable for addressing banking sector problems. Some Directors cautioned that regulatory practices, local market power, rigid labor practices, and public ownership structures could delay the required adjustments. A number of Directors cautioned against both the fiscal costs and the moral hazard that might be associated with public interventions for addressing the problems of the more seriously troubled financial institutions.

Emerging Markets

Directors noted the growing integration of many emerging markets into the global financial system, as

---

[6]The background papers were published as IMF, *International Capital Markets: Developments, Prospects, and Key Policy Issues* (1997), and IMF, *Hedge Funds and Financial Market Dynamics,* IMF Occasional Paper 166 (1998).

evidenced by the record level of private capital flows to these countries in 1996. The scale of such flows reflected improvements in the economic fundamentals in many recipients, the growing international diversification of institutional investor portfolios, and the increased ability of investors to search for higher yields. Directors expressed concern, however, that interest rate spreads on emerging market bonds and syndicated loans might have been bid too low and that many of these investors might not be fully cognizant of the credit risks they faced. Some Directors also thought that the low level of emerging market spreads might reflect investor expectations that systemically important emerging markets would receive official assistance that would allow them to avoid debt-service interruptions. To avoid moral hazard, several Directors cited the need to dispel the notion that the IMF would step in to bail out creditors.

Speculative Attacks and Exchange Rate Regimes

Executive Directors noted that the events in Thailand and neighboring foreign exchange markets had—as during the Mexican and European exchange rate mechanism crises—again demonstrated that the growing integration of financial markets meant that perceived macroeconomic uncertainties and structural weaknesses were more likely to generate large-scale speculative pressures on rigidly managed exchange rate arrangements than on flexible regimes. Many Directors argued that an inflexible exchange rate system could be sustained only if actively supported by strong macroeconomic policies and a sound financial system able to withstand sharp and sometimes sustained increases in interest rates to defend against speculative pressures.

The first line of defense against speculative attack must be sound macroeconomic policies, Directors stressed. When economic fundamentals were broadly correct, the authorities could mount a graduated defense based, first, on sterilized foreign exchange intervention and then, if necessary, unsterilized intervention, allowing short-term domestic interest rates to rise. Even in situations where the cost of maintaining high interest rates was considered excessive, Directors saw only a limited, short-term role for capital controls designed to limit the access of speculators to domestic credit. Such measures, they felt, should be used only in crisis situations to buy time to undertake corrective policies and should not be seen as a substitute for necessary reforms. Some Directors also emphasized that exchange restrictions that discriminated between domestic and foreign residents were inappropriate.

In discussing the appropriateness of fixed exchange rates, a few Directors drew attention to the choice of the peg currency and whether this should be based on the currency composition of trade flows or of external borrowing. Many Directors underscored the importance of moving to more flexible exchange rate systems in the face of sustained market pressures. Some also felt that allowing for more exchange rate flexibility would reduce the need to build up foreign exchange reserves and mitigate the problems in sterilizing sizable capital inflows and the associated cost (see also Chapter VI).

Banking in Emerging Markets

Directors commended the progress made in improving the health of banking systems in several countries but observed that significant problems remained in some others. Several Directors noted that investor concerns about potential vulnerabilities in the banking systems of some Asian emerging markets had contributed to instability in foreign exchange markets. Concerns about the impact of the Thai devaluation echoed similar concerns raised in 1995 in the context of the Mexican financial crisis. Both episodes had underscored the importance of sound risk management and prudential regulation in emerging market banking systems.

Managing Sovereign External Liabilities

Directors stressed the importance of improving the emerging market countries' management of sovereign external liabilities (both gross and net). They generally viewed foreign currency borrowing as necessary for complementing domestic debt instruments, broadening the investor base, and establishing international benchmarks. But they cautioned that such borrowing should be guided by strategic debt-management considerations—namely, the ability to generate corresponding foreign currency revenues—and not be driven by short-term fiscal savings. Cost considerations should be based on the hedged (risk-adjusted) cost for a country. The debt-management strategy should incorporate clear guidelines on currency composition and maturity structure and should take into account foreign borrowing by the private sector, especially by commercial banks. Directors noted the risks and constraints that a large stock of short-term foreign currency debt could impose on macroeconomic policies; they referred to the unfolding Asian turmoil as a clear example of what could occur.

Greater policy transparency and accountability of debt managers in managing foreign assets and liabilities were generally viewed as enhancing the ability to manage exposures to external shocks. In this regard, many Directors highlighted the potential merits of a separate debt-management agency with expertise and experience in risk-management techniques. They also underscored the need for coordination and consistency between such an agency and the monetary and fiscal authorities.

Hedge Funds and Financial Market Dynamics

As a point of departure for their March 1998 discussion on hedge funds, Directors noted that detailed information on these funds was limited. As private investment pools, hedge funds were not subject to most of the reporting and disclosure requirements applicable to banks and mutual funds. More fundamentally, it was difficult to demarcate clearly the boundaries of the hedge fund industry from other institutional investors, or to generalize about its activities given the great diversity of investment strategies pursued by fund managers. Still, several commercial services gathered information on the industry. Excluding "funds of funds" (funds made up of smaller funds), such estimates suggested that hedge fund capital was in the neighborhood of $100 billion as of the third quarter of 1997. Of that, some $25 billion was in the hands of so-called macro funds, that is, funds that take large unhedged positions on changes in global economic conditions and typically leverage their capital through borrowing by a factor of 4 to 7. The remainder was managed by so-called relative value funds that take bets on the relative prices of closely related securities and are less exposed to economic fluctuations; they tend to be more highly leveraged than macro funds. By contrast, the capital of such other institutional investors as investment and commercial banks exceeded $20 trillion in the mature markets alone.

Against this background, Directors differed on the impact of hedge funds on market dynamics. While agreeing that hedge fund capital represented only a fraction of liquidity in global financial markets, several Directors emphasized that highly leveraged hedge funds could take large positions in the smaller emerging markets. They also noted the relative freedom and flexibility of hedge fund activities. Some Directors argued that hedge funds encouraged herding behavior among investors. Others saw only limited evidence that hedge funds contributed significantly to herding and noted their potential role as contrarians or stabilizing speculators.

Hedge Funds and the Asian Crisis

Directors differed on the extent of the involvement of hedge funds in the Asian crisis. Several saw no clear evidence that hedge funds took short positions against Asian currencies any earlier than other investors, or that their trades were necessarily a signal for other investors. Directors noted that while hedge funds had large short positions on the Thai baht, the same did not appear to have been true for Asian currencies in general. Because some governments and central banks limited the ability of offshore counterparties to borrow domestic currency from onshore banks, other investors with better access

to the domestic broker market might have acted as market leaders. The entire constellation of institutional investors, and not merely hedge funds, in the Board's view, had played a role in the market fluctuations of 1997.

A few Directors felt that hedge funds had played a more important role in the crisis than indicated by the staff paper on hedge funds.[7] They argued that hedge funds at times had a strong effect on asset prices, particularly in light of the relative size of their positions in specific markets. Directors generally agreed, however, that the events in Asia highlighted the need for policymakers to pursue sound and prudent macroeconomic policies that were transparent to markets in order to protect their economies against sharp market volatility and speculation. In particular, they recommended avoiding offering one-way bets in the form of inconsistent policies and indefensible currency pegs; maintaining strong, well-regulated, and competitive financial systems; and providing timely and comprehensive information to the public about government policy and private sector financial conditions. While recognizing the role of better information in curbing herd behavior, several Directors cautioned that disclosing market-sensitive information could on occasion trigger or worsen market volatility.

More Regulation?

Board members expressed diverse views on whether hedge funds should be subject to additional regulatory and disclosure requirements. Some argued that, given the scant evidence of market failure associated specifically with hedge funds, the case for new regulations was slim. Some other Directors, however, indicated that further options needed to be explored to render hedge fund operations more transparent and assure officials and market participants that hedge funds were not dominating or manipulating markets.

A number of Directors warned that hedge funds were only one part of the larger constellation of institutional investors, so that, to convey useful information, any system of detailed portfolio and position reporting would also have to encompass, among others, commercial banks, investment banks, insurance companies, and pension funds. It was also noted that reporting systems were more difficult to implement in an over-the-counter environment, such as the foreign exchange market, than on organized exchanges. Moreover, to be totally effective, reporting requirements would have to be applied by all countries. Otherwise, market participants who regarded reporting as onerous would simply book their transactions offshore.

---

[7]Ibid.

CHAPTER IV

European Economic and Monetary Union

During 1997/98, the Executive Board held a series of discussions on issues related to EMU. Early in the year, Directors assessed the implications of EMU for financial markets (see Chapter III); preparations for EMU and EMU in the context of the World Economic Outlook were taken up in May and August 1997 and in March 1998.

At their meeting in May 1997, Directors noted that completion of EMU would represent a milestone in the economic integration of Europe and was of major importance for the international monetary system. They underlined the desirability of completing the project in a timely way, noting that a great deal had been accomplished already in preparing EU economies for EMU and in establishing the policy framework within which economic policies would be conducted once monetary union commenced. The EU authorities needed to follow through on their policy commitments and work closely together to secure the foundations for monetary union to ensure a smooth transition to EMU, Directors noted.

While noting that most EU countries had already achieved a high degree of convergence in the areas required by the Maastricht Treaty—most remarkably with regard to inflation—Directors observed that further progress was needed in the fiscal area in 1997. They underlined that, for most countries, additional fiscal measures would also be needed in 1998 to reduce deficits further in line with the medium-term requirements reflected in the Stability and Growth Pact.

The continuing high structural unemployment in Europe concerned Directors, and they emphasized that urgent action was needed to reduce labor market rigidities in most EU countries. In the context of a common monetary and exchange rate policy, inadequate flexibility in labor markets would impair the ability of individual countries to adjust to asymmetric shocks. Some Directors were concerned that failure to address labor market rigidities would result in persistently high unemployment that could erode public support over time for macroeconomic policies directed at low inflation. Directors also stressed the importance of

factor and product market liberalization to ensure sustainable growth and job creation in the EU.

In establishing a macroeconomic policy framework for the monetary union, it was important to balance policymakers' need for flexibility with the desire to establish rules that would help underpin the credibility of policies in the new environment. Directors thought that the Stability and Growth Pact had struck a reasonable balance between those two considerations. They believed that surveillance by the EU's Council—oriented to giving an early warning of the emergence of excessive deficits—together with the threat of financial penalties, should provide a strong bulwark against fiscal indiscipline.

Directors generally agreed that the euro would, over time, constitute an attractive reserve currency that might rival the dollar. The roles of the euro and the dollar would depend importantly on developments in financial markets in Europe, including the regulatory environment and the variety of instruments available, as well as fundamental economic developments.

When the Executive Board discussed EMU in August 1997 at its review of the World Economic Outlook, Directors again remarked on the impressive degree of economic convergence achieved in Europe, including strengthened public finances, lower inflation and interest rates, and relatively stable exchange rates. Some Directors were of the view that the advances in economic convergence and the strong commitment to begin EMU as envisaged had served to lessen considerably the risks and uncertainties in the run-up to EMU.

A number of Directors stressed that the best way to minimize any remaining uncertainties about the start of EMU, and to ensure that a sustainable and strong EMU began on time, would be for countries to take fiscal action in the remainder of 1997 and in 1998 that continued to demonstrate their commitment to the requirements of the Maastricht Treaty and of the Stability and Growth Pact. Several Directors noted the risk that a number of candidates for membership might slightly exceed the fiscal deficit target. They agreed with the staff, however, that—particularly in view of the reductions achieved in cyclically adjusted deficits and the longer-term framework established with the Stability and Growth Pact on fiscal discipline—small excesses of actual deficits over the reference value should not be viewed as an impediment to EMU proceeding on schedule. In contrast, a few other Directors noted that a strict application of the Maastricht fiscal deficit criterion would be important so as not to impair the credibility of EMU.

Directors noted other challenges to sustain a successful monetary union that still had to be faced during the transition to the single currency. They broadly agreed that, in addition to sound financial policies, improving Europe's labor market performance was critical for the success of EMU. Directors emphasized that comprehensive labor market reforms to reduce structural unemployment would not only help boost medium-term growth and improve fiscal performance, but would also help Europe adjust faster to adverse economic disturbances when monetary union was in place and increase public support for the project. Directors generally agreed that the independence of the European System of Central Banks, and its mandate and capacity to achieve price stability, should be well safeguarded by the provisions that had been put in place relating to its functioning. They generally felt that the exchange rate would not be a suitable nominal anchor for monetary policy in the euro area. Directors felt that the introduction of the euro would be accompanied by a significant restructuring of financial markets and possible instability in money demand

relationships. Directors considered that the European Central Bank (ECB) would likely use a wide range of indicators in conducting monetary policy, especially in the early stages of EMU. It was noted that transparency of monetary policy would be important in securing and maintaining the credibility of the ECB.

A number of Directors observed that despite the considerable progress in fiscal consolidation, budgetary positions in many EU members might worsen in the medium to long term as a result of demographic developments; these problems would have to be addressed, irrespective of EMU.

At their March 1998 discussion of the World Economic Outlook, Directors considered that the objective of establishing a monetary union among a large number of EU member countries was within reach, in accordance with the agreed timetable. Progress in fiscal adjustment and the convergence of inflation and interest rates had been impressive. But further fiscal consolidation was desirable in the near term to strengthen medium-term growth potential and to provide for greater policy flexibility within the Stability and Growth Pact. Directors expressed particular concern, however, that structural reforms in labor and product markets were lagging.

In its April 1998 meeting, the Interim Committee requested the Executive Board to examine further the implications of EMU for IMF operations and for the conduct of IMF surveillance and to report its findings in time for the Committee's next meeting in October 1998.

The Asian Crisis

As the formative event of the financial year, the Asian financial crisis absorbed a large proportion of the Executive Board's time. Directors met frequently—at times, daily—to be briefed on and discuss developments in the countries at the center of the crisis and to guide the work of staff and management with those countries' authorities. IMF-supported adjustment programs, involving very large financial support, for Indonesia, Korea, and Thailand were approved by the Board. The Board also conducted several in-depth reviews—particularly during its World Economic Outlook and International Capital Markets discussions, and in the context of examining the record of IMF surveillance in the region (see Chapter VI)—of the broader questions prompted by the crisis: its origin, the appropriate response of policy, the appropriate role of the international community, and the lessons to be drawn from the experience. This chapter focuses primarily on the Board discussions on these broader issues through the end of the financial year (end-April 1998). Highlights of the IMF's response to the crisis are detailed in Box 1, and summaries of the evolution of IMF-supported adjustment programs for Thailand, Indonesia, and Korea (updated through mid-July 1998) are at the end of the chapter.

Origin and Evolution

The Asian financial crisis took place against the backdrop of severe financial market pressures in several Asian economies, linked in part to concerns about their weak financial systems, large external deficits, inflated property and stock market values, maintenance of relatively fixed exchange rates, and overdependence on short-term capital flows—which tended to be allocated to less-productive investment. In addition, shifts in competitiveness associated with wide swings in the yen/dollar exchange rate were also a contributing factor. The pressures were most acute in Thailand, where fragilities in the financial sector heightened concerns about the sustainability of the pegged exchange rate arrangement. Spillover effects from the crisis were felt by other countries in the region, notably Indonesia, Malaysia, and the Philippines. In all of these countries, acute exchange market pressures eventually led to the adoption of more flexible exchange rate arrangements and sizable depreciations of their currencies, as well as sharp declines in asset values.

In August 1997, several Directors during the Board discussion stressed the importance of containing external current account deficits and reducing the reliance on foreign borrowing—especially short-term borrowing denominated in foreign currency—to diminish the risk of disruptive changes in market sentiment. In this regard, Directors noted that the adoption of a strong adjustment program by the Thai authorities and the solid demonstration of regional and international cooperation would pave the way for a restoration of confidence and a gradual return to Thailand's characteristically strong economic performance. Several Directors observed that to restore economic and financial market stability, it was crucial for all countries in the region to pursue sound macroeconomic and structural policies, strengthen financial supervision, and enhance transparency through timely disclosure of economic and financial data.

By the time of subsequent World Economic Outlook discussions, the crisis had deepened and spread to Korea. In reviewing the reasons for the eruption of turbulence and its unexpectedly strong spillover to other countries, Directors noted that a number of elements had played a role. These included, somewhat ironically, the strong economic performance of the affected countries in recent decades, which had helped attract large capital inflows during the 1990s. The inflows had ultimately put heavy demands on economic policies and institutions, including those intended to promote monetary stability and financial sector soundness. The strength of past performance, moreover, was felt by many Directors to have contributed to initial delays in the implementation of remedial action. External influences had also played an important role. The appreciation of the U.S. dollar—to which the currencies of most of these countries were pegged—and slower export market growth had contributed in 1996–97 to

Box 1
The IMF's Response to the Asian Crisis

In seeking to restore confidence in the region in the wake of the Asian crisis, the IMF responded quickly by:

- helping the three countries most affected by the crisis—Indonesia, Korea, and Thailand—arrange programs of economic reform that could restore confidence and be supported by the IMF. The Philippines' existing IMF-supported program was extended and augmented in 1997, and a Stand-By Arrangement was approved in 1998;
- approving some SDR 26 billion of IMF financial support for reform programs in Indonesia, Korea, and Thailand and spearheading the mobilization of some $77 billion of additional financing commitments from multilateral and bilateral sources in support of these reform programs in 1997. In mid-1998, the IMF's committed assistance for Indonesia was augmented by SDR 1 billion, with an estimated $5 billion from multilateral and bilateral sources. Of the commitments to all three countries, some SDR 18 billion had been disbursed by the IMF by July 23, 1998. (See table.); and
- intensifying its consultations with other members both within and outside the region that, although not necessarily requiring IMF support, were affected by the crisis and needed to take policy steps to ward off contagion.

To implement its response to the crisis, the IMF:

- used the accelerated procedures established under the Emergency Financing Mechanism and the exceptional circumstances clause to meet the exceptional needs of the

Commitments of the International Community and Disbursements of the IMF in Response to the Asian Crisis, as of July 23, 1998[1]
(Billions of U.S. dollars)

Country	Commitments				IMF Disbursements
	IMF	Multilateral[2]	Bilateral[3]	Total	
Indonesia	11.2	10.0	21.1[4]	42.3	5.0
Korea	20.9	14.0	23.3	58.2	17.0
Thailand	4.0	2.7	10.5	17.2	2.8
Total	**36.1**	**26.7**	**54.9[4]**	**117.7**	**24.8**

[1]IMF commitments to the Philippines are not included.
[2]World Bank and Asian Development Bank.
[3]Bilateral contributions to Indonesia and Korea were a contingent second line of defense.
[4]Estimate; amount of new commitments not finalized as of July 23, 1998.

member countries in terms of approval time and access. This was followed by close monitoring of performance under the programs on a continuing basis and the approval of a number of adaptations to the original programs in light of developing circumstances;

- created the Supplemental Reserve Facility to help members experiencing exceptional balance of payments difficulties owing to a large short-term financing need resulting from a sudden loss of market confidence;
- stepped up coordination with other international financial institutions, notably the World Bank and the Asian Development Bank, and with bilateral donors, to augment international support for the affected countries' economic reform programs;
- strengthened its dialogue with a variety of constituencies in the program countries, including consultations with opposition and labor groups and extensive contacts with the press and the public;

- provided staff support to coordinate efforts by international creditor banks and debtors in the affected countries to resolve the severe private sector financing problems at the heart of the crisis;
- posted on the IMF website—with the consent of the governments of Indonesia, Korea, and Thailand—their Letters of Intent, describing in detail their IMF-supported programs, so that details of the programs would be readily available to all interested parties; and
- reinforced means of communication with officials and support for their efforts at consensus building through the appointment of former IMF Deputy Managing Director Prabhakar Narvekar as Special Advisor to the President of Indonesia; the establishment of resident representative posts in Korea and Thailand (in addition to the existing post in Indonesia); and the work of the IMF's new Asia and Pacific Regional Office (see Chapter VI).

worsening the external positions and growth performance of the countries in deepest crisis. Also, international investors, in their drive for higher rates of return, had underestimated the risks in some emerging market economies.

Directors agreed, however, that policy weaknesses in the affected countries had been the most important contributor to the sudden shifts in market sentiment. In particular, inflexible exchange rate arrangements had been maintained for too long—even when funda-

mentals no longer supported them—constraining the response of monetary policy to overheating pressures. Investors had also viewed pegged exchange rates as implicit guarantees of exchange value, which, together with implicit guarantees of support to the banking sector, had encouraged external borrowing and excessive foreign exchange exposure, often at short maturities. Inadequate banking regulation, supervision, and prudential rules had contributed to the inefficient intermediation of these funds, resulting in fragile balance sheets of many banks and nonfinancial corporations. Excessive government intervention and problems with data availability had also—to varying degrees—impeded market discipline on resource allocation and on the volume of capital investment, further distorting the deployment of capital inflows from abroad as well as domestic financial resource intermediation. Significant delays in confronting the problems and adopting the requisite monetary policy and structural reform measures had compounded the affected countries' economic difficulties and the associated contagion effects.

Appropriate Policy Response

At their December 1997 discussion, Directors emphasized that the main responsibility for resolving the turmoil in Asia rested with the affected countries. Hesitation in implementing the needed adjustment and reform measures would only worsen the crisis and exacerbate overshooting in financial markets and contagion to other countries. In this context, a number of Directors questioned the adequacy of the commitments of the authorities in some of the affected countries, arguing that this had added to market turbulence. All Directors agreed that bold actions to address key policy weaknesses were indispensable for restoring confidence and preparing the ground for a solid rebound from the current difficulties. They stressed four areas for action:

- Domestic and foreign investors needed to be reassured that macroeconomic stability would be restored. Directors agreed that the required degree and composition of fiscal adjustment had to strike a balance between several objectives, including the need to contribute sufficiently to current account adjustment and to meet the costs of financial system restructuring, while avoiding excessive compression of domestic demand. Some Directors questioned the need for significant tightening of fiscal policy since the Asian economies in crisis generally did not suffer from fiscal imbalances.

- Monetary policies had to be kept sufficiently firm to resist excessive depreciation of the exchange rate and its inflationary consequences, while ensuring that domestic demand was not unduly squeezed and the banking sector not overly strained. Some Directors stressed the need for a strong, early monetary tightening to restore market confidence quickly, while the requisite banking and other structural reform measures were getting under way. Directors agreed that as confidence was restored, monetary conditions should be allowed to ease—with a gradual lowering of interest rates—to help support activity, but they emphasized the danger of premature easing. It was important to encourage financial institutions and corporations to roll over external short-term loans in cases where the repayment of such loans risked worsening downward pressures on the exchange rate.

- Weaknesses in the financial sector needed to be addressed through bold and comprehensive measures to dispel uncertainties. Although it was necessary to ensure adequate protection for small deposit holders, insolvent institutions had to be closed to facilitate an early restoration of confidence. Weak but viable institutions had to be restructured and recapitalized in ways that were fully transparent and did not inappropriately shield creditors and equity holders from losses or exacerbate problems of moral hazard.

- Public and corporate governance had to be strengthened to enhance transparency and accountability, and data—especially financial and banking sector indicators—had to be provided on an accurate and timely basis.

Directors noted in December 1997 that the prolonged crisis in Southeast Asia and East Asia had raised the prospect that other emerging market countries, which had already experienced some spillovers, could experience an intensification of financial market pressures. While reform efforts had been strengthened considerably among developing countries in recent years, a number of countries remained vulnerable to reversals of market sentiment. The policy requirements in these countries were similar to those in the countries that had already been affected. In addition, several Directors thought that some other emerging market countries should consider whether greater exchange rate flexibility might help to reduce the risk and cost of possible speculative attacks on their currencies. Directors agreed that, whichever exchange arrangement countries chose to follow, protection against currency market turmoil was likely only if it were fully supported by strong macroeconomic policies and robust financial systems.

During their March 1998 discussion, Directors affirmed their support for the programs put in place to restore confidence in the affected countries, including measures to strengthen financial sectors, correct macroeconomic imbalances, and improve data availability, transparency, and governance. Such measures were seen as the most effective means of addressing the causes of the crisis, limiting and reversing currency and stock market overshooting, and restoring sustainable growth.

Directors observed that delays in adopting and implementing reform packages had, in some countries, heightened the panic, deepened the crisis, and delayed its resolution. Delays in implementing critical reforms in Indonesia, in particular, had put stabilization and recovery in doubt. Korea and Thailand, in contrast, had made good progress in stabilizing financial markets and in beginning to rebuild confidence through concrete, timely measures backed by the strong resolve and the consistent message conveyed by the authorities. Directors broadly agreed that the Asian crisis countries would record substantial turnarounds in their current account balances in 1998, from deficit to surplus, as domestic demand declined and improved international competitiveness boosted net exports. Nevertheless, many Directors emphasized that the affected countries had to continue to undertake the necessary adjustment, especially in restructuring financial systems.

Role of the International Community

While financial market conditions remained unsettled, a number of Directors emphasized during their December 1997 discussion that the authorities in the major industrial countries should be cautious in considering any further tightening of monetary policy. Most Directors felt that further tightening should be put on hold, particularly given the prospect in most cases of continuing subdued inflation. Some Directors felt, however, that domestic monetary policy should aim solely at dealing with the condition of the domestic economy.

Directors called for resolute action by the Japanese authorities to address the strains in Japan's financial sector, including through the closure of insolvent institutions, and the well-targeted use of public funds to assist in urgently needed restructuring. Most Directors also called for modest expansionary fiscal measures in Japan to help avoid any further withdrawal of fiscal stimulus until recovery was reestablished. Directors also emphasized the need to speed up deregulation to enhance domestic investment opportunities, thereby reducing Japan's persistently large external surplus.

Directors welcomed the fact that, despite the seriousness of the issues confronting many of the Asian economies, growth in North America and Europe had been sustained and was likely to provide support for the global economy in the period ahead. This meant that the economies in difficulty would benefit from a relatively favorable external environment. Directors stressed that, given the medium-term growth potential of the countries at the center of the crisis, they could reasonably expect to regain market confidence once their authorities had addressed structural weaknesses—especially in the financial sector.

In discussing the role of the international organizations in helping contain the crisis, several Directors were concerned about the possible moral hazard implications of the current crisis resolution mechanisms. They stressed the importance of ensuring to the maximum extent that IMF financing did not serve to bail out private creditors. The IMF, other international financial institutions, and the official sector should not assume the burden of financial support alone; private sector creditors should play a part as well.

Concerns about the IMF's ability to contain financial crises and about moral hazard were reflected in the Executive Board's decision, in December 1997, to adopt the Supplemental Reserve Facility (SRF) (see Chapter VIII). SRF financing carries higher interest rates than are charged on other IMF financing to encourage early repayment, to minimize the risk of moral hazard, and to ensure that only those countries with a compelling need will seek recourse to the facility. In addition, the decision establishing the new facility states that a member using IMF resources under the decision is encouraged to seek to maintain participation of creditors, both official and private, until the pressure on the balance of payments ceases. It also states that all options should be considered to ensure appropriate burden sharing. Similarly, in their February 1998 discussion of IMF policy on sovereign arrears to private creditors (see Chapter VIII), Directors emphasized the need to involve private creditors at an early stage of the crisis to ensure adequate burden sharing and limit moral hazard.

At its April 1998 meeting, the Interim Committee, while noting the difficult issues involved, requested the Board to intensify its consideration of possible steps to strengthen private sector involvement, suggested different mechanisms for meeting this objective, and asked the Board to report on all aspects of its work in these areas at the fall meeting of the Committee.

Early Lessons from Experience

In their regular review of members' policies in the context of IMF surveillance, Executive Directors drew several major lessons from the Asian financial crisis (see Chapter VI). In addition, during their March 1998 World Economic Outlook discussion, Directors pointed to the need for the international community to make greater efforts to identify emerging vulnerabilities for preemptive action; at the same time, they recognized that it was impossible to detect all incipient banking and exchange market crises. They thought that study of the Asian financial crisis could provide useful inputs for developing "vulnerability indicators" and early warning signals of imminent crises. Some Directors, however, were concerned about the reliability of such indicators in view of the complexity of the elements contributing to crises. They stressed that the recent experience amply demonstrated the importance of accurate and timely provision of information and, therefore, underscored the need for continued improvements in the coverage, timeliness, and quality of financial statistics, including indicators of bank profitability, interest rate spreads, levels of nonperforming loans, and indicators of competitiveness. They also called for further study of the contagion process.

One lesson that Directors drew from the crisis was that countries had to prepare carefully for the liberalization of capital account transactions to enjoy the benefits of access to global markets while reducing the risk of disruption. Important preconditions for successful liberalization were consistent domestic policies, a sound financial system, and the removal of economic distortions, as well as progress in transparency and disclosure on the part of governments and financial institutions. Some Directors suggested that emerging market countries—at least during a period of transition that might have to be relatively long—should adopt market-based safeguards aimed at limiting the exposure of financial and corporate sectors to reversals of short-term capital movements. This would reduce the risk that capital inflows could become a source of difficulty, rather than a benefit.

Some Directors also remarked that, while currency pegs had served many countries well, it was important to weigh the costs and benefits of these arrangements in the future, and in some cases design exit strategies. Some other Directors, however, cautioned, that a move toward greater exchange rate flexibility should not be regarded as a prescription for averting a financial crisis. Attention had to be paid to ensuring the consistency of the overall policy framework in order to maintain confidence and avoid excessive currency depreciation; this included the establishment of an alternative monetary anchor or inflation target and a preemptive strengthening of the banking system.

Thailand, Indonesia, and Korea: Evolution of IMF-Supported Adjustment Programs

Thailand

The Asian financial crisis started in Thailand with the baht coming under a series of increasingly serious attacks in May 1997, and the markets losing confidence in the economy. In the face of these pressures, the authorities ceased on July 2 to maintain the exchange rate peg. And on August 20, 1997, the Executive Board approved financial support for Thailand of up to SDR 2.9 billion, equivalent to 505 percent of Thailand's quota, over a 34-month period.

The initial program of economic reform featured:
- financial sector restructuring, focusing first on the identification and closure of unviable financial institutions (including 56 finance companies), intervention in the weakest banks, and the recapitalization of the banking system;
- fiscal measures equivalent to about 3 percent of GDP, to shift the consolidated public sector deficit into a surplus of 1 percent of GDP in 1997/98, to

support the necessary improvement in the large current account deficit, and cover the interest costs of financial restructuring;
- a new framework for monetary policy in line with the new managed float regime; and
- structural initiatives to increase efficiency, deepen the role of the private sector in the Thai economy, and reinforce its outward orientation, including civil service reform, privatization, and initiatives to attract foreign capital.

The program was modified in a Letter of Intent on November 25, 1997, in light of the baht's subsequent larger-than-expected depreciation, a sharper slowdown than anticipated in the economy, and severe adverse regional economic developments. The modifications included:
- additional measures to maintain the public sector surplus at 1 percent of GDP;
- establishment of a specific timetable for implementing financial sector restructuring, including strategies for the preemptive recapitalization and strengthening of the financial system; and
- acceleration of plans to protect the weaker sectors of society.

The program was further modified in a Letter of Intent on February 24, 1998, and again on May 26, 1998, to give clear priority to stabilizing the exchange rate while limiting the magnitude and the negative social impact of the larger-than-expected economic downturn and to set the stage for Thailand's return to the international financial markets. The modifications provided, among other things, for:
- accelerating financial system restructuring, including the privatization of the four banks in which the authorities had intervened;
- adjusting fiscal policy targets from a targeted public sector surplus of about 1 percent of GDP to a deficit of 3 percent of GDP, allowing automatic stabilizers to work, and in part to finance higher social spending;
- ensuring an adequate availability of credit to help foster an economic recovery, while maintaining a tight monetary stance to support exchange rate stability;
- improving governance in both the corporate and government sectors;
- strengthening the social safety net;
- bringing the legal and regulatory framework, including the bankruptcy law, in line with international standards and consistent with the smooth implementation of corporate debt restructuring and the overall economic program; and
- further deepening the role of the private sector, including through initiatives to attract foreign capital.

Table 4 shows selected economic indicators for Thailand.

Table 4
Thailand: Selected Economic Indicators, as of July 23, 1998

	1995	1996	1997[1]	1998[2]
		Percent change		
Real GDP growth	8.8	5.5	−0.4	−4.0 to −5.5
Consumer prices (end of period)	7.4	4.8	7.7	10.0
		Percent of GDP; a minus sign signifies a deficit		
Central government balance	3.0	2.4	−0.9	−2.4
Current account balance	−7.8	−7.9	−2.0	6.9
		Billions of U.S. dollars		
External debt	82.6	90.5	91.8	89.7
Of which: short-term debt	41.1	37.6	29.9	22.8
		Percent of GDP		
External debt	49.1	49.9	59.6	72.5

Data: Thai authorities; and IMF staff estimates. Central government balance data are for financial years (October 1 to September 30).
[1]Estimate.
[2]May 1998 program.

* * *

Chronological Highlights

1997

August 11   With negotiations on an adjustment program well advanced, the IMF convenes a meeting of interested countries in Tokyo; total support pledged for Thailand eventually reaches about $17.2 billion.

August 20   The Board approves an SDR 2.9 billion Stand-By Arrangement for Thailand and releases a disbursement of SDR 1.2 billion.

October 17   The Board reviews the Stand-By Arrangement under the Emergency Financing Mechanism procedures.

November 25   Thailand issues a Letter of Intent detailing additional measures.

December 8   The Board completes the first review under the Stand-By Arrangement and disburses SDR 600 million.

1998

February 24   Thailand issues a Letter of Intent describing further measures.

March 4   The Board completes the second review under the Stand-By Arrangement and disburses SDR 200 million.

May 26   Thailand issues new Letter of Intent.

June 10   The Board completes the third review under the Stand-By Arrangement, approving a disbursement of SDR 100 million and concluding the 1998/99 Article IV consultation.

Indonesia

The shift in financial market sentiment that originated in Thailand exposed structural weaknesses in Indonesia's economy, notably the weakness of the banking system and the large amount of unhedged short-term foreign debt owed by the corporate sector. On November 5, 1997, the Executive Board approved financial support of up to SDR 7.3 billion, equivalent to 490 percent of Indonesia's quota, over the next three years.

The initial program of economic reform envisaged:

• stabilizing the rupiah by retaining a tight monetary policy;

• financial sector restructuring, including closing unviable institutions, merging state banks, and establishing a timetable for dealing with remaining weak institutions and improving the institutional, legal, and regulatory framework for the financial system;

• structural reforms to enhance economic efficiency and transparency, including liberalization of foreign trade and investment, dismantling of domestic monopolies, and expanding the privatization program; and

• fiscal measures equivalent to about 1 percent of GDP in 1997/98 and 2 percent in 1998/99, to yield a public sector surplus of 1 percent of GDP in both years, to facilitate external adjustment and provide resources to pay for financial restructuring. The fiscal measures included cutting low-priority expenditures, including postponing or rescheduling major state enterprise infrastructure projects; reducing government subsidies; eliminating value-added tax (VAT) exemptions; and adjusting administered prices, including the prices of electricity and petroleum products.

Against the background of a continuing loss of confidence in the Indonesian economy and further sharp declines in the value of the rupiah, owing in part to a lack of progress in implementing the program and to uncertainty with respect to the government's commitment to the program, the Indonesian authorities announced a reinforcement and acceleration of the program in a new Memorandum of Economic and Financial Policies on January 15, 1998. Key reinforcing measures included:

• canceling 12 infrastructure projects and revoking or discontinuing financial privileges for the IPTN's (Nusantara Aircraft Industry's) airplane projects and the National Car project;

• strengthening the bank and corporate sector restructuring effort, including the subsequent announcement of a process to put in place a framework for creditors and debtors to deal on a voluntary, case-by-case basis with the external debt problems of Indonesian corporations, the establishment of the Indonesian Bank Restructuring Agency (IBRA), and a government guarantee on bank deposits and credits;

- limiting the monopoly of the national marketing board (BULOG) to rice, deregulating domestic trade in agricultural produce, and eliminating restrictive market arrangements;
- adjusting the 1998/99 budget—to provide for a public sector deficit of about 1 percent of GDP—in order to accommodate part of the impact on the budget of the economic slowdown; and
- taking steps to alleviate the suffering caused by the drought, including ensuring that adequate food supplies were available at reasonable prices.

Subsequently, owing to policy slippages, continuing uncertainty about the government's commitment to elements of the program, and other developments, the rupiah failed to stabilize, inflation picked up sharply, and economic conditions deteriorated. The government issued a Supplementary Memorandum of Economic and Financial Policies on April 10, 1998, adapting the macroeconomic policies to the deteriorated economic situation and further expanding the structural and banking reforms agreed in January. The envisaged measures included:

- a substantial strengthening of monetary policy aimed at stabilizing the rupiah;
- accelerated bank restructuring, with IBRA to continue its takeover or closure of weak or unviable institutions and be empowered to issue bonds to finance the restoration of financial viability for qualified institutions; the elimination of existing restrictions on foreign ownership of banks; and the issuance of a new bankruptcy law;
- an extensive agenda of structural reforms to increase competition and efficiency in the economy, reinforcing the commitments made in January and including the further privatization of six major state enterprises already listed and the identification of seven new enterprises for privatization in 1998/99;
- accelerated arrangements to develop a framework with foreign creditors to restore trade financing and resolve the issues of corporate debt and interbank credit;
- strengthening the social safety net through the temporary maintenance of subsidies on food and other essentials, through support for small and medium-sized enterprises, and through public works programs; and
- enhancing the implementation and credibility of the program through daily monitoring of the reform program by the Indonesian Executive Committee of the Resilience Council, in close cooperation with the IMF, the World Bank, and the Asian Development Bank; substantive actions prior to approval of the program by the Executive Board; and provision for frequent reviews of the program by the Board.

The government issued a Second Supplementary Memorandum of Economic and Financial Policies on June 24, 1998, after the economic situation was made worse and the economic program driven off track by social disturbances and political change in May. The envisaged measures gave high priority to strengthening the social safety net, comprehensively restructuring the banking system, and repairing the weakened distribution system. They included:

- increasing social expenditure to 7.5 percent of GDP, with provision for, among other things, food, fuel, medical, and other subsidies (to be phased out after the economy had begun to improve); the expansion of employment-generating programs, supported by the World Bank, Asian Development Bank, and bilateral donors; and aid to students;
- measures to limit the budget deficit to 8.5 percent of GDP, a level that could be financed with foreign funds, including cuts in infrastructure projects and improvements in the efficiency of state-run operations;
- rehabilitating and strengthening the distribution system, following the disruption caused by social disturbances, to ensure adequate supplies of essential commodities—including the establishment of a special monitoring unit to identify potential shortages of foodstuffs or distribution bottlenecks;
- restructuring the banking system by strengthening relatively sound banks—partly through the infusion of new capital—while moving swiftly to recapitalize, merge, or effectively close weak banks, and maintaining the commitment to guarantee all depositors and creditors. The authorities would also establish a high-level Financial Sector Advisory Committee to advise on the coordination of actions for bank restructuring;
- establishing an effective bankruptcy system, as an essential part of the corporate debt-restructuring strategy envisaged by the June 4 agreement between the government and creditor banks on debt restructuring; and
- strengthening the monitoring of the economic program.

Table 5 shows selected economic indicators for Indonesia.

* * *

Chronological Highlights

1997

November 5   The Executive Board approves a Stand-By Arrangement for Indonesia authorizing drawings of up to SDR 7.3 billion, and disburses SDR 2.2 billion.

Table 5
Indonesia: Selected Economic Indicators, as of July 23, 1998

	1995	1996	1997[1]	1998[2]
	Percent change			
Real GDP growth	8.2	8.0	4.6	–13 to –14
Consumer prices (end of period)	9.0	6.6	11.6	80.6
	Percent of GDP; a minus sign signifies a deficit			
Central government balance	0.9	1.2	–0.9	–8.5
Current account balance	–3.2	–3.3	–1.8	1.6
	Billions of U.S. dollars			
External debt	107.8	110.2	136.1	135.0
Of which: short-term debt	9.5	13.4	18.8	. . .
	Percent of GDP			
External debt	53.3	48.5	64.5	162.7

Data: Indonesian authorities; and IMF staff estimates. Fiscal and external sector data are for Indonesian fiscal years (April 1 to March 31).
[1]Estimate.
[2]June 1998 program.

1998

Mid-January IMF management visits Jakarta to consult with President Suharto on an acceleration of reforms already agreed under the program, after further depreciation of the rupiah.

January 15 Indonesia issues Memorandum of Economic and Financial Policies on additional measures.

January 26 The IMF welcomes Indonesia's plans for a comprehensive program to rehabilitate the banking sector and put into place a framework for creditors and debtors to deal, on a voluntary and case-by-case basis, with the external debt problems of corporations.

April 10 Indonesia issues a Supplementary Memorandum of Economic and Financial Policies on additional measures.

May 4 The Board completes the first review under the Stand-By Arrangement and disburses SDR 734 million.

June 24 Indonesia issues a Second Supplementary Memorandum of Economic and Financial Policies on additional measures.

July 15 The Board completes the second review of the Stand-By Arrangement, disbursing SDR 734 million, and approves an increase in IMF financing under the Stand-By Arrangement by SDR 1 billion. The IMF also announces that additional multilateral and bilateral financing for the program will be made available, in part through an informal arrangement among bilateral creditors that involves debt rescheduling or the provision of new money—for total additional financing of more than $6 billion, including the increase in IMF financing.

Korea

Over a number of decades, Korea transformed itself into an advanced industrial economy. Economic overheating, however, led to an increase in structural problems; in particular, the financial system was undermined by excessive government interference in the economy, close linkages between banks and conglomerates, an inadequate sequencing of capital account liberalization, and the lack of prudential regulation that should accompany liberalization. As the Asian financial crisis spread in the latter part of 1997, a loss of market confidence brought the country close to depleting its foreign exchange reserves. On December 4, 1997, the Executive Board approved financing of up to SDR 15.5 billion, equivalent to 1,939 percent of Korea's quota in the IMF, over the next three years.

The initial program of economic reform featured:

• comprehensive financial sector restructuring that introduced a clear and firm exit policy for weak financial institutions, strong market and supervisory discipline, and more independence for the central bank. The operations of nine insolvent merchant banks were suspended, two large distressed commercial banks received capital injections from the government, and all commercial banks with inadequate capital were required to submit plans for recapitalization;

• fiscal measures expected to yield savings equivalent to about 2 percent of GDP to make room for the costs of financial sector restructuring in the budget, while maintaining a prudent fiscal stance. Fiscal measures included widening the bases for corporate, income, and value-added taxes;

• efforts to dismantle the nontransparent and inefficient ties among the government, banks, and businesses, including measures to upgrade accounting, auditing, and disclosure standards, to require that corporate financial statements be prepared on a consolidated basis and certified by external auditors, and to phase out the system of cross guarantees within conglomerates;

• trade liberalization measures, including setting a timetable to eliminate trade-related subsidies and an import diversification program, as well as streamlining and improving the transparency of import certification procedures;

- capital account liberalization measures to open up the Korean money, bond, and equity markets to capital inflows, and to liberalize foreign direct investment;
- labor market reform to facilitate the redeployment of labor; and
- the publication and dissemination of key economic and financial data.

As described in a Letter of Intent of December 24, 1997, the program was intensified and accelerated as the financial crisis in Korea worsened and concerns about whether international banks would roll over Korean short-term external debt placed additional pressures on international reserves and the won. Announcement of the strengthened program was accompanied by the start of negotiations between the Korean government and creditor banks to extend the maturities of short-term interbank debts. The measures included:

- further monetary tightening and the abolition of the daily exchange rate band;
- speeding up the liberalization of capital and money markets, including the lifting of all capital account restrictions on foreign investors' access to the Korean bond market by December 31, 1997; and
- accelerating the implementation of the comprehensive restructuring plan for the financial sector, including establishing a high-level team to negotiate with foreign creditors and reducing the recourse of Korean banks to the foreign exchange window of the central bank.

A Letter of Intent dated January 7, 1998, provided additional details of the Korean government's external and reserve management strategies and further articulated the financial sector reform program.

In a subsequent Letter of Intent of February 7, 1998, the macroeconomic framework was further revised and the policies that the government intended to pursue for 1998 were set out. These policies, formulated against the background of the January 29 agreement between the Korean authorities and a group of creditor banks on a voluntary debt exchange, included:

- targeting a fiscal deficit of about 1 percent of GDP for 1998 to accommodate the impact of weaker economic activity on the budget and to allow for higher expenditure on the social safety net;
- moving forward to implement a broader strategy of financial sector restructuring, having contained the

Table 6

Korea: Selected Economic Indicators, as of July 23, 1998

	1995	1996	1997	1998[1]
	Percent change			
Real GDP growth	8.9	7.1	5.5	−1 to −2
Consumer prices (end of period)	4.7	4.9	6.6	8.2
	Percent of GDP; a minus sign signifies a deficit			
Central government balance	0.3	0.3	0.0	−1.7
Current account balance	−1.9	−4.7	−1.9	7.3
	Billions of U.S. dollars			
External debt	119.7	157.5	154.4	163.3
Of which: short-term debt	78.7	100.0	68.4	39.6
	Percent of GDP			
External debt	26.4	32.5	34.9	51.5

Data: Korean authorities; and IMF staff estimates. Data are for financial years (January 1 to December 31).
[1]May 1998 program.

immediate dangers of disruptions to the financial system;

- increasing the range and amounts of financial instruments available to foreign investors, increasing the access of Korean companies to foreign capital markets, and liberalizing the scope for mergers and acquisitions in the corporate sector; and
- introducing a number of measures to improve corporate transparency, including strengthening the oversight functions of corporate boards of directors, increasing accountability to shareholders, and introducing outside directors and external audit committees.

In a Letter of Intent of May 2, 1998, the Korean authorities updated the program of economic reform in view of the progress made in resolving the external financing crisis, on the one hand, and the even weaker outlook for economic activity, on the other. Positive developments included the conclusion of the restructuring of $22 billion of Korean banks' short-term foreign debt, a successful return to international capital markets through a sovereign global bond issue of $4 billion, the shifting of the current account into substantial surplus, and an increase in usable reserves to more than $30 billion. The measures cited in the Letter of Intent included:

- accommodation of a larger fiscal deficit of about 2 percent of GDP in 1998, in light of weaker growth and through the operation of automatic stabilizers;
- measures to strengthen and expand the social safety net, including through a widening of the coverage of unemployment insurance and increases in minimum benefit duration and levels, as well as a temporary lowering of minimum contribution periods;

- formation of an appraisal committee, including international experts, to evaluate the recapitalization plans of undercapitalized commercial banks;
- publication by August 15, 1998, of regulations to bring Korea's prudential regulations closer to international best practices, including by strengthening compliance with existing guidelines concerning foreign exchange maturity mismatches; and
- further phased liberalization of the capital account, including loosening restrictions on foreign exchange transactions, foreign ownership of certain assets, and ceilings on foreign equity investment in nonlisted companies.

Table 6 (previous page) shows selected economic indicators for Korea.

* * *

Chronological Highlights

1997

December 3	The IMF notes the successful conclusion of staff discussions with the Korean authorities and the pledges of support coming from the World Bank, ADB, and countries in the group of potential participants in the supplemental financing support package for Korea.
December 4	The Board approves an SDR 15.5 billion Stand-By Arrangement for Korea and releases a disbursement of SDR 4.1 billion.
December 18	The Board concludes the first biweekly review of the Stand-By Arrangement and releases a further SDR 2.6 billion, activating the IMF's new Supplemental Reserve Facility.
December 24	Korea issues a Letter of Intent, providing for an intensification and acceleration of its program. The Managing Director announces his intention to rec-

ommend to the Board a significant acceleration of the resources available to Korea—in light of Korea's Letter of Intent and in the context of the progress between Korean and international banks in dealing with Korea's external debt—and notes that the World Bank and ADB will disburse $5 billion before the year's end.

December 30	The Board approves a request by Korea for a modification of the schedule of drawings, bringing forward part of the amounts originally scheduled for February and May 1998, but without changing overall access to IMF resources, and disburses SDR 1.5 billion.

1998

January 7	Korea issues a Letter of Intent describing additional measures.
January 8	The Board concludes the second biweekly review of the Stand-By Arrangement and disburses SDR 1.5 billion.
January 29	The government, Korean domestic financial institutions, and international banks announce a debt-rescheduling agreement.
February 7	Korea issues a Letter of Intent on additional measures.
February 17	The Board completes the first quarterly review of the Stand-By Arrangement and disburses a further SDR 1.5 billion.
May 2	Korea issues a Letter of Intent describing additional measures.
May 29	The Board completes the second quarterly review of the Stand-By Arrangement, disbursing an additional SDR 1.4 billion and concluding the 1998 Article IV consultation.

CHAPTER VI

Surveillance

Central to the IMF's purposes and operations is the mandate, under its Articles of Agreement, to "exercise firm surveillance over the exchange rate policies of members." To carry out this mandate, the IMF exercises surveillance through both multilateral and bilateral means. Multilateral surveillance consists of Executive Board reviews of developments in the international monetary system based principally on the staff's World Economic Outlook reports and through periodic discussions of developments, prospects, and key policy issues in international capital markets. Bilateral surveillance takes the form of consultations with individual member countries, conducted annually for most members, under Article IV of the IMF's Articles of Agreement. The Board supplements this systematic monitoring of individual country and global developments with informal related discussions.

Traditionally, the IMF's main focus in surveillance has been to encourage countries to correct macroeconomic imbalances, reduce inflation, and undertake key trade, exchange, and other market reforms. But increasingly, and depending on the situation in each country, a much broader range of institutional measures has been seen as necessary for countries to establish and maintain private sector confidence and lay the groundwork for sustained growth (see Box 2). In 1997/98, in addition to its discussions of regular Article IV consultations, the Board met a number of times to develop guidance in each of these areas.

Article IV Consultations in 1997/98

Consultations under Article IV of the IMF's Articles of Agreement are held with each member country, for the most part, every year. An IMF staff team visits the country, collects economic and financial information, and discusses with the authorities the economic developments and the monetary, fiscal, and structural policies they are following. The staff generally prepares a concluding statement for discussion with the authorities at the end of the visit; in some instances, the concluding statement is released to the public. On its return to headquarters, the staff team prepares a report

analyzing the economic situation and evaluating the stance of policies. This report is then discussed by the Executive Board. At the end of the discussion, the Chairman of the Board summarizes the views expressed by Directors during the meeting. This "summing up" is transmitted to the country's authorities. It is then released to the public—at the option of the country—in the form of a Press (now "Public") Information Notice (see Box 3). During 1997/98, the IMF concluded 136 Article IV consultations (Table 7).

To ensure more continuous and effective surveillance, the Board supplements this systematic monitoring of individual country developments with regular informal sessions—sometimes monthly, or even more frequently—on significant developments in selected countries and regions. It also meets regularly to discuss world economic and financial market developments. These continuing assessments by the Board inform and guide the work of IMF staff on member countries and are communicated to national authorities by Executive Directors.

Other Means of Surveillance

Surveillance through Article IV consultations is the main channel for collaboration between the IMF and its members. In addition, for members facing balance of payments difficulties, formal financial arrangements for the immediate use of IMF resources provide a framework for more intensive collaboration (see Chapter VIII). In some cases, members collaborate with the IMF in other ways, such as precautionary financial arrangements, informal staff-monitored programs, and enhanced surveillance.

- *Precautionary Arrangements.* Members agree with the IMF on a Stand-By or Extended Arrangement but do not intend to use resources committed under these arrangements unless circumstances warrant. The country has the right, however, to draw on the resources provided it has met the conditions agreed in the arrangement. Such arrangements help members by providing a framework for economic policy and highlighting the IMF's endorsement of its poli-

Box 2
Second-Generation Reforms

Although macroeconomic stability, lib-eralization, and the basic institutional framework of a market economy are essential for strong growth, the IMF's experience with its member countries has shown that deeper and broader-based reforms are necessary to achieve high-quality growth that is sustainable and more equitably shared. Such reforms—so-called second-generation reforms—cover a number of areas highlighted most recently by the Asian financial crisis.

The IMF, in collaboration with the World Bank, has been contributing to second-generation reforms in member countries through its surveillance (along with other international organi-zations as appropriate), technical assis-tance, and financing, on several fronts:
- helping members strengthen the efficiency and robustness of their financial sectors, including through appropriate prudential oversight;
- helping members enhance the trans-parency of fiscal policy and practices and the quality, timeliness, and dis-semination of economic and finan-cial data to reduce the risk of disrup-tive changes in investor confidence when economic or financial prob-lems appear;
- helping members improve gover-nance by establishing a simple and transparent regulatory environment and a professional and independent judicial system that will uphold the rule of law, including property rights;
- assisting members in redefining the role of the state in the economy as a positive force for private sector activ-ity, including through the restruc-turing and privatization of state-owned enterprises and by gen-erally reducing government inter-vention in areas where market forces provide greater efficiency;
- helping improve the quality of pub-lic expenditure in member countries, for example, through greater atten-tion to education and health spend-ing; and
- helping members promote greater flexibility of labor markets.

cies, thereby boosting confidence in them. They also assure the country that IMF resources will be avail-able if needed and provided the agreed conditions are met.
- *Informal Staff-Monitored Programs.* IMF staff moni-tor the country's economic program and regularly discuss progress under that program with the authorities; however, there is no formal IMF endorsement of the member's policies.
- *Enhanced Surveillance.* This also does not constitute formal IMF endorsement of a member's economic policies. Rather, the emphasis is on close and formal monitoring by the IMF. The procedure was initially established to facilitate debt-rescheduling arrange-ments with commercial banks but has been used occasionally in other situations.

In a few cases, the intensified monitoring described above has been a prelude to an IMF-supported adjust-ment program. More often, monitoring provides the authorities with a framework to reassure interested third parties, such as donors, creditors, or financial markets.

Lessons for Surveillance from the Asian Crisis

In March 1998, the Executive Board undertook its reg-ular review of members' policies in the context of sur-veillance, this time focusing on the lessons for surveillance from the Asian crisis. In their review, Direc-tors noted that the IMF's perfor-mance in identifying emerging tensions in crisis-affected countries at an early stage had been mixed. In the case of Thailand, the IMF had expressed serious concerns about economic developments beginning in 1996—concerns conveyed to the authorities in several ways, including through confidential contacts at the highest level. Indeed, the IMF appeared to have been more aware of the risks in Thailand's economic policy course than had most market observers. In other cases in Asia, however, the IMF—while having identified critical weaknesses, partic-ularly in the financial sector—had been taken by surprise, owing in part to the lack of access to requisite information and also to an inability to see the full consequences of the combination of structural weaknesses in the economy and contagion effects. In particular, in the case of Korea, the IMF had not attached sufficient urgency to the financial tensions that had begun developing in early 1997.

With hindsight it was clear that the affected coun-tries' vulnerabilities had been underestimated, includ-ing by the markets. Directors also remarked that some other emerging market economies had taken timely and sustained policy measures in the face of market pressures and had been able to fend off spreading tur-moil successfully. In those cases, close IMF surveillance had been helpful. Some Directors stressed that it was unrealistic to expect IMF surveillance to detect all problems early and prevent all crises, and that the con-tagion effects of the crisis in Thailand were, to a large extent, unpredictable. Nevertheless, they encouraged the staff, in exercising surveillance, to place increased emphasis on the risks of contagion effects.

Directors agreed that the experience of the past nine months had provided valuable lessons for the IMF and for the international financial community. Events were still unfolding, and many issues would need revisiting, including the design and implementation of IMF-supported programs; the role of the IMF and other official financing for these programs; collaboration between the IMF and other international institutions, especially the World Bank; the role of the private sector in crisis situations; and the IMF's policy on public information. To this end, it was agreed early in the new financial year 1998/99 that a review of the experience with IMF programs in the Asian crisis countries should be undertaken before the October 1998 Annual Meetings to address questions of program orientation and design, implementation, and, to the extent possible, early program results. The experience with the Asian crisis countries would also be examined in 1998/99 as part of the world economic outlook exercise and in the context of the annual report on international capital markets. The lessons from the Asian experience would be reflected in several papers addressing various aspects of strengthening the architecture of the international monetary system, focusing on the availability and the dissemination of economic data, transparency in members' policies and in IMF surveillance, and the role of international standards in assessing countries' policies and practices. There would also be further Board discussion on establishing appropriate incentives for international financial flows by involving the private sector in forestalling or resolving financial crises. The IMF would be incorporating lessons from the Asian crisis in its continuing work on orderly and appropriately sequenced capital account liberalization. In addition, the experience with World Bank–IMF collaboration, notably in the area of financial sector reform, would be reviewed with the aim of identifying areas with scope for improvement.

In March 1998, looking at IMF surveillance, Directors identified five main lessons.

Lesson One

The effectiveness of surveillance depended critically on the timely availability of accurate information. Directors saw some improvement since 1995 in members' provision of data, both to the IMF and to the markets, but felt that further progress was essential. The Asian crisis had revealed the critical importance of certain data that had not been available, either because the authorities had been reluctant to provide them, such as reserve-related liabilities of the central bank, or because systems did not exist to produce timely data, such as that on private short-term debt. The crisis had also demonstrated that adequate provision of data to the public was important for promoting transparency and strengthening market confidence. Directors emphasized that further efforts to strengthen members' provision of data to the IMF and to the public could be realized through the Special Data Dissemination Standard; in both domains, the monitoring of compliance had to be strengthened. Several Directors cautioned

---

Box 3
Enhancing Information on Article IV Consultations

Since May 1997, the Executive Board has been issuing Press (now "Public") Information Notices (PINs) following the conclusion of Article IV consultations with members. PINs set out:
- a background description of the country's economic situation at the time of the consultation;
- the Board's assessment of that situation and the country's policies as detailed in the Chairman's summing up of the Board's discussion; and
- a table of selected economic indicators.

PINs are issued on a voluntary basis, at the request of countries seeking to make public the views of the IMF on their policies and prospects. Of the 136 consultations completed during 1997/98, 77 resulted in the issuance of PINs (see Table 7). The full text of PINs is available on the IMF's website (http://www.imf.org). Collections of PINs are also being published three times a year in a new IMF publication, *IMF Economic Reviews;* the first issue was released in May 1998.

---

that access to highly sensitive data or data for which appropriate standards were not yet universally adopted, such as prudential indicators, had to be handled carefully. Directors particularly stressed the importance of compiling timely and accurate data on short-term external debt, while recognizing that this would require substantial statistical efforts on the part of most countries concerned. It was agreed that, in cases where countries were unable to collect the required data, technical assistance—including from the IMF in its areas of competence—was important. In the meantime, more attention should be paid to using and improving existing data sources, including data from the Bank for International Settlements.

More generally, considering the changing architecture of the international financial system and the variety of data sources, some Directors felt that the IMF needed to begin work with other international organizations, including national regulatory authorities and market participants, toward developing a conceptual framework for data compilation and dissemination. Directors strongly urged the staff to bring to the Board's attention cases where its inability to obtain the necessary data had hampered effective surveillance, and they suggested that ways to strengthen the IMF's reaction to such cases be explored. Some Directors suggested that consideration be given to not concluding Article IV consultations where members' willingness to provide the IMF with the data required for surveillance was in question. This view was endorsed by the Interim Committee, which in its April 1998 meeting recommended that if persistent deficiencies in disclosing relevant data to the IMF seriously impede surveillance, conclusion of Article IV consultations should be delayed.

Lesson Two

The focus of surveillance had to extend beyond short-term macroeconomic issues, while remaining appropri-

Table 7
Article IV Consultations Concluded in 1997/98

Country	Board Date	PIN Issued	Country	Board Date	PIN Issued
Algeria	June 27, 1997	July 23, 1997	India	July 2, 1997	July 16, 1997
Angola	October 8, 1997	—	Indonesia	July 9, 1997	—
Antigua and Barbuda	December 3, 1997	December 17, 1997	Iran, Islamic		
Argentina	February 4, 1998	February 23, 1998	Republic of	January 30, 1998	—
Armenia	February 6, 1998	March 12, 1998	Ireland	July 2, 1997	July 25, 1997
			Israel	February 11, 1998	March 10, 1998
Aruba	May 19, 1997	May 27, 1997			
Austria	June 13, 1997	June 20, 1997	Italy	March 13, 1998	—
Bahamas, the	March 13, 1998	March 31, 1998	Jamaica	September 8, 1997	October 2, 1997
Bahrain	March 4, 1998	—	Japan	July 25, 1997	August 13, 1997
Bangladesh	August 18, 1997	—	Jordan	April 23, 1998	—
			Kazakhstan	June 20, 1997	—
Barbados	January 30, 1998	February 25, 1998			
Belarus	August 21, 1997	—	Kiribati	June 2, 1997	
Belgium	February 23, 1998	March 3, 1998	Kuwait	October 15, 1997	February 3, 1998
Belize	May 12, 1997	June 5, 1997`	Kyrgyz Republic	December 12, 1997	—
Bolivia	September 10, 1997	September 19, 1997	Laos	June 16, 1997	—
			Latvia	March 23, 1998	April 14, 1998
Botswana	March 13, 1998	April 10, 1998			
Brazil	February 11, 1998	March 13, 1998	Lebanon	December 12, 1997	—
Brunei Darussalam	October 6, 1997	—	Lesotho	February 4, 1998	—
Bulgaria	July 23, 1997	July 29, 1997	Lithuania	June 25, 1997	July 14, 1997
Burundi	October 8, 1997	—	Madagascar	September 10, 1997	October 28, 1997
			Malawi	September 12, 1997	—
Cambodia	April 27, 1998	—			
Cameroon	January 7, 1998	January 21, 1998	Malaysia	September 5, 1997	—
Canada	January 30, 1998	February 19, 1998	Malaysia[1]	April 20, 1998	April 27, 1998
Cape Verde	February 20, 1998	March 10, 1998	Maldives	January 26, 1998	—
Chad	June 13, 1997	July 15, 1997	Mali	December 22, 1997	April 1, 1998
			Malta	May 23, 1997	—
Chile	February 11, 1998	February 20, 1998			
China, People's			Mauritania	July 14, 1997	August 27, 1997
Republic of	June 30, 1997	—	Mexico	September 2, 1997	—
Colombia	June 6, 1997	—	Moldova	April 20, 1998	May 27, 1998
Comoros	October 8, 1997	—	Mongolia	July 30, 1997	September 3, 1997
Costa Rica	March 18, 1998	May 14, 1998	Morocco	March 6, 1998	March 31, 1998
Côte D' Ivoire	March 17, 1998	—	Mozambique	April 7, 1998	April 30, 1998
Czech Republic	February 13, 1998	March 6, 1998	Namibia	October 22, 1997	—
Djibouti	May 21, 1997	—	Nepal	May 28, 1997	June 13, 1997
Dominica	May 23, 1997	June 27, 1997	Netherlands	June 12, 1997	July 1, 1997
Dominican Republic	August 21, 1997	September 17, 1997	New Zealand	November 7, 1997	January 12, 1998
Ecuador	September 3, 1997	—	Nicaragua	March 18, 1998	April 9, 1998
Egypt	January 7, 1998	—	Niger	July 28, 1997	—
El Salvador	February 20, 1998	April 6, 1998	Norway	February 23, 1998	March 9, 1998
Equatorial Guinea	February 2, 1998	—	Pakistan	October 20, 1997	November 4, 1997
Eritrea	July 28, 1997		Panama	December 10, 1997	December 22, 1997
Estonia	December 17, 1997	December 24, 1997	Papua New Guinea	January 23, 1998	—
Ethiopia	November 21, 1997	—	Paraguay	October 10, 1997	October 22, 1997
Finland	July 14, 1997	July 23, 1997	Peru	June 25, 1997	—
France	October 22, 1997	November 4, 1997	Philippines	March 27, 1998	—
Gabon	May 21, 1997		Poland	March 16, 1998	March 30, 1998
Gambia, the	October 6, 1997	—	Portugal	October 17, 1997	November 7, 1997
Germany	August 25, 1997	August 29, 1997	Qatar	June 23, 1997	—
Ghana	October 31, 1997	December 1, 1997	Russian Federation	May 16, 1997	—
Greece	August 1, 1997	—	São Tomé and Príncipe	July 16, 1997	—
Grenada	October 6, 1997	October 22, 1997	Senegal	July 28, 1997	August 26, 1997
Guinea	April 3, 1998	April 29, 1998	Sierra Leone	May 5, 1997	
Guinea-Bissau	March 6, 1998	March 26, 1998	Singapore	February 20, 1998	March 16, 1998
Guyana	December 22, 1997	—	Slovak Republic	February 13, 1998	
Hong Kong SAR	January 26, 1998	February 16, 1998	Slovenia	January 9, 1998	January 26, 1998
Hungary	September 8, 1997	—	South Africa	July 11, 1997	August 25, 1997

Table 7 (concluded)

Country	Board Date	PIN Issued	Country	Board Date	PIN Issued
Spain	March 16, 1998	April 6, 1998	Turkey	July 9, 1997	August 5, 1997
Sri Lanka	July 23, 1997	August 5, 1997	Turkmenistan	May 21, 1997	—
St. Kitts and Nevis	June 18, 1997	June 26, 1997	United Arab Emirates	October 8, 1997	—
St. Vincent	December 3, 1997	December 17, 1997	Uganda	April 8, 1998	June 11, 1998
Sudan	February 27, 1998	April 13, 1998	Ukraine	August 25, 1997	—
Suriname	June 4, 1997	—	United Kingdom	October 27, 1997	November 6, 1997
Sweden	August 22, 1997	September 2, 1997	United States	July 28, 1997	August 4, 1997
Switzerland	February 20, 1998	March 6, 1998	Uruguay	June 20, 1997	—
Tajikistan	December 19, 1997	—	Uzbekistan	July 30, 1997	—
Tanzania	December 3, 1997	December 23, 1997	Vietnam	February 2, 1998	—
Thailand	June 13, 1997	—	Yemen	October 29, 1997	—
Togo	January 21, 1998	February 19, 1998	Zambia	October 8, 1997	—
Tunisia	May 23, 1997	June 5, 1997	Zimbabwe	May 21, 1997	—

[1]Malaysia's 1998/99 Article IV consultation was advanced to April 20, 1998.

ately selective. There had been increased coverage and analysis of key structural policies, especially financial sector policies, in emerging market economies since 1995. Problems in the financial sector were often complex and long in gestation, however, and many Directors felt that the IMF needed to develop more expertise in their analysis, including by expanding staff resources with the relevant experience. Noting that the IMF's comparative advantage was in analyzing macroeconomic developments, some Directors felt that financial sector restructuring should be left to other institutions, especially the World Bank. Others considered that, in the context of the Asian crisis, such a distinction had not always been easy to draw, and that the initial intensive role of the IMF in all aspects of the financial sector reforms had been essential. Collaboration with other institutions, it was agreed, had to be close and aimed at avoiding duplication of efforts, especially those of the World Bank, as well as national supervisory authorities and the BIS. Several Directors emphasized the usefulness of developing standards in a variety of areas that could help in the conduct of surveillance and provide information to markets; they suggested that IMF surveillance could usefully encourage members to adapt their practices in line with international standards, such as those laid out in the Basle Committee on Banking Supervision's Core Principles on Banking Supervision.

The vulnerability of many emerging market economies to large capital flows was seen as underlining the importance, also, of close IMF surveillance over capital account issues. Some Directors stressed the need to monitor carefully the sequencing and the pace of moves toward capital account liberalization. In particular, IMF surveillance should focus on the risks posed by the potential reversal of large capital flows, the rapid accumulation of short-term external debt, and the impact of selective capital account liberalization. In this area, too, Directors stressed the critical importance of accurate and timely data. A few speakers proposed that consultation reports systematically address progress toward capital account liberalization. Some other Directors thought that the experience of the previous nine months suggested that selective, well-targeted capital controls could play a useful role in reducing a country's vulnerability. Most Directors, however, were skeptical that introducing controls in economies with already relatively open capital accounts could be helpful, beyond perhaps providing temporary breathing space to put in place more fundamental adjustment policies.

Lesson Three

In an environment of increased financial and trade flows between countries, IMF surveillance at the country level should pay greater attention to policy interdependence and to the risks of contagion. How policies in systemically or regionally important countries affect other countries should receive closer attention, Directors remarked. At the same time, the vulnerability of domestic conditions to external developments should be examined in bilateral consultations, with the objective of urging early, forceful action to mitigate the risks of contagion. Directors noted that multilateral surveillance could help in identifying potential spillover effects; they underlined the importance of more fully integrating the IMF's multilateral surveillance exercises with its bilateral dialogue with members and ensuring that the available staff expertise in capital market and financial sector issues was fully used in bilateral surveillance. Many Directors also supported a more frequent and systematic exchange of views between staff and market participants as part of surveillance; they considered that, in relevant cases, staff reports should include a summary assessment

The establishment of a new Regional Office for Asia and the Pacific in Tokyo reflects the importance of the Asia-Pacific region in the global economy and for the work of the IMF. The Director of the Office, Kunio Saito, administers a staff of 10. The main functions of the Office include the following:

- *Regional Policy Forums.* The Office is responsible for the IMF's dialogue with Asian policymakers that is conducted through various regional policy forums, including the Manila Framework Group, Asia-Pacific Economic Cooperation (APEC), Association of South East Asian Nations (ASEAN), and the Executives' Meeting of East Asian and Pacific Central Banks and Monetary Authorities (EMEAP), and for facilitating regional and mutual surveillance activities. The Manila Framework Group brings together deputies from ministries of finance and central banks of 14 economies across the region. It is the principal new grouping aimed at strengthening surveillance, enhancing cooperation, and promoting financial stability in the region. The Regional Office provides the Secretariat for this Group.

- *Financial Market Surveillance.* The Office monitors and analyzes financial markets in the region with a view to ensuring that the IMF has timely and comprehensive knowledge of market developments and trends. This analysis deepens the IMF's understanding of economic developments in the region and is an important element in strengthening surveillance.

The Office also undertakes a wide range of external relations activities, and facilitates the delivery of technical assistance and training in the region.

of market sentiment. A few Directors cautioned that such contacts should take into account the confidentiality of the IMF's dialogue with members.

Lesson Four

The crucial role of credibility in restoring market confidence underscored the importance of transparency. In this regard, Directors welcomed the decision by the authorities in Indonesia, Korea, and Thailand to release the Letters of Intent to the IMF detailing their adjustment programs. Several Directors also welcomed the fact that an increasing number of countries were agreeing to the release of Press (now "Public") Information Notices, summarizing the content of Article IV consultations in the Board, and felt that it would be desirable if as many countries as possible could agree to do so. Some Directors felt that the IMF could go further in disseminating its views on the economic policies of its members; they suggested revisiting the issue of publication of staff reports for Article IV consultations. Some other Directors, however, advocated a more cautious approach, noting that maintaining confidentiality was key to effective surveillance. A few Directors also supported the suggestion that if, after a period of time, a member continued to ignore IMF warnings expressed confidentially, the IMF should, as a last resort, make use of the provision of Article XII, Section 8, of its Articles of Agreement, to make its concerns known to the public. But most Directors doubted that more public warnings would increase the effectiveness of surveillance. They were particularly concerned that the threat of publicity would jeopardize the frank dialogue between the IMF and member countries and that public warnings could accelerate crises rather than prevent them.

Lesson Five

The effectiveness of IMF surveillance depended crucially on the willingness of members to take its advice. A candid dialogue and the ability of the IMF to focus on the issues of importance to individual members were vital for effective surveillance. In addition, Directors emphasized the opportunity for IMF staff to harness the opinions of the international community by engaging in regional forums more actively; they believed the IMF should work closely with such forums in Asia and elsewhere (Box 4). Some Directors noted the importance of peer pressure both in regional forums and through the Board. Directors welcomed the IMF's involvement in the discussions of the Asia-Pacific Economic Cooperation Council and the Second Manila Framework Meeting in Tokyo.

Government Transparency and Accountability

The IMF has long provided advice and technical assistance to help foster good governance in member countries, including by promoting public sector transparency and accountability. In recent years, increased attention has been focused on issues associated with good governance. In particular, in its Declaration on Partnership for Sustainable Global Growth, adopted in September 1996, the IMF's Interim Committee identified "promoting good governance in all its aspects, including ensuring the rule of law, improving the efficiency and accountability of the public sector, and tackling corruption" as essential for helping economies prosper. Similarly, at its April 1998 meeting, the Interim Committee, in an effort to enhance the accountability and credibility of fiscal policy as a key feature of good governance, adopted a Code of Good Practices on Fiscal Transparency: Declaration on Principles.

In 1997/98, the IMF's Executive Board met a number of times to develop guidance for the institution regarding governance issues and a code of good practices for member countries in the area of fiscal transparency.

Good Governance

In a discussion of the IMF's role in governance issues in May 1997, Executive Directors strongly endorsed the importance of good governance for economic efficiency and growth. It was observed that the IMF's role in this area was evolving pragmatically as more was learned about the contribution that greater attention to governance issues could make to macroeconomic stability and sustainable growth in member countries. Directors strongly supported the role the IMF had been playing in this area in recent years through its policy advice and technical assistance and welcomed the aim of ensuring a more comprehensive treatment, in the context of both Article IV consultations and IMF-supported programs, of governance issues within the IMF's mandate and expertise. Directors stressed the need for evenhandedness in the treatment of governance issues in all member countries. Directors also felt the IMF's efforts to encourage good governance had to be supported by enhanced collaboration with other multilateral institutions—in particular, the World Bank—to make better use of complementary areas of expertise.

Governance issues were, first and foremost, the responsibility of national authorities, Directors stressed. Wherever possible, IMF staff should build on the willingness of those authorities to address such issues. The IMF's mandate did not allow the institution to assume the role of an investigative agency or guardian of financial integrity in member countries.

Directors emphasized that the IMF's involvement in governance should focus on its economic aspects. The IMF could contribute to good governance principally in two spheres: improving the management of public resources and supporting the development and maintenance of a transparent and stable regulatory environment conducive to efficient private sector activities. In this context, Directors emphasized the potential benefits of such reforms as enhancing the transparency and accountability of public sector activities and providing a level playing field for the private sector. In addressing governance issues, the IMF should be guided by an assessment of whether the issue in question would have significant current or potential impact on macroeconomic performance in the short and medium term. Directors cautioned that the IMF should remain apolitical in its dealings on issues relating to governance. At the same time, they acknowledged that a clear delineation between the economic and political dimensions of governance was often difficult in practice: what was important was that the IMF's advice be based on solid economic considerations within its mandate.

Directors emphasized that weak governance that threatened macroeconomic performance should be tackled early on in reform efforts. Although the requirement to safeguard IMF resources was primarily addressed through the implementation of appropriate macroeconomic adjustment policies, Directors recognized that governance issues could influence macroeconomic performance and the effectiveness of those policies. Thus, conditionality could be attached to policy measures relating to governance if those measures were necessary for the achievement of the program's objectives.

In the wake of the May discussion, on July 25, 1997, the Executive Board adopted guidelines addressing the IMF's role in governance issues.[8] The guidelines seek to promote greater attention by the IMF to governance issues, in particular through:

- a more comprehensive treatment in the context of both Article IV consultations and IMF-supported adjustment programs of those governance issues within the IMF's mandate and expertise;
- a more proactive approach in advocating policies and the development of institutions and administrative systems that eliminate the opportunity for bribery, corruption, and fraudulent activity in the management of public resources;
- an evenhanded treatment of governance issues in all member countries; and
- enhanced collaboration with other multilateral institutions, in particular the World Bank, to make better use of complementary areas of expertise.

Transparency in Budgetary Operations

Fiscal transparency can be defined as openness toward the public at large about government structure and functions, fiscal policy intentions, public sector accounts, and projections. It means ready access to reliable, comprehensive, timely, understandable, and internationally comparable information on government activities—including those activities undertaken outside the government sector—so that the electorate and financial markets can accurately assess the government's current and future financial position. Noting that fiscal policy is a key focus of IMF surveillance, and with the aim of strengthening the approach of governments to fiscal policy issues, the Executive Board took up the questions of transparency in government operations and fiscal policy rules in October 1997. And in April 1998, the Board agreed on a draft code of good practices in the area of fiscal transparency for submission to the Interim Committee.

In their October 1997 discussion, Directors agreed that transparency in government operations was conducive to fiscal discipline, sound public sector management, good governance, and improved macroeconomic performance. Moreover, in a globalized economy, where the costs of loss of market confidence had

---

[8]Published as IMF, *Good Governance: The IMF's Role* (1997); also available at http://www.imf.org.

become increasingly clear, fiscal transparency helped instill confidence in a government's economic policies. Fiscal transparency entailed setting out clear fiscal objectives, building clear institutional arrangements (including a proper budgetary process), using transparent and widely accepted accounting methods, and providing timely and reliable information.

The IMF should continue to help its members achieve greater fiscal transparency through surveillance, technical assistance, and program design, Directors agreed. Improving fiscal transparency was a multiyear endeavor, and the priorities for improving transparency could differ among countries. Therefore, the IMF should pay due regard to the specific circumstances of individual countries. Some Directors stressed that the IMF's involvement in fiscal transparency should focus on issues of macroeconomic significance, and they noted the need for an evenhanded approach.

Directors supported greater emphasis in the staff's surveillance work on promoting transparency in government operations. Many favored asking the staff to prepare a brief manual of good practices for fiscal transparency, while some Directors expressed reservations about establishing "best practices." Some others considered that the staff could gradually accumulate an inventory of transparent practices in the context of Article IV consultations. Many Directors cautioned about the resource implications of any such initiative.

Timely and comprehensive reporting of public sector accounts was also important. To this end, Directors urged that the coverage of fiscal accounts be extended to the general government level and include information on off-budget operations and the cost of quasi-fiscal activities. Also, cash-based recording should be supplemented with accrual-based recording of transactions. Where possible, the authorities should publish information on guarantees and unfunded public sector liabilities. Noting that discretionary tax relief, tax exemptions, and arbitrary tax administration were among the most important problems affecting fiscal performance in many countries, Directors also stressed the need for transparent and stable tax systems and for estimates of tax expenditures as part of the budget process.

Fiscal Policy Rules. In October 1997, the Executive Board also discussed the strengths and weaknesses of fiscal policy rules. These included such permanent restraints on fiscal policy as balanced budget or deficit rules, borrowing rules, and debt or reserve rules. Many Directors commented favorably on the potential usefulness of such rules in strengthening or restoring policy credibility in specific circumstances. Some also noted the usefulness of fiscal rules and limits in the context of common currency areas, citing the benefits for fiscal convergence in the European Union that had accrued from the fiscal reference values under the Maastricht Treaty.

At the same time, Directors cautioned that fiscal rules were not a panacea. Good economic performance depended on the political will to implement sound policies; simply promulgating rules without building the political consensus to put in place the implied sound policies was unlikely to yield the desired results. The view was also expressed that it might be difficult in practice for fiscal policy rules to embody all the properties of the model rule outlined by the staff (i.e., that it be well-defined, transparent, adequate, consistent, simple, flexible enough to accommodate exogenous shocks and cyclical fluctuations in activity, enforceable, and efficient).[9] Moreover, attempts at complying with a fiscal rule through excessive reliance on tax rate increases and unsustainable or cosmetic expenditure cuts, or one-off measures, might tend to be counterproductive. Directors indicated that there were circumstances in which fiscal rules could prove useful for countries to institutionalize better macroeconomic policies. Where members were interested in formulating fiscal rules, or incorporating them in the design of adjustment programs, Directors believed that the IMF should be prepared to provide policy advice and technical assistance.

Code of Good Practices on Fiscal Transparency. Following further work by the staff in light of the October 1997 discussion, a draft code of good practices on fiscal transparency was submitted for the Board's consideration in April 1998. The underlying rationale was that fiscal transparency could lead to better-informed public debate about the design and results of fiscal policy, make governments more accountable for the implementation of fiscal policy, and thereby promote good governance, strengthen credibility, and mobilize popular support for sound macroeconomic policies. Because of the IMF's fiscal management expertise, it was well placed to take the lead in promoting greater transparency in this area. The draft presented to the Board set out specific principles and practices that a government could implement to ensure that:

- roles and responsibilities in the government are clear;
- information on government activities is provided to the public;
- budget preparation, execution, and reporting are undertaken in an open manner; and
- fiscal information is subjected to independent assurances of integrity.

Directors generally welcomed the draft code. Most saw merit in reaching a consensus on the broad principles and essential elements of a transparent approach to fiscal management and stressed the importance of moving ahead with a proposed manual to address some of

---

[9]Published as IMF, *Fiscal Policy Rules,* IMF Occasional Paper 162 (1998).

the practical issues that could arise.
They also suggested that the code be
subject to periodic review and
revision.

Directors pointed out that implementation of the code should be tailored to individual country
circumstances, with recognition of
the legitimate differences in
approach that countries might take
to improving fiscal transparency. For
countries with weaker institutions or
binding legal constraints, progress
toward achieving fiscal transparency
consistent with the code might take
time. The IMF had to be prepared
to provide technical assistance, in
cooperation with other international
organizations, to those countries
that requested it.

At its April 1998 meeting, the
Interim Committee adopted the
Code of Good Practices on Fiscal
Transparency—Declaration on Principles (Box 5; the full text is repro-
duced in Appendix VI), recognizing
that implementation would be affected by diversity in
fiscal institutions, legal systems, and implementation
capacity.

Data Issues

Economic policymakers and financial institutions and
markets—public and private—rely on information.
When underlying information about the true economic
and financial situation of countries, banks, and enterprises is poor, when disclosure of available information
is limited, and when potentially damaging information
can be disguised or withheld, national and international
financial systems work less efficiently. Thus, the international community encourages the development and
promulgation of sound information practices, in accord
with broadly accepted international norms.

For its part, the IMF has paid increasing attention in
recent years to data issues—the comprehensiveness,
quality, frequency, and timeliness of the data that
members provide to it, and the data that members disseminate to the public. To guide members in the latter,
the Board has endorsed a two-tiered approach: a Special Data Dissemination Standard (SDDS), established
in March 1996, to guide member countries that have
or might seek access to international financial markets,
and a General Data Dissemination System (GDDS),
approved by the Board in December 1997, to guide all
member countries. In September 1996, the IMF
opened an electronic bulletin board on the Internet
that provides public access to information about the

Box 5
Code of Good Practices on Fiscal Transparency:
Declaration on Principles

The Code's main provisions are as
follows:

Clarity of Roles and Responsibilities
- The government sector should
  be clearly distinguished from the
  rest of the economy, and policy
  and management roles within
  government should be well
  defined.
- There should be a clear legal and
  administrative framework for fiscal
  management.

Public Availability of Information
- The public should be provided with
  full information on the past, current,
  and projected fiscal activity of
  government.
- A public commitment should be
  made to timely publication of fiscal
  information.

Open Budget Preparation,
Execution, and Reporting
- Budget documentation should specify fiscal policy objectives, the macroeconomic framework, the policy
  basis for the budget, and identifiable
  major fiscal risks.
- Budget estimates should be classified
  and presented in a way that facilitates policy analysis and promotes
  accountability.
- Procedures for the execution and
  monitoring of approved expenditures should be clearly specified.
- Fiscal reporting should be timely,
  comprehensive, and reliable and
  identify deviations from the budget.

Independent Assurances of Integrity
- The integrity of fiscal information
  should be subject to public and
  independent scrutiny.

---

data dissemination practices of members that subscribe
to the SDDS (Box 6).

Members' Provision of Information to the IMF

In December 1997, the Board conducted its third
review of progress by members in providing data to the
IMF for surveillance. Directors noted the provision of
core indicators by member countries to the IMF had
continued to improve modestly (this refers to data on
exchange rates, international reserves, reserve or base
money, broad money, interest rates, consumer prices,
exports and imports, external current account balance,
overall government balance, gross domestic product or
gross national income, and external debt). But they
expressed concern that some members did not provide
these data regularly or in a timely way, and that, in a
number of cases, lags in data provision had continued or
even increased. Directors urged members to improve
the timeliness and frequency of their data reporting.

Recent experience had also suggested that the core
indicators needed to be complemented by other data in
light of the circumstances of individual countries, so as
to increase the effectiveness of surveillance in the
period between Article IV consultations and to identify
emerging financial market tensions. Directors identified
reserve-related liabilities, central bank derivative transactions, private sector external debt, and prudential-
type bank indicators as desirable supplementary data.
Within these broad categories, Directors identified a
number of specific data items—including forward

Box 6
Dissemination Standards Bulletin Board

The DSBB is a tool for market analysts and others who track economic growth, inflation, and other economic and financial developments in countries around the world. It describes the statistical practices—such as methodologies and data release calendars—of countries subscribing to the Special Data Dissemination Standard (SDDS) in key areas: the real, fiscal, financial, and external sectors. It also describes steps subscribers have taken to improve practices to move toward full observance of the SDDS by the end of the transition period.

Beginning in April 1997, electronic links (hyperlinks) between the bulletin board and actual data on national data sites have been established, enabling users to move directly from the bulletin board to current economic and financial data on an Internet site maintained by the subscriber. (The links do not indicate IMF endorsement of the data.) The bulletin board can be accessed on the Internet at http://dsbb.imf.org, or through the IMF's website, http://www.imf.org.

Subscribers to the SDDS as of the end of April 1998 are listed below; those for which hyperlinks were in place are indicated by an asterisk:

Argentina*	France	Korea	Singapore*
Australia	Germany	Latvia	Slovak Republic
Austria	Hong Kong SAR*	Lithuania	Slovenia*
Belgium	Hungary	Malaysia	South Africa*
Canada*	Iceland	Mexico*	Spain
Chile	India	Netherlands	Sweden
Colombia*	Indonesia	Norway	Switzerland*
Croatia	Ireland	Peru*	Thailand
Czech Republic	Israel*	Philippines	Turkey*
Denmark	Italy	Poland	United Kingdom*
Ecuador	Japan*	Portugal	United States
Finland			

transactions (outright or arising from swaps), the maturity structure of external debt, the composition of short-term external debt, information on foreign exchange reserves, and information on the financial sector. Some Directors suggested that the definition of core data should be expanded to include these additional data, given their critical importance in identifying emerging tensions at an early stage. And some Directors suggested consideration of a common standard for timeliness and frequency of data provided to the IMF.

On the related issue of data quality, inadequate coverage and deficiencies in compilation methods had often compromised the usefulness of the reported data and posed problems for the design and monitoring of members' programs, particularly with regard to national accounts, government finance, and balance of payments statistics. Directors therefore urged the staff to continue its work on the assessment of data quality. Several Directors stressed the high cost of technical assistance and suggested monitoring recipient countries' implementation of recommendations. Directors agreed that efforts to improve data quality must be part of a broad effort to build solid statistical frameworks in member countries, consistent with efforts undertaken

for the Special Standard and the General System. Some Directors suggested that staff papers indicate clearly data adjustments to help identify for the authorities the data deficiencies and required improvements.

Members' Dissemination of Data to the Public

Review of Special Data Dissemination Standard. In their first review of the Special Data Dissemination Standard, in December 1997, Directors noted that the number of subscribers (43) had been about as expected and hoped that, over time, more members would subscribe. They welcomed the growing external use of the Dissemination Standards Bulletin Board, especially since the introduction of hyperlinks from the bulletin board to national data sites (see Box 6). Directors believed the SDDS provided incentives and a structure for improvements in data dissemination practices; subscribers' views on their initial experience with the Special Standard had been generally positive.

Directors agreed that the proposals for updating the SDDS were timely, given the economic and financial developments in Southeast Asia and elsewhere. They endorsed the procedures for modifying the SDDS, which were in keeping with the consultative and transparent process underlying the Special Standard. These entailed the shifting of the data components for countries' reserve-related liabilities from an "encouraged" to a "prescribed" component and adding a prescribed component for net commitments under derivative positions. Some Directors expressed reservations in this regard, pointing to definitional problems and issues of confidentiality.

Directors agreed that the procedure for modifying the SDDS to include indicators of financial soundness should await the development of standards for the disclosure of macroprudential data and should draw on the work of other organizations, including the BIS. They also agreed to consider in the next review of the SDDS the possibility of establishing a more precise timetable for the dissemination by subscribing countries of data on international investment positions, which would include data on the short-term external indebtedness of the private nonbank sector.

Directors considered that in the period ahead, the credibility of the IMF and of the SDDS subscribers would depend on ensuring that subscribers had implemented the necessary changes to their dissemination practices so that they would fully comply with the Special Standard by the end of 1998. Noting that a number of current subscribers had made limited progress in completing the outstanding actions, Directors urged members to implement rapidly their announced transition plans and asked staff to give priority to assisting subscribers in successfully concluding the transition period. Directors agreed it would be prudent for members intending to subscribe during 1998 to assess carefully the likelihood of fully observing the Special Standard by the end of the transition period. On the same point, in its April 1998 meeting, the Interim Committee emphasized the importance of subscribers being in full observance of the standards by the end of the transition period in December 1998.

In discussing how to deal with possible nonobservance by a subscriber after the end of the transition period, some Directors cited the need to differentiate between minor and serious breaches; Directors agreed to reconsider the issue of possible nonobservance during the next review of the SDDS. Although some Directors suggested exploring some form of cost recovery, the Board agreed that, for the present, the costs associated with the Special Standard and maintenance of the associated bulletin board should not be borne by users on the grounds that the wide reach of the bulletin board benefited the entire international community.

General Data Dissemination System. In contrast to the Special Data Dissemination Standard, whose focus is on dissemination in countries that generally already meet high standards of data quality, the General Data Dissemination System aims primarily to improve the quality of data for all members. It focuses on the development and dissemination of a full range of economic, financial, and sociodemographic data with objectives for comprehensive statistical frameworks—comprising national accounts for the real sector, central government accounts for the fiscal sector, a broad money survey for the financial sector, and balance of payments accounts for the external sector, as well as a set of sociodemographic indicators. In December 1997, in approving the proposal to establish the GDDS, Directors recognized that it was an important step for all IMF members—not only in guiding the provision of data to the public, but also in encouraging improvements in the quality and accessibility of data.

Directors recognized that for many countries improvements in data quality were a necessary precursor to enhanced dissemination of data to the public and that the GDDS was a useful framework for developing a broad range of statistics. Directors favored the General System's focus on a set of core frameworks and indicators, supplemented by improved data systems and categories; this made the General System relevant to a broad range of countries and provided a clear set of links

between the General System and the Special Standard. These links were particularly helpful to countries that wished to use participation in the GDDS as a step toward subscription to the SDDS. Most Directors supported including in the General System a set of sociodemographic indicators because of the importance of these data in assessing economic developments in many countries. Some Directors reiterated that the responsibility for developing social indicators should be left mainly to other international organizations, and some expressed doubts about the appropriateness of including these data in the GDDS. Directors agreed that the IMF should cooperate closely with regional and other international organizations in developing social indicators.

The Board acknowledged that, as aspects of openness and transparency, the issues of access and integrity were important dimensions of the GDDS. The principles embodied in these dimensions were not yet standard practice in many countries, and it was therefore appropriate that the General System focus on developing these dimensions in the practices of data compiling and disseminating agencies.

Most Directors supported a phased approach in implementing the GDDS, focusing first on education and training through appropriate documentation, seminars, and workshops (Box 7). The Board recognized that the General System was an ambitious project, both for the IMF and for countries that might wish to participate, and many Directors agreed that a longer-term approach to implementing the General System was appropriate, taking into account the substantial resource costs to the IMF and to countries, as well as the absorptive capacity of participating countries.

Strengthening IMF-Bank Collaboration on Financial Sector Reform

The IMF and World Bank have long collaborated on financial sector issues (see also Appendix IV). In August 1997, the Board discussed this collaboration, stressing that it was crucial to maximizing the effectiveness of both institutions in helping countries strengthen their financial systems and saw improving this cooperation as an urgent priority.

Although the 1989 agreement between the IMF and the World Bank on Bank-IMF collaboration in assisting member countries in their respective areas of expertise continued to provide an appropriate overall framework, Directors felt that the roles of the two institutions on financial sector issues needed to be clarified and collaboration procedures improved. They stressed the role of collaboration in ensuring that emerging financial sector problems in all countries are promptly identified, that each institution would take the lead in its own areas of primary responsibility, that duplication of activity in areas of mutual interest be avoided, and that the IMF's macroeconomic analysis and the Bank's

How the GDDS Will Work

Participation in the General Data Dissemination System (GDDS), which is voluntary, consists of three steps:

- commitment to using the GDDS as a framework for statistical development;
- designation of a country coordinator; and
- preparation of descriptions of current statistical production and dissemination practices, and plans for short- and long-term improvements in these practices that could be disseminated by the IMF on the Internet.

The GDDS will be implemented in two phases. The first will focus on education and training, and the second on direct country work. The training phase will include eight regional seminars and workshops, beginning in mid-1998 and ending in the fall of 1999, for up to 120 member countries. Following the training phase, IMF staff will work directly with member countries to assist them in assessing their practice against those of the GDDS and developing plans for improvement.

As of April 1998, some 25 countries had indicated preliminary interest in the GDDS by appointing a country coordinator. Formal invitations to participate have been sent to all member countries that have not subscribed to the Special Data Dissemination Standard (SDDS) following completion of guidance materials on the GDDS.

sectoral policy recommendations be fully coordinated. In this context, the two institutions would also have to pay due regard to the responsibility of the Basle Committee in the area of banking supervision.

Many Directors remarked that they would have liked a clearer delineation of the spheres of responsibility of the two institutions, while recognizing that overlap in some areas—especially banking supervision and regulation, and banking legislation—was probably unavoidable. Most Directors stressed that banking system restructuring was the primary responsibility of the World Bank. Nevertheless, many Directors felt that the IMF had to play a role in banking system restructuring in crisis situations, especially in countries where it had been more actively involved. They emphasized, however, that those instances were expected to be rare, that the IMF's involvement in such cases should be temporary, and that the implementation of restructuring programs should be handled by the Bank. In light of the IMF's mandate, some Directors expected the IMF to focus on the macroeconomic implications of such reforms. But Directors hoped that the Bank, by strengthening its financial sector activities—including the establishment of the Financial Sector Board—would be better able to respond quickly and flexibly to help design financial sector restructuring programs in crisis situations. Directors also emphasized the Bank's role—and early involvement—in helping to identify specific benchmarks for banking system restructuring to be incorporated in IMF financial programs.

Exchange Rate Issues

The Board considered two surveillance-related exchange rate issues in 1997/98: the methodology for assessing exchange rates and strategies for moving from a fixed to a flexible exchange rate regime ("exit strategies").

Exchange Rate Assessments and IMF Surveillance

In discussing the methodology of exchange rate assessments and its application in IMF surveillance over major industrial countries, the Board emphasized in October 1997 that the IMF, as the central institution of the international monetary system, must continuously seek to strengthen its analysis and surveillance over exchange rate policies. The IMF had the advantage of a global perspective and a blend of technical expertise and practical policy experience that enabled its staff to add value in advancing the analytical framework and making judgments on exchange rate issues. In this context, Directors also pointed to the need for cooperation with the academic community.

Directors concurred with the view that the macroeconomic balance methodology used by IMF staff (Box 8) complemented rather than substituted for the various measures of international competitiveness and financial market conditions that had traditionally played a major role in IMF surveillance over members' exchange rates and exchange rate policies. Directors generally agreed it was not possible to identify precisely "equilibrium" values for exchange rates and that point estimates of notional equilibrium rates should generally be avoided. Nevertheless, they agreed that a rigorous, systematic, and transparent methodology was important to underpin IMF surveillance. They considered the existing methodology to be a useful starting point.

Directors emphasized that it was essential to consider the appropriateness of exchange rates against the background of prevailing cyclical positions and the attainment of overall macroeconomic objectives. Deviations of exchange rates from their medium-term equilibrium levels might be warranted, and even helpful, in cases of divergence in the cyclical positions of the major industrial countries. For these reasons, Directors advocated a case-by-case approach in considering what actions, if any, should be taken when exchange rates appeared to deviate substantially from their medium-term equilibrium values.

Many Directors considered that the current methodology for assessing exchange rates could be applied more broadly, in particular to nonindustrial countries of regional importance with access to international capital markets. Some Directors recognized, however, that data deficiencies and the diversity of economic conditions might limit the applicability of the methodology in the case of emerging and developing economies.

Exit Strategies: Policy Options for Countries Seeking Greater Flexibility

In January 1998, in their discussion of a staff paper[10] on strategies for exiting from relatively fixed exchange rate regimes to regimes of greater exchange rate flexibility, Directors acknowledged that the choice of exchange rate regime was a complex issue that depended on the specific circumstances of individual countries. Particularly relevant were the structural characteristics of the economy and its historical inflation performance, the degree of vulnerability to shocks and the nature of those shocks, the extent of export and import diversification, and the degree of capital account liberalization and exposure to global capital markets. More generally, whatever regime was chosen, macroeconomic and structural policies needed to be credibly consistent with the regime, and the authorities needed to be transparent about policy objectives and how they intended to achieve them.

Several Directors noted that currency pegs, currency unions, or currency boards have served countries well in a number of cases, including small, open economies and a number of developing and transition economies, at least at some stage of their development and stabilization efforts. In the case of transition economies, a few Directors noted that the balance of costs and benefits tended to shift in favor of greater exchange rate flexibility as inflation subsided and the transition proceeded.

Most Directors were of the view that the increasing globalization of financial markets had made pegged regimes more difficult to manage. Many Directors particularly cited the heightened risk posed by fixed rates in encouraging unhedged exposure by borrowers. While some countries, with the appropriate supportive policies, would continue to benefit from a fixed rate—it being emphasized that there was no presumption that all countries would be better off with flexible rates—Directors noted that some countries with fixed or relatively fixed exchange rate regimes might now wish to move to more flexible arrangements. It was

---

[10]Published as IMF, *Exit Strategies: Policy Options for Countries Seeking Greater Flexibility,* IMF Occasional Paper 168 (1998).

> **Box 8**
> **A Methodology for Exchange Rate Assessments**
>
> Oversight of members' exchange rate policies is at the core of the IMF's surveillance mandate. The methodology used for assessing the appropriateness of current account positions and exchange rates for major industrial countries embodies four steps:
> - applying a trade-equation model to calculate the underlying current account positions that would emerge at prevailing market exchange rates if all countries were producing at their potential output levels;
> - using a separate model to estimate a normal or equilibrium level of the saving-investment balance consistent with medium-run fundamentals, including the assumption that countries were operating at potential output;
> - calculating the amount by which the exchange rate would have to change, other things being equal, to equilibrate the underlying current account position with the medium-term saving-investment norm; and
> - assessing whether the estimates of exchange rates consistent with medium-term fundamentals suggest that any currencies are badly misaligned.

therefore desirable to consider the best ways to engineer an exit.

Directors emphasized that careful attention needed to be given, when exiting a peg, to the design of the new macroeconomic policy framework. In light of the many, often complex, considerations in the decision to exit—even from a position of strength—Directors believed that the IMF could play an important role in providing timely and candid advice to member countries on the appropriate exit strategy and the timing of such action. Too rapid an abandonment of the peg could be as harmful to credibility as too protracted a defense of the peg was to the level of foreign exchange reserves. It was suggested that the IMF's regular Article IV consultations with its member countries should, when appropriate, give greater priority to discussing these issues.

Most Directors agreed that if a case for moving to a flexible regime existed, the best time to do so was during a period of relative calm in exchange markets or when there were pressures for appreciation of the currency, rather than when the exchange rate was under downward pressure. They noted, however, that much judgment was involved and it was often difficult to make such a decision when times were good and there seemed no reason to tinker with an apparently successful regime.

There was no question, Directors agreed, that it was much more difficult to exit a peg during a crisis, when some degree of exchange rate volatility was likely. To minimize depreciation and bolster policy credibility in such circumstances, it was essential that a country implement a strong and credible package of policy measures, including macroeconomic policies and accelerated structural reforms, and ensure the complementarity of those measures. Directors also stressed the need for an alternative policy framework after the exit to provide an anchor for inflation expectations.

Directors differed on how much macroeconomic policy should be tightened in these circumstances. Some pointed to the recent situation in East Asia as one where early and concerted monetary policy actions had not been sufficiently strong to prevent a continuing slide in a number of currencies in the region. Some other Directors noted that very high interest rates could increase pressures on already fragile banking and corporate sectors in most of these countries and could risk accentuating the resulting economic contraction. For similar reasons, some Directors argued that a more flexible approach to fiscal policy might be desirable in some cases, especially in countries where fiscal policy had been on a sustainable footing before the crisis.

The difficulties posed by financial sector problems for the choice of exchange rate regime were discussed at some length. Directors noted that financial fragility made the defense of a pegged rate through higher interest rates more problematic, since higher rates would exacerbate debt-servicing problems and further weaken the financial sector. As East Asia illustrated, however, depreciation of the currency after a long period of exchange rate stability could also endanger the soundness of financial and nonfinancial institutions, to the extent that they had tended not to hedge foreign currency exposures. The ideal solution was clearly to strengthen prudential regulations and supervision, and limit unhedged exposure, before the exit. Directors were divided on whether the absence of such measures merited delaying a needed move to greater exchange rate flexibility. Some pointed mainly to the further weakening of the financial and corporate sectors associated with the defense of the peg, while others noted that in some cases it was essential to begin financial restructuring and reduce unhedged foreign currency exposure before any large exchange rate depreciation. Several Directors suggested that further analysis of second-best policies for countries with less than robust financial sectors would be helpful, including ways to strengthen banking and prudential standards and establish clear bankruptcy legislation as rapidly as possible.

A number of Directors saw merit in imposing selective capital controls to limit the severity of the currency depreciation in the aftermath of an exchange rate crisis, as well as to reduce the risks of crises in the first instance. Several other Directors, however, cautioned that such controls were likely to be ineffectual beyond the short run and could even prove counterproductive, by leading to a surge in capital outflows. A better approach, these speakers felt, was to strengthen prudential regulation and supervision of financial and nonfinancial institutions. Areas to be governed by such regulation could include short-term foreign currency borrowing by domestic corporations and reporting requirements for foreign financial institutions.

Monetary Policy in Dollarized Economies

"Dollarization," the holding by residents of a large share of their assets in instruments denominated in foreign currency, is common in developing and transition countries. Among countries that have undertaken IMF-supported adjustment programs over the past 10 years, almost half could be regarded as dollarized and a significant number of the others as largely dollarized.

In a review of the economic effects of dollarization in January 1998, the Board agreed that in a globalized economy with increasingly free capital movements and deregulated financial markets, most countries experienced some degree of dollarization—whether in the form of currency substitution, asset substitution as part of currency diversification of asset holdings, or a combination of the two. Several Directors saw this as a benign feature of the modern economic environment, to which all countries should adapt. Others were less sure, citing such issues as the policy adaptations required to cope with the challenges posed by currency substitution. Although Directors agreed that dollarization was an important feature in the advanced countries as well—and would become even more so with the introduction of the euro—their discussion centered on the effects of dollarization in developing and transition economies. In many of these countries, dollarization indicated a lack of confidence in the ability of the domestic currency to perform its functions effectively.

Benefits and Risks of Dollarization

Dollarization was seen as presenting both benefits and risks for developing countries. In some circumstances, foreign currency deposits could promote the growth of the domestic financial sector, for example, by allowing domestic banks to compete with cross-border accounts. Dollarization was sometimes the only effective way to remonetize an economy in cases of extreme price instability and capital flight. But, especially in weak and immature financial systems, dollarization could increase risks in the financial sector. Such risks could stem from a deterioration in the quality of the foreign currency loan portfolio in the case of a sharp devaluation of the domestic currency, as well as from the limited ability of the central bank to act as the lender of last resort. Countries with large cash holdings of foreign money would also lose seigniorage revenues.

With regard to the implications of dollarization for exchange rate and monetary policy, Directors noted that the likely higher volatility of money demand in economies with high currency substitution would tend to make the exchange rate more unstable and limit the effectiveness of monetary policy. Several Directors favored the adoption of a fixed rate or a currency board arrangement supported by appropriate macroeconomic policies to handle these types of monetary shocks. A number of Directors, however, stressed that the degree of currency substitution was only one of many elements to be taken into account in choosing an exchange rate regime; also significant were such considerations as the importance of real shocks, the degree of capital mobility, the scope for fiscal adjustment, and the overall macroeconomic situation.

What of the effects of dollarization for inflation? Although this was essentially an empirical question without a unique answer, Directors felt that the relevance of foreign currency aggregates should not be discounted and despite measurement difficulties, these aggregates should be included among the broader set of indicators monitored by the monetary authorities. Some Directors thought that certain dollarized economies could suitably adopt an inflation-targeting framework for monetary policy.

Directors generally preferred that monetary operations be conducted in domestic currency. They recognized, however, that monetary instruments denominated in foreign currency could be useful in highly dollarized economies where the bulk of credits and interbank operations were already denominated in that currency. Similar qualifications applied to the provision of foreign currency interbank settlement on the books of the central bank. In this regard, however, Directors advised that such operations be backed by ample international reserves, as well as effective measures to limit settlement risk.

Special vigilance was needed to limit prudential risk in highly dollarized economies, Directors stressed. Because of the impact of dollarization on credit risk, as well as risks to the banking system, dollarization argued for banks in developing countries to exceed Basle guidelines for capital adequacy. Directors noted that a central bank had limited ability to act as a lender of last resort in foreign currency and that sizable currency reserves and contingent credit lines could usefully contribute to limiting systemic liquidity risk in these circumstances. While recognizing the difficulties in monitoring limits on foreign exchange positions given the sophistication of financial markets, Directors stressed the importance of closely monitoring off-balance-sheet operations, as well as the maturity and composition of foreign exchange exposures.

Most Directors agreed that the focus of monetary policy should be on macroeconomic stabilization. In their view, measures to improve the attractiveness of the domestic currency were generally preferable to those for discouraging the use of foreign currency. Thus, Directors broadly agreed that dollarization should not be tackled by restricting residents' ability to maintain accounts in foreign currency or imposing punitive reserve requirements on foreign currency deposits. Such measures would be counterproductive, weakening financial intermediation or leading to capital outflows. Interest rate liberalization, measures to increase financial deepening, an effective domestic payments system, and an independent monetary authority were the best avenues for limiting dollarization over the medium term. Also important—particularly in countries with weak financial systems—was an appropriate sequence of financial liberalization measures, supported by strong macroeconomic policies. Although Directors recognized that indexed financial instruments could also limit dollarization, the risks of promoting inflationary inertia had to be carefully weighed when contemplating such instruments.

Dollarization and the Design of IMF-Supported Adjustment Programs

The Board stressed the need to consider the prevalence of dollarization in designing adjustment programs supported by the IMF. Although dollarization had not seriously hampered the attainment of growth and inflation objectives, Directors argued that velocity and the money multiplier appeared to be more variable in dollarized economies, pointing to potential problems in selecting intermediate monetary aggregates.

In the Board's view, programs should continue to apply conditionality in a way that would take into account the presence of dollarization, rather than attacking it directly, and to address the more fundamental policies needed to restore confidence and the long-term credibility of the domestic currency. Programs should continue to focus on the underlying causes of dollarization, the development of domestic financial systems, and, where necessary, the adoption of prudential measures. Noting that the costs of dollarization might outweigh the benefits, a few Directors saw greater merit in pursuing an active de-dollarization strategy. In view of the uncertain duration of foreign currency deposits in the banking system, the Board generally agreed that domestic banks' reserves with the central bank against foreign currency deposits be considered part of the central bank's liabilities for purposes of measuring net international reserves.

CHAPTER VII

Strengthening the Architecture of the International Monetary System

Following the Mexican financial crisis of 1994–95, the IMF adopted several initiatives to strengthen the international monetary system and the IMF's central role in the system. These included more intensive surveillance of financial sectors of member countries, closer monitoring of developments in capital markets, more candid policy discussions with country authorities, and greater emphasis on members' dissemination of information—both to the IMF and to financial markets. The financial crisis in Asia, however, made clear that to meet fully the challenges posed by a global economy and global financial markets, more far-reaching measures were needed to tackle potential weaknesses in financial systems, prevent the emergence of inappropriate debt profiles, and ensure greater transparency in both public and private sector activity. Successful implementation of these measures would involve not only the commitment of individual countries, but also broad-based cooperative efforts of the entire international community, including the private sector.

In April 1998, the IMF's Executive Board, reflecting on lessons learned from the Asian crisis and drawing on earlier discussions, identified a series of approaches for strengthening the international monetary system. These approaches were subsequently broadly endorsed by the Interim Committee, which sketched out a comprehensive framework for strengthening the architecture of the monetary system (see Appendix VI).

The Board discussion in April, as well as the Interim Committee communiqué, centered on five aspects of a strengthened international monetary system:

- reinforcing international and domestic financial systems;
- strengthening IMF surveillance;
- promoting more widely available and transparent data on member countries' economic situation and policies;
- underscoring the central role of the IMF in crisis management; and
- increasing the involvement of the private sector in forestalling or resolving financial crises.

Strengthening Financial Systems

It is now well recognized that vulnerable and unstable financial systems can severely disrupt macroeconomic performance and that weak financial systems increase vulnerability to economic crises and deepen such crises when they occur. There was thus broad agreement in the Board that the IMF should work actively with other organizations and members to help members design improved banking and financial systems. Directors are also agreed that:

- Members should give priority to strengthening financial sector supervisory and regulatory frameworks and to establishing the independence of central banks. Sound financial systems also require strengthening governance, including in the corporate sector, and improving accounting practices to conform with international standards.
- The international community's responsibility lay in ensuring that work continued in developing such standards for banking supervision, accounting and disclosure, auditing and valuation of bank assets, and guidelines for effective corporate governance. Increased international cooperation would also be required in areas beyond the establishment of standards, including in the sharing of information among regulators, especially among those with supervisory authority over institutions operating in major financial centers. Regulators also should seek and examine carefully information on flows from offshore centers and off-balance-sheet items, the lack of which could obscure analysis of a country's exposure and delay the identification of potential balance of payments problems.

Directors recognized that the issues were complex and that both the IMF and the international community would need to develop expertise and devote resources to be able to offer detailed advice in each of the areas. They agreed that the IMF could play an important role, especially in its surveillance activities, by disseminating internationally agreed standards and encouraging members to adopt best practices. The Board noted that it would continue discussions on the scope of the IMF's work in developing and disseminating international standards. At its April 1998 meeting, the Interim Committee endorsed this approach.

Strengthening IMF Surveillance

The Board, and subsequently the Interim Committee, reaffirmed the centrality of IMF surveillance in preventing crises. The measures taken after the Mexican financial crisis in 1994–95 were important in helping the IMF adapt its surveillance to the rapidly changing global environment, especially with respect to emerging market economies. At the same time, IMF surveillance needed reinforcing in a number of areas:

- The IMF should intensify its surveillance of financial sector issues and collaborate with other institutions, including the World Bank and the Bank for International Settlements, as well as with the private sector, to offer its members the best possible advice in this regard.
- IMF surveillance should pay more attention to capital account issues. Although the benefits for the world economy of an open and liberal system of capital movements were widely recognized, the sequencing and pace of capital account liberalization had to be monitored carefully. In particular, IMF surveillance should focus on the risks of potential large reversals of capital flows, the rapid accumulation of short-term debt, unhedged exposure to currency fluctuations, and the impact of selective capital account liberalization.
- IMF surveillance should pay greater attention to policy interdependence and the risks of contagion, and to the policies of countries of particular importance to the international monetary system.
- More frequent and systematic exchange of views with market participants was needed so that IMF surveillance was fully cognizant of market perceptions; in turn, this would enable markets to better understand IMF views and analyses. At the same time, such contacts must take into account the confidentiality of the IMF's dialogue with members and ensure evenhanded dealings with market participants.
- Effective IMF surveillance depended crucially on the willingness of IMF members to take its advice. This implied, on the part of the IMF, the best analysis possible, as well as concentration on issues of importance to individual member countries.
- The IMF's views must be communicated effectively to members, possibly through a series of incremental steps. A member could be asked to respond to the IMF's concerns within a specified time, so that the member's reaction could be brought expeditiously to the Board's attention. In cases where a member's policies appeared to depart from the advice of IMF staff, the nature of the concerns in question could be shared with the Board at an early stage, while protecting the confidentiality of the communication with the member. On this issue, the Interim Committee requested the Board "to develop a 'tiered response,' whereby countries believed to be seriously off course in their policies would be given increasingly strong warnings" by the IMF.

Greater Availability and Transparency of Information

The IMF actively encourages its members to be transparent with respect to information on economic developments and policymaking. Despite progress in members' provision of data on core indicators to the IMF in a continuous and timely manner, both Directors and the Interim Committee saw a need for further improvement, particularly on data timeliness. It was also important to complement core indicators by broadening the IMF's Special Data Dissemination Standard to cover additional financial data. Consideration should also be given to increasing the Special Standard's usefulness, its accessibility to the public and market participants, and publication of members' record of compliance.

Directors and Interim Committee members also supported the steps the IMF had taken to promote greater transparency in economic policymaking. These included encouraging members to release Letters of Intent for their programs, which complemented the longstanding IMF policy of encouraging members to release the Policy Framework Papers that members prepare with IMF and World Bank staff assistance in connection with drawings under the Enhanced Structural Adjustment Facility.

It was noted at the Board's April discussion that the IMF had steadily become more transparent with respect to its own policy advice, most recently through the issuance of a Press (now "Public") Information Notice following the conclusion of a member's Article IV consultation (see Box 3). Directors emphasized that clear, concise, and analytically sound staff reports—as well as frank and comprehensive assessments by the Board—were vital for the effectiveness of the PIN process, and they agreed to return to these issues, including ways to expedite PIN publication. In April 1998, the Interim Committee specifically encouraged more members to release PINs. The Committee also asked the IMF "to continue its efforts to increase dissemination of information on its policy recommendations and encouraged member countries to increase the transparency of their policies."

IMF's Central Role in Crisis Management

Directors recognized at their April meeting that it was unrealistic to expect that every crisis could be anticipated or prevented. In case of a crisis, the international community had to be prepared to respond quickly with policy advice, well-integrated technical assistance, and, if necessary, adequate financing. The World Bank and the Asian Development Bank had provided critical technical and financial support for the Asian countries' adjustment efforts; bilateral support had also been important. The Board cited the need for the IMF to coordinate carefully assistance from different sources and ensure, in particular, that such assistance complemented the conditionality of IMF arrangements.

In April 1998, the Interim Committee endorsed the central role of the IMF, in particular its role in supporting the necessary reforms through conditionality. The Committee also welcomed the timely response to the Asian crisis by the international community, including the IMF, and stated that the IMF could not be expected to be able to finance every balance of payments deficit. Its catalytic role was essential for attracting other sources of financing in support of members' adjustment efforts, as was its role, when needed, to coordinate support from other sources.

Involving the Private Sector in Preventing and Resolving Crises

Directors agreed that the world financial community must strengthen its capacity to respond to balance of payments crises in ways that ensure the appropriate involvement of all groups of creditors, including the private sector. Such involvement was required to share the burden equitably with the official sector and to limit moral hazard. Specifically, Directors believed that the means used to resolve one crisis should not encourage imprudent or unsustainable behavior by creditors or debtors, thereby increasing the potential magnitude and frequency of future crises.

In recent crises, many groups of private creditors had sustained large losses. Equities and long-term debt instruments had lost value, and investors in bankrupt enterprises had received no special treatment. A serious challenge had emerged, however, with respect to creditors with short-term claims, where concerns were raised about moral hazard. Such claims were normally highly liquid, which could make it easier for creditors to "bolt for the exit." Members had tried to avoid defaults on such claims because of the potential impact on the stability of their financial systems and their countries' access to international capital markets. Thus, efforts were made to roll over, extend, or restructure the maturing obligations to external creditors. This issue

underscored the importance of preventive measures to discourage excessive reliance on short-term financing. Such measures included appropriate macroeconomic and debt-management policies; nondistortionary tax systems; effective prudential supervision of financial systems; the provision of timely and comprehensive data to financial markets, including on the debt of the corporate sector; and appropriate sequencing of steps to open the capital account.

Directors also cited the importance of strengthening countries' capacity to withstand sudden shifts in market sentiment, in particular, by strengthening their financial systems. Nevertheless, it was recognized that such efforts were not foolproof: circumstances would likely arise in which prevention would not be fully effective and countries would experience balance of payments crises. In most such cases, Directors emphasized, the IMF's approach should be to ensure that the appropriate adjustment programs included the continued involvement of private creditors (see the section on Policy on Sovereign Arrears to Private Creditors in Chapter VIII). At its April 1998 meeting, the Interim Committee endorsed this view, agreeing that ways had to be found to involve private creditors at an early stage. The Committee asked that the Board consider more actively ways to increase private sector involvement in crisis prevention and burden sharing, including devoting efforts to strengthen incentives for creditors and investors to better use information to analyze risks appropriately and avoid excessive risk taking. The Committee suggested the following mechanisms to meet this objective:

- closer contacts with private creditors to better explain IMF-supported arrangements and to develop modes of private sector financing that would help "bail in" private creditors in times of crisis;
- studying further the possibility of introducing provisions in bond contracts for bondholders to be represented, in case of nonpayment, in negotiations on bond contract restructuring;
- extending the IMF's policy of providing financing to members in arrears to include sovereign bonds ("lending into arrears") when appropriate;
- encouraging the adoption of strong bankruptcy laws to improve operation of both domestic and international capital markets; and
- advising members to exercise caution with respect to public guarantees to reduce the risk of a private debt problem turning into a sovereign debt problem.

CHAPTER VIII

Support for Member Countries' Adjustment

In 1997/98, the Executive Board approved the creation of the Supplemental Reserve Facility; reviewed the role of trade liberalization in IMF-supported adjustment programs and IMF policy on members' sovereign arrears to private creditors; discussed IMF monitoring of member country policies after the conclusion of IMF-supported programs; and reviewed the program of group travel by Executive Directors (Box 9). This chapter briefly describes these developments and provides summary information on financial arrangements with IMF member countries—Stand-By Arrangements, Extended Fund Facility Arrangements, and ESAF Arrangements—approved by the Board in 1997/98.

Supplemental Reserve Facility

In December 1997, the Executive Board established a new short-term lending facility for member countries, the Supplemental Reserve Facility (SRF). The facility was created to deal with the circumstances of a member experiencing exceptional balance of payments problems owing to a large short-term financing need resulting from a sudden and disruptive loss of market confidence reflected in pressure on the capital account and the member's reserves. SRF assistance is available when there is a reasonable expectation that implementation of strong adjustment policies and adequate financing will result, in a short period, in early correction of the balance of payments difficulties. Although resources under IMF facilities are available to all members, the SRF is likely to be used where the magnitude of the outflows may create a risk of contagion that could potentially threaten the international monetary system. In approving a request for the use of IMF resources under the SRF, the IMF takes into account the financing provided by other creditors. To minimize moral hazard, a member using resources under the SRF is encouraged to maintain the participation of creditors—both official and private—until the pressure on the balance of payments ceases.

Financing under the SRF, available in the form of additional resources under a Stand-By or Extended Arrangement, is committed for up to one year and generally available in two or more tranches. The first tranche is available at the time of approval of the financing, which normally coincides with the approval of the corresponding arrangement.

The IMF determines the amount of financing available under the SRF by taking into account the needs of the member; its capacity to repay, including in particular the strength of its economic program; its outstanding use of IMF credit; its record in using IMF resources in the past and cooperating with the IMF in surveillance; and the IMF's liquidity position.

Countries borrowing under the SRF are expected to repay within 1–1½ years of the date of each disbursement; the Board may, however, extend this repayment period by up to one year, at which point the borrower is obligated to repay. During the first year from the date of approval of financing to a country under the SRF, borrowers pay a surcharge of 300 basis points above the rate of charge on IMF drawings.[11] This rate increases by 50 basis points at the end of the first year and every six months thereafter until the surcharge reaches 500 basis points.

Trade Liberalization in IMF-Supported Programs

In October 1997, the Board considered a staff report on trade reform in medium-term, IMF-supported adjustment programs.[12] Directors felt that trade liberalization, as a complement to appropriate macroeconomic and other structural policies, should play an increasingly important role in IMF-supported programs designed to foster sustainable high-quality growth and that closer cooperation with the World Bank and the

---

[11]The credit provided by the IMF is denominated in SDRs, whose value is determined on the basis of a basket of the five leading currencies. The SDR interest rate, which forms the basis for the charges paid by members using IMF credit, is a weighted average of short-term interest rates in the domestic money markets of the five countries whose currencies are included in the valuation basket (typically the rates on short-term government paper, such as treasury bills).

[12]Published as IMF, *Trade Liberalization in IMF-Supported Programs,* World Economic and Financial Surveys (1998).

Group Travel by Executive Directors

Travel by a group of Executive Directors to selected countries was initiated to help broaden Directors' understanding of the economic problems and policies in individual member countries, with a view to enhancing their contribution to Board discussion of member country policies. In February 1998, a group of Directors traveled to Cameroon, Côte d'Ivoire, and Mali. Previous group trips were to Egypt, Jordan, and the Republic of Yemen in June 1996; and to Georgia, Hungary, and Ukraine in October 1996.

In reviewing the trial program of group travel by Executive Directors in June 1997, the Board agreed that the number of annual trips should be flexible, but the aim would normally be for two trips a year, each to two or three countries. Many thought the focus should be on program and intensive-surveillance countries, and that participation by a Director (or Directors) from a program country in a group visit would be useful, but they favored maintaining flexibility in the selection process.

World Trade Organization would be important toward achieving that end. There was also a need to promote trade liberalization in nonprogram countries through the IMF's surveillance activities. Trade reform was important in promoting transparency and good governance—reducing the scope for administrative discretion, incentives for lobbying for protection, and opportunities for rent seeking.

Since most countries covered by the staff's review had started out with restrictive trade regimes, trade liberalization had clearly been needed. Directors observed that broader and more rapid liberalization should have been targeted in a significant number of the programs and urged the staff to aim for further liberalization in future programs. Many Directors supported front-loaded liberalization measures as well as the use of prior actions, performance criteria, structural benchmarks, and reviews to monitor implementation of trade reforms, in order to signal their importance in accelerating economic growth. Other Directors cautioned that trade-related conditionality should be applied flexibly and should take into account each country's initial conditions, the degree of political support, and the authorities' own commitment to reforms. Far-reaching trade reform was a long-term process; it demanded a well-specified, comprehensive, and publicly announced program of measures and the avoidance of policy slippages.

Directors underscored the importance of mutually reinforcing trade and fiscal reforms. Trade liberalization did not have to affect the government's fiscal position adversely; the effects would depend on a country's circumstances and the mix of components in the reform package. For trade reform to succeed, Directors remarked that it should be broadly based and should initially replace nontariff barriers with tariffs, while eliminating customs duties exemptions and trade-related subsidies, all of which would tend to strengthen the government's fiscal position, or at least avoid revenue losses.

Policy on Sovereign Arrears to Private Creditors

A key outcome of the Executive Board's February 1998 discussion of IMF policy on sovereign arrears to private creditors was the emphasis given to involving private creditors at an early stage of a crisis, both to ensure adequate burden sharing and to limit moral hazard. The globalization of international capital markets and improved market access had increased the importance of private capital as a source of external financing for many developing countries; at the same time, such access had made these countries more vulnerable to shifts in market sentiment. This underscored the need for early, forceful adjustment measures on the part of borrowing countries in the face of emerging difficulties; for restraint in both public and private foreign borrowing, particularly at the shorter maturities; and for a cautious approach to the waiver of sovereign immunities, particularly by central banks.

With regard to how the IMF could respond to a liquidity crisis that posed the risk of a member defaulting on international sovereign bonds within the existing legal and institutional frameworks, Directors noted that a balance had to be struck between promoting effective balance of payments adjustments and orderly debtor-creditor relations and limiting moral hazard with respect to both creditor and debtor behavior. Many Directors called for consideration of extending the IMF's policy on providing support by "lending into arrears," that is, continuing to provide financing to countries even when they were behind in their debt payments to some private creditors. They recognized that such lending should be limited and provided only where prompt IMF support was essential for the successful implementation of the member's adjustment program; where negotiations between the member and its private creditors on a restructuring had begun; and where there were firm indications that the sovereign borrower and its private creditors would negotiate in good faith to agree on a debt-restructuring plan. All drawings under an IMF-supported adjustment program with a member with sovereign arrears to private creditors had to be subject to financing reviews to allow the Executive Board to monitor closely unexpected developments—including any litigation—in creditor relations. Some Directors opposed lending into arrears, at least in the absence of further protection. This strategy, they believed, would risk aggressive litigation by individual creditors, thus adversely affecting safeguards on the IMF's resources.

Directors noted that the toleration of arrears to bondholders and other private creditors under IMF-supported adjustment programs may be seen by market participants as lowering the cost of a default to debtors, thereby creating debtor moral hazard. They felt, however, that even under a policy of lending into arrears, the cost to debtors of default would remain substantial, and that IMF conditionality would provide an effective limitation on debtor moral hazard.

Directors considered, on a preliminary basis, three suggestions for possible improvements to existing mechanisms for resolving sovereign liquidity crises. Regarding the first suggestion, modification of the legal provisions of bond contracts, a number of Directors felt that the introduction of sharing provisions, collective representation of bondholders, and qualified majorities to alter the terms of bond contracts could help facilitate the orderly resolution of liquidity crises. Directors noted, however, that there had been no market response to the Group of Ten Deputies' proposals in this area. Therefore, a number of Directors felt that progress was likely to require some kind of official action, possibly in the form of leadership by major industrial country borrowers in introducing such provisions into their own bond offerings. Regarding the second suggestion, a sovereign bankruptcy mechanism, most Directors continued to believe that proposals for establishing a formal international debt-adjustment mechanism were cumbersome and impractical and should not be pursued. Finally, Directors gave preliminary consideration to the possibility of a modification of Article VIII, Section 2(*b*), of the IMF's Articles of Agreement to allow the IMF to sanction a temporary stay on creditor litigation, thus providing members with protection from litigation in the context of the IMF lending into arrears. Directors believed that this raised complex issues of legal procedures and interpretation that would need to be considered further before moving in this area.

Postprogram Monitoring

In October 1997, the Board considered a proposal that the IMF continue monitoring member country policies after the conclusion of an IMF-supported adjustment program in cases involving very high access to IMF resources. Directors broadly supported a policy of postprogram monitoring in cases where IMF credit outstanding remained in excess of 300 percent of a member's quota. With respect to the use of postprogram monitoring in cases of access below the 300 percent threshold, the Board asked the staff to study further possible modalities for such monitoring and to suggest draft guidelines for its further consideration.

Member Countries' Use of IMF Facilities

In 1997/98, the IMF approved nine new Stand-By Arrangements, four new Extended Fund Facility Arrangements, and eight new arrangements under the Enhanced Structural Adjustment Facility. Arrangements with Korea included disbursements by means of the newly created Supplemental Reserve Facility (described above). There were also four drawings under the policy on emergency postconflict assistance.

- *Stand-By Arrangements* typically cover periods of one to two years and focus both on macroeconomic policies and on structural policy measures. Drawings are generally made in quarterly installments. Repayments of each drawing are made in eight quarterly installments beginning 3¼ years after the drawing.
- *Extended Fund Facility Arrangements* provide support for medium-term programs that generally run for three years (up to four years in exceptional circumstances). Typically, a program states the general objectives for the three-year period and the specific policies for the first year; policies for subsequent years are spelled out in program reviews. Repayments are made over 4½ to 10 years.
- *Enhanced Structural Adjustment Facility Arrangements* provide support, in the form of highly concessional loans, to low-income member countries facing protracted balance of payments problems. Eligible members seeking ESAF resources must develop, with the assistance of the staffs of the IMF and the World Bank, a policy framework paper (PFP) for a three-year adjustment program. The PFP, which is updated annually, describes the authorities' economic objectives, macroeconomic and structural policies during the three-year period, and associated external financing needs and major sources of financing. ESAF loans are disbursed semiannually and repaid in 10 equal semiannual installments, beginning 5½ years and ending 10 years after the date of each disbursement. The interest rate on ESAF loans is 0.5 percent a year.
- *Emergency assistance* to help members overcome balance of payments problems arising from natural disasters or postconflict situations is normally limited to 25 percent of a member's quota and is available only if the member intends to move within a relatively short period of time to a Stand-By or Extended Arrangement, or to an arrangement under the ESAF. Repayments are made in eight quarterly installments beginning 3¼ years after the drawing.

Albania

Financial Support. On November 7, 1997, the IMF approved a credit of SDR 8.8 million under its emergency postconflict assistance.

Program Objectives. Limit the decline of real GDP to 8 percent in 1997 and achieve real growth of about 12 percent in 1998; contain the annual inflation rate to a range of 51–54 percent in 1997, and reduce it to 15–20 percent in 1998; and keep gross international reserves to the equivalent of some 3.5 months' imports through 1998.

Policies. Fiscal policy would aim at limiting the domestically financed budget deficit to about 13 percent of GDP in 1997 and to below 10 percent in 1998. This would be accomplished by first restoring and then improving tax collection; raising tax rates, including a significant increase in the value-added tax rate; and exercising expenditure restraint, including through reductions in the public sector workforce. The Bank of Albania would support the inflation reduction effort by maintaining an appropriately tight monetary stance. Under the program, the authorities plan a broad range of structural reforms, including progress toward privatization or liquidation of two of the three state-owned commercial banks; winding up the companies that had operated pyramid schemes; civil service reform; a resumption of enterprise privatization; and creation of a functioning agricultural land market. In the short term, there would be a temporary expansion of the social safety net. To this end, the government would accelerate disbursements of social assistance and would also introduce public works and community service schemes for social assistance beneficiaries who could work.

Argentina

Financial Support. On February 4, 1998, the IMF approved a three-year EFF credit for SDR 2.1 billion. The authorities announced their intention to treat the arrangement as precautionary and to draw only if adverse external circumstances made it necessary.

Program Objectives. Consolidate the gains in macroeconomic performance and the structural improvements achieved in recent years through a further strengthening of the fiscal position and the completion of the structural reform agenda. Reduce the overall federal government deficit from the equivalent of 1.4 percent of GDP in 1997 to 1 percent in 1998, and to 0.3 percent by 2000. Strengthen confidence by maintaining a sound financial system under the currency board arrangement and provide for an adequate cushion of liquidity that could compensate for the limited role of the central bank as a lender of last resort in a crisis.

Policies. The program would put in place a reform of the labor market by mid-1998. Comprehensive tax reform would seek to improve the efficiency and equity of the tax system and promote the competitiveness of the economy. Reforms in budgetary procedures would aim at promoting transparency and efficiency in public spending and include widening the coverage of the budget, moving to a pluriannual process, preparing annual assessments of the cost of fiscal benefits and incentives, and introducing the use of expenditure efficiency indicators. Initiatives in health care would include a revision of the regulatory framework for private health care providers and the final phases of the

restructuring of the health insurance system for retirees and of health organizations run by unions. The government would continue restructuring social programs better to target budgetary resources toward vulnerable groups. As part of a broader initiative to reform the judiciary system, the program would also include steps to modify judicial procedures to speed up the resolution of tax cases and increase legal security in credit markets.

Armenia

Financial Support. On June 24, 1997, the IMF approved a second annual ESAF loan for SDR 33.8 million.

Program Objectives. Achieve a real GDP growth rate of about 6 percent in 1997, bring down inflation to less than 10 percent, and increase gross reserves to the equivalent of 2.8 months of imports.

Policies. Fiscal policy would aim at reducing the overall deficit to below 7 percent of GDP in 1997 by increasing revenue through further improvements in tax administration, fully implementing the tax arrears payment scheme, establishing an operational legal framework to enforce revenue collections, and adopting a series of revenue measures aimed at rationalizing and simplifying the structure of several important taxes. The authorities would also further reduce current expenditure to about 18.5 percent of GDP through elimination of open-ended price subsidies to privileged groups, cuts in defense expenditures, and lower interest payments. Monetary policy would be consistent with achieving the program's inflation targets.

The authorities expressed a commitment to accelerating the implementation of structural reforms. In addition to the reforms under way in the banking sector and tax administration, the 1997 program would follow a three-pronged approach toward continued privatization to lay the basis for sustained growth, improvement of financial discipline through enterprise restructuring, and reforms in the energy, health, and education sectors. The authorities decided to take several measures during the program period to improve the targeting of social safety net benefits to alleviate poverty and improve income distribution.

Azerbaijan

Financial Support. On December 22, 1997, the IMF approved a total credit of SDR 48.7 million—with SDR 29.2 million available in two equal semi-annual installments under the second-year ESAF, and SDR 17.5 million under the second year of the EFF.

Program Objectives. Speed up the transition to a market economy and develop the country's oil resources without adverse impact on the rest of the economy. Use both macroeconomic and structural policies to dampen the pressures of domestic demand and encourage domestic savings. Use supply-side policies to remove the obstacles to growth in the non-oil sector inherited from the planning era. Use fiscal policies to reduce the deficit of the general government to less than 1 percent of GDP during the next three years. Use monetary policy to maintain low levels of inflation. For 1998, aim to accelerate growth to 7 percent, while maintaining inflation below 5 percent and limiting the external current account deficit to some 27 percent of GDP, including imports related to development of the oil sector.

Policies. High priority has been placed on public sector management reform, bank restructuring and privatization, and an equitable process of enterprise and land privatization. A comprehensive program to overhaul the public sector, based on the appropriate role of the state in a market economy, would be designed and implemented with the objective of eliminating the state's commercial and industrial activities and focusing on regulatory and policymaking functions. It would aim at establishing a modern, efficient, and professional civil service capable of managing public resources, together with a competent and impartial judiciary and legal system that can enforce property rights and contracts. Over 70 percent of state enterprises—by asset value and employment rate—would be transferred to private hands through 2000. The government is committed to substantial reforms in the health sector, in response to deteriorating quality and access problems.

Bolivia

Financial Support. On September 10, 1997, the IMF approved a third annual ESAF loan for SDR 33.7 million and an extension of the loan's period through September 1998. For support under the HIPC Initiative, see Chapter IX.

Program Objectives. Raise sustainable economic growth and alleviate poverty, while ensuring progress toward lower inflation and a viable balance of payments. The capitalization and privatization program and the pension reform should help achieve these goals, but the reforms will incur additional fiscal costs over the next several years. Thus, design fiscal policy to absorb these costs gradually to ensure that domestic savings continue to increase and to help promote further development of local capital markets. Also, strengthen social programs to reduce poverty further. Reduce inflation to 7 percent and achieve GDP growth of 5 percent.

Policies. The combined public sector deficit is expected to widen between 1996 and 1997–98 and then return to its 1996 level by early in the next decade. With respect to structural policies, the government intends to continue with privatization. The government is committed to adopting Basle norms for risk weighting of bank assets from mid-1998 and raising

the minimum ratio for capital-to-risk-weighted assets to 10 percent from 8 percent starting in 1999. A superintendency of pensions would ensure that the new private pension funds can operate effectively as financial intermediaries. To improve governance and public accountability, the government would intensify judicial reform and reforms of public service and customs. It would continue to strengthen the sectoral superintendencies that regulate public utility sectors and introduce a program to improve commercial and property registers. The authorities would continue to implement education reform; implement an integrated national health plan that covers, in particular, mothers, infants, and elderly citizens in needy urban and rural areas; accelerate land titling to strengthen the property rights of small farmers; and increase investment in rural infrastructure.

Burkina Faso

Financial Support. On September 8, 1997, the IMF approved a second annual ESAF loan for SDR 13.3 million. For support under the HIPC Initiative, see Chapter IX.

Program Objectives. Further increase the ratio of budgetary revenue to GDP and accelerate structural reforms. Achieve a real GDP growth rate above 6 percent, contain inflation at 3 percent, and reduce the external current account deficit to 10.5 percent of GDP. Improve the quality of economic statistics.

Policies. Fiscal policy would aim at increasing the primary budgetary surplus to 1.9 percent of GDP in 1997 through a rise in the revenue-to-GDP ratio to 12.9 percent of GDP. The revenue increases would reflect the full-year impact of a September 1996 rise in the value-added tax rate to 18 percent from 15 percent and further efforts to strengthen customs revenues. Budgetary expenditure would be better monitored through computerization of the budgetary cycle. Monetary policy would seek to contain bank credit expansion, in line with the program's inflation objectives.

Structural reform measures would include steps to expedite privatization and a strategy to open public utilities; judicial system reform; and deregulation of rice and sugar sectors, elimination of nontariff barriers to agricultural trade, and restructuring of the cotton sector by reinforcing farmers' cooperatives. To address social needs, the government set quantitative objectives in the education and health sectors to correct past major weaknesses. The enrollment rates in primary schools and for girls would be increased gradually, as would the numbers of health centers.

Cameroon

Financial Support. On August 20, 1997, the IMF approved a three-year ESAF loan for SDR 162.1 million.

Program Objectives. Place the economy on a sustainable growth path and restore internal and external viability. Rebuild the physical and economic infrastructure with a firm and long-term commitment to structural reforms with a view to unlocking the country's considerable resources. Over the three-year period, aim to achieve real annual GDP growth of at least 5 percent, limiting average annual consumer price inflation to 2 percent and stabilizing the external current account deficit at about 2 percent of GDP.

Policies. At the core of the program would be a comprehensive structural reform agenda aimed at further reducing the public sector's burden on the economy, liberalizing the energy and transport sectors, deepening the financial market, and consolidating the gains in external competitiveness. Key policies in support of the government's medium-term strategy would include maintaining external competitiveness through efficiency-enhancing structural reforms; reducing fiscal imbalances through a steady increase in the ratio of non-oil revenue to GDP and firm control over expenditure; and strengthening the efficiency of the tax system by strictly enforcing tax laws, combating fraud and corruption, introducing a value-added tax, rationalizing income taxes, reforming forestry and agricultural taxation, and phasing out export taxes. A new tax regime for the forestry sector and a requirement for sustainable forest management plans before concessions were granted would benefit conservation. Further priorities include increasing public expenditure on social services, especially health and education, and rehabilitating infrastructure; accelerating state enterprise reforms; completing financial sector reform, including insurance companies and the social security system; and improving public sector management and efficiency.

Cape Verde

Financial Support. On February 20, 1998, the IMF approved a 14-month Stand-By Arrangement for SDR 2.1 million. The authorities indicated that they would treat the arrangement as precautionary and would draw on it only if adverse circumstances made it necessary.

Program Objectives. Achieve real GDP growth of 4 percent in 1998 and an average inflation rate of 3.5 percent. The external current account balance (excluding transfers) would target a deficit of 15.7 percent of GDP in 1998, and tightening fiscal policy would reduce the overall fiscal deficit to 8.7 percent of GDP in 1998 from an estimated 15 percent in 1997.

Policies. The authorities would introduce administrative measures to strengthen budgetary execution. They would also maintain a pegged exchange rate and thus gear monetary policy to balancing the private sector's credit needs against the reserve accumulation targets of the program. The government would liberalize further

the trade regime by replacing the few remaining import quotas with tariffs and then rationalizing and reducing overall tariffs. Objectives in the social area and in poverty alleviation would be achieved through higher growth, lower inflation, and continued budgetary support of efforts to improve primary health and education.

Chad

Financial Support. On April 29, 1998, the IMF approved a third annual ESAF loan for SDR 16.5 million.

Program Objectives. Achieve real GDP growth of 6 percent, limit inflation to 3.5 percent, and contain the current account deficit at 17 percent of GDP in 1998.

Policies. The government would strengthen the fiscal adjustment effort of previous years. Although the overall budget deficit, on a commitment basis, would be limited to 8.6 percent of GDP, the current budget for 1998 projects a surplus of 0.7 percent, reflecting an increase in revenues of 36 percent, to 9 percent of GDP, to be achieved through more efficient revenue collection, tightened controls on exemptions, and strengthened and computerized operations in the customs directorate. Expenditures would be restructured in favor of health and education, and a comprehensive reform of the civil service would be initiated. The regional monetary authorities would maintain a prudent policy stance, in line with the program objectives for low inflation, while consolidating foreign exchange reserves. Structural reforms would be pursued to enhance the efficiency of the productive sectors of the economy and improve government revenues. Social policies designed to reduce poverty substantially would continue to be implemented.

Côte d'Ivoire

Financial Support. On March 17, 1998, the IMF approved a three-year ESAF credit for SDR 285.8 million. For support under the HIPC Initiative, see Chapter IX.

Program Objectives. Under the medium-term adjustment strategy for 1998–2000, achieve real GDP growth of about 6 percent a year, allowing per capita income to rise by more than 2 percent annually; maintain inflation of about 3 percent a year, consistent with the exchange rate peg; and reduce the external current account deficit to 2 percent of GDP by 2000. Bring the fiscal position close to balance by 2000 and achieve a surplus thereafter; adopt structural reforms to promote private sector development and investment; and reduce poverty, especially through well-targeted measures in the education and health sectors.

Policies. To consolidate the fiscal situation, the authorities would strengthen revenue performance by improving tax and customs administration, reducing exemptions, and continuing to fight against fraud and evasion. They would follow a prudent expenditure policy while providing adequately for basic health and education services and infrastructure maintenance. Monetary policy, conducted at the regional level, would be consistent with the fixed exchange rate regime and a further improvement of the CFA franc zone's net foreign asset position.

Regarding structural reforms, trade liberalization would be pursued in the context of regional arrangements, while privatization would be accelerated with the sale of 15 enterprises in 1998. The authorities decided to liberalize fully the marketing of coffee and cocoa, beginning with the liberalization of coffee in October 1998. To reduce poverty, public spending would continue to be redirected in favor of education and health, with a system being established to monitor poverty indicators.

Djibouti

Financial Support. On May 21, 1997, the IMF approved a request for the extension of a Stand-By Arrangement for SDR 4.6 million through the end of March 1998 and augmentation of the amount available under it by SDR 2 million. A further extension through the end of June 1998 was approved in March 1998.

Program Objectives. Regain control of the fiscal situation and implement structural measures in a number of areas to improve the economy's supply responsiveness and competitiveness.

Policies. Policies would include intensified efforts to reduce further current expenditures and improve the quality of the tax system, as well as the overall regulatory framework for economic activities; enhance flexibility in factor inputs and create conditions conducive to a resumption of investment; and create new job opportunities.

Estonia

Financial Support. On December 17, 1997, the IMF approved a 15-month Stand-By Arrangement for SDR 16.1 million. The authorities indicated they would treat their arrangement as precautionary and would draw on it only if adverse external circumstances made it necessary.

Program Objectives. Achieve an annual growth rate of real GDP of over 5 percent and reduce inflation further to about 8 percent in 1998. To reduce demand pressures, expand the general government surplus to 1.8 percent of GDP. Reduce the current account deficit.

Policies. The program would follow a three-pronged approach: implement tighter fiscal policies to restrain domestic demand; adopt monetary measures (within the limited policy options available under the currency board) to reduce the rate of credit expansion and to

raise banking system prudential standards, plus an intensification of financial system surveillance; and accelerate structural reforms to improve productivity and raise private savings. On the fiscal side, tax revenues would be expected to continue to improve through further economic expansion, some new tax measures, and stronger tax administration. At the same time, the ratio of general government expenditures to GDP would decline.

The authorities would reinforce measures to address the growth in domestic credit and improve the soundness of the financial system, such as raising capital adequacy ratios and the level of required bank reserves. Banks' minimum capital requirements would be raised and prudential regulations imposed on a consolidated basis for banks and their nonbank financial subsidiaries. The authorities intend to adopt a more aggressive approach to financial sector surveillance to reduce systemic risks and improve supervision of bank and nonbank financial institutions. They would also implement measures to strengthen securities and capital markets. Other structural reforms would focus on faster implementation of enterprise privatization and land reform, thus would improve the scope for noninflationary growth by minimizing distortions and reducing constraints on potential output.

Ghana

Financial Support. On March 23, 1998, the IMF approved a second annual ESAF loan for SDR 82.2 million.

Program Objectives. Secure a stable macroeconomic environment that supports private-sector-led economic growth, thereby creating jobs, boosting incomes, and reducing poverty. Achieve annual real GDP growth of 5.6 percent, or 2.5 percent on a per capita basis; reduce annual inflation to 11 percent by the end of 1998, further halving it to 5.5 percent by the end of 1999; and contain the current account deficit at 7.3 percent of GDP in 1998 while maintaining gross official reserves at 2.7 months of imports.

Policies. The government would strengthen the fiscal adjustment effort launched in 1997 and increase 1998 tax revenue by about 1 percent of GDP, in part by improving sales tax revenue collections, introducing the value-added tax effective December 1, 1998, and intensifying tax system reforms. Inflation would be brought down through control of the money supply, conditioning any action to lower interest rates on the abatement of inflation expectations. Structural reforms would be pursued to enhance private investment and improve resource allocation; to further deregulate the petroleum and cocoa sectors; to pursue the divestiture program aggressively; to liberalize the financial sector; and to reform the civil service and autonomous government agencies.

Guinea

Financial Support. On April 3, 1998, the IMF approved a second annual ESAF loan for SDR 23.6 million.

Program Objectives. Implement tight financial policies and further structural reforms to consolidate the stabilization under way and to create the conditions for sustainable and diversified economic growth. Achieve growth of 5 percent in real terms; reduce inflation to about 3.5 percent; contain the current account deficit at 7.7 percent of GDP (excluding official transfers); and increase gross official reserves to 3.4 months of imports.

Policies. Fiscal measures would include pursuing further improvements in tax and customs administration, ensuring compliance with the VAT, and introducing a new, unified real estate tax and a lower VAT threshold for enterprises in the service sector, with the aim of raising total revenues to 11.6 percent of GDP. Allocations to the priority sectors of health, primary education, and rural development and roads would be increased, and sufficient local counterpart funds provided for foreign-financed investment projects. Budget management would be reformed to improve efficiency and transparency, and a new computerized expenditure monitoring system put into operation. Monetary policy would be designed to support the external sector and achieve inflation objectives. Bank supervision would be tightened and prudential regulations enforced more strictly. Structural reforms would include accelerating privatization, public sector restructuring, and judicial sector reform; reinforcing the efficiency of the civil service; extending the cost-reduction program in public enterprises to the mining and energy sectors and preparing a divestiture timetable by the end of June 1998; and improving the legal environment for business activity by creating an arbitration court and preparing reforms to reinforce transparency and efficiency in the judicial system. The authorities would continue to reorient resources toward primary education and to increase nonwage expenditure on health.

Guinea-Bissau

Financial Support. On July 25, 1997, the IMF approved a third annual ESAF loan for SDR 4.7 million and an extension of the period through the end of March 1998. The ESAF Arrangement was augmented by SDR 1.1 million.

Program Objectives. Maintain annual economic growth of about 5 percent; lower the average annual rate of inflation to about 6 percent in 1999 from 51 percent in 1996; and reduce the external current account deficit (excluding grants) by about 5 percentage points to 16 percent of GDP by 1999. Maintain the level of investment at 22 percent of GDP, while enhancing its efficiency through a projected rise in gross domestic saving to 4 percent of GDP in 1999.

Policies. Fiscal policy would be the key focus of the authorities' economic policy, with a twofold objective of further raising the current primary surplus through an increase in the revenue-GDP ratio and overhauling the tax system. The government would introduce a general sales tax and a major reform of external tariffs, reduce export taxes, and revise excise taxes, particularly on petroleum. On the expenditure side, the program was to focus on containing nonessential outlays and on further streamlining the civil service. A major strengthening of budgetary procedures was to be introduced, with prior authorization of the Ministry of Finance Budget Directorate required for all expenditure commitments. In the monetary field, domestic credit policy would be kept tight to quell inflation. Structural reforms would continue to focus on accelerating public enterprise privatization; increasing efficiency in the energy sector; enhancing the role of the private sector in agriculture, fisheries, and forestry; improving social services; and reforming the civil service.

Guyana

For support under the HIPC Initiative, see Chapter IX.

Indonesia

Financial Support. On November 5, 1997, the IMF approved a Stand-By Arrangement for SDR 7.3 billion over three years. In approving the request, the IMF used the accelerated procedures established under the Emergency Financing Mechanism. On July 15, 1998, the IMF approved an additional SDR 1 billion.

Program Objectives and Policies. For details, see Chapter V.

Korea

Financial Support. On December 4, 1997, the IMF approved a three-year Stand-By Arrangement for SDR 15.5 billion. In approving the request, the IMF used the accelerated procedures established under the Emergency Financing Mechanism. On December 18, the Board concluded its first review of the arrangement and activated the new Supplemental Reserve Facility.

Program Objectives and Policies. For details, see Chapter V.

Latvia

Financial Support. On October 10, 1997, the IMF approved an 18-month Stand-By Arrangement for SDR 33 million. The authorities indicated they would treat the arrangement as precautionary and would draw on it only if adverse external circumstances made it necessary.

Program Objectives. Attain a real GDP growth of 4 percent for 1997 and 5 percent for 1998; reduce the annual rate of inflation to 9 percent in 1997 and 7 percent in 1998; and narrow the external current account deficit to 6.1 percent of GDP in 1997 and to 4.9 percent in 1998. Target gross international reserves at the equivalent of about three months of imports for 1997 and 1998. Reduce the general government fiscal deficit to 0.9 percent of GDP in 1997 and 0.5 percent in 1998.

Policies. The program emphasized the acceleration of structural reforms, including the completion of enterprise privatization and the strengthening and extension of private property rights, with the aim of establishing Latvia firmly as a market economy, encouraging restructuring, and stimulating saving and domestic and foreign investment. Virtually all remaining state-owned enterprises, including large companies, would be privatized by mid-1998. In this context, steps would be taken to resolve the issue of consumer arrears and to ensure that energy tariffs were set on a cost-recovery basis. Other structural reforms, including land registration and a reduction in the number of business regulations, would also advance under the program. Trade liberalization would continue, and legislation would be submitted to parliament by mid-1998 for a further substantial reduction in agricultural tariffs. Measures to improve tax administration and expenditure productivity, including through civil service reform, would make possible increased expenditures on social services and infrastructure. The government would take steps to improve the efficiency of social spending, including through a reform of the national health insurance system.

Mauritania

Financial Support. On July 14, 1997, the IMF approved a third annual ESAF loan for SDR 14.3 million.

Program Objectives. Achieve real GDP growth of 4.9 percent in 1997, hold inflation at 5 percent, and limit the external current account deficit (excluding official transfers) to 5.5 percent of GDP. In fiscal policy, achieve an overall government surplus of 4.1 percent of GDP in 1997, reflecting the further rationalization and control of expenditure, and containment of the decline in total revenues in relation to GDP, mainly on account of lower fishing royalties.

Policies. Monetary policy under the program would be consistent with the achievement of the program's inflation and balance of payments objectives. The government took a number of actions to reform the legal, judicial, and regulatory framework, including notably accelerating procedures for establishing new enterprises and adopting measures to encourage private sector investment in the mining sector. Legislation was also being prepared to encourage private sector participation, particularly in the transport and utilities sectors. The authorities were committed to observing minimum levels of expenditure on health and education and

were adopting measures to further improve the quality and coverage of services in these areas.

Mongolia

Financial Support. On July 30, 1997, the IMF approved a three-year ESAF loan for SDR 33.4 million.

Program Objectives. Reduce inflation to single-digit rates, achieve annual real growth of 6 percent, and increase official gross international reserves to the equivalent of over 15 weeks of import cover. Reduce the budget deficit to 6 percent of GDP by 2000 and raise national savings over the medium term. Achieve fiscal adjustment by reducing the size of the public sector and adopting reforms in public administration and taxation.

Policies. Monetary policy would be geared to maintaining positive real interest rates on central bank bills and limiting commercial bank access to central bank credit to the refinancing and rediscount facilities. The elimination of import duties and the large up-front cost of bank restructuring—fundamental components of the reform strategy—were projected to cause the budget deficit to rise to 10.5 percent in 1997. The deficit would be reduced significantly, however, in 1998 as the costs of bank restructuring decline and further tax reforms are phased in. Public administration reforms are to be aimed at improving expenditure control and accountability to set the stage for decentralized decision making. The government is committed to reforming education and health to improve the delivery of services and restructuring other aspects of the social welfare system to reduce budgetary costs and improve targeting.

Mozambique

Financial Support. On June 23, 1997, the IMF approved a second annual ESAF loan for SDR 25.2 million. For support under the HIPC Initiative, see Chapter IX.

Program Objectives. Increase nonenergy GDP by 5 percent in 1997 and total GDP by 6 percent, cut end-of-period inflation to 14 percent in 1997, and increase gross international reserves to the equivalent of about five months of imports of goods and nonfactor services.

Policies. The program would envisage a tight monetary policy and maintenance of a floating exchange rate system. The focus of fiscal policy would be on strengthening tax administration, reducing exemptions, and modernizing the direct and indirect tax systems to encourage compliance and remove distortions. The government would continue its program of privatization, with a view to completing it by mid-1999. Another major priority would be the reform and strengthening of public administration. Plans would include greater decentralization of decision making, increased transparency and accountability in government, and civil service reforms. Mozambique would be committed to expanding the share of the social sectors in total spending and to improving the effectiveness of social expenditure. The 1997/98 program targeted an increase in such spending to reduce poverty and improve the human capital base.

Nicaragua

Financial Support. On March 18, 1998, the IMF approved a three-year ESAF loan for SDR 100.9 million.

Program Objectives. Move toward sustainable public finance and external sector positions, carry out structural reform, and promote growth to alleviate poverty and reduce unemployment. Increase public saving by 6 percentage points of GDP and achieve a small surplus in the combined public sector balance (after grants) by 2000. Increase gross reserves—net of central bank paper—to three months of imports, achieve real GDP growth of about 6 percent, and reduce inflation to about 5 percent. Within this medium-term strategy, the 1998 program, supported by the first annual ESAF loan, seeks to increase gross reserves—net of central bank paper—to the equivalent of 1.8 months of imports, achieve a real GDP growth rate of 4.8 percent, and limit inflation to 8.0 percent.

Policies. The government would reduce the size of the public sector and increase central government revenues by broadening the tax base, increasing the transparency of the tax system, and eliminating a large number of discretionary VAT and customs exemptions. Central government current expenditures would be frozen and export subsidies eliminated. Monetary policy would be geared to supporting the external sector and inflation objectives. Public sector reforms would continue to improve services and efficiency, and the executive branch would be restructured to reduce the number of government ministries and agencies reporting directly to the president. A comprehensive judicial reform would be prepared, designed to improve legal procedures and enhance enforcement of contracts and property rights. Discriminatory treatment against foreign investors would be eliminated, reform of the state banking sector completed, and public utilities, state oil distribution, and the services of the major ports privatized.

Niger

Financial Support. On July 28, 1997, the IMF approved a second annual ESAF loan for SDR 19.3 million.

Program Objectives. Raise real GDP growth to 4–5 percent a year, thereby allowing real per capita income to increase by at least 1 percent a year; reduce inflation to 3 percent by the end of 1997; and contain the external current account deficit (excluding official transfers) at 11.1 percent of GDP in 1997, lowering it to 10.5 percent of GDP in 1998. Raise budgetary revenue to the equivalent of 9.3 percent of GDP in 1997 and to 10.7 percent in 1998.

Policies. The government would reduce the overall budget deficit to 7.3 percent of GDP by 1998 through enhanced revenue mobilization and a cautious expenditure policy. Expenditure policies would continue to ensure that wages and salaries do not crowd out other essential expenditures, especially those on maintenance and key social services. The government would take steps to streamline the regulatory framework and to reduce its involvement in those areas of interest to the private sector. It would continue efforts to strengthen legal provisions governing commercial transactions and, in particular, the recovery of commercial bank loans. Current budgetary expenditures allocated to health and education would be increased by 10 percent a year in real terms during 1997–2000.

Pakistan

Financial Support. On October 20, 1997, the IMF approved a three-year financing package for SDR 1.14 billion, with SDR 682.4 million available under the ESAF and SDR 454.9 million under the EFF.

Program Objectives. Raise the average annual growth rate of real GDP to the 5–6 percent range; progressively reduce annual inflation to about 7 percent; and reduce the external current account deficit (excluding official transfers) to the range of 4–4.5 percent of GDP, with a view to strengthening external reserves substantially. Design fiscal policy to cut the overall budget deficit to 4 percent of GDP by the third year of the program, which would help boost national savings to about 15 percent of GDP in 1999/2000.

Policies. The government would further rationalize the public sector, shifting more of the primary productive role to the private sector, and strengthen local institutional capacity. In the public sector, the domestic tax base would be broadened, tax administration strengthened, government expenditure shifted toward the social services and human capital formation, and key public enterprises restructured. The government had also resolved to enhance the authority and the ability of the State Bank of Pakistan to regulate and supervise banks, improve the legal and judiciary process for enforcing financial contracts, privatize the state-owned banks and financial institutions, and develop the capital market. In the external sector, the interbank foreign exchange market would be deepened and exchange rate policy guided increasingly by market developments.

Panama

Financial Support. On December 10, 1997, the IMF approved a three-year EFF credit for SDR 120 million.

Program Objectives. Deepen and broaden structural reforms in the context of continued prudent fiscal policy and low inflation, with the goal of promoting sustainable output and employment growth and reducing poverty. Raise GDP growth to 5 percent by 2000, while holding annual inflation at about 1½ percent.

Policies. Structural measures would focus on further privatization, import tariff reduction, and financial sector reform during the first half of the program period. Reforms relating to taxation, civil service, and social security would be implemented during the second half of the program period. The authorities would implement an ambitious privatization program, and a new round of substantial tariff reform would take place to further increase transparency and efficiency to attract foreign investment. A comprehensive tax study would be completed in 1998 and its recommendations implemented in the second half of 1999, to improve tax collection by 2000. The authorities would strengthen the social safety net for the most vulnerable groups in society. Efforts would also be made to improve efficiency in the provision of basic health and education service, through investment income from privatization proceeds.

Philippines

Financial Support (I). On July 18, 1997, the IMF approved the extension of an arrangement under the EFF for SDR 474.5 million through December 31, 1997, and its augmentation by SDR 316.7 million. In approving the extension and augmentation of the EFF, the IMF used, for the first time, the accelerated procedures under the Emergency Financing Mechanism.

Program Objectives. Achieve economic growth of 6.3 percent in 1997, reduce average inflation to 6.5 percent, contain the external current account deficit to about 4½ percent of GNP, and hold adjusted reserve cover equivalent to 2.1 months of imports of goods and services by year-end.

Policies. The new floating exchange rate policy would be supported by strong monetary and fiscal policies. Interest rates would be kept high until the foreign exchange market stabilized, and base money growth reduced to keep annual growth in broad money (including foreign currency deposits) at 23 percent—a rate consistent with inflation and growth targets. Fiscal policy would be tightened in the second half of 1997 to offset slippages in the first half and achieve a public sector surplus of 0.3 percent of GNP for the year as a whole. The fiscal tightening would include revenue-enhancing measures as well as expenditure cuts. The government would also seek passage of the remaining elements of the Comprehensive Tax Reform Package, a vital element of its policies to strengthen savings performance. It would further strengthen the financial system with the help of

recently adopted measures to tighten the limits on the exposure of banks to the real estate market and to discourage the growth of foreign currency liabilities through new liquidity requirements and by removing tax disincentives on peso deposits.

Financial Support (II). On March 27, 1998, the IMF approved a two-year Stand-By Arrangement for SDR 1.0 billion. The authorities expressed their intention to treat the arrangement as precautionary and would draw on it only if adverse external circumstances made it necessary.

Program Objectives. Contain the slowdown of real GNP growth to 3 percent in 1998 and to 5 percent in 1999; limit inflation to 8 percent in 1998 and to 6.5 percent in 1999; and reduce the current account deficit to 3.1 percent of GNP in 1998 and 2.7 percent in 1999, with adjusted reserve cover rising to 1.9 months of imports in 1998 and to 2.3 months of imports in 1999.

Policies. The consolidated public sector deficit would be limited to 0.9 percent of GNP in 1998, followed by balance in 1999. Higher interest payments would be compensated for by cuts in other current and capital expenditures. In implementing the cuts, programs directed at poverty reduction would be protected. Monetary policy would be designed to be consistent with the inflation objective and restoring confidence in the peso, within the overall framework of base money targets and a floating exchange rate regime. Comprehensive and proactive banking sector reforms would be implemented to contain the effects of the slowdown in growth, the peso depreciation, and higher interest rates. Capital requirements would be increased further, provisioning requirements tightened, regulatory oversight strengthened, disincentives to peso intermediation reduced, and a resolution strategy for problem banks adopted. Reforms would be implemented to strengthen the corporate sector, including continuing trade and investment liberalization, comprehensive reform of the power sector, and further privatization. Agriculture would be strengthened, along with improvements in education and health services—with a focus on primary education and the rural areas—helping to reduce poverty. To cushion the impact of the regional crisis on the poor, the availability of rice stocks and other basic commodities would be ensured, the inflationary impact of the peso depreciation on socially sensitive petroleum products contained, and best efforts made to protect social programs in the budget, especially those directed at poverty reduction and the poorest regions.

Rwanda

Financial Support. On December 12, 1997, the IMF approved a credit for SDR 6.0 million, the second of two drawings under the IMF's policy of emergency postconflict assistance, bringing total disbursements for calendar year 1997 to SDR 14.9 million.

Program Objectives. Aim at fiscal consolidation, including a reduction in the primary budget deficit, through tax reform and improvements in budget and treasury management. Initiate reforms of the civil service and public enterprise sector, and consolidate financial sector restructuring.

Policies. The Ministry of Finance, Economy, and Planning established an administrative unit to spearhead the reform of the public enterprises; three enterprises were privatized, and eight were offered for sale. The demobilization program was initiated with the departure of 5,000 soldiers. The National Assembly had approved support for genocide survivors, and the government—assisted by nongovernmental organizations and other members of the international community—was implementing various programs for helping other vulnerable groups.

Senegal

Financial Support. On April 20, 1998, the IMF approved a three-year ESAF loan for SDR 107 million.

Program Objectives. Seek to achieve real GDP growth of 5–6 percent a year, thereby allowing per capita income to rise by 2–3 percent a year; keep inflation below 3 percent; and reduce the external current account deficit (excluding official transfers) to less than 7 percent of GDP by 2000.

Policies. Fiscal policy would be geared toward limiting the overall fiscal deficit, on a commitment basis and excluding grants, to 2 percent of GDP in 1998. On the revenue side, the authorities would implement the West African Economic and Monetary Union's (WAEMU's) Common External Tariff, substantially reducing average import duties. The short-term revenue losses from the tariff reform would be offset over time by measures to broaden the tax base, drastically reduce exemptions, and improve the efficiency of the tax system. On the expenditure side, the government would maintain strong financial discipline, while reordering priorities in favor of social services and the investment program. Monetary policy would support WAEMU's growth, inflation, and external sector objectives.

The authorities would speed up the implementation of their unfinished reform agenda, particularly public enterprise and energy sector reforms, and undertake new reforms to modernize public administration. The government would design an action plan for public sector reform that would seek to promote good governance, further strengthen the judicial system, and build more constructive relations with the private sector.

Sierra Leone

Financial Support. On May 5, 1997, the IMF approved a third annual ESAF loan for SDR 10.1 million.

Program Objectives. Intensify the postconflict recovery by further strengthening the ongoing macroeconomic and structural reforms. Target real GDP growth at about 10 percent, inflation at 8 percent, and gross international reserves at 1.8 months of imports. Aim to reduce the overall budget deficit and improve the quality of expenditure.

Policies. To achieve the targeted fiscal deficit reduction, the government would significantly increase revenue and substantially cut military expenditure, in line with the improvement in the security situation. It would achieve the ambitious revenue target for 1997 through discretionary measures and strengthen income tax and customs administration. On the expenditure side, the authorities would use the shift in budgetary resources away from military outlays to education, health, economic services, and capital expenditure to improve the quality of expenditure. Inflation would be kept under control, the reserve position strengthened, and the economic recovery and the reintroduction of money in rural areas supported. Key reforms would include rationalizing the government workforce to improve the quality and efficiency of public services, streamlining public enterprise reform to further reduce government involvement in the economy, and simplifying legal requirements for foreign and domestic investment. Judicial reforms would seek to make legal procedures more transparent and to simplify adjudication of civil and commercial cases to afford greater protection to economic agents. Further reform would be designed to improve fisheries surveillance and deregulate the prices of petroleum products. Increases in budgetary spending on social and economic services would be targeted primarily on enhancing human capital development.

Tajikistan

Financial Support. On December 19, 1997, the IMF approved a credit for SDR 7.5 million under its policy of emergency postconflict assistance. On April 1, 1998, the IMF approved a second emergency postconflict credit of SDR 7.5 million.

Program Objectives. Establish financial stability through further fiscal adjustment, tight monetary policy, and enhanced financial discipline in the enterprise sector. Achieve real GDP growth of 4–5 percent in 1998, a fall in inflation to about 18 percent, and a rise in gross international reserves to about 1.5 months of imports by the end of 1998. Design fiscal policy to reduce the government deficit to less than 3 percent of GDP in 1998 and eliminate budgetary wage and cash compensation arrears, while reducing central bank credit to the government.

Policies. The program placed considerable emphasis on structural policy measures and institution building to sustain economic recovery and enhance policy implementation capacity. Particularly important for structural reform were privatization, land reform, bank restructuring, and enterprise reform. The authorities intended to ensure a continued open trade and exchange regime by refraining from introducing restrictions on exports or imports during the program. Tajikistan would continue to use technical assistance from multilateral and bilateral institutions to build on progress in a number of areas, including the compilation of statistics, tax administration, building a treasury system, bank supervision, and central bank operations. On the monetary front, the government would reduce the annual growth rate of broad money to less than 25 percent in 1998. It would normalize relations with external creditors, clear external debt-service arrears, and avoid new debt-service arrears. Sustainable and balanced economic growth would be facilitated by banking sector reform. Smaller businesses would be privatized, and medium- and large-scale enterprises restructured or sold. Tax administration would continue to be strengthened, introduction of a treasury system finalized, and the government would begin to align fiscal accounts with international standards and increase outlays on the social safety net.

Tanzania

Financial Support. On December 3, 1997, the IMF approved a second annual ESAF loan for SDR 71.4 million, incorporating an increase in the initial amount of SDR 51.4 million by SDR 20 million to help Tanzania deal with the effects of drought.

Program Objectives. Achieve real GDP growth of 4.7 percent, reduce inflation to not more than 13 percent, and limit the external current account deficit (excluding official transfers) to 14.4 percent of GDP.

Policies. Fiscal policy would target a surplus on the current government budget of 1.1 percent of GDP in 1997/98 and rationalization of the structure of both revenues and expenditures, including the introduction of a value-added tax in July 1998. Monetary policy under the program would be consistent with achieving the program's inflation and balance of payments objectives. The government would continue with reforms of the banking and the parastatal sectors, and with civil service reform. The scope of privatization had been widened to include the utilities and other core parastatals, and its pace was being accelerated. Key steps would be taken to strengthen the delivery of health and education services.

Thailand

Financial Support. On August 20, 1997, the IMF approved a Stand-By Arrangement for SDR 2.9 billion under the accelerated procedures of the Emergency Financing Mechanism.

Program Objectives and Policies. For details, see Chapter V.

Togo

Financial Support. On June 30, 1997, the IMF approved a third annual ESAF loan for SDR 21.7 million.

Program Objectives. Correct weaknesses that occurred in 1996, particularly in the fiscal consolidation effort, and accelerate the implementation of agreed structural reforms. Achieve average annual real GDP growth of more than 5.5 percent; reduce annual average inflation to 3 percent by the end of the program period; and lower the external current account deficit (excluding grants) to an annual average of less than 5 percent of GDP. Reduce the overall fiscal deficit to 4.3 percent of GDP, while improving the primary balance to a surplus of 0.8 percent of GDP.

Policies. The authorities would correct weaknesses in fiscal consolidation and accelerate structural reforms. Reforms of the tax system and of tax administration would be continued, with technical support from the IMF. The authorities would increase outlays in real terms for the health and education sectors, and for the rehabilitation and maintenance of infrastructure, while curtailing nonpriority spending. Budgetary and treasury procedures would enhance the control of expenditures, and the government would also undertake a comprehensive restructuring of its domestic debt. The government would pursue the fight against poverty through an appropriate investment policy in the areas of health, basic education, and vocational training. To protect the most vulnerable segments of society, the government would also continue its labor-intensive public works projects.

Uganda

Financial Support. On November 10, 1997, the IMF approved a three-year ESAF loan for SDR 100.4 million. For support under the HIPC Initiative, see Chapter IX.

Program Objectives. Sustain high and broad-based economic growth and ensure that the poor would be able to participate in, and benefit from, increased economic activity. Maintain macroeconomic stability, liberalize further the economy to promote private sector and export-oriented growth, and undertake structural and institutional reforms to further reduce impediments to growth and job creation. Achieve real GDP growth of at least 7 percent a year on average, reducing annual inflation to about 5 percent and increasing gross international reserves to the equivalent of 4.9 months of imports of goods and nonfactor services. Increase the gross-investment-to-GDP ratio to about 23 percent in 1999/2000, and reduce the overall fiscal deficit by about 1.7 percent of GDP over the program period.

Policies. The authorities would improve customs and tax administration substantially, reduce the incidence of smuggling, and prevent other forms of revenue leakages while exercising considerable expenditure restraint. Monetary policy would continue to build upon the major gains achieved in reducing inflation, taking into account projected balance of payments developments, the need for adequate provision of credit to the private sector, and increased savings by the government in the banking system. The government would deepen and broaden structural reforms in the financial sector, civil service, tax and customs administration, trade liberalization, privatization program, and enterprise restructuring, and more generally improve the environment for private sector activity through deregulation. The authorities would reduce the incidence of poverty through increased social expenditures and intensify efforts to measure and monitor the outcome of these expenditures.

Ukraine

Financial Support. On August 25, 1997, the IMF approved a one-year Stand-By Arrangement for SDR 398.9 million.

Program Objectives. Lay the basis for the resumption of economic growth through structural reforms. Reduce inflation to 15 percent during 1997 and to 12 percent during 1998. Increase gross international reserves to the equivalent of 6.0 weeks of imports in 1997, and to 7.4 weeks of imports in 1998. Design fiscal policy to reduce existing arrears on wages, pensions, and social benefits, while avoiding new arrears. Accelerate privatization, demonopolization (particularly in the agricultural sectors), and deregulation to provide a conducive environment for private sector development.

Policies. The main thrust of structural policies would be further deregulation, privatization, and demonopolization. With small-scale privatization virtually complete, the focus would shift to privatizing medium- and large-scale enterprises. The consolidated budget deficit would be limited to 4.6 percent in 1997 and 4.5 percent of GDP in 1998. Structural reforms would include establishing more efficient labor markets through increased wage flexibility, implementing faster land reform and privatization within the agro-industrial complex, and widening and deepening energy sector restructuring. As part of its outward-oriented growth strategy, the government would maintain a liberal and transparent trade regime. Social policies would include a further strengthening of means testing of social programs, streamlining the diverse set of allowances to provide a higher level of benefits to the most needy recipients, and rationalizing the pension and unemployment insurance systems.

Uruguay

Financial Support. On June 20, 1997, the IMF approved a 21-month Stand-By Arrangement for SDR 125 million. The authorities intended to treat the arrangement as precautionary and would draw on it only if adverse external circumstances made it necessary.

Program Objectives. Reduce inflation to single-digit levels by the end of 1998 in an environment of sustained output and employment growth and maintain a viable external position. Achieve real GDP growth of at least 3 percent in 1997 and 1998, led by expanded investment and exports; reduce inflation to 14–17 percent by the end of 1997; and strengthen the international reserve position.

Policies. Policies would be designed to consolidate public finances; adopt prudent credit and wage measures—including gradual deindexation of wages and administered public sector prices; and continue structural reforms. State reform would be expected to reduce civil service positions by eliminating vacancies, outsourcing, and cutting employment. The government would also increase the participation of the private sector in activities previously reserved for public entities. Special efforts would be made under the program further to assist the most vulnerable groups in society through targeted programs.

Yemen

Financial Support. On October 29, 1997, the IMF approved a financial package for SDR 370.6 million, with SDR 264.8 million under the ESAF and SDR 105.9 million under the EFF.

Program Objectives. Achieve real non-oil GDP growth of 6 percent a year on average over the three-year program period, a core inflation rate of at most 5 percent a year on average, a reduction in the external current account deficit to 2 percent of GDP on average by 2000, and maintain sufficient foreign exchange reserves to cover 4.5 months of imports. Seek significant improvements in social indicators through substantially higher budgetary allocations for education and health as well as strengthened social safety net arrangements.

Policies. The authorities would continue to maintain a tight fiscal stance and appropriately supportive monetary policies directed at ensuring positive real interest rates. Structural reforms would focus on expenditure reorientation toward the social sectors and public investment in infrastructure; direct and indirect tax reforms; the elimination of subsidies; civil service, pension fund, customs administration, and budget management reforms; financial sector reforms focused on indirect monetary control, the quality of the banking system, and prudential supervision; and a broad privatization program.

CHAPTER IX

The ESAF and the HIPC Initiative

Since the mid-1980s, the IMF has provided concessional financing through the Enhanced Structural Adjustment Facility (ESAF) and its predecessor, the Structural Adjustment Facility (SAF), to respond to the balance of payments difficulties confronting many of the world's poorest developing countries. In December 1993, the Board enlarged and extended the ESAF to ensure continued concessional support by the IMF for low-income countries, and in September 1996, it approved an overall framework for continuing ESAF operations. As of April 30, 1998, SDR 1.8 billion had been disbursed under the 38 SAF arrangements approved for 37 countries, and SDR 6.4 billion had been disbursed under the 71 ESAF arrangements approved for 48 countries (see also Chapter XII).

Notwithstanding the efforts of the international community to channel external finance and debt relief to developing countries through a wide range of mechanisms, many heavily indebted poor countries (HIPCs) have continued to experience difficulty in meeting their external debt-service obligations. To address the problems of those countries, in September 1996, the IMF and the World Bank approved an Initiative to provide special assistance to HIPCs pursuing sound adjustment and reform programs supported by the IMF and World Bank, but for which traditional debt-relief mechanisms were not adequate to secure a sustainable external debt position over the medium term. For eligible countries, all creditors would provide assistance sufficient to reduce the debt burden to sustainable levels. The IMF's contribution to the HIPC Initiative is in the form of grants in most cases—with the possibility of escrowed loans in others—that are used to meet part of indebted members' debt-service obligations to the IMF. World Bank contributions are channeled mainly through the International Development Association (IDA)–administered HIPC Trust Fund (which is also a vehicle for other creditors).

Mobilizing Financing

The Board met twice during the financial year to discuss the status and possible options for the financing of the ESAF and the HIPC Initiative. It reaffirmed the overall framework agreed in September 1996 (see Box 10), including the estimate of total financing needs of SDR 2.8 billion. Pledges of bilateral contributions toward meeting these needs were roughly SDR 1.25 billion at the time of the Board's November 1997 review of the situation and increased only very slightly during the remainder of the financial year. These pledges were subject to clarification regarding amount, timing, and form of contribution, and some were subject to special conditions. To ensure the full funding of the IMF's commitments under the HIPC Initiative in the first stage of its implementation, the Board authorized—as a bridge to the full funding of the ESAF and of the HIPC Initiative—the transfer, as needed, of up to SDR 250 million from the ESAF Trust Reserve Account to the Special Disbursement Account to be used in providing Trust grants or Trust loans to the HIPCs. In addition, the Board decided to forgo the reimbursement to the General Resources Account (GRA) of the costs of administering the ESAF Trust in 1997/98 and 1998/99 and to transfer the corresponding amounts from the ESAF Trust Reserve Account to the ESAF-HIPC Trust.

In their November 1997 discussion, Directors stressed the urgency of securing the additional resources required to fully finance the ESAF and the HIPC Initiative, citing the costs of delays in terms of lost investment income. Directors believed that further efforts should be made to secure additional bilateral contributions, but most speakers felt that there would remain a need to supplement such contributions from the IMF's own resources. Although most Directors, in this context, continued to favor sales of gold of up to 5 million ounces to "optimize the management of the institution's reserves," a few remained opposed. Directors agreed that it was important to have broad support for such a decision and that the Board should return to the matter in 1998.

At its meeting in Washington in April 1998, the Interim Committee noted the need to reactivate the efforts by the IMF to secure the full financing of the

Box 10
ESAF Resources

Given the Board consensus that the ESAF was, and should remain, the centerpiece of the IMF's support for the poorest countries—including in the context of the HIPC Initiative—Directors agreed in September 1996 on a framework for continuing ESAF operations. Existing ESAF resources are expected to meet demands until about the end of 2000. Resources to fund a *self-sustained ESAF*, with a commitment capacity of about SDR 0.8 billion a year, will then become available in the year 2005, or perhaps earlier, as reserves previously set aside to provide security for ESAF lenders against the risk of nonpayment by borrowers are freed as lenders are repaid. This will leave an *interim ESAF* period of about four years during which financing of an estimated SDR 1.7 billion will need to be mobilized to cover interest subsidies. In addition, SDR 1.1 billion is estimated to be needed for special ESAF operations under the HIPC Initiative.

ESAF and the HIPC Initiative. In view of the current and expected future commitments under the HIPC Initiative, and the significant costs resulting from delay in mobilizing the necessary financial resources, the Committee urged all members to move quickly to complete the financing of these initiatives as soon as possible and asked the Executive Board to report back to it on this issue at the Committee's next meeting in October 1998.

Progress in Implementing the HIPC Initiative

To obtain assistance under the HIPC Initiative, a country must be eligible for concessional assistance from the IMF and World Bank, face an unsustainable debt burden even after the application of traditional debt-relief mechanisms, and establish a track record of reform and sound policies through IMF- and World Bank–supported programs. Stages in the decision-making process under the Initiative are set out in Figure 4; these include a so-called *decision point,* when the Board of the IDA, which administers funds for the Initiative for the World Bank Group, and the Board of the IMF formally decide on a country's eligibility and precommit assistance under the Initiative; and a *completion point,* when the two Boards decide that a country has met the conditions for assistance, allowing that assistance to be disbursed.

In April 1998, Uganda became the first country to reach the completion point under the HIPC Initiative, as performance under its ESAF- and IDA-supported programs remained strong, and Uganda's other creditors pledged satisfactory assurances of action. Uganda would receive assistance equivalent to approximately $350 million in net present value terms. This amount would reduce Uganda's ratio of net present value of debt to exports to 196 percent, well within the 192–212 percent target range agreed at the decision point; the saving in nominal debt service would be nearly $650 million. The IMF's assistance would lower the present value of its claims on Uganda by $69 million; this would cover 22 percent of Uganda's annual debt service to the IMF on average over the next nine years.

In addition, during 1997/98, five countries reached the decision point: Burkina Faso (in September 1997), Bolivia (in September 1997), Guyana (in December 1997), Côte d'Ivoire (in March 1998), and Mozambique (in April 1998). The assistance committed to these five countries at the decision point totaled about $2.6 billion in net present value terms, which was estimated to reduce debt service in nominal terms by some $5.0 billion. The five countries were scheduled to reach their completion points under the Initiative at various dates between September 1998 and March 2001 (see Table 8).

In March and April 1998, the Boards of the IMF and IDA discussed preliminary HIPC documents for Mali and Guinea-Bissau and indicated that the countries were approaching their decision points and could qualify for assistance under the Initiative. Based on the guidance of the Boards, final HIPC documents were expected to be presented to the Boards after consultation with other creditors.

ESAF Resources for Commercial Debt- and Debt-Service-Reduction Operations

In June and July 1997, the Board discussed the use of ESAF resources for commercial debt- and debt-service-reduction operations for members qualifying for assistance under the ESAF. Most Directors agreed to the use of ESAF resources in the few cases where resources available under the IDA Debt-Reduction Facility and from donors and the member might not be sufficient to finance the up-front costs of such operations, and for which the use of the IMF's General Resources Account would be inappropriate.

Such use of ESAF resources would be guided by the same general principles of the existing policy for supporting debt- and debt-service-reduction operations, including, among other things, conditionality, the efficient use of IMF resources, and market-based operations. In addition, the use of ESAF resources would complement the highly concessional resources available from IDA and other sources and be provided only in the context of appropriately ambitious ESAF-supported programs.

To ensure that the use of ESAF resources for debt- and debt-service-reduction operations would be strictly limited, consideration was given to restricting such

Figure 4

Initiative for Heavily Indebted Poor Countries

First Stage

- *Paris Club* provides flow rescheduling on Naples terms, that is, rescheduling of debt service on eligible debt falling due during the three-year consolidation period (up to 67 percent reduction on eligible maturities on a net present value basis).

- *Other* bilateral and commercial creditors provide at least comparable treatment.

- *Multilateral institutions* continue to provide adjustment support in the framework of World Bank- and IMF-supported adjustment programs.

- *Country* establishes first three-year track record of good performance (performance prior to the start of the HIPC Initiative can be taken into account).

Decision Point

Exit

- Paris Club stock-of-debt operation under Naples terms (up to 67 percent present value reduction of eligible debt) and comparable treatment by other bilateral and commercial creditors judged adequate for the country to reach sustainability by the completion point— country not eligible for HIPC Initiative.

Eligible

- Paris Club stock-of-debt operation (on Naples terms) judged not sufficient for the country's overall debt to become sustainable by the completion point—country requests additional support under the HIPC Initiative and IMF and World Bank Boards determine eligibility.

Second Stage

- *Paris Club* goes beyond Naples terms to provide more concessional debt reduction of up to 80 percent in present value terms.

- *Other* bilateral and commercial creditors provide at least comparable treatment.

- *Donors and multilateral institutions* provide enhanced support through interim measures.

- *Country* establishes a second track record of good performance under IMF- and Bank-supported programs.

Completion Point

- *All creditors* take coordinated action to provide sufficient assistance to reduce the country's debt to a sustainable level.

- *Paris Club* provides deeper stock-of-debt reduction of up to 80 percent in present value terms on eligible debt.

- *Other* bilateral and commercial creditors provide at least comparable treatment on stock of debt.

- *Multilateral institutions* take action to reduce the net present value of their claims, taking into account the assistance provided by nonmultilateral creditors and their own preferred creditor status.

Borderline

- For borderline cases, where there is doubt about whether sustainability would be achieved by the completion point under a Naples terms stock-of-debt operation, the country would receive further flow reschedulings under Naples terms.

- *If* the outcome at the completion point is better than or as projected, the country would receive a stock-of-debt operation on Naples terms from Paris Club creditors and comparable treatment from other bilateral and commercial creditors.

- *If* the outcome at the completion point is worse than projected, the country could receive additional support under the HIPC Initiative, so as to be able to exit from unsustainable debt.

Table 8
HIPC Initiative: Status of Early Cases[1]

Country (in order of expected decision point within groups)	Decision Point	Completion Point	NPV-of-Debt-to-Export Target (in percent)	Assistance at Completion Point (millions of U.S. dollars, present value at completion point)					Percentage Reduction in NPV of Debt[2]	Estimated Total Nominal Debt-Service Relief (millions of U.S. dollars)	Satisfactory Assurances from Other Creditors
				Total	Bilateral	Multilateral	IMF	World Bank			
Completion point reached											
Uganda	April 97	April 98	202	347	73	274	69	160	20	650	Received
Decision point reached and assistance committed by IMF and World Bank											
Burkina Faso	Sept. 97	April 2000	205	115	21	94	10	44	14	200	Being sought
Bolivia	Sept. 97	Sept. 98	225	448	157	291	29	54	13	600	Being sought
Guyana	Dec. 97	Dec. 98	107[3]	253	91	161	35	27	25	500	Being sought
Côte d'Ivoire	March 98	March 2001	141[3]	345	163	182	23	91	6[4]	800	Being sought
Mozambique	April 98	June 99	200	1,442	877	565	105	324	57	2,900	Being sought
Total assistance provided or committed	...	...	...	2,950	1,382	1,567	271[5]	700	...	5,650	...
Preliminary HIPC document issued; targets based on majority view in preliminary discussions at World Bank and IMF Boards; assistance based on preliminary HIPC documents and subject to change											
Mali	Mid-98	Dec. 99	200	196	63	133	20	65	...	...	...
Guinea-Bissau	98:QIII	Mid-2001	200	300	148	153	8	73	...	...	...
Debt judged sustainable											
Benin	July 97	...	...	...	...	...	...	...	...	...	...
Senegal	April 98	...	...	...	...	...	...	...	...	...	...

Sources: IMF and World Bank Board decisions, completion point documents, final HIPC documents, preliminary HIPC documents, and staff calculations.

[1] Other countries that could reach the decision point within the coming year include Chad, Guinea, Mauritania, Senegal, Togo, and possibly Ethiopia and Vietnam. Not all would be expected to require assistance under the HIPC Initiative.

[2] In percent of net present value (NPV) of debt at completion point, after full use of traditional debt-relief mechanisms.

[3] Eligible under fiscal/openness criteria; NPV-of-debt-to-export target chosen to meet NPV-of-debt-to-revenue target of 280 percent.

[4] Nonreschedulable debt to non-Paris Club official bilateral creditors and the London Club, which was already subject to a highly concessional restructuring, is excluded from the NPV of debt at the completion point in the calculation of this ratio.

[5] Equivalent to SDR 200 million.

assistance to countries that had qualified for assistance under the HIPC Initiative. Several Directors expressed concern about the possible resource implications of the proposal, as the financing of the interim ESAF and IMF participation in the HIPC Initiative had not yet been secured. It was noted, however, that the use of ESAF resources for debt- and debt-service-reduction operations would be decided by the Board in each individual case. In addition, the overall use of ESAF resources for these operations would be subject to Board review if the aggregate resource use for that purpose appeared likely to exceed a predetermined level. Directors expressed the view that ESAF financing for debt- and debt-service-reduction operations should be used in a subsidiary, or "last resort," role, only if other financing options were not available. And there should be no strict rules on burden sharing; each case should be subject to discussion, considering both the prospects for bilateral contributions and the use of the country's own resources.

In dealing with the possibility that a debt- and debt-service-reduction operation might materialize at a time that was not well synchronized with the disbursement of ESAF resources, most Directors favored the option of incorporating into the ESAF Trust Instrument a provision for a special disbursement for the sole purpose of financing part of such an operation. This provision was expected to be used only when the disbursement for that operation could not be part of a normal semiannual disbursement.

Review of Experience Under ESAF-Supported Arrangements

In July 1997, the Board discussed a staff study assessing the experience of 36 countries that had availed themselves of SAF and ESAF financing in support of 68 multiyear programs during 1986–95.[13] This internal review was complemented by an external evaluation that was discussed by the Board in March 1998 (see below).

Internal Evaluation of the ESAF

Directors, in their review of the internal evaluation (see Box 11), agreed that most countries that had undertaken reform and adjustment programs with the support of the SAF and ESAF now had economies that were materially stronger and more market oriented than a decade earlier. Fiscal imbalances had been reduced, and macroeconomic policies had eliminated almost all instances of very high inflation. Liberalization and structural reforms had taken hold and, in

---

[13]Published as IMF, *The ESAF at Ten Years: Economic Adjustment and Reform in Low-Income Countries,* IMF Occasional Paper 156 (1997).

Box 11
Strengthening ESAF-Supported Programs

The main recommendations of the internal review of ESAF for the design of future programs called for:
- stronger and reoriented fiscal adjustment based on durable cuts in budget outlays, particularly from civil service reform and reduced support for public enterprises, while protecting growth-enhancing expenditures on health and education;
- more resolve in reducing inflation to single-digit levels through the use of monetary or exchange rate anchors where appropriate;
- a more concerted effort to adopt so-called second-generation reforms, especially enhanced trade liberalization, public enterprise reform, bank restructuring, and strengthened property rights; and
- steps to reduce policy slippage and encourage more sustained policy implementation, including through more intensive program monitoring in selected cases, greater use of contingency planning in program design, and more proactive technical assistance to build institutional capacity.

---

some instances, had gathered momentum in recent years. Furthermore, economic growth and living standards had improved, with progress toward external viability in many countries.

At the same time, progress had been uneven, and most countries continued to perform below their potential—in many cases despite multiple ESAF-supported programs. Per capita GDP growth in many ESAF countries remained below the average in developing countries, indicators of openness remained relatively weak, and inflation had not been brought down to acceptable levels on a sustained basis in a number of countries. Moreover, debt-service burdens remained unmanageably high in several countries.

Directors noted that this disappointing performance largely reflected shortcomings in a number of policy areas, both macroeconomic and structural. A widespread failure to move ahead decisively with civil service reform and reduce the direct and indirect burdens of public enterprises on the state budget had contributed to missed fiscal targets . Hesitant reforms to the administration of tax systems and countries' banking systems had failed to address fundamental operational weaknesses. Significant barriers to international economic integration had also remained, while the development of the private sector had been held back by problems of poor governance, excessive regulation, and ill-defined or inadequately enforced property rights. Several Directors emphasized the importance of developing institutional capacity while recognizing the difficulties that this entailed. Future ESAF-supported programs should tackle persistent weaknesses in these crucial areas, Directors concluded.

Policies and Program Design. Directors considered that the mutually reinforcing ESAF objectives of growth and external viability called for ambitious strategies, consistently implemented, but tailored to the situation and implementation capacity of countries, and set over a realistic time frame. Better-coordinated and more effective collaboration with the World Bank would also be important, and Directors asked management and staff to propose concrete suggestions to that end. Most Directors emphasized that bolder strategies, with more decisive fiscal adjustment at their core, were needed to achieve a significant increase in national savings. Fiscal reforms should be durable, based on a realistic appraisal of the country's institutional capacities, and founded on systemic changes to the structure of revenues and expenditures and on policies to strengthen budgetary institutions. Reforms should be sought in the structure and administration of tax systems—including greater reliance on consumption-based taxes and reductions in trade taxes—with a view to raising revenues and putting taxes on a permanently sounder and more rational basis.

Noting that rapid population growth and lack of investment in human capital had contributed to holding back per capita income growth in ESAF countries, Directors agreed that high-priority social expenditures—such as on health and education—should be protected, in both the planning and the execution of state budgets. Many felt that programs should make greater use of core budgets to insulate these expenditures against possible revenue shortfalls. Social safety nets should continue to be integrated in ESAF-supported programs to protect vulnerable groups that might be adversely affected by reforms. Furthermore, countries needed to improve the transparency of the fiscal accounts, in particular to reflect extrabudgetary operations. Although Directors also emphasized that major improvements needed to be sought in the data required to assess the adequacy and efficiency of social spending, they saw that as primarily within the World Bank's field of expertise.

Directors expressed concern about the persistence of inflation at double-digit rates in many countries—often despite adherence to program targets for credit expansion and the budget deficit—as evidence suggested a close, positive association between low inflation and economic growth. Noting that the restraint of domestic credit growth was typically not adequate to achieve the desired inflation targets, Directors underscored the need for careful, case-by-case analysis of the root cause of persistent inflation and suggested that future programs attach more weight to policies aimed at bringing about a lasting reduction in inflation to single-digit levels within the period of a three-year arrangement. Although several Directors supported greater use of nominal anchors in the form of an exchange rate peg, money supply ceilings, or announced inflation targets, most felt that those should be used cautiously and selected on a case-by-case basis.

Directors endorsed the importance, in ESAF-supported programs, of structural measures to stimulate private investment and entrepreneurship. Such measures included further liberalization of foreign trade and investment, public enterprise reform, the creation of a sound banking system, and legislation to strengthen property rights. Directors felt that the responsibility for helping countries formulate policies in most of these areas should continue to fall primarily to the World Bank. Particular attention was given to the problem of weak financial discipline in the public enterprise sector and the generally poor record of improvement in this area under ESAF-supported programs. Some Directors argued that this problem was unlikely to be addressed satisfactorily without privatization, and they encouraged a further shift in that direction in future programs. It was agreed that greater efforts were needed to enforce budget constraints on those enterprises that remained in the public sector, which would be possible only with adequate information on their financial position. It was noted that the persistent financial problems in the public enterprise sector had continued to impair banks' portfolios, adding to the difficulties and expense of bank-restructuring programs. More complete information on the financial status of countries' banking systems and the likely fiscal costs of restructuring was needed at the outset of programs—not only to facilitate reform, but also to help safeguard IMF resources, particularly where the solvency of a country's financial system was a concern. To promote more comprehensive implementation of banking system reform, Directors also proposed that conditionality in ESAF-supported programs should focus to a greater extent on sound operational practices, drawing on the Basle Committee's *Core Principles for Effective Supervision.*

Sustaining Programs. The high frequency with which ESAF-supported programs had been interrupted because of policy weaknesses was seen by Directors as a cause for concern. A more active and coordinated approach to providing technical assistance could help if supported fully by the national authorities. Given the vulnerability of ESAF countries to external shocks, many Directors supported more consistent contingency planning and allowing more intensive program monitoring where it would aid policy implementation. They noted that the frequency of IMF staff missions and program reviews, the number of resident representatives, and total staff resources per country had all been low in ESAF countries relative to countries making use of Stand-By and Extended Arrangements; yet these countries typically had weaker administrative and institutional capacities. Many Directors favored phasing

Box 12
Key Findings of External Evaluators of the ESAF

In reviewing the ESAF, the external evaluators offered the following recommendations:

Social Impact

• The IMF should seek ex ante assessments by the World Bank of the likely impact that ESAF-supported programs would have on the incomes of the poor and of the real projected value of social service provision. These impact assessments could be taken into account at the program design stage and should be updated during program implementation.

• In program design, the IMF should explicitly analyze trade-offs between the short run and long run. The analysis would address sequencing issues, front-loading of structural reforms, and the efficiency costs of revenue measures.

• In the area of fiscal policy, IMF–World Bank collaboration should be increased to allow for more joint analysis and to address overlaps concerning the macroeconomic con-

cerns of the IMF and the microeconomic concerns of the Bank.

• The ESAF should have a new role in the poststabilization environment to help reforming governments build reputations and to enable the IMF to play a role in potential ESAF countries that currently reject the facility.

External Viability

• ESAF financing should be provided as budget support, rather than to central banks.

• Equal or more weight should be given to indicators that relate total debt and debt service to GDP rather than to the traditional export-based indicators, as the latter are overly sensitive to an economy's openness.

Ownership and Governance

• Countries have primary responsibility for economic reform programs and should develop and build a consensus behind a program capable of achieving sustainable growth. The

IMF should make the negotiation process and conditionality regime more supportive of country ownership.

• Specifically, the IMF should ensure greater flexibility in the negotiating frameworks (e.g., formulate alternative program paths through negotiation, leaving it to the country to decide, with IMF staff advice, what best suits its circumstances); develop systematic mechanisms for ex post support for country-initiated programs; strengthen resident representative missions in ESAF countries; engage in regular informal policy dialogue with the country's political leadership; and find ways to improve the IMF's image.

• Countries should create economic management teams comprising representatives of economic and social sector ministries and political leaders to oversee the reform process and hold national conferences where alternatives and trade-offs can be openly debated.

disbursements and program monitoring along the lines of Extended Arrangements, with quarterly performance criteria and half-yearly reviews in selected cases. Directors asked the staff to offer concrete proposals for stronger monitoring.

Most Directors agreed that more focused technical assistance, contingency planning, and program monitoring, although constructive and worthwhile, were unlikely by themselves to reduce significantly the incidence of program interruptions. The record suggested that many discontinuities or weaknesses in policy implementation were related to political factors. In view of such difficulties, and taking into account administrative limitations, some Directors felt that programs needed to anticipate a slower pace of reform and adjustment than in the past. Many Directors, however, felt that more selectivity was needed in approving arrangements. They favored greater use of prior actions by member countries and indicators of commitment by governments to forge a political consensus for change and aggressively pursue the objectives of the program.

External Evaluation of the ESAF

In the spring of 1997, a panel of outside experts began work on an independent evaluation of SAF/ESAF-sup-

ported programs.[14] This was the first time that an external evaluation of aspects of the IMF's work had been commissioned by the Executive Board. The panel—Dr. Kwesi Botchwey, Harvard Institute for International Development and former Finance Minister of Ghana; Professor Paul Collier, Oxford University; Professor Jan Willem Gunning, Free University, Amsterdam; and Professor Koichi Hamada, Yale University—completed its study in January 1998. On the basis of the terms of reference for the study adopted by the Executive Board, the evaluators used a case-study approach to examine social policies and the composition of government spending; developments in countries' external positions; and the determinants and influence of differing degrees of national ownership of ESAF-supported programs. The Board discussed the external evaluation (Box 12) in March 1998.

Directors saw a high degree of complementarity between the report of the external evaluators and the IMF staff review. All supported the fundamental view underlying the evaluators' findings that the ESAF was a valuable instrument to assist low-income countries and

---

[14]Published as IMF, *External Evaluation of the ESAF* (1998), and available on the IMF's website (http://www.imf.org).

that the IMF's work with this instrument could be improved. Directors agreed with many of the views expressed by the external evaluators and noted that the report provided an opportunity to broaden the debate by offering a different perspective and to promote a better understanding of the IMF's work.

Implications for Social Policy. Directors agreed with the external evaluators that economic reforms, while "generally having positive effects on growth and income distribution," did entail temporary costs for certain segments of the population. This called for appropriate compensatory measures to be built into the design of the program to protect such groups, including the provision of well-targeted assistance to the more vulnerable groups and the allocation of adequate resources for social sectors. In addition, the sequencing of fiscal and other structural reforms should be further analyzed to minimize any adverse social impact. These actions would help policymakers to build a domestic consensus in favor of important but difficult reform measures.

The IMF was already making important efforts to advise countries to protect low-income groups from the impact of adjustment measures and to safeguard social expenditures during fiscal consolidation, Directors observed. They welcomed the proposals by the evaluators to draw more extensively on the expertise and data of the World Bank for a more refined ex ante assessment of the likely impact of adjustment measures on low-income groups. They also agreed that it would be desirable to review the effects of the adjustment measures on those groups on an ongoing basis as part of the regular ESAF program reviews.

Fiscal Issues and External Viability. Transparency and clarity of the breakdown of the deficits were essential, and Directors were generally satisfied with staff presentations on fiscal positions. Directors agreed that short-term revenue objectives should be pursued with sensitivity to the important longer-term implications of the tax system for economic efficiency.

An assessment of progress toward external viability required a broad range of indicators, and Directors continued to favor traditional export-based indicators. On other external aspects, Directors did not share the view of the evaluators that the ESAF constituted an inadvertent tax on exports since most ESAF funds were disbursed to central banks. They endorsed the staff view that the macroeconomic effects of ESAF disbursements did not depend on the initial recipient of ESAF resources.

National Ownership. Directors noted with concern the evaluators' assessment—which they saw as a key contribution of the report—that a common perception at the country level was "a feeling of loss of control over the policy content and the pace of implementation of reform programs." They agreed it was, first and fore-

most, the obligation of national governments to ensure transparency in policymaking and to promote wide public debate of policy issues. They therefore recommended that governments seriously consider the suggestions of the evaluators concerning the organization of national conferences and regular meetings with academic, business, and labor groups to allow open debate on trade-offs and policy options and to broaden public support. Economic management teams were seen as important for overseeing the reform efforts.

Directors agreed with the evaluators that the IMF staff should consider the political constraints faced by the national authorities. IMF staff, however, should not be put in a position of having to judge what was and was not politically feasible. Directors noted that some of the recommended measures to ensure ownership might prolong the initial stages of negotiations but considered that the investment would be compensated for over the period of implementation. Directors also recognized the importance of striking the right balance between ownership and securing a strong program. Unless a government was committed to pursuing the program objectives, the program would have little chance of success and would thus not merit ESAF support. In this connection, Directors agreed that the IMF should be more cautious in providing ESAF support where the authorities' commitment was in question.

Flexibility in IMF Programs. On the point of perceived inflexibility by IMF staff, many Directors felt that the evaluators might have inadvertently conveyed an inconsistent message. While criticizing perceived inflexibility, the evaluators noted that "the failure to frontload structural reforms with long gestational lags may well be the most serious defect of structural adjustment as currently designed." Often this failure reflected the IMF's willingness to accommodate government resistance to specific reforms.

Finding the proper balance between negotiating flexibility and supporting only programs that adequately addressed economic problems was indeed a delicate matter. These trade-offs and the sequencing of reform issues would continue to be at the center of future Board discussions of ESAF programs. On sequencing reform measures, Directors agreed with the staff that member countries often needed to take advantage of windows of opportunity, without being overly constrained by strict sequencing considerations. Directors also felt that, in several cases, what appeared to be sequencing problems were in reality problems of lack of implementation of agreed policy measures.

Better Public Understanding. Improved public understanding of the IMF in countries receiving ESAF support was important, including through public explanations of the purpose and benefits of economic reform programs by the governments. The steps being taken to increase resident representatives' external relations activities and to enhance collaboration with national authorities and civil society conformed with the evaluators' views.

Continued IMF Presence. Directors agreed that there were many cases in which the IMF must stay engaged in ESAF-eligible countries after the initial macroeconomic stabilization had been achieved. As the evaluators had suggested, Directors saw a window of opportunity in several African economies that had stabilized and were now approaching high rates of growth as a result of policy reform. Investment rates in these economies, however, remained far too low for these growth rates to continue over the longer term, and significant external capital had to be attracted to supplement only slowly rising domestic saving rates. To attract external savings from public and private sources in an environment perceived by markets to be risky, an IMF signal of policy adequacy was often essential to help reduce uncertainty.

With regard to the scope for ESAF financing in the poststabilization phase, several Directors emphasized that the ESAF was not a long-term aid transfer mechanism, as the evaluators seemed to imply. Therefore, disbursements of ESAF support could not be provided over the long term, particularly for programs that aimed at little, if any, further reform. Directors expressed interest in more extensive use, in the poststabilization phase, of precautionary arrangements with the IMF, under which members agreed to an IMF arrangement but without intending to draw on IMF resources. This could have the advantage of conferring the IMF's stamp of approval on a country's reform efforts, to catalyze financial support from other sources. Directors also saw the need for a greater role for the World Bank and other donors in supporting the reform efforts of ESAF countries in the poststabilization period.

The evaluators recommended that the IMF develop more systematic mechanisms for providing continuing support in situations where stabilization had been achieved but where agreement between the government and the IMF was delayed, or, for mainly political reasons, the government was unable to agree on a conventional IMF arrangement. The evaluators favored a move from negotiation to certification. But many Directors were concerned that IMF support for such programs might not be workable. In particular, the absence of ex ante agreement on a framework for policies might mean that any ex post judgment and disbursement of ESAF resources would pose difficulties, as the IMF must avoid arbitrary judgments and unequal treatment of member countries.

Directors took note of the evaluators' suggestion that World Bank and IMF cooperation could be improved in some country cases and recognized the importance of seeking ways to strengthen this collaboration; these issues had also surfaced in the internal evaluation of the ESAF and on other occasions. Some Directors felt that it might not be useful to establish further formal rules on coordination, recommending that priority be given to promoting an open and free flow of information between the IMF and the Bank.

On March 13, 1998, following soon after the Board's consideration of the report, the IMF released the study and other documentation to the public at a press conference at IMF headquarters. Three of the four external evaluators, as well as the chairman of the Evaluation Group of IMF Executive Directors, participated in the briefing.

In its April 1998 meeting, the Interim Committee expressed its appreciation for the work of the external evaluators of the ESAF. It also welcomed the intention of the Board to draw operational conclusions from the issues raised by both the internal and external evaluations so as to strengthen the IMF's ability to foster sustained growth and external viability in poor countries.

CHAPTER X

Capital Movements Under an Amendment of the IMF's Articles

During 1997/98, the Executive Board met to discuss various aspects of an amendment to the IMF's Articles of Agreement with respect to liberalization of capital movements and the IMF's role, including the methodology and scope of jurisdiction; the treatment of inward direct investment, transitional arrangements, and approval policies; and the legal aspects of capital movements, including considerations regarding financing and conditionality. In their discussions, Directors emphasized that, given the scope and complexity of the issues involved, their views remained preliminary and without prejudice to their final positions.

At the Annual Meetings in Hong Kong SAR in September 1997, the Interim Committee issued a Statement on the Liberalization of Capital Movements Under an Amendment of the IMF's Articles of Agreement (Box 13). The statement invited the Board to complete its work on a proposed amendment of the IMF's Articles to make the liberalization of capital movements one of the purposes of the IMF and extend, as needed, the IMF's jurisdiction through the establishment of carefully defined and uniformly applied obligations regarding the liberalization of such movements.

Seminar on Capital Account Liberalization

To help inform its work on bringing the liberalization of capital movements within its mandate, the IMF hosted a seminar on the subject in March 1998 to elicit views from a wide range of private and official observers outside the IMF. Participants included senior government officials, private sector representatives, academicians, and representatives from international organizations. IMF senior staff, management, and members of the Executive Board also participated.

Seminar participants generally agreed that the Asian financial crisis confirmed the importance of orderly and properly sequenced liberalization of capital movements, the need for appropriate macroeconomic and exchange rate policies, and the critical role of a sound financial sector. Participants broadly recognized that, in the current globalized environment, the trend toward greater liberalization was here to stay. The real issues were

how, when, and under what circumstances capital flows should be liberalized. A number of speakers noted that weakness in the financial sector lay at the heart of the crises in Indonesia, Korea, and Thailand. The main problems were the limited capacity of financial institutions to assess and manage risks, inadequate prudential supervision, and ad hoc liberalization of capital movements. With respect to the latter, it was noted that it was not liberalization per se, but its form and sequence that rendered countries vulnerable to changes in market sentiment. A number of speakers felt that the Asian crisis demonstrated that liberalization should be approached cautiously in concert with progress in other areas to realize fully the benefits of liberalization. Participants acknowledged that the IMF had a central role to play in promoting the orderly liberalization of capital movements, but views differed as to whether IMF "advocacy" of freer capital markets or "jurisdiction" over its members' capital flows was the more appropriate means for the IMF to achieve this goal.

Is Liberalization Necessary?

The trend toward capital account convertibility is "irreversible," IMF Managing Director Michel Camdessus said at a luncheon address on March 9, and "all countries have an important stake in seeing that the process takes place in an orderly way," no matter where they stood on the opening of their own capital accounts. The benefits of open capital markets were well known, but free-flowing capital could be highly disruptive, as several speakers noted, creating financial crises that threatened the stability of the international monetary system. Certainly, massive capital flows were a major element behind the financial crisis in Asia. If the trend toward open capital movements was irreversible, and if the benefits from free access to capital markets were undeniable, how, then, could the costs and risks be minimized? Seminar participants noted the importance of an orderly and properly sequenced approach to liberalization of capital movements. In this context, they discussed the role the IMF could play in encouraging the orderly liberalization of capital movements, includ-

Box 13
Interim Committee Statement on Liberalization of Capital Movements Under an Amendment of the IMF's Articles, as Adopted, Hong Kong SAR, September 21, 1997

1. It is time to add a new chapter to the Bretton Woods agreement. Private capital flows have become much more important to the international monetary system, and an increasingly open and liberal system has proved to be highly beneficial to the world economy. By facilitating the flow of savings to their most productive uses, capital movements increase investment, growth, and prosperity. Provided it is introduced in an orderly manner, and backed both by adequate national policies and a solid multilateral system for surveillance and financial support, the liberalization of capital flows is an essential element of an efficient international monetary system in this age of globalization. The IMF's central role in the international monetary system, and its near universal membership, make it uniquely placed to help this process. The Committee sees the IMF's proposed new mandate as bold in its vision, but requiring cautious implementation.

2. International capital flows are highly sensitive to, among other things, the stability of the international monetary system, the quality of macroeconomic policies, and the soundness of domestic financial systems. The recent turmoil in financial markets has demonstrated again the importance of underpinning liberalization with a broad range of structural measures, especially in the monetary and financial sector, and

within the framework of a solid mix of macroeconomic and exchange rate policies. Particular importance will need to be attached to establishing an environment conducive to the efficient use of capital and to building sound financial systems solid enough to cope with fluctuations in capital flows. This phased but comprehensive approach will tailor capital account liberalization to the circumstances of individual countries, thereby maximizing the chances of success, not only for each country but also for the international monetary system.

3. These efforts should lead to the establishment of a multilateral and nondiscriminatory system to promote the liberalization of capital movements. The IMF will have the task of assisting in the establishment of such a system and stands ready to support members' efforts in this regard. Its role is also key to the adoption of policies that would facilitate properly sequenced liberalization and reduce the likelihood of financial and balance of payments crises.

4. In light of the foregoing, the Committee invites the Executive Board to complete its work on a proposed amendment of the Fund's Articles that would make the liberalization of capital movements one of the purposes of the Fund and extend, as needed, the Fund's jurisdiction through the establishment of carefully defined and uniformly applied

obligations regarding the liberalization of such movements. Safeguards and transitional arrangements are necessary for the success of this major endeavor. Flexible approval policies will have to be adopted. In both the preparation of an amendment to the IMF's Articles and its implementation, the members' obligations under other international agreements will be respected. In pursuing this work, the Committee expects the IMF and other institutions to cooperate closely.

5. Sound liberalization and expanded access to capital markets should reduce the frequency of recourse to Fund resources and other exceptional financing. Nevertheless, the Committee recognizes that, in some circumstances, there could be a large need for financing from the Fund and other sources. The Fund will continue to play a critical role in helping to mobilize financial support for members' adjustment programs. In such endeavors, the Fund will continue its central catalytic role while limiting moral hazard.

6. In view of the importance of moving decisively toward this new worldwide regime of liberalized capital movements, and welcoming the very broad consensus of the membership on these basic guidelines, the Committee invites the Executive Board to give high priority to the completion of the required amendment of the Fund's Articles of Agreement.

ing a possible amendment of the Articles of Agreement to extend IMF jurisdiction to include capital movements.

Preconditions

Although it was not possible to say with any certainty how long a country should hold off opening its capital account, there was consensus, according to IMF First Deputy Managing Director Stanley Fischer, that "liberalization without a necessary set of preconditions in place may be extremely risky." The absence of such preconditions could promote a crisis or reveal weaknesses in the financial system that could have been

overcome had the authorities been allowed more time to strengthen the system before the capital markets were opened.

Participants generally recognized that the Asian financial crisis had not negated the contribution that substantial inflows of capital had made to economic progress in the Asian countries before the crisis erupted. The crisis demonstrated the risks of liberalization that is not properly sequenced and adequately supported by sound policies on a wide range of other fronts. Some speakers noted, however, that appropriate sequencing should not mean that liberalization should, or could, wait for other reforms to be completed.

Rather, both should proceed hand in hand to take advantage of windows of political opportunity. Most speakers stressed the importance of making progress in:

- achieving sound and consistent macroeconomic policies, sustainable current account positions, and appropriate exchange rate regimes;
- having sound and well-supervised domestic financial systems, including improved supervision and prudential regulations covering capital adequacy, lending standards, asset valuation, effective loan recovery mechanisms, and provisions ensuring that insolvent institutions were dealt with promptly;
- improving transparency through disclosure of accurate financial and economic information, based on internationally recognized standards and practices; and
- liberalizing financial services to allow for greater competition and the transfer of skills, capital, and best practices.

Path to Liberalization Should Be Orderly

The Asian experience demonstrated the need for adapting the pace of liberalization to the circumstances of individual countries in order to limit their vulnerability to wide fluctuations in capital movements. A number of seminar speakers advocated a gradual opening of the capital account, noting that for many developing countries the costs of disruption occasioned by reversals in capital flows were high, given their limited capacity to absorb risk and the absence of institutional structures to deal with such reversals.

Several speakers considered it important to avoid ad hoc liberalization that might create a bias toward short-term inflows. They suggested that in the initial stages, the emphasis should be on liberalizing medium- and long-term investments. For emerging market economies, the improper management of the opening of financial markets could easily lead to a boom-and-bust cycle during the transition period.

Speakers noted that the experience of countries— not just in Asia—demonstrated that appropriate regulatory requirements and controls could help discourage volatile short-term capital inflows. A number of speakers argued that appropriate prudential measures, aimed particularly at limiting banks' external exposures, were necessary. A fairly wide cross-section of participants— from developed and developing countries and representing both the public and private sectors—saw scope for introducing controls on short-term inflows in some circumstances, even for well-managed economies; to be effective, they concluded, any such controls should be market based, transparent, and temporary. At the same time, a number of speakers were wary of controls, noting that, like tariffs, they were generally undesirable. Such controls could easily become permanent and a way of avoiding necessary policy adjustment.

Institutionalizing Liberalization

All seminar participants agreed that, given its mandate to oversee the international monetary system, the IMF had an important role to play in promoting the orderly liberalization of capital movements and was better placed than other international organizations to do so. Differing views were expressed, however, about whether the IMF could best achieve that goal through advocacy or jurisdiction.

A few speakers argued that an amendment to extend jurisdiction to capital movements was not necessary to achieve the goal of capital market liberalization. In their view, the IMF was already promoting capital account convertibility in the context of surveillance, conditionality, and technical assistance. Although an amendment of Article I to make the liberalization of capital movements a purpose of the IMF could be useful, further amending the Articles to extend IMF jurisdiction to cover both payments and transfers and the underlying transactions would not provide an effective mechanism for promoting liberalization. Furthermore, these participants contended, it would involve the IMF in activities beyond its designated responsibilities in the balance of payments area and could raise difficulties of overlap and potential conflict with other international treaties.

Those favoring extending IMF jurisdiction to capital movements held that the IMF was the ideal agency to undertake this function, because it could deal with each country on a case-by-case basis, adjusting the progress toward full liberalization to the country's individual capacity and complementary structural reforms. Although the IMF had encouraged countries with IMF-supported adjustment programs to free up their capital accounts, legal jurisdiction would allow the IMF to apply the principles of capital liberalization to all member countries through its surveillance activities, not just those using its financial resources. Furthermore, as an organization that promoted good governance among its members, the IMF had to set an example by ensuring that the legal basis for its activities was transparent. Such transparency would also clarify, rather than undermine, the IMF's relationship with other organizations. Speakers from other international organizations, such as the World Trade Organization, the Organization for Economic Cooperation and Development, and the European Union, noted the complementarity of the IMF's role in this area with that of their own organizations and considered that a well-defined code of conduct for capital movements would help clarify the respective roles of the IMF and other international institutions.

Some speakers cautioned that without commitment, advocacy carried little conviction. A country's resolution to open its capital account and its agreement not to impose restrictions at a later date would not be credible without the commitment, transparency, and conviction imparted by its obligations as a member of the IMF to proceed toward an open capital account. Nevertheless, the seminar discussion highlighted that, given the undefined and open-ended transition period, obligations themselves would imply no more conviction than advocacy.

Some private sector representatives pressed for greater transparency in the IMF's deliberations on an amendment. In particular, they would like to see specific language on the proposed amendment before lending their support to an amendment.

Future Considerations

In summing up the seminar, First Deputy Managing Director Stanley Fischer cited several issues yet to be resolved. Despite considerable enthusiasm for an amendment of the IMF's Articles—from both official sources and the private sector—he noted that some "severe doubts" had been expressed, both on whether capital account liberalization per se was a good idea and on whether advocacy was not sufficient and legalized jurisdiction too painful, complicated, and unnecessary.

A pressing unresolved issue, Fischer said, was how the international system could ensure that banking supervisory standards and the quality of banking systems were improved and what could be done at the international level. Also unresolved was how to determine when an economy was sufficiently insulated by preconditions to risk opening the capital account. Fischer noted that some seminar participants had expressed the fear that too much talking about preconditions might discourage countries that would end up waiting forever for preconditions to be in place. On the other hand, some participants suggested that change did not happen until it was forced. Such a way of proceeding was "pretty risky," said Fischer, since the consequences of potential accidents were very large.

The consequences of uncontrolled short-term flows posed another set of problems. Aside from their dislocating effect on the economy, short-term flows could do serious damage to a vulnerable banking system. There was no established body of analysis on capital controls—what worked and what did not—and a "host of questions" had to be examined. A capital account amendment of the IMF's Articles, Fischer said, would provide an appropriate context in which to conduct such an analysis.

Finally, other international organizations and institutions were closely associated with both the regulation and liberalization of capital movements. It was clear, Fischer said, that if the IMF's Articles were amended to include jurisdiction over capital movements, the existing close cooperation between the IMF and these organizations would have to be strengthened further.

Next Steps

At an April 1998 discussion following the seminar, the Executive Board agreed that the IMF and its members faced a world vastly different from that of the 1940s, when the IMF's Articles—with their emphasis on the liberalization, and financing, of current account transactions—were conceived. The benefits for the world economy of an open and liberal system of capital movements were now widely recognized. Balance of payments difficulties associated with the capital account, although stemming from underlying policy issues, also dominated many of the problems the IMF was dealing with now, which would no doubt be even more the case in the future. Directors thus saw a tension between the focus of the existing Articles and the realities faced by the IMF that had to be addressed.

The increasing openness and integration of capital markets was being driven to a large extent by markets themselves and by the advantages that members saw in liberalization. This phenomenon should not be reversed. One lesson of the Asian financial crisis, Directors agreed, was that it was necessary to achieve a better pace and sequencing of liberalization with other reforms, most notably in the domestic financial sector, and for countries to adopt appropriate macroeconomic and exchange rate policies. Given the IMF's mandate and its universal membership, Directors saw the institution as uniquely placed to foster prudent, well-considered, and orderly liberalization worldwide. It could do this while respecting the interests and roles of other organizations active in this area.

In reporting to the Interim Committee in April 1998, the Managing Director noted that Executive Directors had reaffirmed that the orderly liberalization of capital movements should be one of the IMF's purposes and had reached provisional agreement on the text of an amendment that would express that purpose in general terms. Directors would continue work on other aspects, including policy issues, jurisdiction, and financing.

Subsequently, at its April 1998 meeting, the Interim Committee reaffirmed its view, expressed in its Hong Kong communiqué of September 1997, that it was time to add a new chapter to the Bretton Woods agreement by making the liberalization of capital movements one of the IMF's purposes and extending, as needed, the IMF's jurisdiction for this purpose. The Committee noted the progress made to date and the provisional agreement reached by the Executive Board on that part of an amendment dealing with the IMF's purposes. It asked the Board to pursue with determination its work on other aspects, including policy issues, with the aim of submitting an appropriate amendment of the Articles for the Committee's consideration as soon as possible.

CHAPTER XI

Technical Assistance and Training

Member countries' demand for IMF technical assistance and training remained strong in 1997/98. Technical assistance continued to focus on the monetary and fiscal aspects of macroeconomic management, but also addressed statistics, financial law, IMF financial organization and operations, and information technology (Figure 5). A large number of departments in the IMF provided assistance, and the Technical Assistance Committee—composed of senior staff from each of the IMF's functional, area, and support departments— advised IMF management on priorities and policies and coordinated assistance activities among IMF departments. In the field, assistance was delivered by IMF staff and the assignment of short- and long-term advisors.

At headquarters and abroad, training courses and seminars on a variety of topics were given by the IMF Institute and other departments providing technical assistance and training. In 1997/98, the Institute's program at headquarters included basic, intermediate, and advanced courses on financial programming and policies, shorter courses on such specialized topics as exchange rate policies and monetary and inflation targeting, and a high-level seminar on trade reform and regional integration in Africa. In addition, other functional departments—including Fiscal Affairs, Monetary and Exchange Affairs, Policy Development and Review, and Statistics—conducted seminars and courses in their areas of expertise in collaboration with the Institute. The Institute's overseas training program continued to focus on issues related to the formulation and implementation of economic adjustment programs.

Technical assistance has been described as forming the third leg of the IMF stool—the other two legs

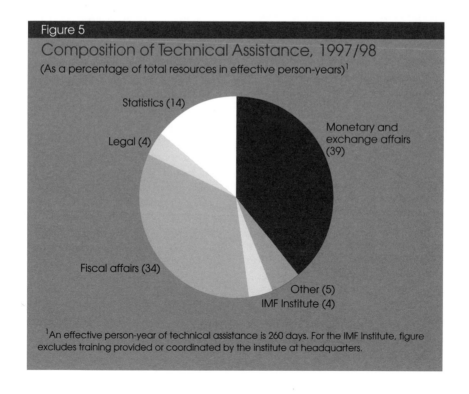

Figure 5

Composition of Technical Assistance, 1997/98
(As a percentage of total resources in effective person-years)[1]

- Statistics (14)
- Legal (4)
- Monetary and exchange affairs (39)
- Fiscal affairs (34)
- Other (5)
- IMF Institute (4)

[1]An effective person-year of technical assistance is 260 days. For the IMF Institute, figure excludes training provided or coordinated by the institute at headquarters.

being its surveillance work and its financial assistance under IMF-supported adjustment programs. Member countries and the IMF have become increasingly convinced that the timely provision of effective technical assistance is a key ingredient in supporting governments' efforts to sustain policy and institutional reform. In 1997/98, technical assistance activity represented about 17 percent of total IMF administrative expenditures.

The increased attention being placed on the promotion of better governance and on creating or maintaining conditions for sustainable and equitable growth have highlighted the need for more attention to strengthening governments' human resource and institutional capacities for effective economic management. Without such improvements, the IMF's surveillance and program financing activities would likely have a less durable impact. The IMF's technical assistance and training are specifically aimed at strengthening economic management capacity so that, in the long run, members will have less need for IMF financing and a greater ability to engage in a productive dialogue with the IMF during surveillance operations. This can be described as the *preventive* aspect of IMF technical assistance and training. Given available resources, much of the IMF's technical assistance was inevitably *remedial* in nature—directed toward immediate problem solving or helping governments implement economic and financial reforms within the context of an IMF-supported program.

The IMF quantifies the technical assistance it delivers in units of "person-years of services provided," both by its staff as well as by the experts it recruits. Using this measurement, the annual volume of IMF technical assistance in the past few years has been about 300 person-years (see Table 9). The cost in U.S. dollar terms per unit of input increased over the period owing to increases in compensation for outside experts and greater use of short-term experts.

The regional distribution of IMF technical assistance and training has shifted markedly since 1995, when the

Table 9
Technical Assistance Delivery
(Effective person-years)[1]

	1994/95	1995/96	1996/97	1997/98[2]
Fund technical assistance resources	**220.0**	**211.4**	**172.7**	**189.6**
Staff	115.7	108.6	97.1	103.9
Headquarters-based consultants	22.1	23.5	20.1	20.8
Experts	82.3	79.3	55.5	64.9
External technical assistance resources	**80.5**	**97.5**	**104.2**	**96.2**
United Nations Development Programme	16.6	25.0	21.5	24.4
Japan	51.4	65.0	67.3	55.6
Other	12.4	7.5	15.4	16.2
Total technical assistance resources	**300.6**	**309.0**	**277.0**	**285.7**
Total resources by department				
Monetary and Exchange Affairs Department	138.1	137.3	114.6	110.6
Fiscal Affairs Department	95.1	99.8	96.2	98.8
Statistics Department	37.9	39.2	36.6	39.0
IMF Institute	14.6	14.0	11.0	12.1
Legal Department	7.9	11.0	9.3	10.3
Other[3]	7.0	7.7	9.3	14.9
Total regional use by department	**271.1**	**280.1**	**251.0**	**258.7**
African Department	60.6	62.4	54.5	65.8
Asia and Pacific Department[4]	n.a.	n.a.	49.0	42.5
Central Asia Department	27.7	27.5	n.a.	n.a.
Southeast Asia and Pacific Department	23.6	25.0	n.a.	n.a.
European I Department	27.8	24.4	22.5	23.8
European II Department	79.3	73.5	57.6	52.6
Middle Eastern Department	16.9	23.4	26.5	29.5
Western Hemisphere Department	27.4	32.3	31.2	35.2
Interregional	7.9	11.7	9.6	8.6
Nonregional use	**29.6**	**28.9**	**26.1**	**26.9**
Total technical assistance use	**300.6**	**309.0**	**277.0**	**285.6**

[1]An effective person-year of technical assistance is 260 days.
[2]Estimated.
[3]"Other" includes the Policy Development and Review Department, Bureau of Computing Services, and Technical Assistance Secretariat.
[4]Effective January 1, 1997, the Central Asia and Southeast Asia and Pacific Departments were merged into a single Asia and Pacific Department.

countries of the two IMF European Departments absorbed 40 percent of technical assistance resources. This proportion dropped back to 30 percent in 1997/98, while the share of countries in the African and the Middle Eastern Departments, taken together, rose to 37 percent from 28 percent over the same period.

One of the features of IMF technical assistance and training over the past few years has been its involvement in postconflict countries. In such situations the traditional "request-and-response" mode of operation has been considered inadequate to address the urgent need to rehabilitate these countries' basic economic

Box 14

IMF Institute and Regional Institutions

Europe. The IMF, in collaboration with the World Bank and certain other international institutions, has established the Joint Vienna Institute (JVI) to provide training to officials of former centrally planned economies that are in transition to market-based systems. In addition to a comprehensive course in applied market economics jointly presented by all sponsoring organizations, the IMF Institute and other IMF departments offer an extensive seminar program covering macroeconomic analysis and policy, banking supervision, payment systems, monetary and exchange operations, fiscal policy, public expenditure management, value-added taxes, social safety nets, financial sector law, and macroeconomic statistics. Recently the Board extended the IMF's support for the JVI for another five years.

Capacity building in Africa. The Institute has a long-standing cooperative relationship with the regional training institutions in Francophone Africa, namely, the training centers of the Central Bank of West African States (West African Training Center for Banking Studies—COFEB) and the Bank of Central African States. The Institute offers a yearly regional course on Financial Programming and Policies or External Sector Policies, as well as periodic lecturing assistance to the centers. The regional courses benefit from cofinancing from the United Nations

Development Programme and the European Union. In collaborating with these centers, the Institute continues to place emphasis on "capacity building" by training trainers, both in financial macroeconomics and in managerial fields linked to teaching.

To respond to the growing need for training in Africa, the Institute helped establish in 1997 the nine-member Macroeconomic and Financial Management Institute of Eastern and Southern Africa (MEFMI) in Zimbabwe and the West African Institute for Financial and Economic Management (WAIFEM) in Nigeria.

Asia. Effective May 4, 1998, the IMF-Singapore Regional Training Institute (STI) commenced the offering of training on policy-related economics to selected government officials, mainly from developing countries in the Asia and the Pacific region. In 1998/99, 13 courses and seminars are scheduled on macroeconomic adjustment and reform policies, financial programming, the problems of transition economies, monetary and exchange operations, public finance, banking supervision, and macroeconomic statistics. The STI is viewed as a precursor to similar regional training centers in other parts of the world.

South-East Asian Central Banks Research and Training Center (SEACEN). Relations between the IMF Institute and SEACEN (Kuala

Lumpur, Malaysia) developed in the 1970s when the Institute began to send senior staff to assist SEACEN in the formulation of its training program. Since the early 1980s, the Institute has also provided lecturing assistance to SEACEN and coordinated lecturing assistance from other IMF departments, and in the early 1990s began to conduct joint courses.

The Arab Monetary Fund. The IMF Institute has maintained a close relationship with the training branch of the Arab Monetary Fund (AMF), the Economic Policy Institute (EPI), since its inception in 1988. Since then, it has regularly provided the EPI with lecturing assistance in connection with the AMF course on Macroeconomic Management and also participated in the AMF course on External Sector Management, first offered in March 1995. Cooperation between the IMF Institute and the AMF includes joint courses and seminars and participation by Institute staff in AMF-sponsored seminars.

In addition, the Institute has been providing lecturing assistance for courses organized by the Center for Latin American Monetary Studies for several years; has been cooperating with the Islamic Development Bank on regional training courses since 1994; and conducted its first cooperative training venture with the Asian Development Bank in 1995.

---

and financial management capacities. This has given rise to the practice of preparing large-scale, integrated, multiyear technical assistance programs cofinanced with other donors. Such technical assistance programs have now been implemented—or are being implemented—in such postconflict countries as Angola, Cambodia, Haiti, Lebanon, Namibia, Rwanda, and Yemen; plans are under way for a similar approach for Liberia. These programs are usually closely coordinated with, and cofinanced by, the United Nations Development Programme (UNDP) and often involve a number of bilateral donors. In addition, where appropriate, the IMF is developing a regional approach to the delivery of technical assistance and training services. Examples include the Pacific Financial Technical Assistance Centre in Fiji, which channels technical assistance to 15 countries in the Pacific area with financing from

UNDP, Australia, New Zealand, the Pacific Forum, and the Asian Development Bank; the Joint Vienna Institute; the Harare Center; the Cairo Information Center; and the IMF-Singapore Regional Training Institute, which is cofinanced by the IMF and the Government of Singapore (see Box 14).

Japan was the single largest source of external financing for IMF-provided technical assistance and responded with great flexibility during 1997/98 in seeking to ensure that its funding was readily available to help address the new demands for technical assistance that arose from the Asian crisis. The Framework Administered Account for Technical Assistance Activities—established by the IMF in 1995—attracted contributions from Australia, France, Japan (for a scholarship program), and Switzerland. A few countries, such as Sweden and Norway, financed UNDP projects for which the IMF was the executing agency. Others, such as the United Kingdom, the European Union, and the Inter-American Development Bank, agreed to coordinate technical assistance cofinancing arrangements with the IMF. Several developing country members used the proceeds from World Bank credits to finance IMF-provided technical assistance. In 1996/97, 30 percent of the IMF's total technical assistance and training activities were financed from external sources, and two-thirds of the experts that it recruited to serve in its member countries were also externally financed. This ratio of internal to external financing is likely to remain fairly stable in the immediate future.

During 1997/98, joint evaluations of country technical assistance projects were conducted with the UNDP in China, Haiti, the Pacific, and Yemen. The IMF's Office of Internal Audit and Inspection is currently evaluating the IMF's technical assistance and training operations.

CHAPTER XII

Financial Operations and Policies

During 1997/98, member countries purchased (i.e., borrowed) SDR 19.0 billion from the IMF's General Resources Account (GRA) in the credit tranches—nearly four times the level of the previous year—and made reserve tranche purchases of SDR 1.0 billion.[15] The IMF approved nine new Stand-By Arrangements in 1997/98, with total commitments of SDR 27.3 billion (including SDR 10.0 billion under the Supplemental Reserve Facility), and four new Extended Arrangements, with total commitments of SDR 2.8 billion. In addition, the IMF approved eight new ESAF Arrangements, with commitments totaling SDR 1.7 billion. As of April 30, 1998, 14 Stand-By Arrangements, 13 Extended Arrangements, and 33 ESAF Arrangements were in effect. With the large volume of credit tranche purchases, along with drawings of ESAF loans, total IMF credit outstanding rose to a record SDR 56 billion as of April 30, 1998, from SDR 40.5 billion a year earlier.

With the very high demand for the use of IMF resources, the IMF's net uncommitted usable resources fell by SDR 20.9 billion during 1997/98, and its liquidity position weakened considerably. At a review in March 1998, the Board considered the IMF's liquidity position vulnerable and expected it to remain under considerable strain in the period immediately ahead. Executive Directors cited the pressing need for the agreed quota increase under the Eleventh General Review to take early effect and called for a rapid conclusion of the adherence process for the New Arrangements to Borrow (NAB).

The IMF earned a net income of SDR 164 million in the financial year, which was placed to reserves, increasing the IMF's reserves to SDR 2.1 billion as of the end of 1997/98. The level of outstanding overdue financial obligations to the IMF increased slightly to SDR 2.3 billion in 1997/98, with the number of members in protracted arrears remaining at seven.

Membership and Quotas

In 1997/98, the Republic of Palau became the 182nd member of the IMF, with an initial quota of SDR 2.25 million. The Federal Republic of Yugoslavia (Serbia/Montenegro) has not completed arrangements for succession to membership in the IMF. The Board decided on December 10, 1997, that the country had until June 14, 1998, to complete such arrangements; on June 10, 1998, this period was extended for a further six months.

Five member countries (Democratic Republic of the Congo, Iraq,[16] Liberia, Somalia, and Sudan) have not been able to consent to their quota increases under the Ninth General Review of Quotas because of their arrears to the General Resources Account. The Executive Board approved on December 30, 1997, a six-month extension of the periods for consent to and payment of increases in quotas under the Ninth Review. In its report to the Board of Governors on the Eleventh General Review of Quotas[17] (see below), the Board recommended that the period for consent to quota increases under the Ninth Review be extended to the effective date of the quota increase under the Eleventh Review, and the period for payment of quota increases under the Ninth Review be extended to 30 days after that date.

The Board began its work on the Eleventh General Review of Quotas in August 1995, and it reported its recommendations regarding quota increases to the Board of Governors in December 1997. The Board's Report and the Proposed Resolution of the Board of Governors (Resolution No. 53-2, adopted January 30, 1998) are shown in Appendix III.

The Board's recommendation to increase total IMF quotas by 45 percent (to SDR 212 billion from

---

[15]As of April 30, 1998, the U.S. dollar/SDR exchange rate was SDR 1 = US$1.34666.

[16]Iraq has not made payments to the IMF in view of sanctions under UN Security Council Resolution No. 661, adopted on August 6, 1990.

[17]The Board of Governors concluded the Tenth General Review of Quotas without an increase in quotas.

SDR 146 billion) took into account a range of factors, including the growth of world trade and payments; the scale of potential payments imbalances, including those that may stem from sharp changes in capital flows; the prospective demand for the use of IMF resources in support of member countries' economic programs; and the rapid globalization and associated liberalization of trade and payments—including on capital account—that have characterized the world economy since the last increase in quotas in 1990. The Board also considered the IMF's liquidity position and the adequacy of its borrowing arrangements. The Board reiterated that the IMF should continue to rely on its quota resources as its principal form of financing and resort to borrowing only in exceptional circumstances.

As regards the distribution of the overall increase in quotas, the Board was guided by the views of the Interim Committee expressed in its communiqué of April 1997, which stated that "the proposed distribution should be predominantly equiproportional while contributing to a correction of the most important anomalies in the present quota distribution." Meeting in Hong Kong SAR in September 1997, the Interim Committee agreed that 75 percent of the overall increase would be distributed in proportion to present quotas; 15 percent would be distributed in proportion to members' shares in calculated quotas (based on 1994 data), so as to better reflect the relative economic positions of members; and the remaining 10 percent would be distributed among those members whose current quotas are "out of line with their positions in the world economy (as measured by the excess of their share in calculated quotas over their share in actual quotas), of which 1 percent of the overall increase would be distributed among five members whose current quotas are far out of line with their relative economic positions, and which are in a position to contribute to the IMF's liquidity over the medium term." The Interim Committee reiterated its view that the formulas used to calculate quotas should be reviewed by the Board promptly after the completion of the Eleventh Review.

In reaching agreement on the size and distribution of the quota increase, the Board confirmed that it did not intend to reopen the issues of the size and composition of the Board and that the existing representation of developing countries should not be affected.

At its April 1998 meeting, the Interim Committee called for rapid implementation of the quota increase approved by the Board of Governors in January 1998. The resolution approved by the Board of Governors asked member countries to consent to the quota increase before January 29, 1999. The quota increase will not take effect until members having not less than 85 percent of total quotas as of December 23, 1997, have consented.

IMF Liquidity and Borrowing

The IMF's liquidity position weakened considerably in 1997/98 as a result of large new demands for use of IMF resources arising from the crisis affecting several Asian countries, along with sustained demand from other member countries—including, in particular, the Russian Federation, as well as Algeria, Argentina, Bulgaria, and the Philippines. Total purchases (gross drawings, including reserve tranche and under the SRF) rose sharply to an unprecedented SDR 20.0 billion in 1997/98, owing largely to heavy frontloading of purchases by Indonesia, Korea, and Thailand under their Stand-By Arrangements. Net of repurchases (i.e., repayments) by members, IMF credit outstanding in the GRA increased by SDR 15.2 billion to reach a historic high of SDR 49.7 billion at the end of 1997/98.

General Resources

The liquid resources of the IMF consist of usable currencies and SDRs held in the GRA. Usable currencies, the largest component of liquid resources, are holdings of currencies of members whose balance of payments and reserve positions are considered sufficiently strong to warrant the inclusion of their currencies in the operational budget for use in the financing of IMF operations and transactions (Box 15). The exclusion of six members from the list of sufficiently strong countries during 1997/98 reduced the stock of usable currencies by about SDR 2.4 billion, while the inclusion of three other members on the list added about SDR 3.0 billion to the stock of usable currencies. More significantly, however, purchases during the year far exceeded repurchases and the IMF's usable resources declined to SDR 47.3 billion at the end of April 1998 from SDR 62.7 billion a year earlier.

The stock of uncommitted usable resources, that is, usable resources less the amount of resources committed under current arrangements and considered likely to be drawn, also declined sharply during the period, to SDR 32.0 billion at the end of April 1998 from SDR 55.7 billion a year earlier. The IMF's net uncommitted usable resources (adjusted to reflect the requirement to maintain adequate working balances of currencies) amounted to SDR 22.6 billion as of April 30, 1998, compared with SDR 43.5 billion a year earlier.

The IMF's liquid liabilities at the end of April 1998 totaled SDR 50.3 billion, consisting entirely of reserve tranche positions (as the IMF had no outstanding borrowing), a substantial rise from the level of SDR 36.1 billion a year earlier. The ratio of the IMF's net uncommitted usable resources to its liquid liabilities—the traditional liquidity ratio—declined to 44.8 percent at the end of April 1998 (Figure 6) from 120.5 percent a year earlier.

Box 15
Operational Budget

The quarterly operational budget is the mechanism through which the IMF makes its resources available to member countries. Reflecting the cooperative character of the IMF and the revolving nature of its resources, IMF financial assistance is provided through the use of SDRs and the currencies of a wide range of members—large and small, including advanced, developing, and transition economies. Members whose balance of payments and reserve positions are judged sufficiently strong for their currencies to be included in the operational budget make foreign exchange available to members with weak balance of payments positions in need of external financing. In return for the use of their currencies through the operational budget, members receive a liquid claim on the IMF that earns a market-related rate of return.

Guidelines underlying the preparation and implementation of the operational budget are established by the Board. During 1997/98, the Board reviewed the procedures governing the assessment of members' balance of payments and reserve strength. It concluded that assessments should continue to rely on a relatively simple system, based on criteria set out in the Articles of Agreement (balance of payments and reserve positions and developments in exchange markets), supplemented by a small set of additional indicators bearing on a member's external financial strength, including in particular indicators of short-term external debt and debt service.

Borrowing

The IMF is a quota-based institution. At the same time, it has authority under its Articles of Agreement to borrow to provide temporary supplements to its usable quota resources, if needed.

General Arrangements to Borrow. During the financial year, the IMF renewed the General Arrangements to Borrow (GAB) for a further five-year period from December 26, 1998.

The GAB is a set of arrangements under which 11 industrial countries or their central banks have agreed to provide resources to the IMF to forestall or cope with an impairment of the international monetary system. The amount potentially available under the GAB is SDR 17 billion, with an additional SDR 1.5 billion available under an associated agreement with Saudi Arabia. Table 10 shows the amounts of credit arrangements of participants in the GAB.

New Arrangements to Borrow. The amount of resources potentially available to the IMF through borrowing in circumstances similar to those covered by the GAB was enhanced by the Board's adoption on January 27, 1997, of a decision on the New Arrangements to Borrow (NAB). The NAB represents the culmination of intensive efforts since the June 1995 Halifax meeting of the Group of Seven countries, which called for doubling the amount of resources available to the IMF under the GAB to respond to financial emergencies.

The New Arrangements do not replace the General Arrangements, which remain in force. The NAB will be the facility of first and principal recourse, unless a GAB participant (all GAB participants are also participants in the NAB) requests the use of IMF resources. A proposal for calls may be made by the IMF under either of the arrangements, and if a call under the NAB is not accepted, then such a proposal may be made under the GAB. The amount potentially available under the NAB is up to SDR 34 billion, which is also the maximum combined amount available under the two arrangements. Table 11 shows the amounts of credit arrangements of participants under the NAB, which are based on relative economic strength—as measured by the actual IMF quotas of the participants as a predominant criterion. The credit arrangements under the NAB may be activated for the benefit of an IMF member, either a participant or a nonparticipant, under circumstances similar to those specified in the GAB, except that activation of the GAB for the benefit of a nonparticipant requires additionally that, after consulting with the participants, the Managing Director judges that the IMF faces an inadequacy of resources.

The NAB will enter into force when the decision has been adhered to by potential participants with credit arrangements amounting to not less than SDR 28.9 billion, including the five members or institutions with the largest credit arrangements. As of April 30, 1998, two-thirds of the participants, representing some 55 percent of the potential resources under the arrangements, had adhered to the decision.

Access Policy and Limits on Use of IMF Resources

The IMF's current policies on access to its resources reflect the Board's decision in 1994 to raise the annual access limit under the credit tranches and the Extended Fund Facility (EFF) for a period of three years to 100 percent of quota from 68 percent, while keeping the cumulative access limit unchanged at 300 percent of quota. The Board reviews access policies annually. At the November 1997 review, it decided to maintain the annual and cumulative access limits set in 1994 until the next review of access policies, to be held not later than October 1998.

The access policies and limits applicable to the credit tranches and the EFF do not apply to the IMF's special facilities, including the Supplemental Reserve Facility, established in December 1997. Under the SRF, the IMF makes financial assistance available to member countries for a period of up to one year in case of exceptional balance of payments difficulties attributable to a large short-term financing need resulting from a sudden and disruptive loss of market confidence. SRF drawings are made within the context of a Stand-By or Extended Arrangement but are not subject to a specific quota limit. Repurchases (i.e., repayments) under the SRF are expected within 1–1½ years of each purchase, although the Board may extend this period by up to one year at which point the member is obligated to repurchase.

Members' Use of IMF Resources and Credit Outstanding

In 1997/98, members' purchases from the GRA, excluding reserve tranche purchases,[18] amounted to SDR 19.0 billion, nearly four times the 1996/97 level of SDR 4.9 billion (Table 12; see also Appendix II, Table II.7). These purchases consisted of SDR 16.1 billion under Stand-By Arrangements (compared with SDR 1.8 billion in 1996/97) and SDR 2.8 billion under Extended Arrangements (SDR 2.8 billion in 1996/97). During 1997/98, there were also purchases of SDR 30 million under the policy on emergency postconflict assistance; no purchases were made under the Compensatory and Contingency Financing Facility (CCFF) (SDR 0.3 billion in 1996/97).

The largest users of IMF resources in 1997/98 were Asian members. Korea drew SDR 11.2 billion, including SDR 7.1 billion under the SRF; Indonesia SDR 2.2 billion; and Thailand SDR 2.0 billion. Russia was the next largest user, drawing a total of SDR 1.5 billion. Other members making significant purchases were the Philippines (SDR 0.8 billion), Algeria (SDR 0.3 billion), Argentina (SDR 0.2 billion), Bulgaria (SDR 0.2 billion), and Ukraine (SDR 0.2 billion). By region, purchases by Asian countries amounted to SDR 16.2 billion and purchases by European countries (including the Baltic States, Russia, and other countries of the former Soviet Union) amounted to SDR 2.0 billion. Purchases by Latin American, Middle Eastern, and African countries combined totaled SDR 0.7 billion.

Repurchases in the GRA during 1997/98 totaled SDR 3.8 billion, compared with SDR 6.7 billion in the previous financial year (Figure 7; see also Appendix II,

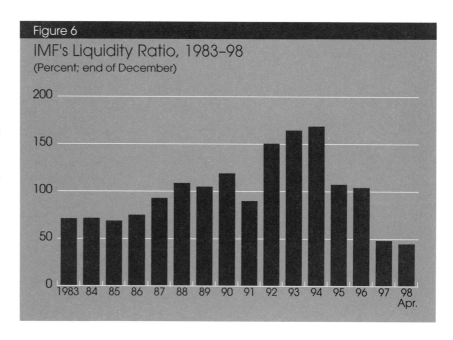

Figure 6

IMF's Liquidity Ratio, 1983–98
(Percent; end of December)

Table II.8). The largest repurchases were made by Argentina (SDR 0.5 billion); India, Mexico, and Russia (roughly SDR 0.4 billion each); and Algeria, South Africa, and Venezuela (roughly SDR 0.3 billion each). Actual repurchases in 1997/98 were higher than the scheduled level of SDR 3.5 billion, owing to a repurchase by Algeria as a result of CCFF overcompensation (SDR 0.2 billion) and a voluntary advance repurchase by Hungary (SDR 0.1 billion). Given the sharp rise in the use of IMF resources in the recent past and the revolving nature and medium-term maturity of IMF financial assistance, scheduled repurchases are likely to

---

Table 10

General Arrangements to Borrow (GAB)

Participant	Amount (millions of SDRs)
United States	4,250.0
Deutsche Bundesbank	2,380.0
Japan	2,125.0
France	1,700.0
United Kingdom	1,700.0
Italy	1,105.0
Swiss National Bank	1,020.0
Canada	892.5
Netherlands	850.0
Belgium	595.0
Sveriges Riksbank	382.5
Total	**17,000.0**
Associated agreement with Saudi Arabia	1,500.0
Total	**18,500.0**

---

[18]Reserve tranche purchases totaling SDR 1.1 billion were made by Indonesia (SDR 288 million), Korea (SDR 444 million), and Thailand (SDR 317 million) in 1997/98, whereas there were no reserve tranche purchases in 1996/97. Reserve tranche purchases represent members' use of their own IMF-related assets and not use of IMF credit.

Table 11
New Arrangements to Borrow (NAB)[1]

Participant	Amount (millions of SDRs)
Australia	810
Austria	412
Belgium	967
Canada	1,396
Denmark	371
Deutsche Bundesbank	3,557
Finland	340
France	2,577
Hong Kong Monetary Authority	340
Italy	1,772
Japan	3,557
Korea	340
Kuwait	345
Luxembourg	340
Malaysia	340
Netherlands	1,316
Norway	383
Saudi Arabia	1,780
Singapore	340
Spain	672
Sveriges Riksbank	859
Swiss National Bank	1,557
Thailand	340
United Kingdom	2,577
United States	6,712
Total	34,000

[1]The arrangements will enter into force when the NAB decision has been adhered to by potential participants with credit arrangements amounting to not less than SDR 28.9 billion, including the five members or institutions with the largest credit arrangements.

increase over the next several years. A sizable amount is scheduled to be repurchased in 1999 under the SRF, under which purchases are expected to be repurchased within 1–1½ years.

Taking into account both purchases and repurchases, IMF credit outstanding in the GRA increased by SDR 15.2 billion in 1997/98, to SDR 49.7 billion as of April 30, 1998 from SDR 34.5 billion a year earlier (Appendix II, Table II.9). If net disbursements under the SAF and ESAF are also included (see below), IMF credit outstanding under all facilities increased by SDR 15.5 billion in 1997/98, to SDR 56.0 billion on April 30, 1998 (Figure 8) from SDR 40.5 billion a year earlier.

Stand-By and Extended Arrangements
In 1997/98, the IMF approved commitments under nine new Stand-By Arrangements totaling SDR 27.3 billion (Appendix II, Table II.1). Stand-By Arrangements totaling SDR 26.7 billion were approved for

Indonesia (SDR 7.3 billion), Korea (SDR 15.5 billion), the Philippines (SDR 1.0 billion), and Thailand (SDR 2.9 billion). The arrangement for Korea—the largest in the IMF's history—included SDR 10.0 billion available until December 1998 under the SRF. Stand-By Arrangements totaling SDR 0.6 billion were also approved for Cape Verde, Estonia, Latvia, Ukraine, and Uruguay.[19] As of April 30, 1998, 14 countries had Stand-By Arrangements with the IMF, with total commitments of SDR 28.3 billion and undrawn balances of SDR 12.4 billion (Appendix II, Tables II.2 and II.3).

During 1997/98, four new Extended Arrangements with commitments totaling SDR 2.8 billion were approved for Argentina, Pakistan, Panama, and Yemen, with the arrangement for Argentina (SDR 2.1 billion) the largest approved during the year.[20] In addition, the Extended Arrangement for the Philippines was augmented by SDR 0.3 billion. The Extended Arrangements for Pakistan and Yemen were approved in conjunction with ESAF Arrangements. As of April 30, 1998, 13 countries had Extended Arrangements, with commitments totaling SDR 12.3 billion and undrawn balances of SDR 6.8 billion (Appendix II, Tables II.2 and II.4).

Overall, new commitments of IMF resources under Stand-By and Extended Arrangements amounted to SDR 30.4 billion (including the augmentation of the Extended Arrangement for the Philippines) in 1997/98. Of this total, nearly 90 percent was approved for Asian countries directly affected by the regional financial crisis.

Special Facilities and Outright Purchases
The IMF's special facilities consist of the CCFF and the Buffer Stock Financing Facility. The latter has not been used since 1983. During 1997/98, no member used the CCFF. At a meeting in November 1997, Directors suggested that the merits of the CCFF be reviewed. Three countries (Albania, Rwanda, and Tajikistan) made purchases totaling SDR 30 million under the IMF's policy on emergency postconflict assistance in 1997/98.

SAF and ESAF
The IMF continued to provide concessional financial support to low-income countries under the ESAF in 1997/98.[21] Eight new ESAF Arrangements with commitments totaling SDR 1.7 billion were approved

---

[19]The authorities of Cape Verde, Estonia, Latvia, the Philippines, and Uruguay indicated their intention not to draw under their respective arrangements, which were precautionary.

[20]The Argentine authorities indicated their intention not to draw under the arrangement, which was precautionary.

[21]The SAF has been phased out; the last annual SAF Arrangement expired in December 1996.

Table 12
Selected Financial Indicators
(Millions of SDRs)

	Financial Year Ended April 30								
	1990	1991	1992	1993	1994	1995	1996	1997	1998
	During Period								
Total disbursements	**5,266**	**6,823**	**5,903**	**5,877**	**5,903**	**11,178**	**12,303**	**5,644**	**19,924**
Purchases by facility (GRA)[1]	4,440	6,248	5,294	5,284	5,241	10,592	10,826	4,939	18,951
Stand-By and first credit tranche	1,183	1,975	2,343	2,940	1,052	7,587	9,127	1,836	16,127
Extended Fund Facility	2,449	2,146	1,571	2,254	746	1,595	1,554	2,820	2,824
Compensatory and Contingency Financing Facility	808	2,127	1,381	90	718	287	9	282	—
Systemic Transformation Facility	—	—	—	—	2,725	1,123	136	—	—
Loans under SAF/ESAF arrangements	826	575	608	593	662	587	1,477	705	973
Special Disbursement Account resources	584	180	138	49	68	19	185	—	—
ESAF Trust resources	242	395	470	544	594	568	1,292	705	973
By region	5,267	6,823	5,903	5,877	5,903	11,178	12,303	5,644	19,924
Africa	1,289	577	740	377	1,185	1,022	2,304	992	876
Asia	525	1,714	1,476	1,806	690	383	367	181	16,446
Europe	268	1,960	1,516	1,343	3,258	2,896	5,156	3,381	2,170
Middle East	66	—	333	26	11	76	129	153	148
Western Hemisphere	3,119	2,572	1,838	2,325	758	6,801	4,427	937	283
Repurchases and repayments	**6,399**	**5,608**	**4,770**	**4,117**	**4,509**	**4,231**	**7,100**	**7,196**	**4,385**
Repurchases	6,042	5,440	4,768	4,081	4,343	3,984	6,698	6,668	3,789
Trust Fund and SAF/ESAF loan repayments	357	168	2	36	166	247	402	528	596
	End of Period								
Total outstanding credit provided by IMF	**24,388**	**25,603**	**26,736**	**28,496**	**29,889**	**36,837**	**42,040**	**40,488**	**56,026**
Of which:									
General Resources Account	22,098	22,906	23,432	24,635	25,533	32,140	36,268	34,539	49,701
Special Disbursement Account	1,549	1,729	1,865	1,879	1,835	1,651	1,545	1,220	922
Administered accounts									
Trust Fund	326	158	158	158	105	102	95	90	90
ESAF Trust[2]	416	811	1,281	1,824	2,416	2,944	4,132	4,639	5,314
Percentage change in total outstanding credit	−4	5	4	7	5	23	14	−4	38
Number of indebted countries	87	81	82	90	93	99	97	95	94

[1]Excludes reserve tranche purchases.
[2]Includes Saudi Fund for Development associated loans.

in 1997/98 (for Cameroon, Côte d'Ivoire, Mongolia, Nicaragua, Pakistan, Senegal, Uganda, and Yemen) (Appendix II, Tables II.1 and II.5). As of April 30, 1998, 33 ESAF Arrangements were in effect. Cumulative commitments under all approved SAF and ESAF Arrangements (excluding undisbursed amounts under expired and canceled arrangements) totaled SDR 10.3 billion as of April 30, 1998,[22] compared with SDR 8.8 billion a year earlier. Total ESAF disbursements amounted to SDR 1.0 billion during 1997/98, com-

pared with SDR 0.7 billion in 1996/97; cumulative SAF and ESAF disbursements through April 30, 1998 amounted to SDR 8.1 billion.

The ESAF has been financed mainly from contributions in the form of loans and grants by member countries to the ESAF Trust, administered by the IMF, and also from SAF resources in the Special Disbursement Account (SDA). SAF resources were made available in conjunction with loans from the ESAF Trust until February 1994, when the Board decided to cease approving new commitments of SAF resources under ESAF Arrangements. As of April 30, 1998, total disbursements of SDA resources under SAF and ESAF Arrangements amounted to SDR 2.2 billion.

---

[22]Cumulative commitments under the SAF amounted to SDR 1.8 billion, while cumulative ESAF commitments amounted to SDR 8.5 billion.

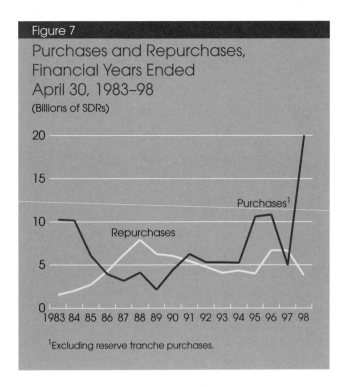

Figure 7

Purchases and Repurchases, Financial Years Ended April 30, 1983–98

(Billions of SDRs)

[1]Excluding reserve tranche purchases.

The enlarged and extended ESAF Trust, which became effective on February 23, 1994, has a target for total loan resources of SDR 10.1 billion. Financing toward this goal has been provided by a broad cross-section of the IMF's membership. Total effective commitments by lenders to the ESAF Trust amounted to SDR 9.7 billion as of April 30, 1998. The commitment period for ESAF Trust loans to eligible members runs through December 31, 2000, with disbursements to be made through the end of 2003.

Contributions to the Subsidy Account enable loans from the ESAF Trust to be provided at a highly concessional rate of interest (currently 0.5 percent a year). The total value of bilateral subsidy contributions is estimated at SDR 3.7 billion. In addition, the Board transferred SDR 0.4 billion from the SDA to the Subsidy Account in early 1994. This contribution by the IMF, including the interest it will earn, is valued at SDR 0.6 billion.

The availability of resources in the Subsidy Account, net of subsidies already paid, rose from SDR 1,562 million as of April 30, 1997, to SDR 1,629 million as of April 30, 1998. The ESAF Trust made interest payments of SDR 172 million to lenders in 1997/98, of which SDR 23 million was financed by payments of interest by borrowers from the Trust and the balance of SDR 149 million was drawn from the resources of the Subsidy Account.

Details of SAF and ESAF arrangements, and of borrowing agreements and subsidy contributions for the ESAF Trust, are provided in Appendix II (Tables II.1, II.5, and II.10).

ESAF-HIPC Trust

The ESAF-HIPC Trust was established in February 1997 to make grants or loans, or both, to eligible members that qualify for assistance under the Initiative for Heavily Indebted Poor Countries (HIPC) and to subsidize the interest rate on interim ESAF operations to ESAF-eligible members (see Chapter IX). Contributions to the Trust have been received from six countries. To proceed quickly with the implementation of the HIPC Initiative, the Board amended the ESAF Trust Instrument to permit the transfer of up to SDR 250 million from the Reserve Account of the ESAF Trust to the SDA for financing special ESAF operations, provided other resources are not available. All creditors to the Loan Account of the ESAF Trust consented to such a transfer. In addition, to augment the resources available in the ESAF-HIPC Trust, the Board decided to forgo the reimbursement to the GRA of the costs of administering the ESAF Trust in 1997/98 and to transfer SDR 40.7 million from the ESAF Trust Reserve Account to the ESAF-HIPC Trust. The Board also decided that no reimbursement would be made to the GRA in 1998/99 and authorized quarterly transfers totaling an estimated SDR 45 million from the ESAF Trust Reserve Account to the ESAF-HIPC Trust.

In April 1998, Uganda reached its completion point under the HIPC Initiative and SDR 51.5 million was disbursed in the form of a grant, which is being held in an administered account to be used to service a part of Uganda's debt to the IMF under a schedule agreed with the Ugandan authorities.[23] Resources available to the ESAF-HIPC Trust from bilateral contributions (including accrued interest) amounted to SDR 3.6 million at the end of April 1998.

IMF Income, Charges, and Burden Sharing

At the beginning of each financial year, the IMF sets the rate of charge on the use of its resources as a proportion of the weekly SDR interest rate to achieve a target amount of net income to add to its reserves. This method of setting the rate of charge has been in use for a number of years. By ensuring that its operational income closely reflects its operational costs, which depend largely on the SDR interest rate, the IMF tries to minimize the possible need for a discrete increase in the rate of charge during the financial year.

---

[23]On April 7, 1998, the IMF established the "Umbrella Account for HIPC Operations" to receive and administer resources on behalf of eligible member countries that qualify for assistance under the terms of the ESAF-HIPC Trust. Within the umbrella account, the IMF will establish an individual subaccount for each member receiving resources from the ESAF-HIPC Trust. These resources were used to meet part of the member's debt-service payments on existing debt to the IMF.

In April 1997, the proportion of the rate of charge to the SDR interest rate for 1997/98 was set at 109.6 percent to achieve a net income target of SDR 99 million—or 5 percent of the IMF's reserves at the beginning of the financial year—with the proviso that any income in excess of the target (excluding operational income generated from the use of credit under the SRF, discussed below) be used to reduce retroactively the proportion of the rate of charge for the year. Following a review of the IMF's income position at midyear, the proportion of the rate of charge to the SDR interest rate was reduced retroactively to 107.0 percent for 1997/98, and SDR 31 million was returned to members that had paid charges through the third quarter of the financial year. Furthermore, at the end of the financial year, after actual income exceeding the target of SDR 22 million had been returned to members that paid charges during the year, the proportion of the rate of charge to the SDR interest rate was reduced retroactively to 105.6 percent for 1997/98. The average rate of charge on the use of IMF resources in 1997/98 was 4.41 percent, before adjustments for burden sharing, which are discussed below (Appendix II, Table II.14).

As described above, in December 1997, the IMF established the Supplemental Reserve Facility. The IMF levies a surcharge, in addition to the regular rate of charge, on the use of credit under the SRF. During the first year from the date of approval of financing under this facility, the surcharge is set at 300 basis points above the basic rate of charge; it increases by an additional 50 basis points at the end of the first year, and every six months thereafter, until the surcharge reaches 500 basis points. Net operational income generated from the use of credit under the SRF during 1997/98, after meeting the expenses of administering the ESAF Trust, amounted to SDR 65 million, which was placed to the General Reserve.

The IMF pays remuneration to a member on the amount by which its norm for remuneration exceeds the IMF's holdings of its currency, excluding holdings that reflect the member's use of IMF credit. The norm for remuneration is calculated as the sum of 75 percent of the member's quota on April 1, 1978, plus any increases in quota consented to and paid after that date. For members joining the IMF after April 1, 1978, the norm is calculated as the sum of (1) a percentage of

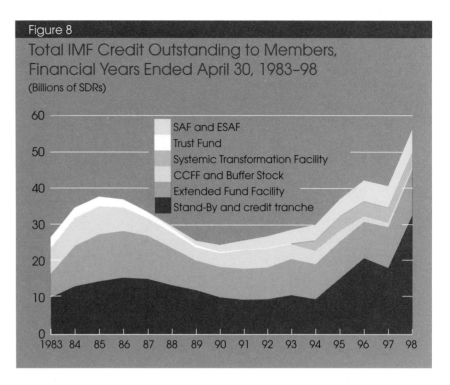

Figure 8

Total IMF Credit Outstanding to Members, Financial Years Ended April 30, 1983–98

(Billions of SDRs)

- SAF and ESAF
- Trust Fund
- Systemic Transformation Facility
- CCFF and Buffer Stock
- Extended Fund Facility
- Stand-By and credit tranche

the member's quota equal to the weighted average of the norms of all existing members relative to quota on the date of the member's admission, and (2) any increases in the member's quota consented to and paid after that date. The rate of remuneration, before the adjustments under the burden-sharing mechanisms discussed below, is set at 100 percent of the SDR interest rate, which averaged 4.18 percent in 1997/98.

The IMF continues to have measures in place to strengthen its financial position, in view of the existence of overdue financial obligations. First, a target amount of net income is determined each year to be added to IMF reserves, which provide protection against administrative deficits and losses of a capital nature. Second, debtor and creditor members share equally—through adjustments to the rate of charge and the rate of remuneration—the financial costs to the IMF of deferred overdue charges and of the allocation to the first Special Contingent Account (SCA-1), which, for 1997/98, was set at 5 percent of reserves at the beginning of the year (SDR 99 million). These adjustments, however, cannot reduce the rate of remuneration to less than 85 percent of the SDR interest rate. The SCA-1 was established as a precautionary measure to protect the IMF against the risks associated with overdue obligations; as of April 30, 1998, SCA-1 balances amounted to SDR 884 million. These burden-sharing procedures have been extended by the Board through 1998/99.

As part of the strengthened cooperative strategy to resolve the problem of protracted overdue financial

Table 13

Arrears to the IMF of Countries with Obligations Overdue by Six Months or More

(Millions of SDRs; end of period)

	Financial Year Ended April 30					
	1993	1994	1995	1996	1997	1998
Amount of overdue obligations	3,006.4	2,911.3	2,982.6	2,174.9	2,212.2	2,261.2
Number of countries	12	9	8	6	7	7
Of which:						
General Department	2,767.9	2,729.2	2,808.8	2,001.3	2,023.1	2,066.5
Number of countries	11	8	7	5	5	5
SDR Department	50.2	51.7	46.6	53.4	73.3	79.1
Number of countries	12	9	8	6	7	7
Trust Fund	188.3	130.4	127.2	120.2	115.8	115.6
Number of countries	6	4	4	3	3	3
Number of ineligible members	7	5	5	4	4	4

adjustments to the basic rate of charge of 18 basis points and to the rate of remuneration of 21 basis points during 1997/98. The adjusted rate of charge and the adjusted rate of remuneration averaged 4.59 percent and 3.97 percent, respectively, during the financial year.

Following the retroactive reductions of charges totaling SDR 53 million, net income of SDR 164 million for 1997/98 was placed to the IMF's reserves, of which SDR 65 million was placed to the General Reserve. Total reserves increased to SDR 2.1 billion as of April 30, 1998, from SDR 2.0 billion a year earlier. For 1998/99, the Board agreed to set the proportion of the rate of charge to the SDR interest rate at 107 percent, so as to achieve a target amount of net income of SDR 107 million, in addition to the amount of net income generated under the SRF.

Precautionary balances generally available to protect the IMF's financial position against the consequences of overdue repurchases in the GRA—that is, reserves plus the balances in the SCA-1—totaled SDR 3.0 billion as of April 30, 1998, equivalent to 293 percent of outstanding GRA credit to member countries in arrears to the IMF by six months or more (SDR 1.0 billion). Total precautionary balances—reserves and the balances in the two Special Contingent Accounts—amounted to SDR 4.0 billion, equivalent to 8.1 percent of total outstanding GRA credit as of April 30, 1998.

In April 1998, the Board considered the level and adequacy of the IMF's precautionary balances. In reaching a judgment on the adequacy and the appropriate rate of accumulation of precautionary balances, Directors were guided by two general principles: precautionary balances should cover fully the credit outstanding to members in protracted arrears to the IMF; and precautionary balances should include a margin for the risk exposure related to credit extended to members currently meeting their payment obligations to the IMF in a timely manner. After taking into account the significant expansion of outstanding IMF credit during 1997/98—and such qualitative factors as the strength and perseverance of members' adjustment programs and members' progress toward medium-term balance of payments viability—Directors agreed to accelerate the rate of accumulation of the IMF's precautionary balances. As mentioned above, the rate of charge for 1998/99 was set at 107 percent of the SDR interest rate to generate non-SRF income of SDR 107 million, equivalent to 5 percent of the IMF's reserves at the beginning of the financial year, and an equal amount is

obligations to the IMF, extended burden-sharing arrangements were established in July 1990 that provided for further adjustments to the rate of charge and the rate of remuneration. The additional precautionary balances generated under these arrangements were placed to a second Special Contingent Account (SCA-2). The SCA-2 was established as a safeguard against potential losses on credit extended from the GRA under a successor arrangement, following successful completion of a "rights accumulation program" (under which a country in protracted arrears accumulates "rights" to future IMF purchases through its adjustment and reform efforts; see next section), and also to provide additional liquidity for financing the encashment of accumulated rights. The adjustments under the extended burden-sharing arrangements ended in 1996/97, after the target amount of SDR 1 billion had been accumulated in the SCA-2.

Settlements of overdue charges previously deferred amounted to SDR 6.5 million in 1997/98, of which SDR 1.2 million had given rise to burden-sharing adjustments. When deferred charges that have resulted in burden-sharing adjustments are settled, an equivalent amount is refunded to the members that paid additional charges or received reduced remuneration. Cumulative refunds amounted to SDR 961.9 million as of April 30, 1998. Balances in the SCA-1 will be returned to contributors when all overdue financial obligations have been settled or at such earlier time as the IMF may decide. Balances in the SCA-2 will be returned when all outstanding purchases related to the encashment of rights have been repurchased or at such earlier time as the IMF may decide.

Unpaid charges due by members in protracted arrears and contributions to the SCA-1 resulted in

Table 14

Arrears to the IMF of Countries with Obligations Overdue by Six Months or More, by Type and Duration, as of April 30, 1998

(Millions of SDRs)

| | | By Type | | | By Duration | | | |
	Total	General Department (incl. SAF)	SDR Department	Trust Fund	Less than one year	1–2 years	2–3 years	3 years or more
Afghanistan, Islamic State of	2.5	—	2.5	—	1.2	1.1	0.3	—
Congo, Democratic Republic of the	334.0	328.6	5.4	—	35.0	34.9	29.5	234.7
Iraq	33.0	—	33.0	—	4.1	3.7	4.1	21.1
Liberia	454.6	407.4	16.4	30.8	10.9	10.4	11.2	421.9
Somalia	194.3	180.4	6.2	7.7	6.2	6.9	7.3	173.9
Sudan	1,156.2	1,079.0	0.1	77.1	25.4	25.2	29.0	1,076.6
Yugoslavia, Federal Republic of (Serbia/Montenegro)	86.6	71.1	15.5	—	5.5	9.1	9.7	62.3
Total	2,261.2	2,066.5	79.1	115.6	88.3	91.3	91.2	1,990.3

to be added to the SCA-1. Furthermore, net operational income from the SRF for 1998/99, after meeting the expenses of administering the ESAF Trust, will be placed to the IMF's General Reserve at the end of the financial year.

Overdue Financial Obligations

The level of outstanding overdue financial obligations to the IMF increased slightly in 1997/98 to SDR 2.3 billion on April 30, 1998, from SDR 2.2 billion a year earlier.[24] There were no new cases of protracted arrears in 1997/98, and the number of countries in arrears to the IMF by six months or more remained at seven. Selected data on arrears to the IMF are shown in Table 13, and further information on countries' overdue obligations by type and duration is shown in Table 14.

As of April 30, 1998, four countries were ineligible to use the general resources of the IMF, pursuant to declarations under Article XXVI, Section 2 (a)—the Democratic Republic of the Congo (formerly Zaïre), Liberia, Somalia, and Sudan. These four countries accounted for 95 percent of total overdue obligations to the IMF on that date. Declarations of noncooperation—a further step under the strengthened cooperative strategy (see below)—were in effect with respect to three countries: the Democratic Republic of the Congo (issued February 14, 1992), Liberia (March 30, 1990), and Sudan (September 14, 1990). The voting rights of two countries remained suspended in 1997/98: the Democratic Republic of the Congo (effective June 2, 1994) and Sudan (August 9, 1993).

---

[24]The data in this section include the overdue financial obligations of the Federal Republic of Yugoslavia (Serbia/Montenegro), which has not yet completed arrangements for succession to IMF membership.

Progress Under the Strengthened Cooperative Strategy

The strengthened cooperative strategy to resolve the problem of protracted overdue obligations to the IMF has been in effect since May 1990. The three key elements of the strategy—prevention, intensified collaboration, and remedial measures—continued to be implemented in 1997/98 to prevent the emergence of new arrears and to help overdue countries find solutions to their arrears problems.

The main *preventive element* against the emergence of new arrears is the specification and implementation of a strong and comprehensive macroeconomic adjustment program supported by an IMF arrangement. Such a program would include appropriate conditionality with respect to the use of IMF resources, technical assistance in the formulation and implementation of the program, and the assurance, through multilateral efforts as necessary, of adequate financing in support of the program. In addition, assessments of member countries' medium-term balance of payments viability and capacity to repay the IMF play an important role.

The *intensified collaborative aspect* of the arrears strategy was designed to help cooperating member countries in arrears to the IMF resolve their arrears problems. It provides a framework for members in arrears to establish a strong track record of policy performance and payments to the IMF, and in turn, to mobilize bilateral and multilateral financial support for their adjustment efforts and to clear arrears to the IMF and other creditors. Pursuit of the intensified collaborative approach, including use of the rights approach described below, has succeeded in resolving several cases of members with large and protracted arrears. It has also contributed to an improvement in policy performance and payments to the IMF by some other overdue members.

The rights approach, established in 1990, allows an eligible member (limited to the 11 members that were in protracted arrears to the IMF at the end of 1989) to establish a track record of policy performance and payments to the IMF to serve as a basis for the accumulation of "rights" to disbursements from the IMF under a subsequent arrangement following the clearance of arrears to the IMF. In light of the risks associated with large disbursements to countries previously in protracted arrears, the SCA-2 was established as an added precautionary measure and to provide additional liquidity to assist in the financing of encashments of rights under arrangements in the GRA. To allay concerns about access to ESAF resources by these countries, the IMF pledged to mobilize up to three million ounces of gold, in respect of encashments of rights under ESAF arrangements, in the event of a potential shortfall in resources available to meet ESAF Trust obligations.

The deadline for entry into a rights accumulation program has been extended on a number of occasions. Most recently, in March 1998, the Board agreed to extend the availability of the rights approach until the spring 1999 meeting of the Interim Committee. The rights approach was instrumental in the clearance of arrears and normalization of IMF relations with three members—Peru, Sierra Leone, and Zambia. Five other rights-eligible members—Cambodia, Guyana, Honduras, Panama, and Vietnam—settled their arrears without recourse to the rights approach. Of the 11 rights-eligible countries, Liberia, Somalia, and Sudan continue to have outstanding overdue obligations to the IMF.

The preventive and collaborative elements of the arrears strategy are complemented by *remedial measures* that seek to protect the IMF's resources from further use by members in arrears and set in motion a concerted effort to resolve the problems of those members. These measures consist of concrete actions to be taken on the basis of a specified timetable. This timetable provides a framework for the Board's consideration of various measures, which are implemented if the Board considers that, taking into account the particular circumstances of the case, the member concerned is not cooperating with the IMF in addressing the problem of its overdue obligations.

When a member country has been in arrears to the IMF for a month, the Managing Director notifies the Board concerning the member's overdue financial obligations. Six such notifications were issued in 1997/98. In five of these cases, the arrears were cleared before the issuance of a complaint, which occurs after arrears have been outstanding for two months. Prior to the issuance of a complaint, when a member has been in arrears for six weeks, the Managing Director is to consult with and recommend to the Board that a com-munication concerning the member's situation be sent to all, or selected, IMF Governors. Two such consultations took place in 1997/98. In the event, as the arrears that gave rise to one of them were cleared shortly thereafter, only one set of telexes was sent to selected Governors. A complaint (with regard to arrears in the General Department) was subsequently issued under Rule K-1 with respect to this member. This complaint was withdrawn following clearance of the member's arrears in October 1997.

The Board reviewed Liberia's overdue obligations to the IMF on March 2, 1998, for the first time in three years, following an improvement in the political and security situation in Liberia. The Board decided not to proceed with the next step under the timetable of remedial measures—namely, initiating the procedure on suspending the member's voting rights—in light of Liberia's recent efforts to cooperate with the IMF, including making regular monthly payments to the IMF, and the authorities' commitment to implement further policy reforms in the period ahead. The Board decided to review Liberia's overdue obligations again within six months.

The Board reviewed the decision suspending the voting rights of the Democratic Republic of the Congo on two occasions during 1997/98. At the most recent review, on March 18, 1998, the Board regretted the further increase in the Democratic Republic of the Congo's arrears to the IMF and noted the intention of the authorities to resume payments to the IMF; the Board urged the authorities to finalize agreement with the staff on a schedule of regular monthly payments. While the Board welcomed the authorities' recent policy efforts, it urged them to maintain a close policy dialogue with the staff with a view to formulating, as early as conditions permitted, a comprehensive adjustment and reform program that could be monitored by the staff. The Board decided to review the Democratic Republic of the Congo's overdue obligations to the IMF again by June 29, 1998; at that time, it would consider initiating the procedure on compulsory withdrawal, unless the Congo had resumed cooperation with the IMF in the areas of policy implementation and payments performance.

Compulsory withdrawal is the final and most severe sanction in the scale of remedial measures. In the case of Sudan, which has the largest and most protracted arrears to the IMF, the procedure for compulsory withdrawal was initiated on April 8, 1994, with a complaint issued by the Managing Director. The Board considered this complaint on two occasions during 1997/98. At the most recent review, on February 27, 1998, the Board again deferred action on a recommendation to the Board of Governors, in the light of Sudan's regular monthly payments to the IMF and continued satisfactory implementation of the program of economic adjustment presented to the IMF in 1997; its adoption of a strengthened program for 1998 to be monitored by the IMF staff; and its proposed payments schedule for 1998, which would lead to a further reduction in Sudan's arrears to the IMF. The decision provided that the next review of the Managing Director's complaint with respect to Sudan's compulsory withdrawal would be held within 12 months, or at the next Article IV consultation, whichever was earlier. The Board further decided that if Sudan failed to continue its satisfactory performance, the Board would meet promptly to review the situation and recommend compulsory withdrawal to the Board of Governors. The Board encouraged Sudan to enter into discussions with IMF staff on measures to extend and broaden the staff-monitored program and to make all efforts to increase payments to the IMF and to regularize relations with other creditors, as the basis for closer cooperation with the IMF in the medium term.

SDR Department

The SDR is an international reserve asset created by the IMF under the First Amendment to its Articles of Agreement to supplement existing reserve assets. First allocated in January 1970, total SDR allocations amount to SDR 21.4 billion. SDRs are held largely by IMF member countries—all of which are participants in the SDR Department—with the balance held in the IMF's General Resources Account and by official entities prescribed by the IMF to hold SDRs. Prescribed holders do not receive SDR allocations, but they can acquire and use SDRs in transactions and operations with participants in the SDR Department and with other prescribed holders under the same terms and conditions as participants. During 1997/98, the number of prescribed holders remained unchanged at 15.[25]

The SDR is the unit of account for IMF operations and transactions. It is also used as a unit of account, or the basis for a unit of account, by a number of other international and regional organizations and international conventions. In addition, to a very limited extent, the SDR has been used to denominate financial instruments created outside the IMF by the private sector (private SDRs). At the end of 1997/98, the currencies of four member countries were pegged to the SDR.

Following a broad review of the role and functions of the SDR in the light of changes in the world financial system, and to ensure that all participants in the SDR Department would receive an equitable share of cumu-

---

[25]Prescribed holders of SDRs are the African Development Bank, African Development Fund, Arab Monetary Fund, Asian Development Bank, Bank of Central African States, Bank for International Settlements, Central Bank of West African States, East African Development Bank, Eastern Caribbean Central Bank, International Bank for Reconstruction and Development, International Development Association, International Fund for Agricultural Development, Islamic Development Bank, Latin American Reserve Fund, and Nordic Investment Bank.

Table 15
SDR Valuation Basket
(As of January 1, 1996)

Currency	Percentage Weight	Amount of Currency Units
U.S. dollar	39	0.582
Deutsche mark	21	0.446
Japanese yen	18	27.2
French franc	11	0.813
Pound sterling	11	0.105

lative SDR allocations, the Board of Governors adopted a resolution in September 1997 proposing a Fourth Amendment to the IMF's Articles of Agreement.[26] If approved by the membership, the amendment would provide the authority under Article XV for a special one-time allocation of SDR 21.4 billion, which would raise all participants' ratios of cumulative SDR allocations to quota under the Ninth General Review of Quotas to a common benchmark ratio of 29.315788813 percent. Appendix II, Table II.11 shows the amount of SDRs each participant will be eligible to receive under the special allocation. The proposed amendment, which will become effective when approved by three-fifths of the members having 85 percent of the total voting power, also provides for future participants to receive a special allocation following the later of (1) the date of their participation or (2) the effective date of the Fourth Amendment. The proposed amendment would not affect the IMF's existing power to allocate SDRs based on a finding of a long-term global need to supplement reserves as and when that need arises.

SDR Valuation and Interest Rate Basket

Since January 1, 1981, the value of, and interest rate on, the SDR has been based on a basket of five currencies. In September 1995, the Board reviewed the valuation of the SDR, and the valuation basket was revised effective January 1, 1996. The currencies included in the current basket, which are those of the five member countries with the largest exports of goods and services during the five-year period ended one year prior to the date of the revision, are the same as those in the previous basket. The weights of the currencies were modified, however, to reflect changes in their relative importance in international trade and reserves, as measured by the value of exports of goods and services of the countries issuing them and the balances of the currencies held as reserves by members of the IMF. The initial weights and the corresponding amounts of each of the five currencies in the revised basket are shown in Table 15.

---

[26]See Appendix III.

Table 16
Transfers of SDRs
(In millions of SDRs)

	Annual Averages[1]					Financial Years Ended April 30			1/1/70–
	1/1/70– 4/30/78	5/1/78– 4/30/81	5/1/81– 4/30/83	5/1/83– 4/30/87	5/1/87– 4/30/95	1996	1997	1998	4/30/98
Transfers among participants and prescribed holders									
Transactions with designation									
From own holdings	221	294	815	165	—	—	—	—	5,016
From purchase of SDRs from IMF	43	1,150	1,479	1,744	123	—	—	—	14,727
Transactions by agreement	439	771	1,262	3,121	6,031	8,931	7,411	8,567	94,132
Prescribed operations	—	—	277	520	1,156	1,951	88	86	14,009
IMF-related operations	—	—	—	43	244	704	606	901	4,335
Net interest on SDRs	42	161	259	285	345	319	268	284	6,116
Total	744	2,377	4,092	5,878	7,899	11,905	8,372	9,893	138,336
Transfers from participants to General Resources Account									
Repurchases	306	809	702	991	1,695	5,572	4,364	2,918	36,756
Charges	259	620	1,233	2,574	1,766	1,985	1,616	1,877	36,386
Quota payments	24	1,703	175	1,591	1,625	70	—	—	25,097
Interest received on General Resources Account holdings	16	135	551	307	136	53	51	44	4,102
Assessments	1	1	2	4	4	4	4	4	75
Total	606	3,269	2,662	5,466	5,226	7,683	6,035	4,844	102,417
Transfers from General Resources Account to participants and prescribed holders									
Purchases	208	1,474	2,227	2,554	2,631	6,460	4,060	4,243	56,629
Repayments of IMF borrowings	—	88	86	614	1,091	—	—	—	11,620
Interest on IMF borrowings	4	27	183	443	254	—	—	—	4,286
In exchange for other members' currencies									
Acquisitions to pay charges	—	3	95	896	324	49	224	20	6,666
Acquisitions to make quota payments	—	114	—	—	—	—	—	—	341
Reconstitution	175	33	—	—	—	—	—	—	1,551
Remuneration	26	165	604	1,536	987	1,092	1,055	1,220	19,333
Other	29	7	22	17	59	259	27	90	1,226
Total	442	1,911	3,217	6,059	5,346	7,859	5,366	5,574	101,655
Total transfers	1,792	7,556	9,971	17,404	18,472	27,448	19,773	20,256	342,408
General Resources Account holdings at end of period	1,371	5,445	4,335	1,960	1,001	825	1,494	764	764

[1]The first column covers the period from the creation of the SDR until the Second Amendment to the Articles of Agreement; the second column covers the period of the SDR allocations in the third basic period and the Seventh General Review quota increases; after an intervening period represented by the third column, the fourth column covers the period of the Eighth General Review quota increases and before the introduction of the two-way arrangements to facilitate transactions by agreement; and the fifth column covers, except for the three most recent financial years, the period since the designation mechanism became of a precautionary nature.

Since August 1, 1983, the SDR interest rate has been calculated weekly as a weighted average of interest rates on selected short-term instruments in the five countries whose currencies are included in the valuation basket. With effect from January 1, 1991, the interest rates and instruments are the market yield on three-month treasury bills in the United States and the United Kingdom, the three-month interbank deposit rate in Germany, the three-month rate on certificates of deposit in Japan, and the three-month rate for treasury bills in France.

SDR Transactions and Operations
Total transfers of SDRs in 1997/98 increased slightly to SDR 20.3 billion from SDR 19.8 billion in 1996/97. An increase in transfers among participants and prescribed holders (SDR 1.5 billion) more than offset a decline in transfers involving the GRA

(SDR 1.0 billion). Contributing to the increase in transfers among participants and prescribed holders was a significant reduction in the SDR holdings of prescribed holders. Summary data on transfers of SDRs by participants, the GRA, and prescribed holders are presented in Table 16 (see also Appendix II, Table II.12).

Transfers of SDRs from participants to the GRA fell to SDR 4.8 billion in 1997/98 from SDR 6.0 billion in 1996/97, reflecting mainly a fall in repurchase obligations discharged in SDRs to SDR 2.9 billion in 1997/98 from SDR 4.4 billion in 1996/97. Because the expansion of credit outstanding took place in the second half of the financial year, charges paid in SDRs increased only slightly, to SDR 1.9 billion in 1997/98 from SDR 1.6 billion in 1996/97.

Transfers of SDRs from the GRA to participants and prescribed holders were constrained by the lower receipts of SDRs from participants, but rose slightly to SDR 5.6 billion in 1997/98 from SDR 5.4 billion in 1996/97. Members' purchases made in SDRs of SDR 4.2 billion represented the largest category of transfer, followed by remuneration payments of SDR 1.2 billion to members with creditor positions.

Transfers among participants and prescribed holders rose to SDR 9.8 billion in 1997/98, from SDR 8.4 billion in 1996/97, largely reflecting increases in transactions by agreement and in IMF-related operations.[27] Transactions by agreement totaled SDR 8.6 billion during 1997/98, compared with SDR 7.4 billion in 1996/97. Participants continued to acquire substantial amounts of SDRs in transactions by agreement in order to discharge their financial obligations to the IMF; they also sold in transactions by agreement most of the SDRs they received in purchases and ESAF loan disbursements. For the most part, transactions by agreement continued to be conducted with the assistance of 12 members with standing arrangements with the IMF to buy or sell SDRs for one or more freely usable currencies at any time provided that their SDR holdings remained within certain limits. These "two-way" arrangements accommodated a very substantial propor-

---

[27]IMF-related operations are those between members and the IMF conducted through the intermediary of a prescribed holder.

Box 16
Designation Plan

Article XIX of the IMF's Articles of Agreement provides for a designation mechanism under which participants whose balance of payments and reserve positions are deemed sufficiently strong are obliged, when designated by the IMF, to provide freely usable currencies in exchange for SDRs up to specified amounts. The designation mechanism ensures that, in case of need, participants can use their SDRs to obtain freely usable currencies at short notice. To ensure that such use is not for the sole purpose of changing the composition of reserves, a participant wishing to sell SDRs in a transaction with designation is required to make a representation to the IMF that it has a need to use its SDRs.

The designation mechanism is executed through quarterly designation plans, approved by the Board, which list participants subject to designation and set maximum limits to the amounts of SDRs that they can be designated to receive during the quarter.

Apart from a participant being "sufficiently strong" for designation, the amounts of designation for individual participants are determined in a manner that over time promotes equality in the "excess holdings ratios" of participants (i.e., SDR holdings above or below allocations as a proportion of participants' official gold and foreign exchange reserves).

Since September 1987, there have been no transactions with designation because potential exchanges of SDRs for currencies have been accommodated through voluntary transactions by agreement with other participants, primarily the 12 participants that have established with the IMF standing arrangements to buy or sell SDRs for one or more freely usable currencies at any time, provided that their SDR holdings remain within a certain range. These arrangements have helped accommodate members' desires to both buy and sell SDRs and have facilitated the circulation of SDRs in the system.

---

tion of desired acquisitions and sales of SDRs, obviating the need for recourse to the designation mechanism (Box 16). In this regard, the reduction in the holdings of prescribed holders during the year (by SDR 0.9 billion) was accommodated largely through transactions by agreement with members with two-way arrangements and had the effect of making more SDRs available for use by participants. Despite the improved supply of SDRs for transactions by agreement, requests for acquisitions totaling SDR 0.2 billion by a number of participants could not be met as of the end of the financial year. IMF-related operations, representing the use of SDRs in connection with the SAF and ESAF, increased to SDR 0.9 billion in 1997/98 from SDR 0.6 billion in 1996/97.

Pattern of SDR Holdings

The distribution of SDR holdings among various groups of holders changed somewhat in 1997/98, reflecting transfers during the year, with the IMF playing the major role in the circulation and redistribution of SDRs. In making transfers of SDRs under the quarterly operational budgets, the IMF has sought since early 1993 to maintain its SDR holdings in a range of SDR 1.0–1.5 billion by transferring each quarter the SDRs it receives to debtor members in connection with their purchases and to creditors in the payment of remuneration. To meet part of the substantial demand for use of IMF resources that developed in the second half of the year, the IMF reduced its SDR holdings to levels below the lower end of its target range, while maintaining adequate provisions for the payment of remuneration to its creditor members. The GRA held SDR 0.8 billion as of April 30, 1998.

Debtor countries received more SDRs in purchases from the IMF and in transactions by agreement than they sold to obtain freely usable currencies or used to meet their financial obligations to the IMF, resulting in an increase in their SDR holdings relative to their net cumulative allocations (Appendix II, Table II.13). In terms of net cumulative allocations, the SDR holdings of nonindustrial countries increased from 60.5 percent to 69.4 percent during 1997/98, while the holdings of industrial countries increased from 99.8 percent to 107.0 percent. The latter was mainly because the industrial countries absorbed the reduction in the holdings of prescribed holders, which decreased during 1997/98 from SDR 1.3 billion to SDR 0.4 billion, largely as a consequence of changes in the IMF's investments of SAF and ESAF resources in official SDRs maintained with the Bank for International Settlements.

Organization, Staffing, and Budget

The IMF's organizational structure is set out in its Articles of Agreement, which provide for a Board of Governors, an Executive Board, a Managing Director, and a staff of international civil servants. The Articles require that staff appointed to the IMF demonstrate the highest standards of efficiency and technical competence and reflect the organization's diverse membership.

Executive Board

As the IMF's permanent decision-making organ, its 24-member Executive Board, conducts the day-to-day business of the IMF. In 1997, the Board held 166 meetings, consisting of 132 formal discussions, 6 informal meetings, 6 seminars, and 22 private meetings.

The Executive Board carries out its work largely on the basis of papers prepared by IMF management and staff. In 1997, the Board spent 58 percent of its time on member country matters (Article IV consultations and reviews and approvals of arrangements) and 36 percent of its time on policy issues (such as the world economic outlook, developments in international capital markets, the IMF's financial resources, surveillance, data issues, the debt situation, and issues related to IMF facilities and program design).

Departments

The IMF staff is organized primarily in departments with regional (or area), functional, information and liaison, and support functions (Figure 9). These departments are headed by directors who report to the Managing Director.

Area Departments

Six area departments—*African, Asia and Pacific, European I, European II, Middle Eastern,* and *Western Hemisphere*—advise management and the Executive Board on economic developments and policies in countries in their region. Their staff also negotiate arrangements for the use of IMF financial resources and review performance under IMF-supported arrangements. Together with relevant functional departments, they provide member countries with pol-

icy advice and technical assistance and maintain contact with regional organizations and multilateral institutions in their geographic areas. Supplemented by staff in functional departments, area departments carry out much of the IMF's bilateral surveillance work through direct contacts with member countries. In addition, 70 area department staff members are assigned to member countries as IMF resident representatives (see Box 17).

Functional and Special Services Departments

The *Fiscal Affairs Department* is responsible for activities involving public finance in member countries. It participates in area department missions on fiscal issues, reviews the fiscal content of IMF policy advice and IMF-supported adjustment programs, and provides technical assistance in public finance. It also conducts research and policy studies on fiscal issues, as well as on income distribution and poverty, social safety nets, public expenditure policy issues, and the environment.

The *IMF Institute* provides training for officials of member countries—particularly developing countries—in such topics as financial programming and policy, external sector policies, balance of payments methodology, national accounts and government finance statistics, and public finance.

The *Legal Department* advises management, the Board, and the staff on the applicable rules of law. It prepares most of the decisions and other legal instruments necessary for the IMF's activities. The department serves as counsel to the IMF in litigation and arbitration cases, provides technical assistance on legislative reform, and responds to inquiries from national authorities and international organizations on the law of the IMF.

The *Monetary and Exchange Affairs Department* provides technical assistance to central banks in such areas as monetary and exchange rate policies, banking supervision, prudential regulation, and payment systems issues. It also assigns experts to central banks where long-term technical assistance is sought. In the

Figure 9

International Monetary Fund: Chart of Organization

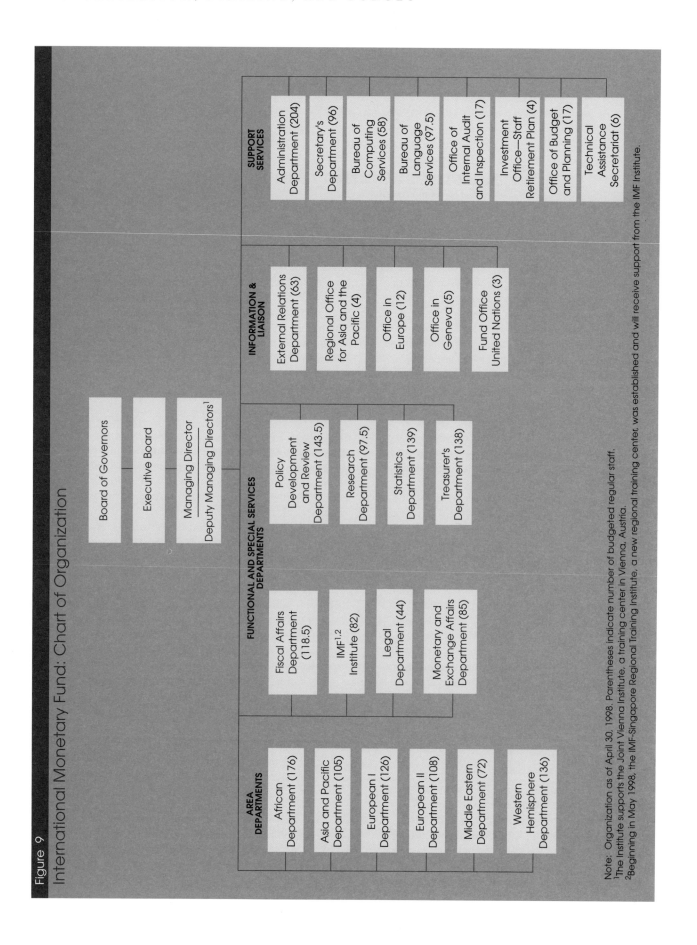

Board of Governors

Executive Board

Managing Director
Deputy Managing Directors[1]

AREA DEPARTMENTS

African Department (176)

Asia and Pacific Department (105)

European I Department (126)

European II Department (108)

Middle Eastern Department (72)

Western Hemisphere Department (136)

FUNCTIONAL AND SPECIAL SERVICES DEPARTMENTS

Fiscal Affairs Department (118.5)

IMF[1,2] Institute (82)

Legal Department (44)

Monetary and Exchange Affairs Department (85)

Policy Development and Review Department (143.5)

Research Department (97.5)

Statistics Department (139)

Treasurer's Department (138)

INFORMATION & LIAISON

External Relations Department (63)

Regional Office for Asia and the Pacific (4)

Office in Europe (12)

Office in Geneva (5)

Fund Office United Nations (3)

SUPPORT SERVICES

Administration Department (204)

Secretary's Department (96)

Bureau of Computing Services (58)

Bureau of Language Services (97.5)

Office of Internal Audit and Inspection (17)

Investment Office—Staff Retirement Plan (4)

Office of Budget and Planning (17)

Technical Assistance Secretariat (6)

Note: Organization as of April 30, 1998. Parentheses indicate number of budgeted regular staff.
[1]The Institute supports the Joint Vienna Institute, a training center in Vienna, Austria.
[2]Beginning in May 1998, the IMF-Singapore Regional Training Institute, a new regional training center, was established and will receive support from the IMF Institute.

context of surveillance and requests for the use of IMF resources, the Monetary and Exchange Affairs Department works with area departments in its areas of expertise. It also contributes to the exercise of IMF jurisdiction on exchange practices and restrictions.

The *Policy Development and Review Department* plays a central role in the design and implementation of IMF financial facilities and operations, in surveillance policies, and in other areas. Together with the Research Department, it takes the lead in multilateral surveillance, policy coordination, and associated review and support activities. With area departments, the Policy Development and Review Department helps mobilize other financial resources for member countries using IMF resources, including work on debt and program financing (through the Paris Club and international banks).

The *Research Department* conducts policy analysis and research in areas relating to the IMF's work. The department plays a prominent role in the development of IMF policy concerning the international monetary system and surveillance and cooperates with other departments in formulating IMF policy advice to member countries. It coordinates the semiannual World Economic Outlook exercise and prepares the annual *International Capital Markets* report, as well as analysis for the Group of Seven policy coordination exercise and the Executive Board's seminars on World Economic and Market Developments. The department also maintains contacts with the academic community and with other research organizations.

The *Statistics Department* maintains databases of country, regional, and global economic and financial statistics and reviews country data in support of the IMF's surveillance role. It is also responsible for developing statistical concepts in balance of payments, government finance, and money and financial statistics, as well as producing methodological manuals. The department provides technical assistance and training to help members develop statistical systems and produces the IMF's statistical publications. In addition, it is responsible for developing and maintaining standards for the dissemination of data by member countries.

Box 17
IMF Resident Representatives

At the end of 1997/98, the IMF had 70 resident representatives in 64 countries. These posts—typically filled by a single staff member—are intended to enhance the provision of IMF policy advice and are often set up in conjunction with an IMF-supported adjustment program.

To evaluate their effectiveness, the IMF's Office of Internal Audit and Inspection reviewed the program in 1997. The review concluded that resident representative positions have a major impact on the quality of the IMF's country work; in particular, resident representatives alert the IMF and the host country to potential policy slippages and facilitate program implementation. The review highlighted the importance of placing broadly equal emphasis on policy and program support and activities to strengthen underlying macroeconomic capacities and institutions and enhance transparency. It also underscored the need to view these posts as transitional.

At their discussion, many Directors cited the exceptional access that resident representatives had to key national policymakers, which was an important asset for the IMF. Directors were generally highly satisfied with resident representatives, but there were problems in about one-third of the posts, which undermined their effectiveness. Directors urged the IMF staff to implement recommendations to improve this record. Most Directors agreed there should be no single model for the situations in which a resident representative could be used, but they supported a greater focus on the resident representatives' comparative advantage—that is, in providing on-site macroeconomic advice and program support. Directors stressed the need to ensure a consistently high quality of staff in these posts, with particular attention to strong economic policy and communication skills, self-confidence, and initiative. Given high start-up costs, Directors favored two- to three-year assignments. They also emphasized that member country receptiveness was vital to the success of a resident representative; the IMF staff needed to work closely with the national authorities to define objectives for the post and prioritize joint work.

The *Treasurer's Department* formulates the IMF's financial policies and practices; conducts and controls financial operations and transactions in the General Department, SDR Department, and Administered Accounts (including the ESAF Trust and related accounts); effects and controls expenditures under the administrative and capital budgets; and maintains IMF accounts and financial records. The department's responsibilities also include quota reviews, IMF financing and liquidity, borrowing, investments, the IMF's income, and operational policies on the SDR.

Information and Liaison

The *External Relations Department* edits, produces, and distributes the IMF's nonstatistical publications; provides information services to the press and general public; maintains contacts with nongovernmental organizations and parliamentary bodies; and manages the IMF's website.

The IMF maintains four offices—in Asia and the Pacific, in Europe, in Geneva, and at the United Nations—to foster close contacts with other international and regional institutions.

Table 17

Nationality Distribution of Professional and Managerial Staff by Region

(Percent)

Region[1]	1980	1990	1997
Africa	3.8	5.8	5.2
Asia	12.3	12.7	15.0
Japan	1.4	1.9	1.6
Other Asia	10.9	10.8	13.4
Europe	39.5	35.1	33.2
France	6.9	5.5	4.5
Germany	3.7	4.3	3.8
Italy	1.7	1.4	2.8
United Kingdom	8.2	8.0	7.0
BRO countries[2]	...	...	1.1
Other Europe	19.0	15.9	14.0
Middle East	5.4	5.5	6.1
Western Hemisphere	39.1	41.0	40.5
Canada	2.6	2.8	3.5
United States	25.9	25.9	25.5
Other Western Hemisphere	10.6	12.3	11.5
Total	**100.0**	**100.0**	**100.0**

[1]Regions are defined on the basis of the country distribution of the IMF's area departments. The European region includes countries in both the European I Department and the European II Department. The Middle East region includes countries in North Africa.

[2]The Baltics, Russia, and other former Soviet Union countries.

Support Services

The *Administration Department* manages recruitment, training, and career planning programs; supervises the operation of the IMF's headquarters building and leased space; provides administrative services to the organization; and administers the Joint Fund-Bank Library.

The *Secretary's Department* assists management in preparing and coordinating the work program of the Executive Board and other official bodies, including scheduling and assisting in the conduct of Board meetings. The department also manages the Annual Meetings, in cooperation with the World Bank, and is responsible for the IMF's archives, communications, and security program.

The IMF's *bureaus, offices,* and *secretariats* are responsible for computer services; translation services; auditing, evaluation, and work practices; budget matters; technical assistance; and investments under the staff retirement plan.

See Figure 9 for staffing by department as of April 30, 1998.

Staff

As mentioned above, the Managing Director appoints a staff whose sole responsibility is to the IMF; whose effi-

ciency and technical competence are to be of the "highest standards"; and whose diversity reflects the IMF's membership, by giving "due regard to the importance of recruiting personnel on as wide a geographical basis as possible." To these ends, and to provide the continuity and institutional memory necessary to maintain a close working relationship with member countries, the IMF's employment policy is designed to recruit and retain a corps of international civil servants interested in spending a career, or a significant part of a career, at the IMF. At the same time, a number of Board members see the need for greater movement of staff into and out of the IMF to promote skill renewal and introduce new blood into the institution. In the case of a number of skills and jobs, mainly relating to technology, certain services, and highly specialized skills in economics, business considerations have called for contractual employment relationships or outsourcing of activities.

As of December 31, 1997, the IMF had 693 assistant staff and 1,488 professional and managerial staff (approximately two-thirds of whom were economists). Some 480 additional positions fall into the category of "other authorized staff" (experts, consultants, Economic Program participants, and other nonregular resources). Of the IMF's 182 member countries, 122 were represented on the staff. (See Table 17 for the evolution of the nationality distribution of IMF professional and managerial staff since 1980.)

During 1997/98, 2,941 staff-years were used in the IMF, compared with 2,904 in 1996/97. Included in the 1997/98 total were 1,988 regular staff-years (1,999 in 1996/97), supplemented by other resources including Economist Program staff, overtime, and contractual and other temporary staff-years for a total of 2,585 staff-years (2,545 in 1996/97); 230 staff-years for the Office of Executive Directors (232 in 1996/97); and 125 staff-years for externally financed technical assistance experts and related overhead resources (127 in 1996/97).

Recruitment and Retention

During 1997, 149 new staff members joined the organization (84 economists, 26 professionals in specialized career streams, and 39 assistants)—compared with the 133 staff members hired in 1996. Of the new hires in 1997, 49 were mid-career economists (up from 30 in 1996), and 31 entered the Economist Program, a two-year program whose purpose is to familiarize "entry level" economists with the work of the IMF by placing them in two different IMF departments each for a 12-month period. Candidates for the Economist Program typically are completing a Ph.D. in macroeconomics or a related field, or have already finished their graduate studies and have one or two years' work experience. Economist Program participants who perform well dur-

Table 18
Gender Distribution of Staff by Level

Staff Level	1980		1990		1997	
	Number	Percent	Number	Percent	Number	Percent
All staff						
Total (all levels)	1,444	100.0	1,774	100.0	2,181[1]	100.0
Women	676	46.8	827	46.6	1,014	46.5
Men	768	53.2	947	53.4	1,167	53.5
Support staff						
Total	613	100.0	642	100.0	693	100.0
Women	492	80.3	540	84.1	593	85.6
Men	121	19.7	102	15.9	100	14.4
Professional staff						
Total	646	100.0	897	100.0	1,179	100.0
Women	173	26.8	274	30.5	390	33.1
Men	473	73.2	623	69.5	789	66.9
Economists						
Total	362	100.0	529	100.0	770	100.0
Women	42	11.6	70	13.2	150	19.5
Men	320	88.4	459	86.8	620	80.5
Specialized career streams						
Total	284	100.0	368	100.0	409	100.0
Women	131	46.1	204	55.4	240	58.7
Men	153	53.9	164	44.6	169	41.3
Managerial staff						
Total	185	100.0	235	100.0	309	100.0
Women	11	5.9	13	5.5	31	10.0
Men	174	94.1	222	94.5	278	90.0
Economists						
Total	99	100.0	184	100.0	250	100.0
Women	4	4.0	9	4.9	17	6.8
Men	95	96.0	175	95.1	233	93.2
Specialized career streams						
Total	86	100.0	51	100.0	59	100.0
Women	7	8.1	4	7.8	14	23.7
Men	79	91.9	47	92.2	45	76.3

[1]Some 480 additional positions fall into the category of "other authorized staff" (experts, consultants, Economist Program participants, and other non-regular resources).

ing the two-year period are offered regular staff appointments.

During 1997, 137 staff separated from the IMF, an increase of 22 over 1996. The separation rate of professional staff rose to 7 percent (104 staff) in 1997 from 5½ percent (82 staff) in 1996, which had been close to the long-term average. The increase in turnover was attributable largely to a sudden and sharp rise in resignations of economists joining private sector financial firms.

Salary Structure

To recruit and retain the staff it needs, the IMF has developed a compensation and benefits system that is designed to be competitive, to reward performance, and to take account of the special needs of a multinational and largely expatriate staff. The IMF's staff salary structure is reviewed and, if warranted, adjusted annually on the basis of a comparison with salaries paid by selected private financial and industrial firms and public sector organizations in the United States, France, and Germany. On the basis of updated analyses of comparator salaries, the salary structure was increased by 4.3 percent in 1997/98, and the Board approved an increase of 4.3 percent for 1998/99.

Diversity

The IMF views staff diversity as an important asset for improving its effectiveness as an international institution. With the support of the Managing Director, the IMF's Special Advisor on Diversity has designed a number of initiatives to enhance nationality as well as gender diversity (Table 18) in the organization—working closely with departments to identify issues and

Table 19
Estimated Cost of Major IMF Activities, Financial Years 1997–99[1]
(Millions of U.S. dollars)

Activity	Financial Year 1997	Percent of Total	Financial Year 1998	Percent of Total	Budget Financial Year 1999	Percent of Total
Staff and management						
Surveillance	132.4	28.1	141.1	28.5	149.6	28.8
Use of IMF resources	116.7	24.7	104.3	21.1	126.3	24.3
Technical assistance	65.7	13.9	81.6	16.5	80.3	15.5
External relations	21.2	4.5	23.2	4.7	24.1	4.6
Administrative support	78.5	16.6	90.1	18.2	80.8	15.6
Subtotal	414.6	87.9	440.3	88.9	461.1	88.8
Executive Board[2]	36.4	7.7	35.4	7.1	37.7	7.3
Board of Governors[3]	20.6	4.4	19.6	4.0	20.7	4.0
Subtotal	57.0	12.1	55.0	11.1	58.4	11.2
Total	471.6	100.0	495.3	100.0	519.5	100.0

Note: Details may not add to total because of rounding.
[1]Cost estimates for financial years 1997 and 1998 are based on year-end data.
[2]The Executive Board costs include salaries and benefits of Executive Directors, Alternates, and Assistants; business and other travel; communications; building occupancy; books and printing; supplies and equipment; data processing; other miscellaneous costs of Executive Directors' offices; and the costs of staff support services provided for Executive Directors.
[3]The costs of the Board of Governors consist mainly of the travel and subsistence of Governors, the costs of staff support services provided for the Board of Governors, including the costs of the Annual Meetings, and other miscellaneous administrative services.

opportunities and to develop departmental diversity action plans. In 1997/98, departments began implementing these plans—which typically include mentoring, recognition of diversity needs in career development, flexible work arrangements, more emphasis on diversity considerations in recruitment, and grade and salary equity initiatives—and submitted their first progress reports to the Managing Director. The IMF has also placed greater emphasis on cultivating and strengthening the managerial qualities needed to develop the skills of its increasingly diverse staff.

Expanded monitoring of diversity data has revealed some progress in recruitment, promotions, and overall representativeness in all staff groups (and across most grade groups) earlier identified as having unequal opportunities. The achievement of satisfactory diversity of staff, however, will take some time.

Administrative and Capital Budgets

Medium-Term Budget Outlook

The IMF's Administrative and Capital Budgets are considered respectively in the context of rolling three-year and five-year medium-term budget outlooks that are reviewed each year by the Executive Board. At its discussion of the medium-term outlook in January 1998, the Board supported management's proposal for a modest increase in the authorized staff in 1998/99 to carry out the additional work arising from the financial crisis in Asia and other priority work activities. The proposal stipulated that once the crisis in Asia abated, the budgetary consolidation policy begun in 1994/95 would continue, with staffing reductions in financial years 2000 and 2001. Despite the proposed increase in staffing, administrative expenses were projected to continue to remain relatively flat in real terms over the medium term. Implementing the medium-term proposals would require the continuation of internal redeployment of resources from lower priority activities to front-line activities to ensure that the institution continued to meet the changing needs of its membership, in particular the strengthening of IMF surveillance (including banking sector and related financial sector issues, the proposed amendment to the Articles of Agreement, and data dissemination standards); the work associated with the use of IMF resources; strengthening the IMF's financial resources; and provision of internally and externally financed technical assistance to members.

The five-year outlook for the Capital Budget remained consistent with the strategy to continue and finalize the major building projects that had already been approved, and to continue with other capital investments that would result in cost savings or are required to comply with building codes or to maintain existing buildings and equipment inventory.

Budgets and Expenditure in 1997/98

The IMF's Administrative Budget for the financial year ended April 30, 1998 (1997/98) was $503.7 million. For the Capital Budget, $27.2 million was approved for projects beginning in financial year 1998 and $17.0 million was approved for Part 3 of the Building Fit-Out Project (Phase III). The estimated cost of major IMF activities is shown in Table 19. Actual administrative expenditures during the year totaled $495.3 million, and capital project disbursements totaled $56.3 million, including $40.5 million for major building projects (Table 20).

During 1997/98, Administrative Budget resources were used to support the IMF's work in the following proportions: surveillance and use of IMF resources, with over 115 countries classified as programs/intensive, 70 resident representatives located in 64 coun-

Table 20

Administrative and Capital Budgets, Financial Years 1996–99[1]

(Thousands of U.S. dollars)

	Financial Year Ended April 30, 1996: Actual Expenses	Financial Year Ended April 30, 1997: Actual Expenses	Financial Year Ended April 30, 1998: Actual Expenses	Financial Year Ending April 30, 1999: Budget
Administrative Budget				
I. Personnel expenses				
Salaries	210,216	216,350	229,150	247,270
Other personnel expenses	131,115	129,550	117,213	126,019
Subtotal	341,331	345,901	346,363	373,289
II. Other expenses				
Business travel	39,624	39,302	46,831	44,515
Other travel	26,458	26,960	28,010	29,470
Communications	9,869	10,693	10,506	11,681
Building occupancy	40,242	41,899	42,877	44,585
Books and printing	8,371	8,579	9,669	10,228
Supplies and equipment	7,219	7,941	8,164	8,754
Data processing	18,129	19,735	25,765	25,500
Miscellaneous	12,831	9,924	12,930	13,635
Subtotal	162,743	165,033	184,752	188,368
III. Reimbursements	−33,239	−39,368	−35,836	−42,124
Total Administrative Budget	**470,836**	**471,564**	**495,279**	**519,533**
Less: Reimbursement for administering the SDR Department	−5,841	−5,914	−6,000	−5,800
Reimbursement for administering the SAF/ESAF	−35,634	−43,788	. . .[2]	. . .[3]
Net Administrative Budget expenses[4]	429,361	421,862	489,279	513,733
Capital Budget				
Capital project budgets[5]	152,500	20,123	27,240	14,440
Capital project disbursements	34,800	151,500	56,061	46,391

[1]Administrative Budget as approved by the Board for the financial year ending April 30, 1999, as compared with actual expenses for the financial years ended April 30, 1996, April 30, 1997, and April 30, 1998; and Capital Budgets as approved by the Board for capital projects in financial years 1996, 1997, 1998, and 1999. Due to rounding, details may not add to total.

[2]The reimbursement of $55,500 was not included in the Administrative Budget by Executive Board decision.

[3]The reimbursement of $61,800 will not be included in the Administrative Budget by Executive Board decision.

[4]Net Administrative Budget expenses exclude valuation or loss on administrative currency holdings.

[5]Multiyear Capital Budgets for projects beginning in each financial year.

tries, and an estimated 285 person-years of technical assistance (66.1 percent of expenses); external relations activities to continue to provide a greater openness of the IMF's policies and operations (4.7 percent); administrative support, where investments in technology and continuing work practice improvements continue to produce a series of savings in the diverse activities within this category (18.2 percent); Board of Governors (4.0 percent); and Executive Board (7.1 percent). The distribution of estimated administrative costs by major IMF activities is shown in Figure 10.

Budgets and Expenditure in 1998/99

The IMF's work program for 1998/99 will focus on:

- strengthening multilateral, regional, and bilateral surveillance, including seeking ways to strengthen the architecture of the international monetary system;
- an increase in work associated with the use of IMF resources as a result of the ESAF and the HIPC Initiative;
- ensuring that the IMF continues to meet the changing and expanding needs of its membership, including the provision of technical assistance; and
- intensified efforts in external relations and communication to the general public of the IMF's role and work.

In support of this work program, the Board, in April 1998, approved an Administrative Budget for 1998/99 of $519.5 million, a 3.1 percent increase over the approved budget for the previous year. In addition, a capital projects budget of $14.4 million was approved

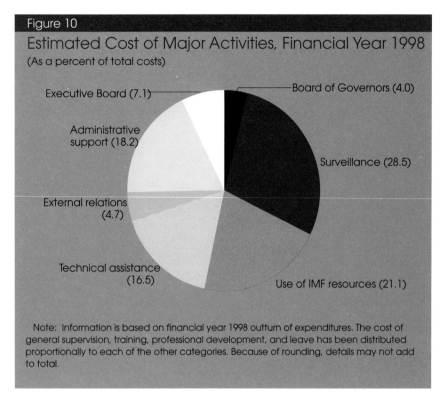

Figure 10

Estimated Cost of Major Activities, Financial Year 1998

(As a percent of total costs)

Executive Board (7.1)
Board of Governors (4.0)
Administrative support (18.2)
Surveillance (28.5)
External relations (4.7)
Technical assistance (16.5)
Use of IMF resources (21.1)

Note: Information is based on financial year 1998 outturn of expenditures. The cost of general supervision, training, professional development, and leave has been distributed proportionally to each of the other categories. Because of rounding, details may not add to total.

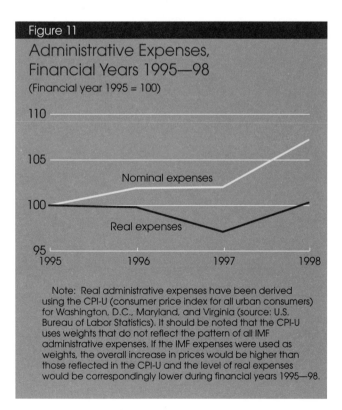

Figure 11

Administrative Expenses, Financial Years 1995—98

(Financial year 1995 = 100)

Nominal expenses

Real expenses

Note: Real administrative expenses have been derived using the CPI-U (consumer price index for all urban consumers) for Washington, D.C., Maryland, and Virginia (source: U.S. Bureau of Labor Statistics). It should be noted that the CPI-U uses weights that do not reflect the pattern of all IMF administrative expenses. If the IMF expenses were used as weights, the overall increase in prices would be higher than those reflected in the CPI-U and the level of real expenses would be correspondingly lower during financial years 1995—98.

for facility improvements, new technology, and data-processing equipment. The 1998/99 Administrative Budget includes an increase of 32.5 positions in the authorized staffing level to meet the very heavy workload associated with the financial crisis in Asia that was not anticipated in the previous medium-term plan, for a number of other priority work activities, and to increase the number of participants in the IMF's Economist Program. The increase in authorized staffing will allow the IMF to attend to priority work activities, to reduce the very high level of uncompensated overtime being worked by many staff, and to reduce accumulated leave balances. To resume the medium-term strategy of budgetary consolidation in the staffing area, the additional positions authorized to carry out the work on the Asian crisis will be eliminated once the crisis has abated and work returns to more normal levels. The one-time increase in the intake of economists into the Economist Program is meant to expand the IMF's flexibility over the medium term and rebuild the economist ranks. Notwithstanding the increase in authorized staffing, the 1998/99 budget maintains the existing policy of budgetary consolidation by keeping administrative expenses relatively flat in real terms, compared with the 1997/98 budget. The Administrative Budget in nominal and real terms is shown in Figure 11. The Capital Budget represents a continuation of plans for completing major building projects, replacing older facilities and electronic data-processing equipment, and other medium-term programs.

Building Projects

The addition to the headquarters building (Phase III) is essentially completed, and in March 1998 staff began to move out of leased space and to occupy the building. The PEPCO building (Phase IV) adjacent to headquarters will be ready for occupancy after the current tenant has vacated and the building has been renovated. When the Phase IV project has been completed, staff will be housed in two immediately adjacent buildings owned by the IMF, overall occupancy costs will be reduced, and the IMF's long-term space and budget strategies will have been realized.

Contents

International Reserves

During 1997, total international reserves increased by 4 percent to SDR 1.4 trillion at the end of the year (Table I.1). Nongold reserves increased by 9 percent to SDR 1.2 trillion while the market value in SDR terms of the official holdings of gold by monetary authorities declined by 18 percent to SDR 191 billion.[1] The rates of increase in 1997 for both total and nongold reserves were lower than those in the previous two years. The growth of nongold reserves can be attributed largely to an increase of SDR 84 billion in foreign exchange reserves. IMF-related assets increased by SDR 11 billion, reflecting an increase in industrial countries' reserve positions in the IMF associated with purchases of their currencies by certain Asian countries toward the end of 1997.

Foreign Exchange Reserves

Foreign exchange reserves[2] constitute the largest component of countries' official holdings of reserve assets, accounting for 94 percent of nongold reserves for all countries. Total foreign exchange reserves were valued at SDR 1.1 trillion at the end of 1997, representing an increase of 8 percent relative to the level at the end of 1996. During 1997, the stock of foreign exchange reserves rose by SDR 19 billion for industrial countries (4 percent since 1996) and by SDR 64 billion for developing countries (12 percent). Developing countries have gradually increased their share of holdings of foreign exchange during the 1990s; at the end of 1997, these countries held 53 percent of total foreign exchange reserves. Foreign exchange accounts for 98 percent of developing countries' total nongold reserves, compared with 90 percent for industrial countries. Foreign exchange reserves of oil exporting developing countries rose by SDR 8 billion during 1997 (a 16 percent increase). Non-oil-exporting developing countries increased their foreign exchange reserves by SDR 58 billion (12 percent). Of the foreign exchange reserves held by developing countries, net debtor countries accounted for

about 78 percent. Reflecting private capital inflows, the stock of foreign exchange reserves held by net debtor countries grew by 15 percent in 1997. Foreign exchange reserves of countries without debt-servicing problems increased by SDR 51 billion (18 percent); these reserves increased by SDR 9 billion (8 percent increase) for countries with debt-servicing problems.

Holdings of IMF-Related Assets

Total holdings of IMF-related assets increased by 20 percent in 1997, to SDR 68 billion at the end of the year. Much of that increase can be attributed to an increase of SDR 9 billion in members' reserve positions in the IMF, which comprise their reserve tranche and creditor positions. The increase of SDR 9 billion in members' reserve tranche positions during 1997 mainly reflects purchases of hard currencies by East Asian nations from other IMF members. IMF-related assets represented 6 percent of total nongold reserve assets for all countries at the end of 1997. Industrial countries hold a substantial fraction of total IMF-related reserves, accounting for 84 percent in 1997.

Members' holdings of SDRs—which had been drawn down substantially during 1992 to pay for the reserve asset portions of quota increases under the Ninth General Review—appear to have stabilized after a sharp increase from 1992 to 1995 resulting from the IMF's policy of decreasing its SDR holdings to replenish members' holdings. IMF member countries now hold 20.5 billion of the total of 21.4 billion SDRs allocated by the IMF in two allocations since 1970. At the end of 1997, the IMF held 630 million SDRs, compared with 8.6 billion SDRs at the end of 1992, and other prescribed institutions held the remaining 340 million SDRs.

Gold Reserves

The market value of the stock of official gold reserves held by monetary authorities declined by 18 percent during 1997, to SDR 191 billion at the end of the year. This decline mainly reflected a 16 percent fall in the SDR market price of gold. The physical stock of gold reserves held by monetary authorities declined only marginally (by 2 percent). The share of gold holdings in total reserves has declined steadily since the 1980s, when the average for the decade was 44 percent, to 14 percent in 1997. Industrial countries hold 83 percent of the world's gold reserves; gold holdings accounted for about 21 percent of their total reserves in 1997. Gold holdings accounted for only 5 percent of total reserves of developing countries at the end of 1997, compared with an average share of 10 percent in the early 1990s.

---

[1]Official monetary authorities comprise central banks and also currency boards, exchange stabilization funds, and treasuries, to the extent they perform monetary authorities' functions.

[2]The coverage of foreign exchange reserves is in the process of being expanded to include new members of the IMF. Revisions are also under way to incorporate more comprehensive data on reserves obtained under new data reporting standards instituted by the IMF. These revisions, which are currently in a preliminary stage, are not incorporated here but will appear in the IMF's *International Financial Statistics* database later in 1998.

Table I.1

Official Holdings of Reserve Assets, 1992–March 1998[1]
(In billions of SDRs)

	1992	1993	1994	1995	1996	1997	Mar. 1998
All countries							
Total reserves excluding gold							
IMF-related assets							
Reserve positions in the Fund	33.9	32.8	31.7	36.7	38.0	47.1	50.1
SDRs	12.9	14.6	15.8	19.8	18.5	20.5	20.3
Subtotal, IMF-related assets	46.8	47.4	47.5	56.4	56.5	67.6	70.4
Foreign exchange	646.9	718.4	776.7	893.4	1,033.8	1,117.3	1,151.7
Total reserves excluding gold	693.7	765.9	824.2	949.9	1,090.3	1,184.8	1,222.1
Gold[2]							
Quantity (millions of troy ounces)	927.5	922.0	918.0	908.7	906.4	889.7	880.5
Value at London market price	224.8	262.2	241.0	236.4	232.8	191.4	198.4
Total reserves including gold	918.5	1,028.1	1,065.2	1,186.3	1,323.0	1,376.2	1,420.5
Industrial countries							
Total reserves excluding gold							
IMF-related assets							
Reserve positions in the Fund	29.5	28.3	27.4	31.6	32.6	41.3	44.3
SDRs	10.5	11.5	12.5	15.0	14.5	15.5	15.7
Subtotal, IMF-related assets	40.0	39.8	39.9	46.6	47.1	56.8	60.0
Foreign exchange	356.8	373.7	393.9	441.1	501.7	520.9	527.9
Total reserves excluding gold	396.7	413.4	433.8	487.7	548.8	577.7	587.9
Gold[2]							
Quantity (millions of troy ounces)	785.2	770.8	768.0	755.0	748.2	732.5	723.1
Value at London market price	190.3	219.2	201.6	196.4	192.1	157.5	162.9
Total reserves including gold	587.1	632.7	635.5	684.1	740.9	735.2	750.8
Developing countries							
Total reserves excluding gold							
IMF-related assets							
Reserve positions in the Fund	4.4	4.5	4.3	5.0	5.4	5.7	5.8
SDRs	2.4	3.2	3.3	4.8	4.0	5.0	4.6
Subtotal, IMF-related assets	6.8	7.7	7.6	9.8	9.4	10.8	10.4
Foreign exchange	290.1	344.8	382.8	452.4	532.1	596.4	623.8
Total reserves excluding gold	296.9	352.4	390.4	462.2	541.5	607.1	634.2
Gold[2]							
Quantity (millions of troy ounces)	142.3	151.2	149.6	153.7	158.2	157.2	157.4
Value at London market price	34.5	43.0	39.4	40.0	40.6	33.8	35.5
Total reserves including gold	331.4	395.4	429.7	502.2	582.1	640.9	669.7
Net debtors							
Total reserves excluding gold							
IMF-related assets							
Reserve positions in the Fund	2.8	2.7	2.9	3.5	3.9	4.2	4.3
SDRs	1.7	2.3	2.4	3.8	2.9	3.9	3.5
Subtotal, IMF-related assets	4.5	5.0	5.2	7.3	6.9	8.1	7.7
Foreign exchange	184.9	233.1	264.6	329.2	401.5	462.2	487.8
Total reserves excluding gold	189.4	238.1	269.8	336.5	408.3	470.3	495.6
Gold[2]							
Quantity (millions of troy ounces)	116.1	125.0	123.7	128.1	132.6	131.8	132.0
Value at London market price	28.1	35.5	32.5	33.3	34.0	28.3	29.7
Total reserves including gold	217.6	273.6	302.3	369.8	442.4	498.7	525.3
Countries without debt-servicing problems							
Total reserves excluding gold							
IMF-related assets							
Reserve positions in the Fund	2.3	2.3	2.4	3.1	3.5	3.8	3.8
SDRs	1.1	1.2	1.3	2.8	1.8	3.0	2.6
Subtotal, IMF-related assets	3.4	3.5	3.7	5.9	5.3	6.8	6.5
Foreign exchange	119.2	155.4	179.7	234.6	281.3	332.4	346.4
Total reserves excluding gold	122.6	158.9	183.4	240.5	286.5	339.2	352.8
Gold[2]							
Quantity (millions of troy ounces)	70.3	78.6	77.1	79.7	83.5	86.7	87.7
Value at London market price	17.0	22.3	20.2	20.7	21.4	18.6	19.8
Total reserves including gold	139.6	181.3	203.6	261.2	308.0	357.8	372.6

Note: Components may not sum to totals because of rounding.

Source: International Monetary Fund, *International Financial Statistics*.

[1]End-of-year figures for all years except 1998. "IMF-related assets" comprise reserve positions in the IMF and SDR holdings of all IMF members. The entries under "Foreign exchange" and "Gold" comprise official holdings of those IMF members for which data are available and certain other countries or areas.

[2]One troy ounce equals 31.103 grams. The market price is the afternoon price fixed in London on the last business day of each period.

Table I.2

Share of National Currencies in Total Identified Official Holdings of Foreign Exchange, End of Year 1988–97[1]
(In percent)

	1988	1989	1990	1991	1992	1993	1994	1995	1996	1997	Memorandum: ECU-Dollar Swaps Included with Dollars[2] 1997
All countries											
U.S. dollar	54.6	51.4	49.4	50.0	54.2	55.6	55.7	56.4	59.6	57.1	61.3
Pound sterling	2.3	2.3	2.8	3.2	3.0	2.9	3.3	3.2	3.4	3.4	3.5
Deutsche mark	14.2	17.8	17.0	15.6	13.6	14.0	14.4	13.8	13.1	12.8	13.1
French franc	1.0	1.4	2.3	2.8	2.5	2.2	2.4	2.3	1.8	1.2	1.2
Swiss franc	1.8	1.4	1.3	1.2	1.0	1.1	0.9	0.8	0.7	0.7	0.7
Netherlands guilder	1.0	1.1	1.0	1.0	0.6	0.6	0.5	0.4	0.3	0.4	0.4
Japanese yen	6.9	7.2	7.9	8.4	7.6	7.7	7.9	6.5	5.7	4.9	5.0
ECUs	11.7	10.8	10.1	10.6	10.1	8.6	8.1	7.1	6.2	5.0	n.a.
Unspecified currencies[3]	6.6	6.6	8.2	7.0	7.4	7.3	6.9	9.6	9.1	14.6	14.9
Industrial countries											
U.S. dollar	53.9	47.9	44.9	43.1	48.4	49.9	50.8	51.8	56.1	57.5	66.7
Pound sterling	1.1	1.1	1.4	1.6	2.2	2.0	2.3	2.1	2.0	1.9	2.0
Deutsche mark	15.2	20.4	19.4	18.0	14.9	16.2	16.3	16.4	15.6	16.6	17.4
French franc	0.7	1.1	2.3	3.0	2.8	2.5	2.4	2.3	1.7	0.9	0.9
Swiss franc	1.5	1.1	0.9	0.8	0.4	0.3	0.2	0.1	0.1	0.2	0.2
Netherlands guilder	1.0	1.1	1.1	1.1	0.4	0.4	0.3	0.2	0.2	0.3	0.3
Japanese yen	6.2	7.4	8.5	9.5	7.5	7.7	8.2	6.6	5.6	5.4	5.7
ECUs	16.3	15.3	14.5	16.6	16.7	15.2	14.6	13.4	12.0	10.7	n.a.
Unspecified currencies[3]	4.1	4.5	6.9	6.3	6.7	5.8	5.0	7.0	6.7	6.5	6.8
Developing countries											
U.S. dollar	56.5	59.8	59.5	62.0	63.1	63.1	61.7	61.6	63.3	56.7	56.7
Pound sterling	5.2	5.3	6.1	5.8	4.2	4.0	4.5	4.4	4.8	4.7	4.7
Deutsche mark	11.6	11.4	11.5	11.5	11.5	11.1	12.1	10.9	10.5	9.5	9.5
French franc	2.0	2.1	2.3	2.5	2.1	1.9	2.4	2.2	2.0	1.4	1.4
Swiss franc	2.3	2.2	2.0	2.0	2.0	2.2	1.8	1.5	1.4	1.1	1.1
Netherlands guilder	1.0	0.9	0.8	1.0	1.0	0.9	0.8	0.6	0.5	0.5	0.5
Japanese yen	8.6	6.6	6.6	7.0	7.9	7.6	7.5	6.3	5.9	4.4	4.4
ECUs	—	—	—	—	—	—	—	—	—	—	n.a.
Unspecified currencies[4]	12.8	11.7	11.2	8.2	8.4	9.3	9.2	12.5	11.6	21.6	21.6

Note: Components may not sum to total because of rounding.

[1]Note that ECUs are treated as a separate currency except in the last column. Only IMF member countries that report their official holdings of foreign exchange are included in this table.

[2]This column is for comparison and indicates the currency composition of reserves when ECUs issued against dollars are assumed to be dollars and all other ECUs are ignored.

[3]The residual is equal to the difference between total foreign exchange reserves of IMF member countries and the sum of the reserves held in the currencies listed in the table.

[4]The calculations here rely to a greater extent on IMF staff estimates than do those provided for the group of industrial countries.

Developments in the First Quarter of 1998

In the first quarter of 1998, total international reserves rose by SDR 44 billion. Of this, SDR 34 billion can be attributed to an increase in foreign exchange reserves. IMF-related assets increased by SDR 3 billion while the market value of official gold holdings rose by SDR 7 billion. For industrial countries, total nongold reserve assets increased by SDR 10 billion, reflecting an increase of SDR 3 billion in reserve positions at the IMF and an increase of SDR 7 billion in foreign exchange. The market value of gold reserves held by industrial countries increased by SDR 5 billion. Foreign exchange reserves of developing countries increased by SDR 27 billion during the first quarter of 1998; there were no significant changes in these countries' holdings of other official reserve assets.

Currency Composition of Reserves

During the past 10 years, the degree of diversification in the currency composition of foreign exchange reserves has not changed significantly (Table I.2). The U.S. dollar remains the dominant international reserve currency, accounting for 57 percent of the identified foreign exchange reserves in 1997.[3] The dollar share of total foreign exchange reserves declined from 1987 through 1990. This decline was reversed by 1993; the share of dollars has since remained over 55 percent, com-

[3]Table I.2 includes European currency units (ECUs) as a separate currency except in the last column, where the dollar-swap component of ECU liabilities of the European Monetary Institute (EMI) is classified as dollars and all other ECUs are omitted from the calculation.

parable with its share in the early 1980s. The share of the deutsche mark peaked in 1989 at 18 percent and gradually declined thereafter to 13 percent in 1997. The share of Japanese yen peaked in 1991 at 9 percent but fell to 5 percent by the end of 1997. The share of pound sterling has remained at between 2 percent and 3 percent during the past two decades. The shares of French francs, Swiss francs, and Dutch guilders have all declined throughout the 1990s; together they represented 2 percent of total identified official foreign exchange holdings in 1997. The increase in the share of unspecified currencies in foreign exchange reserves since 1995 principally reflects data problems, especially for the developing country group.[4] In particular, many transition economies that have become IMF members in recent years report only their total holdings of foreign exchange reserves and information on the currency composition of those reserves is not incorporated into Table I.2. The unspecified currency component of foreign exchange reserves rose sharply to 15 percent at the end of 1997, indicating that the evolution of currency shares discussed here should be interpreted with considerable caution.

For industrial countries, the share of U.S. dollars in foreign exchange reserves was 58 percent at the end of 1997, representing an increase of 14 percentage points since 1991. The shares of the deutsche mark and the Japanese yen in foreign exchange reserves have declined gradually during the 1990s for both industrial and developing countries. Their combined share of industrial country foreign exchange reserves stood at 22 percent in 1997, compared with 28 percent in 1990; their combined share of foreign exchange reserves of developing countries stood at 14 percent in 1997. The share of identified hard currency holdings in total foreign exchange reserves of developing countries declined markedly in 1997 as the share of unspecified currency holdings jumped to 22 percent. As noted earlier, this largely reflects reporting deficiencies, especially for countries that have only recently become IMF members.

In the calculation of currency shares in Table I.2, the ECU (European currency unit) is treated as a separate currency. Official ECU reserves, held mainly by European countries, are in the form of claims both on the private sector and the European Monetary Institute (EMI). The ECU reserves that represent claims on the EMI are issued in exchange for deposits equal to 20 percent of both gold and dollar reserves. These swaps are renewed every three months, and changes in member's holdings of dollars and gold—as well as changes in the market price of gold and in the foreign exchange value of

the dollar—affect the amount of ECUs outstanding.[5] Quantity changes in ECU holdings therefore depend in part on the evolution of the two components of the EMI swaps.[6] The other component of ECU foreign exchange reserves is official claims on the private sector, usually in the form of ECU deposits and bonds.

The share of ECUs in total foreign exchange reserves of industrial countries has declined gradually from 16 percent in 1988 to 11 percent at the end of 1997. Most of the recent fall in the share of ECUs is a result of the decline in official ECU reserves in the form of claims on the private sector.

In the last column of Table I.2, the SDR value of ECU swaps issued against dollars is counted as a part of the dollar component of foreign exchange reserves. This increases the share of U.S. dollars to 61 percent of total foreign exchange reserves for all countries in 1997 and to 67 percent for industrial countries. The broad trends in the currency composition of foreign exchange reserves are unaffected by this alternative treatment of ECU reserves.

Changes in the SDR value of foreign exchange reserves can be decomposed into quantity and valuation (price) changes for each of the major currencies as well as the ECU (Table I.3). In 1997, total official holdings of reserves in the major identifiable currencies increased by SDR 71 billion, reflecting a quantity increase of SDR 48 billion and a valuation increase of SDR 23 billion.

Official reserves held in U.S. dollars increased by SDR 59 billion in 1997, attributable to an increase of SDR 19 billion in the quantity of dollar holdings and an increase of 7 percent in the SDR value of the U.S. dollar during 1997. The quantity of reserves held in deutsche mark increased by SDR 26 billion during 1997, although this was partially offset by a decrease of SDR 10 billion in the value of those reserves. Reserves held in Japanese yen fell by SDR 1 billion owing to a 5 percent decline in the SDR value of Japanese yen. Holdings of pound sterling increased by SDR 5 billion, aided by both quantity and valuation increases. French franc and ECU reserves, on the other hand, experienced both quantity and valuation decreases during 1997, resulting in total declines of SDR 5 billion and SDR 4 billion, respectively. Foreign exchange reserves held in Swiss francs and Netherlands guilders increased in quantity but experienced some valuation declines.

---

[4]Unspecified currencies include currencies other than those listed in Table I.2, as well as foreign exchange reserves for which no information on currency composition is available from the reporting country or from other sources. For developing countries as well as transition economies that have recently become IMF members, a large share of this classification probably indicates a lack of information on currency composition.

[5]In calculating the value of the gold holdings of the EMI in terms of ECUs, the ECU swap price is set equal to the lower of two values: the average of the prices recorded daily at the two London price fixings during the previous six calendar months, and the average price at the two price fixings on the penultimate working day of the period.

[6]The quarterly swaps are arranged at the end of the first weeks of January, April, July, and October. Changes in the number of ECUs outstanding thus depend on the exchange rate and the gold price on these dates, whereas changes in the SDR value of ECU holdings are calculated at the SDR-ECU exchange rate at the end of each quarter.

Table I.3

Currency Composition of Official Holdings of Foreign Exchange, End of Year 1989–97[1]
(In millions of SDRs)

	1989	1990	1991	1992	1993	1994	1995	1996	1997
U.S. dollar									
Change in holdings	11,736	16,374	16,089	34,363	47,420	31,616	72,730	109,808	59,021
Quantity change	6,157	36,710	18,404	22,478	46,064	54,779	77,298	92,887	19,406
Price change	5,580	-20,336	-2,315	11,885	1,356	-23,163	-4,568	16,921	39,615
Year-end value	251,697	268,072	284,161	318,524	365,943	397,559	470,289	580,097	639,118
Pound sterling									
Change in holdings	1,569	3,929	2,587	-395	1,360	4,356	3,143	6,434	5,146
Quantity change	2,627	2,558	3,057	3,082	1,698	4,477	3,699	2,590	3,716
Price change	-1,058	1,372	-470	-3,476	-338	-122	-556	3,844	1,430
Year-end value	11,495	15,424	18,011	17,616	18,976	23,332	26,475	32,909	38,055
Deutsche mark									
Change in holdings	24,545	5,255	-3,455	-9,129	12,380	11,063	12,020	12,755	15,539
Quantity change	18,129	713	-1,564	-7,468	18,199	6,385	5,763	18,620	25,533
Price change	6,416	4,542	-1,881	-1,661	-5,819	4,678	6,257	-5,865	-9,994
Year-end value	86,983	92,238	88,794	79,665	92,044	103,107	115,127	127,882	143,421
French franc									
Change in holdings	2,494	5,472	3,544	-1,324	-60	2,656	1,559	-1,113	-4,687
Quantity change	2,026	5,098	3,526	-1,115	872	2,046	322	-514	-3,427
Price change	468	374	18	-209	-932	610	1,237	-598	-1,260
Year-end value	6,989	12,461	16,005	14,681	14,622	17,278	18,837	17,724	13,037
Swiss franc									
Change in holdings	-774	-60	-132	-623	1,344	-1,075	54	433	621
Quantity change	-800	-758	177	-423	1,362	-1,535	-710	1,270	714
Price change	26	698	-308	-200	-18	459	764	-837	-93
Year-end value	6,962	6,902	6,771	6,147	7,492	6,417	6,471	6,903	7,525
Netherlands guilder									
Change in holdings	865	328	295	-2,238	299	-299	-282	-154	1,226
Quantity change	514	90	371	-2,241	557	-493	-505	2	1,513
Price change	351	238	-76	3	-258	194	222	-156	-287
Year-end value	5,265	5,593	5,888	3,650	3,949	3,651	3,368	3,214	4,440
Japanese yen									
Change in holdings	4,887	8,029	5,693	-3,940	5,544	5,698	-2,049	1,738	-1,381
Quantity change	8,852	8,247	2,534	-6,019	408	2,903	802	6,615	1,471
Price change	-3,966	-218	3,160	2,079	5,136	2,795	-2,851	-4,877	-2,851
Year-end value	35,087	43,116	48,810	44,870	50,413	56,111	54,062	55,800	54,420
European currency unit									
Change in holdings	1,207	1,974	5,360	-498	-2,820	959	1,665	985	-4,493
Quantity change	-1,079	-724	6,283	3,845	1,503	-1,035	-1,157	1,833	-736
Price change	2,287	2,697	-923	-4,342	-4,323	1,994	2,822	-849	-3,757
Year-end value	52,638	54,611	59,971	59,473	56,654	57,613	59,278	60,262	55,769
Sum of the above[2]									
Change in holdings	46,528	41,301	29,992	16,216	65,467	54,975	88,839	130,885	70,993
Quantity change	36,425	51,934	32,788	12,138	70,665	67,528	85,513	123,302	48,190
Price change	10,103	-10,633	-2,795	4,077	-5,197	-12,553	3,326	7,583	22,803
Year-end value	457,116	498,417	528,410	544,625	610,093	665,068	753,907	884,792	955,785
Total official holdings[3]									
Change in holdings	50,761	48,586	31,764	21,543	71,529	58,260	116,745	140,338	83,194
Year-end value	545,020	593,607	625,371	646,914	718,443	776,703	893,448	1,033,786	1,117,300

Note: Components may not sum to totals because of rounding.

[1]The currency composition of foreign exchange is based on the IMF's currency survey and on estimates derived mainly, but not solely, from official national reports. The numbers in this table should be regarded as estimates that are subject to adjustment as more information is received. Quantity changes are derived by multiplying the changes in official holdings of each currency from the end of one quarter to the next by the average of the two SDR prices of that currency prevailing at the corresponding dates. This procedure converts the change in the quantity of national currency from own units to SDR units of account. Subtracting the SDR value of the quantity change so derived from the quarterly change in the SDR value of foreign exchange held at the end of two successive quarters and cumulating these differences yields the effect of price changes over the years shown.

[2]Each item represents the sum of the eight currencies above.

[3]Includes a residual whose currency composition could not be ascertained, as well as holdings of currencies other than those shown.

Financial Operations and Transactions

The tables in this appendix supplement the information given in Chapter XII on the IMF's financial operations and policies.

Table II.1

Arrangements Approved During Financial Years Ended April 30, 1953–98

Financial Year	Number of Arrangements					Amounts Committed Under Arrangements (in millions of SDRs)				
	Stand-By	EFF	SAF	ESAF	Total	Stand-By	EFF	SAF	ESAF	Total
1953	2				2	55				55
1954	2				2	63				63
1955	2				2	40				40
1956	2				2	48				48
1957	9				9	1,162				1,162
1958	11				11	1,044				1,044
1959	15				15	1,057				1,057
1960	14				14	364				364
1961	15				15	460				460
1962	24				24	1,633				1,633
1963	19				19	1,531				1,531
1964	19				19	2,160				2,160
1965	24				24	2,159				2,159
1966	24				24	575				575
1967	25				25	591				591
1968	32				32	2,352				2,352
1969	26				26	541				541
1970	23				23	2,381				2,381
1971	18				18	502				502
1972	13				13	314				314
1973	13				13	322				322
1974	15				15	1,394				1,394
1975	14				14	390				390
1976	18	2			20	1,188	284			1,472
1977	19	1			20	4,680	518			5,198
1978	18				18	1,285				1,285
1979	14	4			18	508	1,093			1,600
1980	24	4			28	2,479	797			3,277
1981	21	11			32	5,198	5,221			10,419
1982	19	5			24	3,106	7,908			11,014
1983	27	4			31	5,450	8,671			14,121
1984	25	2			27	4,287	95			4,382
1985	24				24	3,218				3,218
1986	18	1			19	2,123	825			2,948
1987	22		10		32	4,118		358		4,476

Table II.1 *(concluded)*

Financial Year	Number of Arrangements					Amounts Committed Under Arrangements (in millions of SDRs)				
	Stand-By	EFF	SAF	ESAF	Total	Stand-By	EFF	SAF	ESAF	Total
1988	14	1	15		30	1,702	245	670		2,617
1989	12	1	4	7	24	2,956	207	427	955	4,545
1990	16	3	3	4	26	3,249	7,627	37	415	11,328
1991	13	2	2	3	20	2,786	2,338	15	454	5,593
1992	21	2	1	5	29	5,587	2,493	2	743	8,826
1993	11	3	1	8	23	1,971	1,242	49	527	3789
1994	18	2	1	7	28	1,381	779	27	1,170	3357
1995	17	3		11	31	13,055	2,335		1,197	16,587
1996	19	4	1	8	32	9,645	8,381	182	1,476	19,684
1997	11	5		12	28	3,183	1,193		911	5,287
1998	9	4		8	21	27,336	3,078		1,738	32,152

Table II.2

Arrangements in Effect at End of Financial Years Ended April 30, 1953–98

Financial Year	Number of Arrangements as of April 30					Amounts Committed Under Arrangements as of April 30 (in millions of SDRs)				
	Stand-By	EFF	SAF	ESAF	Total	Stand-By	EFF	SAF	ESAF	Total
1953	2				2	55				55
1954	3				3	113				113
1955	3				3	113				113
1956	3				3	98				98
1957	9				9	1,195				1,195
1958	9				9	968				968
1959	11				11	1,013				1,013
1960	12				12	351				351
1961	12				12	416				416
1962	21				21	2,129				2,129
1963	17				17	1,520				1,520
1964	19				19	2,160				2,160
1965	23				23	2,154				2,154
1966	24				24	575				575
1967	25				25	591				591
1968	31				31	2,227				2,227
1969	25				25	538				538
1970	23				23	2,381				2,381
1971	18				18	502				502
1972	13				13	314				314
1973	12				12	282				282
1974	15				15	1,394				1,394
1975	12				12	337				337
1976	17	2			19	1,159	284			1,443
1977	17	3			20	4,673	802			5,475
1978	19	3			22	5,075	802			5,877
1979	15	5			20	1,033	1,611			2,643
1980	22	7			29	2,340	1,463			3,803
1981	22	15			37	5,331	5,464			10,795
1982	23	12			35	6,296	9,910			16,206
1983	30	9			39	9,464	15,561			25,025
1984	30	5			35	5,448	13,121			18,569
1985	27	3			30	3,925	7,750			11,675
1986	24	2			26	4,076	831			4,907
1987	23	1	10		34	4,313	750	327		5,391
1988	18	2	25		45	2,187	995	1,357		4,540
1989	14	2	23	7	46	3,054	1,032	1,566	955	6,608
1990	19	4	17	11	51	3,597	7,834	1,110	1,370	13,911
1991	14	5	12	14	45	2,703	9,597	539	1,813	14,652
1992	22	7	8	16	53	4,833	12,159	101	2,111	19,203
1993	15	6	4	20	45	4,490	8,569	83	2,137	15,279
1994	16	6	3	22	47	1,131	4,504	80	2,713	8,428
1995	19	9	1	27	56	13,190	6,840	49	3,306	23,385
1996	21	7	1	28	57	14,963	9,390	182	3,383	27,918
1997	14	11		35	60	3,764	10,184		4,048	17,996
1998	14	13		33	60	28,323	12,336		4,410	45,069

Table II.3

Stand-By Arrangements in Effect During Financial Year Ended April 30, 1998
(In millions of SDRs)

Member	Arrangement Dates		Amounts Approved		Undrawn Balance	
	Effective date	Expiration date	Through April 30, 1997	In 1997/98	At date of termination	As of April 30, 1998
Argentina	4/12/96	1/11/98	720	—	107	—
Bulgaria	4/11/97	6/10/98	372	—	—	124
Cape Verde[1]	2/20/98	4/19/99	—	2	—	2
Djibouti[2]	4/15/96	6/30/98	5	2	—	3
Egypt[1]	10/11/96	9/30/98	271	—	—	271
El Salvador[1,3]	2/28/97	5/30/98	38	—	—	38
Estonia[1]	7/29/96	8/28/97	14	—	14	—
Estonia[1]	12/17/97	3/16/99	—	16	—	16
Hungary[1]	3/15/96	2/14/98	264	—	264	—
Indonesia	11/5/97	11/4/00	—	7,338	—	5,137
Korea[4]	12/4/97	12/3/00	—	15,500	—	4,300
Latvia[1]	5/24/96	8/23/97	30	—	30	—
Latvia[1]	10/10/97	4/9/99	—	33	—	33
Lesotho[1]	9/23/96	9/22/97	7	—	7	—
Pakistan[5]	12/13/95	9/30/97	563	—	268	—
Papua New Guinea[6]	7/14/95	12/15/97	71	—	36	—
Philippines[1]	4/1/98	3/31/00	—	1,021	—	1,021
Romania	4/22/97	5/21/98	302	—	—	181
Thailand	8/20/97	6/19/00	—	2,900	—	900
Ukraine	8/25/97	8/24/98	—	399	—	218
Uruguay[1]	6/20/97	3/19/99	—	125	—	125
Venezuela	7/12/96	7/11/97	976	—	626	—
Yemen	3/20/96	6/19/97	132	—	—	—
Total			**3,764**	**27,336**	**1,352**	**12,368**

[1]The authorities indicated their intention not to draw under the arrangement.
[2]Extended from June 14, 1997 and March 31, 1998. Increased by SDR 2 million.
[3]Extended from April 27, 1998.
[4]Includes SDR 10 billion available until December 17, 1998 under the Supplemental Reserve Facility.
[5]Extended from March 31, 1997. Original amount of SDR 402 million increased by SDR 161 million.
[6]Extended from January 13, 1997.

Table II.4

Extended Arrangements in Effect During Financial Year Ended April 30, 1998
(In millions of SDRs)

| Member | Arrangement Dates | | Amounts Approved | | Undrawn Balance | |
	Effective date	Expiration date	Through April 30, 1997	In 1997/98	At date of termination	As of April 30, 1998
Algeria	5/22/95	5/21/98	1,169	—	—	84
Argentina[1]	2/4/98	2/3/01	—	2,080	—	2,080
Azerbaijan	12/20/96	12/19/99	59	—	—	26
Croatia	3/12/97	3/11/00	353	—	—	324
Gabon	11/8/95	11/7/98	110	—	—	50
Jordan[2]	2/9/96	2/8/99	238	—	—	47
Kazakhstan[1]	7/17/96	7/16/99	309	—	—	309
Lithuania	10/24/94	10/23/97	135	—	—	—
Moldova	5/20/96	5/19/99	135	—	—	98
Pakistan	10/20/97	10/19/00	—	455	—	398
Panama	12/10/97	12/9/00	—	120	—	110
Peru[3]	7/1/96	3/31/99	300	—	—	140
Philippines[4]	6/24/94	3/31/98	475	317	—	—
Russia	3/26/96	3/25/99	6,901	—	—	3,065
Yemen	10/29/97	10/28/00	—	106	—	97
Total			**10,184**	**3,078**	**—**	**6,828**

[1]The authorities indicated their intention not to draw under the arrangement.
[2]Original amount of SDR 201 million increased by SDR 37 million.
[3]Original amount of SDR 248 million increased by SDR 52 million for debt and debt-service reduction.
[4]Extended from June 23, 1997, December 31, 1997, and January 31, 1998. Increased by SDR 317 million.

Table II.5

Arrangements Under the Enhanced Structural Adjustment Facility in Effect During Financial Year Ended April 30, 1998
(In millions of SDRs)

Member	Arrangement Dates		Amounts Approved		Undrawn Balance	
	Effective date	Expiration date[1]	Through April 30, 1997	In 1997/98	At date of termination	As of April 30, 1998
Armenia	2/14/96	2/13/99	101	—	—	34
Azerbaijan	12/20/96	12/19/99	94	—	—	38
Benin	8/28/96	8/27/99	27	—	—	18
Bolivia	12/19/94	9/9/98	101	—	—	—
Burkina Faso	6/14/96	6/13/99	40	—	—	20
Cambodia	5/6/94	8/31/97	84	—	42	—
Cameroon	8/20/97	8/19/00	—	162	—	108
Chad	9/1/95	8/31/98	50	—	—	17
Congo, Rep. of	6/28/96	6/27/99	69	—	—	56
Côte d'Ivoire	3/11/94	6/13/97	333	—	—	—
Côte d'Ivoire	3/17/98	3/16/01	—	286	—	202
Ethiopia	10/11/96	10/10/99	88	—	—	74
Georgia	2/28/96	2/27/99	167	—	—	56
Ghana[2]	6/30/95	6/29/99	164	—	—	69
Guinea	1/13/97	1/12/00	71	—	—	35
Guinea-Bissau[3]	1/18/95	7/24/98	9	1	—	—
Guyana	7/20/94	4/17/98	54	—	—	—
Haiti	10/18/96	10/17/99	91	—	—	76
Honduras	7/24/92	7/24/97	47	—	14	—
Kenya	4/26/96	4/25/99	150	—	—	125
Kyrgyz Republic	7/20/94	3/31/98	88	—	—	—
Lao PDR	6/4/93	5/7/97	35	—	—	—
Macedonia, FYR	4/11/97	4/10/00	55	—	—	36
Madagascar	11/27/96	11/26/99	81	—	—	54
Malawi	10/18/95	10/17/98	46	—	—	15
Mali	4/10/96	4/9/99	62	—	—	21
Mauritania	1/25/95	7/13/98	43	—	—	—
Mongolia	7/30/97	7/29/00	—	33	—	28
Mozambique	6/21/96	6/20/99	76	—	—	25
Nicaragua	6/24/94	6/23/97	120	—	100	—
Nicaragua	3/18/98	3/17/01	—	101	—	84
Niger	6/12/96	6/11/99	58	—	—	19
Pakistan	10/20/97	10/19/00	—	682	—	455
Senegal	8/29/94	1/12/98	131	—	—	—
Senegal	4/20/98	4/19/01	—	107	—	89
Sierra Leone	3/28/94	5/4/98	102	—	—	5
Tanzania	11/8/96	11/7/99	162	—	—	74
Togo	9/16/94	6/29/98	65	—	—	11
Uganda	9/6/94	11/17/97	121	—	—	—
Uganda	11/10/97	11/9/00	—	100	—	60
Vietnam	11/11/94	11/10/97	362	—	121	—
Yemen	10/29/97	10/28/00	—	265	—	221
Zambia	12/6/95	12/5/98	702	—	—	40
Total			**4,048**	**1,738**	**276**	**2,165**

[1]Expiration of the commitment period or the current annual arrangement, whichever is later.

[2]Extended from June 29, 1998.

[3]Augmented by SDR 1 million.

Table II.6

Summary of Disbursements, Repurchases, and Repayments, Financial Years Ended April 30, 1948–98
(In millions of SDRs)

Financial Year	Disbursements					Repurchases and Repayments				Total Fund Credit Outstanding[2]
	Purchases[1]	Trust Fund loans	SAF loans	ESAF loans	Total	Repurchases	Trust Fund repayments	SAF/ESAF repayments	Total	
1948	606				606					133
1949	119				119					193
1950	52				52	24			24	204
1951	28				28	19			19	176
1952	46				46	37			37	214
1953	66				66	185			185	178
1954	231				231	145			145	132
1955	49				49	276			276	55
1956	39				39	272			276	72
1957	1,114				1,114	75			75	611
1958	666				666	87			87	1,027
1959	264				264	537			537	898
1960	166				166	522			522	330
1961	577				577	659			659	552
1962	2,243				2,243	1,260			1,260	1,023
1963	580				580	807			807	1,059
1964	626				626	380			380	952
1965	1,897				1,897	517			517	1,480
1966	2,817				2,817	406			406	3,039
1967	1,061				1,061	340			340	2,945
1968	1,348				1,348	1,116			1,116	2,463
1969	2,839				2,839	1,542			1,542	3,299
1970	2,996				2,996	1,671			1,671	4,020
1971	1,167				1,167	1,657			1,657	2,556
1972	2,028				2,028	3,122			3,122	840
1973	1,175				1,175	540			540	998
1974	1,058				1,058	672			672	1,085
1975	5,102				5,102	518			518	4,869
1976	6,591				6,591	960			960	9,760
1977	4,910	32			4,942	868			868	13,687
1978	2,503	268			2,771	4,485			4,485	12,366
1979	3,720	670			4,390	4,859			4,859	9,843
1980	2,433	962			3,395	3,776			3,776	9,967
1981	4,860	1,060			5,920	2,853			2,853	12,536
1982	8,041				8,041	2,010			2,010	17,793
1983	11,392				11,392	1,555	18		1,574	26,563
1984	11,518				11,518	2,018	111		2,129	34,603
1985	6,289				6,289	2,730	212		2,943	37,622
1986	4,101				4,101	4,289	413		4,702	36,877
1987	3,685		139		3,824	6,169	579		6,749	33,443
1988	4,153		445		4,597	7,935	528		8,463	29,543
1989	2,541		290	264	3,095	6,258	447		6,705	25,520
1990	4,503		419	408	5,329	6,042	356		6,398	24,388
1991	6,955		84	491	7,530	5,440	168		5,608	25,603
1992	5,308		125	483	5,916	4,768		1	4,770	26,736
1993	8,465		20	573	9,058	4,083		36	4,119	28,496
1994	5,325		50	612	5,987	4,348	52	112	4,513	29,889
1995	10,615		14	573	11,175	3,984	4	244	4,231	36,837
1996	10,870		182	1,295	12,347	6,698	7	395	7,100	42,040
1997	4,939			705	5,644	6,668	5	524	7,196	40,488
1998	20,000			973	20,973	3,789	1	595	4,385	56,026

[1]Includes reserve tranche purchases.
[2]Excludes reserve tranche purchases.

Table II.7

Purchases and Loans from the IMF, Financial Year Ended April 30, 1998

(In millions of SDRs)

Member	Reserve Tranche	Stand-By	Extended Fund Facility	Total Purchases	ESAF Loans	Total Purchases and Loans
Albania[1]	—	—	—	9	—	9
Algeria	—	—	338	338	—	338
Argentina	—	214	—	214	—	214
Armenia	—	—	—	—	34	34
Azerbaijan	—	—	23	23	35	58
Benin	—	—	—	—	5	5
Bolivia	—	—	—	—	34	34
Bulgaria	—	224	—	224	—	224
Burkina Faso	—	—	—	—	7	7
Cameroon	—	—	—	—	54	54
Chad	—	—	—	—	8	8
Côte d'Ivoire	—	—	—	—	83	83
Djibouti	—	1	—	1	—	1
Gabon	—	—	17	17	—	17
Georgia	—	—	—	—	28	28
Ghana	—	—	—	—	41	41
Guinea	—	—	—	—	24	24
Guinea-Bissau	—	—	—	—	5	5
Guyana	—	—	—	—	9	9
Indonesia	288	2,201	—	2,490	—	2,490
Jordan	—	—	80	80	—	80
Korea[2]	444	11,200	—	11,644	—	11,644
Kyrgyz Republic	—	—	—	—	16	16
Lithuania	—	—	21	21	—	21
Macedonia, FYR	—	—	—	—	9	9
Madagascar	—	—	—	—	14	14
Malawi	—	—	—	—	8	8
Mali	—	—	—	—	21	21
Mauritania	—	—	—	—	14	14
Moldova	—	—	15	15	—	15
Mongolia	—	—	—	—	6	6
Mozambique	—	—	—	—	25	25
Nicaragua	—	—	—	—	17	17
Niger	—	—	—	—	19	19
Pakistan	—	—	57	57	227	284
Panama	—	—	10	10	—	10
Philippines	—	—	755	755	—	755
Romania	—	60	—	60	—	60
Russia	—	—	1,500	1,500	—	1,500
Rwanda[1]	—	6	—	6	—	6
Senegal	—	—	—	—	36	36
Sierra Leone	—	—	—	—	5	5
Tajikistan[1]	—	15	—	15	—	15
Tanzania	—	—	—	—	61	61
Thailand	317	2,000	—	2,317	—	2,317
Togo	—	—	—	—	22	22
Uganda	—	—	—	—	64	64
Ukraine	—	181	—	181	—	181
Yemen	—	14	9	23	44	67
Total	1,050	16,127	2,824	20,000	973	20,973

[1]Emergency postconflict assistance.

[2]Stand-By amount includes purchases under Supplemental Reserve Facility of SDR 7.1 billion.

Table II.8

Repurchases and Repayments to the IMF, Financial Year Ended April 30, 1998
(In millions of SDRs)

Member	Stand-By/ Credit Tranche	Extended Fund Facility	CCFF and STF	Total Repurchases	SAF/ESAF and Trust Fund Repayments	Total Repurchases and Repayments[1]
Albania	5	—	—	5	—	5
Algeria[2]	51	—	277	328	—	328
Argentina	38	415	—	453	—	453
Bangladesh	—	—	—	—	83	83
Barbados	1	—	—	1	—	1
Belarus	—	—	6	6	—	6
Benin	—	—	—	—	3	3
Bolivia	—	—	—	—	26	26
Brazil	16	—	—	16	—	16
Bulgaria	62	—	—	62	—	62
Burkina Faso	—	—	—	—	1	1
Burundi	—	—	—	—	6	6
Cambodia	—	—	1	1	—	1
Cameroon	11	—	—	11	—	11
Central African Rep.	5	—	—	5	4	9
Chad	5	—	—	5	4	9
Congo, Republic of	5	—	—	5	—	5
Côte d'Ivoire	9	—	—	9	—	9
Croatia	3	—	—	3	—	3
Dominican Republic	23	—	17	41	—	41
Ecuador	12	—	—	12	—	12
Equatorial Guinea	—	—	—	—	2	2
Estonia	13	—	1	14	—	14
Ethiopia	—	—	—	—	1	1
Gabon	7	—	—	7	—	7
Gambia, The	—	—	—	—	5	5
Ghana	—	11	24	34	86	120
Guinea	—	—	—	—	6	6
Guinea-Bissau	—	—	—	—	1	1
Guyana	4	—	—	4	12	16
Honduras	—	—	—	—	1	1
Hungary[3]	—	119	—	119	—	119
India	430	—	—	430	—	430
Jamaica	15	4	—	19	—	19
Jordan	13	—	—	13	—	13
Kazakhstan	14	—	5	19	—	19
Kenya	—	—	—	—	49	49
Kyrgyz Republic	6	—	3	8	—	8
Lao People's Dem. Rep.	—	—	—	—	4	4
Latvia	26	—	—	26	—	26
Lesotho	—	—	—	—	3	3
Lithuania	27	—	2	29	—	29
Madagascar	—	—	—	—	12	12
Malawi	2	—	—	2	12	14
Mali	—	—	—	—	6	6
Mauritania	—	—	—	—	5	5
Mexico	—	359	—	359	—	359
Moldova	12	—	10	23	—	23
Mozambique	—	—	—	—	11	11
Nepal	—	—	—	—	5	5
Niger	6	—	—	6	7	12
Pakistan	115	—	—	115	76	192
Panama	11	—	—	11	—	11
Peru	—	107	—	107	—	107
Philippines	87	39	—	126	—	126

Table II.8 *(concluded)*

Member	Stand-By/ Credit Tranche	Extended Fund Facility	CCFF and STF	Total Repurchases	SAF/ESAF and Trust Fund Repayments	Total Repurchases and Repayments[1]
Romania	78	—	10	87	—	87
Russia	270	—	90	359	—	359
Rwanda	—	—	—	—	2	2
Senegal	15	—	—	15	31	47
Slovak Republic	35	—	5	40	—	40
South Africa	—	—	307	307	—	307
Sri Lanka	—	—	—	—	54	54
Sudan	6	20	7	33	—	33
Tanzania	—	—	—	—	20	20
Togo	—	—	—	—	8	8
Trinidad and Tobago	9	—	—	9	—	9
Tunisia	—	37	—	37	—	37
Turkey	70	—	—	70	—	70
Uganda	—	—	—	—	42	42
Uruguay	2	—	—	2	—	2
Venezuela	—	329	—	329	—	329
Vietnam	45	—	1	46	—	46
Zimbabwe	—	19	—	19	5	24
Total	**1,565**	**1,458**	**766**	**3,789**	**596**	**4,385**

[1]Includes Comoros, Dominica, Liberia, Mongolia, and São Tomé and Príncipe, each of which had repurchases or repayments totaling less than SDR 500,000.

[2]CCFF overcompensation.

[3]Advance repurchase.

Table II.9

Outstanding IMF Credit by Facility and Policy, Financial Years Ended April 30, 1991–98
(In millions of SDRs and percent of total)

	1991	1992	1993	1994	1995	1996	1997	1998
	Millions of SDRs							
Stand-By Arrangements[1]	9,323	9,469	10,578	9,485	15,117	20,700	18,064	25,526
Extended Arrangements	8,440	8,641	9,849	9,566	10,155	9,982	11,155	12,521
Supplemental Reserve Facility	—	—	—	—	—	—	—	7,100
Compensatory and Contingency Financing Facility	5,142	5,322	4,208	3,756	3,021	1,602	1,336	685
Systemic Transformation Facility	—	—	—	2,725	3,848	3,984	3,984	3,869
Subtotal (GRA)	**22,906**	**23,432**	**24,635**	**25,532**	**32,140**	**36,268**	**34,539**	**49,701**
SAF arrangements	1,377	1,500	1,484	1,440	1,277	1,208	954	730
ESAF arrangements[2]	1,163	1,646	2,219	2,812	3,318	4,469	4,904	5,505
Trust Fund	158	158	158	105	102	95	90	90
Total	**25,603**	**26,736**	**28,496**	**29,889**	**36,837**	**42,040**	**40,488**	**56,026**
	Percent of total							
Stand-By Arrangements[1]	36	35	37	32	41	49	45	46
Extended Arrangements	33	32	34	32	28	24	28	22
Supplemental Reserve Facility	—	—	—	—	—	—	—	13
Compensatory and Contingency Financing Facility	20	20	15	12	8	4	3	1
Systemic Transformation Facility	—	—	—	9	10	9	10	7
Subtotal (GRA)	**89**	**87**	**86**	**85**	**87**	**86**	**85**	**89**
SAF Arrangements	5	6	5	5	3	3	2	1
ESAF Arrangements[2]	5	6	8	9	9	11	12	10
Trust Fund	1	1	1	—[3]	—[3]	—[3]	—[3]	—[3]
Total	**100**	**100**	**100**	**100**	**100**	**100**	**100**	**100**

[1]Includes outstanding credit tranche and emergency purchases.
[2]Includes outstanding associated loans from the Saudi Fund for Development.
[3]Less than ½ of 1 percent of total.

Table II.10

Enhanced Structural Adjustment Facility, Estimated Value of Contributions (Commitments as of April 30, 1998)
(In millions of SDRs)

Contributor	Subsidies (Grant or Grant Equivalent)[1]			Loans[2]	
	Prior to enlargement	For enlargement[3]	Total	Prior to enlargement	For enlargement
Argentina	—	32	32	—	—
Australia	—	14	14	—	—
Austria	42	19	61	—	—
Bangladesh	—	1	1	—	—
Belgium	83	42	125	—	—
Botswana	—	3	3	—	—
Canada	128	67	194	300	200
Chile	—	4	4	—	—
China	—	14	14	—	100
Colombia	—	6	6	—	—
Czech Republic	—	12	12	—	—
Denmark	49	27	76	—	—
Egypt	—	12	12	—	100
Finland	41	—	41	—	—
France	264	250	514	800	750
Germany	193	—	193	700	700
Greece	24	13	37	—	—
Iceland	3	1	4	—	—
India	—	12	12	—	—
Indonesia	—	6	6	—	—
Iran, Islamic Republic of	—	2	2	—	—
Ireland	—	6	6	—	—
Italy	137	42	179	370	210
Japan	454	250	704	2,200	2,150
Korea	50	8	59	65	28
Luxembourg	5	8	13	—	—
Malaysia	33	15	48	—	—
Malta	1	1	2	—	—
Mexico	—	33	33	—	—
Morocco	—	9	9	—	—
Netherlands	81	55	136	—	—
Norway	29	15	44	90	60
Pakistan	—	4	4	—	—
Portugal	—	6	6	—	—
Singapore	21	15	37	—	—
Spain	—	32	32	216	67
Sweden	129	52	181	200	152
Switzerland	56	48	105	—	—
Thailand	12	5	17	—	—
Tunisia	—	2	2	—	—
Turkey	—	10	10	—	—
United Kingdom	334	77	411	—	—
United States	144	78	223	—	—
Uruguay	—	2	2	—	—
Other	—	15	15	—	—
Saudi Arabia	83[4]	—	83[4]	200[4]	—
Subtotal (bilateral)	**2,381[5]**	**1,325**	**3,706**	**5,141**	**4,517**
OPEC Fund	—	—	—	—	37[6]
SDA[7]	—	589	589	—	—
Total	**2,381[5]**	**1,914**	**4,295**	**5,141**	**4,554**

[1]The amounts reported for grant contributions are the "as needed" equivalent of the resources committed, or implicit in loans or deposits at concessional interest rates. The calculations are based on actual interest rates through April 30, 1998 and an assumed rate of 6.0 percent a year thereafter. Grants committed in local currency are valued at April 30, 1998 exchange rates.

[2]Loan contributions are provided either at concessional interest rates or on the basis of weighted averages of market interest rates in the five currencies comprising the SDR basket.

[3]Some of the contributions listed are subject to parliamentary approval or completion of other internal procedures. A few contributions are to be confirmed.

[4]Corresponds to the associated borrowing agreement with the Saudi Fund for Development (SFD).

[5]The sum of individual contributions has been adjusted downward to take into account additional loan costs.

[6]The SDR equivalent of $50 million valued at the exchange rate of April 30, 1998.

[7]Special Disbursement Account.

Table II.11

Special One-Time Allocation of SDRs Pursuant to Schedule M of the Proposed Fourth Amendment of the Articles of Agreement
(In SDRs)

Country	Ninth General Review Quota	Existing Cumulative Allocations	Special Allocation[1]
Afghanistan, Islamic State of	120,400,000	26,703,000	8,593,210
Albania	35,300,000	—	10,348,473
Algeria	914,400,000	128,640,000	139,423,573
Angola	207,300,000	—	60,771,630
Antigua and Barbuda	8,500,000	—	2,491,842
Argentina	1,537,100,000	318,370,000	132,242,990
Armenia	67,500,000	—	19,788,157
Australia	2,333,200,000	470,545,000	213,450,985
Austria	1,188,300,000	179,045,000	169,314,518
Azerbaijan	117,000,000	—	34,299,473
Bahamas, The	94,900,000	10,230,000	17,590,684
Bahrain	82,800,000	6,200,000	18,073,473
Bangladesh	392,500,000	47,120,000	67,944,471
Barbados	48,900,000	8,039,000	6,296,421
Belarus	280,400,000	—	82,201,472
Belgium	3,102,300,000	485,246,000	424,217,716
Belize	13,500,000	—	3,957,631
Benin	45,300,000	9,409,000	3,871,052
Bhutan	4,500,000	—	1,319,210
Bolivia	126,200,000	26,703,000	10,293,525
Bosnia and Herzegovina	121,200,000	20,481,252	15,049,484
Botswana	36,600,000	4,359,000	6,370,579
Brazil	2,170,800,000	358,670,000	277,717,144
Brunei Darussalam	150,000,000	—	43,973,683
Bulgaria	464,900,000	—	136,289,102
Burkina Faso	44,200,000	9,409,000	3,548,579
Burundi	57,200,000	13,697,000	3,071,631
Cambodia	65,000,000	15,417,000	3,638,263
Cameroon	135,100,000	24,462,600	15,143,031
Canada	4,320,300,000	779,290,000	487,240,024
Cape Verde	7,000,000	620,000	1,432,105
Central African Republic	41,200,000	9,325,000	2,753,105
Chad	41,300,000	9,409,000	2,698,421
Chile	621,700,000	121,924,000	60,332,259
China	3,385,200,000	236,800,000	755,598,083
Colombia	561,300,000	114,271,000	50,278,523
Comoros	6,500,000	716,400	1,189,126
Congo, Democratic Republic of the[2]	394,800,000	86,309,000	29,429,734
Congo, Republic of	57,900,000	9,719,000	7,254,842
Costa Rica	119,000,000	23,726,000	11,159,789
Côte d'Ivoire	238,200,000	37,828,000	32,002,209
Croatia	261,600,000	44,205,369	32,484,735
Cyprus	100,000,000	19,438,000	9,877,789
Czech Republic	589,600,000	—	172,845,891
Denmark	1,069,900,000	178,864,000	134,785,625
Djibouti	11,500,000	1,178,000	2,193,316
Dominica	6,000,000	592,400	1,166,547
Dominican Republic	158,800,000	31,585,000	14,968,473
Ecuador	219,200,000	32,929,000	31,331,209
Egypt	678,400,000	135,924,000	62,954,311
El Salvador	125,600,000	24,985,000	11,835,631
Equatorial Guinea	24,300,000	5,812,000	1,311,737
Eritrea	11,500,000	—	3,371,316
Estonia	46,500,000	—	13,631,842
Ethiopia	98,300,000	11,160,000	17,657,420

Table II.11 *(continued)*

Country	Ninth General Review Quota	Existing Cumulative Allocations	Special Allocation[1]
Fiji	51,100,000	6,958,000	8,022,368
Finland	861,800,000	142,690,000	109,953,468
France	7,414,600,000	1,079,870,000	1,093,778,477
Gabon	110,300,000	14,091,000	18,244,315
Gambia, The	22,900,000	5,121,000	1,592,316
Georgia	111,000,000	—	32,540,526
Germany	8,241,500,000	1,210,760,000	1,205,300,735
Ghana	274,000,000	62,983,000	17,342,261
Greece	587,600,000	103,544,000	68,715,575
Grenada	8,500,000	930,000	1,561,842
Guatemala	153,800,000	27,678,000	17,409,683
Guinea	78,700,000	17,604,000	5,467,526
Guinea-Bissau	10,500,000	1,212,400	1,865,758
Guyana	67,200,000	14,530,000	5,170,210
Haiti	60,700,000	13,697,000	4,097,684
Honduras	95,000,000	19,057,000	8,792,999
Hungary	754,800,000	—	221,275,574
Iceland	85,300,000	16,409,000	8,597,368
India	3,055,500,000	681,170,000	214,573,927
Indonesia	1,497,600,000	238,956,000	200,077,253
Iran, Islamic Republic of	1,078,500,000	244,056,000	72,114,782
Iraq[2]	864,800,000	68,463,800	185,059,142
Ireland	525,000,000	87,263,000	66,644,891
Israel	666,200,000	106,360,000	88,941,785
Italy	4,590,700,000	702,400,000	643,399,917
Jamaica	200,900,000	40,613,000	18,282,420
Japan	8,241,500,000	891,690,000	1,524,370,735
Jordan	121,700,000	16,887,000	18,790,315
Kazakhstan	247,500,000	—	72,556,577
Kenya	199,400,000	36,990,000	21,465,683
Kiribati	4,000,000	—	1,172,632
Korea	799,600,000	72,911,200	161,497,847
Kuwait	995,200,000	26,744,400	265,006,330
Kyrgyz Republic	64,500,000	—	18,908,684
Lao People's Democratic Republic	39,100,000	9,409,000	2,053,473
Latvia	91,500,000	—	26,823,947
Lebanon	146,000,000	4,393,200	38,407,852
Lesotho	23,900,000	3,739,000	3,267,474
Liberia[2]	96,200,000	21,007,000	7,194,789
Libya	817,600,000	58,771,200	180,914,689
Lithuania	103,500,000	—	30,341,841
Luxembourg	135,500,000	16,955,000	22,767,894
Macedonia, former Yugoslav Republic of	49,600,000	8,378,694	6,161,937
Madagascar	90,400,000	19,270,000	7,231,473
Malawi	50,900,000	10,975,000	3,946,737
Malaysia	832,700,000	139,048,000	105,064,573
Maldives	5,500,000	282,400	1,329,968
Mali	68,900,000	15,912,000	4,286,578
Malta	67,500,000	11,288,000	8,500,157
Marshall Islands	2,500,000	—	732,895
Mauritania	47,500,000	9,719,000	4,206,000
Mauritius	73,300,000	15,744,000	5,744,473
Mexico	1,753,300,000	290,020,000	223,973,725
Micronesia, Federated States of	3,500,000	—	1,026,053
Moldova	90,000,000	—	26,384,210

Table II.11 (continued)

Country	Ninth General Review Quota	Existing Cumulative Allocations	Special Allocation[1]
Mongolia	37,100,000	—	10,876,158
Morocco	427,700,000	85,689,000	39,694,629
Mozambique	84,000,000	—	24,625,263
Myanmar	184,900,000	43,474,000	10,730,894
Namibia	99,600,000	—	29,198,526
Nepal	52,000,000	8,104,800	7,139,410
Netherlands	3,444,200,000	530,340,000	479,354,398
New Zealand	650,100,000	141,322,000	49,259,943
Nicaragua	96,100,000	19,483,000	8,689,473
Niger	48,300,000	9,409,000	4,750,526
Nigeria	1,281,600,000	157,155,000	218,556,149
Norway	1,104,600,000	167,770,000	156,052,203
Oman	119,400,000	6,262,000	28,741,052
Pakistan	758,200,000	169,989,000	52,283,311
Panama	149,600,000	26,322,000	17,534,420
Papua New Guinea	95,300,000	9,300,000	18,637,947
Paraguay	72,100,000	13,697,000	7,439,684
Peru	466,100,000	91,319,000	45,321,892
Philippines	633,400,000	116,595,000	69,091,206
Poland	988,500,000	—	289,786,572
Portugal	557,600,000	53,320,000	110,144,838
Qatar	190,500,000	12,821,600	43,024,978
Romania	754,100,000	75,950,000	145,120,363
Russia	4,313,100,000	—	1,264,419,287
Rwanda	59,500,000	13,697,000	3,745,894
St. Kitts and Nevis	6,500,000	—	1,905,526
St. Lucia	11,000,000	741,600	2,483,137
St. Vincent and the Grenadines	6,000,000	353,600	1,405,347
Samoa	8,500,000	1,142,000	1,349,842
San Marino	10,000,000	—	2,931,579
São Tomé and Príncipe	5,500,000	620,000	992,368
Saudi Arabia	5,130,600,000	195,526,800	1,308,549,061
Senegal	118,900,000	24,462,000	10,394,473
Seychelles	6,000,000	406,400	1,352,547
Sierra Leone	77,200,000	17,455,000	5,176,789
Singapore	357,600,000	16,475,200	88,358,061
Slovak Republic	257,400,000	—	75,458,840
Slovenia	150,500,000	25,430,888	18,689,374
Solomon Islands	7,500,000	654,400	1,544,284
Somalia[2]	60,900,000	13,697,000	4,156,315
South Africa	1,365,400,000	220,360,000	179,917,780
Spain	1,935,400,000	298,805,000	268,572,777
Sri Lanka	303,600,000	70,868,000	18,134,735
Sudan[2]	233,100,000	52,192,000	16,143,104
Suriname	67,600,000	7,750,000	12,067,473
Swaziland	36,500,000	6,432,000	4,268,263
Sweden	1,614,000,000	246,525,000	226,631,831
Switzerland	2,470,400,000	—	724,217,247
Syrian Arab Republic	209,900,000	36,564,000	24,969,841
Tajikistan	60,000,000	—	17,589,473
Tanzania	146,900,000	31,372,000	11,692,894
Thailand	573,900,000	84,652,000	83,591,312
Togo	54,300,000	10,975,000	4,943,473
Tonga	5,000,000	—	1,465,789
Trinidad and Tobago	246,800,000	46,231,000	26,120,367

Table II.11 *(concluded)*

Country	Ninth General Review Quota	Existing Cumulative Allocations	Special Allocation[1]
Tunisia	206,000,000	34,243,000	26,147,525
Turkey	642,000,000	112,307,000	75,900,364
Turkmenistan	48,000,000	—	14,071,579
Uganda	133,900,000	29,396,000	9,857,841
Ukraine	997,300,000	—	292,366,362
United Arab Emirates	392,100,000	38,736,800	76,210,408
United Kingdom	7,414,600,000	1,913,070,000	260,578,477
United States	26,526,800,000	4,899,530,000	2,877,010,667
Uruguay	225,300,000	49,977,000	16,071,472
Uzbekistan	199,500,000	—	58,484,999
Vanuatu	12,500,000	—	3,664,474
Venezuela	1,951,300,000	316,890,000	255,148,987
Vietnam	241,600,000	47,658,000	23,168,946
Yemen	176,500,000	28,743,000	22,999,367
Yugoslavia, Federal Republic of (Serbia/Montenegro)[2]	335,400,000	56,664,797	41,660,359
Zambia	363,500,000	68,298,000	38,264,892
Zimbabwe	261,300,000	10,200,000	66,402,156
Total[3]	146,223,800,000	21,433,330,200	21,433,330,200

[1]Participants as of September 19, 1997, will receive a special one-time allocation of SDRs in an amount that will result in their cumulative allocations of SDRs being equal to 29.315788813 percent of their Ninth General Review quota.

[2]These countries currently have Eighth General Review quotas. The Federal Republic of Yugoslavia (Serbia/Montenegro) has not completed arrangements for succession to membership and is not currently a participant in the SDR Department.

[3]A country that becomes a participant in the SDR Department after September 19, 1997, and within three months of its membership in the IMF will receive a special one-time allocation of SDRs based on a notional Ninth General Review quota. The Republic of Palau, which became a member and a participant in the SDR Department in December 1997 with an initial quota of SDR 2.25 million, will be entitled to receive a special one-time allocation of SDR 659,605.

Table II.12

Summary of Transactions and Operations in SDRs, Financial Year Ended April 30, 1998
(In thousands of SDRs)

Member	Total Holdings April 30, 1997	Receipts from Participants and Prescribed Holders — Designated	Receipts from Participants and Prescribed Holders — Other	Transfers to Participants and Prescribed Holders — Designated	Transfers to Participants and Prescribed Holders — Other	Receipts from the General Resources Account	Transfers to the General Resources Account	Interest, Charges, and Assessment (Net)	Positions as at April 30, 1998 — Holdings	Positions as at April 30, 1998 — Net cumulative allocations	Positions as at April 30, 1998 — Holdings as percent of cumulative allocations
Participants											
Afghanistan, Islamic State of	—	—	—	—	—	—	—	—	—	26,703	—
Albania	89	—	5,075	—	155	6	4,846	4	173	—	—
Algeria	18,614	—	308,925	—	129,912	210,439	400,958	-4,721	2,387	128,640	1.9
Angola	115	—	—	—	—	—	—	5	120	—	—
Antigua and Barbuda	5	—	—	—	—	—	—	—	5	—	—
Argentina	257,866	—	387,000	—	2,267	112,327	660,728	-5,639	88,559	318,370	27.8
Armenia	28,609	—	—	—	212	53	2,219	1,157	27,389	—	—
Australia	22,438	—	113,260	—	126,601	7,854	—	-18,657	11,634	470,545	2.5
Austria	114,887	—	20,480	—	34,668	19,599	—	-2,159	118,986	179,045	66.5
Azerbaijan	8,572	—	—	—	—	14,242	6,351	268	2,544	—	—
Bahamas, The	104	—	384	—	—	48	—	-421	115	10,230	1.1
Bahrain	11,735	—	—	—	82,072	—	—	229	11,965	6,200	193.0
Bangladesh	59,372	—	30,000	—	—	—	—	-133	7,167	47,120	15.2
Barbados	127	—	348	—	—	3	38	-330	111	8,039	1.4
Belarus	2,136	—	2,300	—	—	7,003	8,923	17	2,533	—	—
Belgium	350,511	—	899	—	—	22,264	—	-5,377	368,298	485,246	75.9
Belize	633	—	—	—	—	79	—	28	740	—	—
Benin	123	—	4,930	—	4,530	—	—	-385	138	9,409	1.5
Bhutan	479	—	—	—	—	14	—	20	513	—	—
Bolivia	26,804	—	16,830	—	16,830	—	—	-1	26,802	26,703	100.4
Bosnia and Herzegovina[1]	585	—	—	—	—	2,227	1,406	-834	572	20,481	2.8
Botswana	29,110	—	20,550	—	—	666	—	1,040	30,816	4,359	707.0
Brazil	52	—	—	—	—	37	1,271	-14,771	4,597	358,670	1.3
Brunei Darussalam	783	—	—	—	—	1,042	—	49	1,873	—	—
Bulgaria	896	—	96,500	—	32,200	33,658	89,398	178	9,634	—	—
Burkina Faso	1,753	—	—	—	900	154	—	-319	688	9,409	7.3
Burundi	159	—	540	—	—	43	—	-563	178	13,697	1.3
Cambodia	9,383	—	—	—	210	7	814	-262	8,104	15,417	52.6
Cameroon	254	—	30,226	—	27,020	54	2,204	-1,007	303	24,463	1.2
Canada	817,677	—	—	—	63,000	22,477	—	1,762	778,916	779,290	100.0
Cape Verde	39	—	—	—	—	—	5	-24	9	620	1.5
Central African Republic	100	—	7,311	—	2,447	11	4,481	-384	111	9,325	1.2
Chad	110	—	8,791	—	8,000	10	420	-379	111	9,409	1.2
Chile	1,322	—	3,800	—	—	1,053	—	-5,001	1,174	121,924	1.0
China	436,393	—	356	—	43,325	37,109	—	8,303	438,836	236,800	185.3

Member										
Colombia	124,012	—	—	—	191	5,032	—	452	129,497	114,271	113.3
Comoros	—	—	217	—	—	9	—	-29	7	716	1.0
Congo, Democratic Republic of the	—	—	—	—	—	—	—	—	—	86,309	—
Congo, Republic of	107	—	949	—	—	13	551	-400	119	9,719	1.2
Costa Rica	267	—	950	—	—	28	4	-976	266	23,726	1.1
Côte d'Ivoire	506	—	1,750	—	—	10	273	-1,553	440	37,828	1.2
Croatia, Republic of[1]	112,871	—	—	—	—	188	11,851	2,606	103,814	44,205	234.8
Cyprus	31	—	250	—	—	748	—	-798	231	19,438	1.2
Czech Republic	—	—	—	—	—	—	—	—	—	—	—
Denmark	158,968	—	199,000	—	130,779	14,124	—	803	242,116	178,864	135.4
Djibouti	61	—	659	—	1,100	1,108	186	-43	498	1,178	42.3
Dominica	7	—	293	—	282	13	—	-24	7	592	1.1
Dominican Republic	1,084	—	2,807	—	—	51	1,872	-1,290	780	31,585	2.5
Ecuador	2,016	—	16,500	—	—	458	17,025	-1,311	638	32,929	1.9
Egypt	94,991	—	69,773	—	49,348	267	685	-1,698	113,300	135,924	83.4
El Salvador	24,981	—	28	—	—	—	24	-5	24,980	24,985	100.0
Equatorial Guinea	112	—	245	—	55	—	—	-239	63	5,812	1.1
Eritrea	39	—	—	—	—	86	—	9	55	—	—
Estonia	218	—	16,494	—	—	13	16,573	—	196	11,160	—
Ethiopia	—	—	421	—	—	—	—	-456	8,369	6,958	1.8
Fiji	8,057	—	—	—	—	264	—	48	—	—	120.3
Finland	166,787	—	308,997	—	275,824	9,828	—	2,391	212,179	142,690	148.7
France	691,261	—	—	—	—	56,793	—	-15,560	732,494	1,079,870	67.8
Gabon	1,099	—	3,612	—	16,000	16,696	—	-573	239	14,091	1.7
Gambia, The	815	—	4,750	—	—	4,694	—	-171	699	5,121	13.7
Georgia	947	—	3,813	—	238	88	3,649	12	974	—	—
Germany	1,322,430	—	—	—	102,166	131,262	—	4,715	1,356,241	1,210,760	112.0
Ghana	15,015	—	111,679	—	87,323	47	36,236	-2,322	860	62,983	1.4
Greece	616	—	1,000	—	—	3,062	—	-4,259	419	103,544	0.4
Grenada	32	—	60	—	—	—	—	-38	54	930	5.8
Guatemala	9,975	—	17,600	—	11,512	—	—	-743	9,232	27,678	33.4
Guinea	1,628	—	2,363	—	2,363	—	—	-667	7,050	17,604	40.0
Guinea-Bissau	79	—	28,110	—	—	—	—	-48	31	1,212	2.6
Guyana	543	—	1,279	—	21,380	5	4,613	-572	2,092	14,530	14.4
Haiti	403	—	—	—	—	19	770	-560	371	13,697	2.7
Honduras	242	—	817	—	—	3	14	-783	265	19,057	1.4
Hungary	1,354	—	4,000	—	—	575	5,575	23	378	16,409	—
Iceland	221	—	410	—	—	183	—	-674	141	681,170	0.9
India	19,244	—	291,000	—	—	965	261,038	-27,518	22,652	238,956	3.3
Indonesia	1,230	—	14,000	—	387,617	—	49,480	-6,190	347,176	244,056	145.3
Iran, Islamic Republic of	239,668	—	7,015	—	2,000	—	—	-108	244,575	68,464	100.2
Iraq	116,868	—	—	—	—	7,408	—	—	—	87,263	—
Ireland	2,362	—	—	—	—	15	161	1,326	125,602	106,360	143.9
Israel	—	—	3,450	—	—	—	—	-4,357	1,309	702,400	1.2
Italy	22,896	—	29,571	—	42,552	—	—	-27,418	67,601	—	9.6

Table II.12 *(continued)*

Member	Total Holdings April 30, 1997	Receipts from Participants and Prescribed Holders Designated	Other	Transfers to Participants and Prescribed Holders Designated	Other	Receipts from the General Resources Account	Transfers to the General Resources Account	Interest, Charges, and Assessment (Net)	Positions as at April 30, 1998 Holdings	Net cumulative allocations	Holdings as percent of cumulative allocations
Jamaica	1,818	—	6,000	—	—	115	4,581	−1,655	1,697	40,613	4.2
Japan	1,855,984	—	399,150	—	543,749	179,949	—	43,860	1,935,194	891,690	217.0
Jordan	125	—	23,032	—	46,422	42,026	13,802	−648	4,311	16,887	25.5
Kazakhstan	256,658	—	79,125	—	—	430	37,476	11,423	310,160	—	—
Kenya	621	—	51,374	—	49,986	14	—	−1,465	558	36,990	1.5
Kiribati	8	—	—	—	—	—	—	—	8	—	—
Korea	86,471	—	37,000	—	570,000	615,917	164,790	444	5,043	72,911	6.9
Kuwait	69,623	—	—	—	—	4,516	—	1,848	75,987	26,744	284.1
Kyrgyz Republic	3,275	—	7,700	—	340	43	10,256	93	516	—	—
Lao People's Democratic Republic	11,548	—	—	—	3,767	—	—	58	7,839	9,409	83.3
Latvia	975	—	29,200	—	—	88	29,401	32	895	—	—
Lebanon	13,579	—	—	—	—	641	—	392	14,612	4,393	332.6
Lesotho	914	—	—	—	—	88	—	−117	885	3,739	23.7
Liberia	—	—	—	—	—	—	—	—	—	21,007	—
Libya	379,733	—	—	—	—	12,104	—	13,543	405,379	58,771	689.8
Lithuania	7,058	—	18,203	—	5,000	20,976	38,358	285	3,164	—	—
Luxembourg	7,819	—	—	—	—	668	—	−374	8,113	16,955	47.8
Macedonia, former Yugoslav Republic of[1]	2,162	—	1,100	—	38	53	2,214	−311	752	8,379	9.0
Madagascar	227	—	780	—	—	—	—	−792	215	19,270	1.1
Malawi	681	—	16,980	—	12,603	14	2,188	−428	2,457	10,975	22.4
Malaysia	118,885	—	—	—	—	15,607	—	−625	133,867	139,048	96.3
Maldives	68	—	—	—	—	27	—	−9	87	282	30.6
Mali	331	—	10,685	—	10,335	126	—	−650	157	15,912	1.0
Malta	40,264	—	14	—	—	1,031	—	1,220	42,529	11,288	376.8
Marshall Islands	—	—	—	—	—	—	—	—	—	—	—
Mauritania	148	—	7,125	—	6,757	—	—	−354	162	9,719	1.7
Mauritius	22,228	—	—	—	—	72	—	268	22,568	15,744	143.3
Mexico	225,472	—	788,563	—	—	8,498	590,980	2,233	433,785	290,020	149.6
Micronesia, Federated States of	953	—	—	—	—	—	—	40	993	—	—
Moldova	1,307	—	27,500	—	11,000	15,252	31,022	56	2,093	—	—
Mongolia	980	—	—	—	160	1	320	27	529	—	—
Morocco	2,219	—	18,000	—	15,568	83	1	−3,409	1,324	85,689	1.5
Mozambique	38	—	—	—	—	—	—	2	40	—	—
Myanmar	465	—	1,900	—	—	—	—	−1,788	577	43,474	1.3
Namibia	13	—	—	—	—	—	—	1	13	—	—

Nepal	150	200	—	102	—	−331	121	8,105	1.5
Netherlands	540,288	793,235	777,091	42,624	—	1,530	600,586	530,340	113.2
New Zealand	311	3,600	—	2,758	—	−5,816	853	141,322	0.6
Nicaragua	208	933	—	216	—	−802	239	19,483	1.2
Niger	1,651	16,060	16,580	—	441	−324	583	9,409	6.2
Nigeria	365	8,100	—	22,674	—	−6,459	2,006	157,155	1.3
Norway	239,285	297,383	322,704	1,158	—	3,257	239,895	167,770	143.0
Oman	9,154	—	—	19,686	—	137	10,449	6,262	166.9
Pakistan	8,414	172,243	102,680	—	81,931	−6,820	8,912	169,989	5.2
Palau	—	—	—	—	—	—	—	—	—
Panama	1,301	16,575	—	747	15,936	−1,005	1,682	26,322	6.4
Papua New Guinea	583	2,002	—	40	1,698	−378	550	9,300	5.9
Paraguay	73,967	147,679	—	378	143,779	2,513	76,858	13,697	561.1
Peru	885	121,000	—	852	106,992	−3,728	1,910	91,319	2.1
Philippines	1,927	—	349,000	355,691	—	−4,639	17,987	116,595	15.4
Poland	3,296	—	—	808	—	150	4,253	53,320	—
Portugal	70,926	—	—	11,108	—	888	82,922	12,822	155.5
Qatar	22,825	—	—	848	—	427	24,101	75,950	188.0
Romania	60,153	655,000	—	60,993	60,540	−785	59,821	13,697	78.8
Russia	405	—	749,000	917,921	822,636	664	2,355	—	—
Rwanda	20,690	378	1,795	18	812	200	18,680	742	136.4
St. Kitts and Nevis	1,425	—	—	—	—	28	1,453	354	196.0
St. Lucia	73	—	—	—	—	−12	69	1,142	—
St. Vincent and the Grenadines	2,110	—	—	7	—	40	2,157	620	19.4
Samoa	271	—	—	7	—	12	354	—	188.9
San Marino	6	169	162	70	—	−25	7	—	—
São Tomé and Príncipe	—	—	—	19	—	—	—	—	1.1
Saudi Arabia	488,752	49,900	—	19,470	16,683	12,475	520,697	195,527	266.3
Senegal	3,470	—	32,518	30	—	−909	3,290	24,462	13.4
Seychelles	24	—	—	21	—	−16	30	406	7.4
Sierra Leone	5,200	4,000	610	7,458	—	−403	8,187	17,455	46.9
Singapore	44,474	1,600	—	228	49,541	1,309	54,841	16,475	332.9
Slovak Republic	6,001	50,000	—	174	—	213	6,901	25,431	1.2
Slovenia, Republic of[1]	279	900	—	6	6	−1,045	301	654	1.1
Solomon Islands	11	17	—	—	—	−27	7	13,697	—
Somalia	680	—	—	542	252,305	−8,847	—	220,360	20.1
South Africa	323,001	304,211	—	39,801	—	1,520	44,282	298,805	121.9
Spain	1,437	—	—	—	—	−2,837	364,321	70,868	2.4
Sri Lanka	—	58,499	55,376	7,447	5,303	−2,144	1,723	52,192	—
Sudan	—	—	—	—	—	18	—	7,750	—
Suriname	8,221	—	—	—	—	−22	8,239	6,432	106.3
Swaziland	5,930	—	—	39	—	−15	5,947	—	92.5
Sweden	211,381	299,343	230,200	14,372	—	4,911	294,881	246,525	119.6
Switzerland	87,309	884,670	839,739	37,115	—	−1,509	174,265	36,564	—
Syrian Arab Republic	—	—	—	1,894	—	—	386	—	1.1

Table II.12 (concluded)

Member	Total Holdings April 30, 1997	Receipts from Participants and Prescribed Holders		Transfers to Participants and Prescribed Holders		Receipts from the General Resources Account	Transfers to the General Resources Account	Interest, Charges, and Assessment (Net)	Positions as at April 30, 1998		
		Designated	Other	Designated	Other				Holdings	Net cumulative allocations	Holdings as percent of cumulative allocations
Tajikistan	2,058	—	—	—	12,500	15,018	819	101	3,858	—	—
Tanzania	388	—	44,988	—	43,562	—	—	−1,280	533	31,372	1.7
Thailand	44,533	—	404	—	1,082,750	1,420,189	44,781	4,101	341,695	84,652	403.6
Togo	142	—	11,360	—	10,860	36	—	−450	192	10,975	1.7
Tonga	78	—	—	—	—	—	—	4	118	—	—
Trinidad and Tobago	712	—	2,100	—	—	11	376	−1,899	549	46,231	1.2
Tunisia	23,244	—	50,018	—	8,332	167	43,356	−835	20,907	34,243	61.1
Turkey	7,162	—	70,000	—	—	513	70,767	−4,557	2,351	112,307	2.1
Turkmenistan	—	—	—	—	—	—	—	—	—	—	—
Uganda	1,096	—	64,085	—	59,332	—	—	−1,075	4,774	29,396	16.2
Ukraine	29,590	—	7,234	—	—	75,099	79,958	956	32,921	—	—
United Arab Emirates	57,776	—	—	—	—	1	—	785	58,562	38,737	151.2
United Kingdom	314,480	—	803,150	—	755,044	38,738	—	−66,876	334,448	1,913,070	17.5
United States	7,122,454	—	—	—	—	346,501	—	96,596	7,565,552	4,899,530	154.4
Uruguay	1,270	—	3,618	—	—	2	2,284	−2,032	574	49,977	1.1
Uzbekistan	2,356	—	5,486	—	—	181	7,758	24	290	—	—
Vanuatu	383	—	—	—	—	64	—	17	464	—	—
Venezuela	320,807	—	150,000	—	—	4,000	379,199	−4,429	91,180	316,890	28.8
Vietnam	2,466	—	54,550	—	1,208	127	51,470	−1,713	2,752	47,658	5.8
Yemen, Republic of	57,268	—	57,825	—	2,290	14,564	5,926	1,940	123,383	28,743	429.3
Yugoslavia, Federal Republic of (Serbia/Montenegro)[1]	—	—	—	—	—	—	—	—	—	56,665	—
Zambia	754	—	8,909	—	4,207	464	—	−2,782	3,138	68,298	4.6
Zimbabwe	2,461	—	29,400	—	760	160	25,080	−334	5,847	10,200	57.3
Total participants	18,696,850	—	8,976,618	—	8,013,726	5,573,506	4,795,000	−76,442	20,361,807	21,433,330	95.0
Prescribed holders											
Arab Monetary Fund	42,503	—	45,076	—	52,228	—	—	1,031	36,382	—	—
Bank of Central African States	886	—	16,654	—	15,853	—	—	88	1,775	—	—
Bank for International Settlements	1,256,584	—	515,905	—	1,472,444	—	—	40,304	340,348	—	—
East African Development Bank	169	—	—	—	—	—	—	7	176	—	—
Eastern Caribbean Central Bank	2,077	—	—	—	—	—	—	86	2,163	—	—

International Bank for Reconstruction and Development	2,286	—	—	—	95	—	2,381
Islamic Development Bank	2,438	—	—	—	103	—	2,541
Total prescribed holders	1,306,942	577,634	1,540,526	—	41,715	385,765	—
General Resources Account	1,494,149	4,795,000	5,573,506	4,795,000	48,782	764,424	—
Total	21,497,941	14,349,252	15,127,758	5,573,506	14,055	21,511,996	21,433,330

[1]The assets and liabilities of the former Socialist Federal Republic of Yugoslavia were assumed by five successor states. As of April 30, 1998, the Federal Republic of Yugoslavia (Serbia/Montenegro) had not completed arrangements for succession to membership in the IMF.

Table II.13

Holdings of SDRs by All Participants and by Groups of Countries as Percent of Their Cumulative Allocations of SDRs and of Their Non-Gold Reserves, at End of Financial Years Ended April 30, 1974–98

| | | | | | Nonindustrial Countries | | |
| | | | | | | Net debtor countries | |
Financial Year	All Participants[1]	Industrial Countries[2]	All nonindustrial countries	Net creditor countries	All net debtor countries	With arrears and/or rescheduling[3]	Without arrears and/or rescheduling
			Holdings of SDRs as percent of cumulative allocations				
1974	94.6	106.2	64.3	100.0	64.3	72.5	58.7
1975	94.5	106.5	63.1	100.0	63.1	71.9	57.1
1976	95.1	108.4	59.8	100.0	59.8	71.8	51.7
1977	91.7	105.7	54.9	100.0	54.9	70.5	44.3
1978	85.3	95.6	58.1	100.0	58.0	73.9	47.3
1979	90.3	97.0	74.5	100.0	73.8	82.4	67.9
1980	91.9	96.8	81.0	176.5	77.3	83.4	73.0
1981	74.5	81.0	60.8	154.8	55.9	64.3	50.2
1982	74.6	81.8	59.1	154.0	54.2	57.3	52.1
1983	79.8	95.0	47.4	267.6	35.9	39.0	33.8
1984	69.8	80.3	47.4	224.6	38.1	38.1	38.1
1985	78.4	95.1	42.8	218.3	33.6	37.6	31.0
1986	87.3	105.2	49.0	233.6	39.4	43.9	36.3
1987	90.8	110.0	49.9	236.7	40.2	42.4	38.7
1988	96.2	115.8	54.4	262.1	43.6	41.2	45.2
1989	93.1	116.3	43.5	240.2	33.3	16.5	44.7
1990	97.2	121.9	44.4	262.9	33.0	15.7	44.8
1991	96.8	120.7	45.9	193.9	38.1	18.5	51.5
1992	96.8	121.2	44.6	200.1	36.5	13.1	52.4
1993	63.0	73.1	41.6	166.6	35.1	20.0	45.7
1994	71.0	77.9	56.3	222.5	47.7	51.2	45.2
1995	90.9	105.1	60.4	263.9	49.8	36.9	58.8
1996	91.4	102.4	67.9	285.5	56.6	39.5	68.6
1997	87.2	99.8	60.5	303.6	47.8	37.3	55.3
1998	95.0	107.0	69.4	323.7	56.2	32.4	72.9
			Holdings of SDRs as percent of non-gold reserves				
1974	7.2	9.2	3.6	—	4.3	2.9	7.4
1975	6.0	8.9	2.4	—	3.4	2.0	7.6
1976	5.4	8.3	2.0	—	3.0	2.0	5.2
1977	4.4	7.4	1.4	—	2.1	1.6	2.9
1978	3.5	5.3	1.4	—	1.9	1.7	2.2
1979	4.6	5.8	2.9	0.5	3.4	2.9	4.1
1980	5.6	7.1	3.5	1.4	4.1	3.4	4.8
1981	4.8	6.2	2.9	1.3	3.6	3.5	3.6
1982	5.3	6.9	3.0	1.3	3.7	4.0	3.5
1983	5.3	7.2	2.3	2.3	2.3	2.8	2.0
1984	4.2	5.6	2.0	2.1	2.0	2.3	1.8
1985	4.4	6.3	1.6	1.9	1.6	1.9	1.4
1986	5.0	6.7	2.0	2.4	1.9	2.5	1.6
1987	4.7	5.7	2.0	2.8	1.8	3.1	1.4
1988	4.4	5.1	2.0	3.4	1.8	3.2	1.4
1989	3.9	4.7	1.5	3.3	1.2	1.2	1.2
1990	3.8	4.6	1.5	5.0	1.1	1.1	1.1
1991	3.4	4.3	1.3	3.3	1.1	1.0	1.1
1992	3.2	4.4	1.0	3.4	0.9	0.6	0.9
1993	2.2	2.8	0.9	3.2	0.8	0.8	0.8
1994	2.1	2.7	1.1	4.8	0.9	1.8	0.7
1995	2.6	3.5	1.1	5.2	0.9	1.3	0.8
1996	2.1	2.9	0.9	4.6	0.8	0.9	0.7
1997	1.7	2.6	0.7	4.8	0.5	0.7	0.5
1998	1.8	2.7	0.7	5.3	0.6	0.6	0.6

[1]Consists of member countries that are participants in the SDR Department. At the end of 1997/98, of the total SDRs allocated to participants in the SDR Department (SDR 21.4 billion), SDR 1.2 billion was not held by participants but instead by the IMF and prescribed holders.
[2]Based on *IFS* classification (International Monetary Fund, *International Financial Statistics,* various years).
[3]Countries that incurred external payments arrears or rescheduled their debts during the period 1993–97.

Table II.14

Key IMF Rates, Financial Year Ended April 30, 1998
(In percent)

Period Beginning	SDR Interest Rate and Unadjusted Rate of Remuneration[1]	Basic Rate of Charge[1]	Period Beginning	SDR Interest Rate and Unadjusted Rate of Remuneration[1]	Basic Rate of Charge[1]
1997					
April 28	4.09	4.32	November 3	4.21	4.45
			November 10	4.32	4.56
May 5	4.06	4.29	November 17	4.33	4.57
May 12	3.99	4.21	November 24	4.31	4.55
May 19	3.96	4.18			
May 26	3.95	4.17	December 1	4.32	4.56
			December 8	4.39	4.64
June 2	3.90	4.12	December 15	4.32	4.56
June 9	3.98	4.20	December 22	4.37	4.61
June 16	3.92	4.14	December 29	4.38	4.63
June 23	3.95	4.17			
June 30	4.01	4.23	**1998**		
			January 5	4.37	4.61
July 7	4.02	4.25	January 12	4.21	4.45
July 14	4.02	4.25	January 19	4.24	4.48
July 21	4.08	4.31	January 26	4.21	4.45
July 28	4.11	4.34			
			February 2	4.25	4.49
August 4	4.13	4.36	February 9	4.22	4.46
August 11	4.15	4.38	February 16	4.26	4.50
August 18	4.15	4.38	February 23	4.27	4.51
August 25	4.12	4.35			
			March 2	4.32	4.56
September 1	4.14	4.37	March 9	4.22	4.46
September 8	4.11	4.34	March 16	4.20	4.44
September 15	4.07	4.30	March 23	4.25	4.49
September 22	4.06	4.29	March 30	4.30	4.54
September 29	4.02	4.25			
			April 6	4.26	4.50
October 6	4.09	4.32	April 13	4.23	4.47
October 13	4.15	4.38	April 20	4.24	4.48
October 20	4.14	4.37	April 27	4.24	4.48
October 27	4.19	4.42			

[1]Under the decision on burden sharing, the rate of remuneration is adjusted downward and the rate of charge is adjusted upward to share the burden of protecting the IMF's income from overdue charges and of contributing to the IMF's precautionary balances. The amounts generated from burden sharing are refundable when overdue charges are paid and when overdue obligations cease to be a problem. The basic rate of charge presented is the effective rate following the retroactive reduction that was implemented after the end of the financial year. The basic rate of charge, which was set at 109.6 percent of the SDR interest rate, at the beginning of the year, was reduced to 105.6 percent of the SDR interest following after the retroactive reduction.

Table 11.15

Members That Have Accepted the Obligations of Article VIII, Sections 2, 3, and 4 of the Articles of Agreement

Member	Effective Date of Acceptance	Member	Effective Date of Acceptance
Algeria	September 15, 1997	Iceland	September 19, 1983
Antigua and Barbuda	November 22, 1983	India	August 20, 1994
Argentina	May 14, 1968	Indonesia	May 7, 1988
Armenia	May 29, 1997	Ireland	February 15, 1961
Australia	July 1, 1965	Israel	September 21, 1993
Austria	August 1, 1962	Italy	February 15, 1961
Bahamas, The	December 5, 1973	Jamaica	February 22, 1963
Bahrain	March 20, 1973	Japan	April 1, 1964
Bangladesh	April 11, 1994	Jordan	February 20, 1995
Barbados	November 3, 1993	Kazakhstan	July 16, 1996
Belgium	February 15, 1961	Kenya	June 30, 1994
Belize	June 14, 1983	Kiribati	August 22, 1986
Benin	June 1, 1996	Korea	November 1, 1988
Bolivia	June 5, 1967	Kuwait	April 5, 1963
Botswana	November 17, 1995	Kyrgyz Republic	March 29, 1995
Brunei Darussalam	October 10, 1995	Latvia	June 10, 1994
Burkina Faso	June 1, 1996	Lebanon	July 1, 1993
Cameroon	June 1, 1996	Lesotho	March 5, 1997
Canada	March 25, 1952	Lithuania	May 3, 1994
Central African Republic	June 1, 1996	Luxembourg	February 15, 1961
Chad	June 1, 1996	Madagascar	September 18, 1996
Chile	July 27, 1977	Malawi	December 7, 1995
China	December 1, 1996	Malaysia	November 11, 1968
Comoros	June 1, 1996	Mali	June 1, 1996
Congo, Republic of	June 1, 1996	Malta	November 30, 1994
Costa Rica	February 1, 1965	Marshall Islands	May 21, 1992
Côte d'Ivoire	June 1, 1996	Mauritius	September 29, 1993
Croatia	May 29, 1995	Mexico	November 12, 1946
Cyprus	January 9, 1991	Micronesia, Federated States of	June 24, 1993
Czech Republic	October 1, 1995	Moldova	June 30, 1995
Denmark	May 1, 1967	Mongolia	February 1, 1996
Djibouti	September 19, 1980	Morocco	January 21, 1993
Dominica	December 13, 1979	Namibia	September 20, 1996
Dominican Republic	August 1, 1953	Nepal	May 30, 1994
Ecuador	August 31, 1970	Netherlands	February 15, 1961
El Salvador	November 6, 1946	New Zealand	August 5, 1982
Equatorial Guinea	June 1, 1996	Nicaragua	July 20, 1964
Estonia	August 15, 1994	Niger	June 1, 1996
Fiji	August 4, 1972	Norway	May 11, 1967
Finland	September 25, 1979	Oman	June 19, 1974
France	February 15, 1961	Pakistan	July 1, 1994
Gabon	June 1, 1996	Palau	December 16, 1997
Gambia, The	January 21, 1993	Panama	November 26, 1946
Georgia	December 20, 1996	Papua New Guinea	December 4, 1975
Germany	February 15, 1961	Paraguay	August 22, 1994
Ghana	February 21, 1994	Peru	February 15, 1961
Greece	July 7, 1992	Philippines	September 8, 1995
Grenada	January 24, 1994	Poland	June 1, 1995
Guatemala	January 27, 1947	Portugal	September 12, 1988
Guinea	November 17, 1995	Qatar	June 4, 1973
Guinea-Bissau	January 1, 1997	Romania	March 25, 1998
Guyana	December 27, 1966	Russian Federation	June 1, 1996
Haiti	December 22, 1953	St. Kitts and Nevis	December 3, 1984
Honduras	July 1, 1950	St. Lucia	May 30, 1980
Hungary	January 1, 1996	St. Vincent and the Grenadines	August 24, 1981

Table 11.15 (concluded)

Member	Effective Date of Acceptance	Member	Effective Date of Acceptance
Samoa	October 6, 1994	Tanzania	July 15, 1996
San Marino	September 23, 1992	Thailand	May 4, 1990
Saudi Arabia	March 22, 1961	Togo	June 1, 1996
Senegal	June 1, 1996	Tonga	March 22, 1991
Seychelles	January 3, 1978	Trinidad and Tobago	December 13, 1993
Sierra Leone	December 14, 1995	Tunisia	January 6, 1993
Singapore	November 9, 1968	Turkey	March 22, 1990
Slovak Republic	October 1, 1995	Uganda	April 5, 1994
Slovenia	September 1, 1995	Ukraine	September 24, 1996
Solomon Islands	July 24, 1979	United Arab Emirates	February 13, 1974
South Africa	September 15, 1973	United Kingdom	February 15, 1961
Spain	July 15, 1986	United States	December 10, 1946
Sri Lanka	March 15, 1994	Uruguay	May 2, 1980
Suriname	June 29, 1978	Vanuatu	December 1, 1982
Swaziland	December 11, 1989	Venezuela	July 1, 1976
Sweden	February 15, 1961	Yemen, Republic of	December 10, 1996
Switzerland	May 29, 1992	Zimbabwe	February 3, 1995

Table II.16

Exchange Rate Arrangements as of April 30, 1998[1]

Pegged				
Single currency			Currency composite	
U.S. dollar	French franc	Other	SDR	Other
Angola	Benin	Bhutan (Indian rupee)	Jordan	Bangladesh
Antigua and Barbuda	Burkina Faso	Bosnia and Herzegovina	Latvia	Botswana
Argentina	Cameroon	(deutsche mark)	Libyan Arab	Burundi
Bahamas, The[5]	Central African Rep.	Bulgaria (deutsche mark)	Jamahiriya[5,6]	Cyprus[8]
Barbados	Chad	Brunei Darussalam	Myanmar[5]	Fiji
		(Singapore dollar)		
Belize	Comoros	Cape Verde (Portugese escudo)		Iceland[10]
Djibouti	Congo			Kuwait
Dominica	Côte d'Ivoire	Estonia (deutsche mark)		Malta
Grenada	Equatorial Guinea	Kiribati[11] (Australian dollar)		Morocco
Iraq[5]	Gabon	Lesotho (South African rand)		Samoa
		Namibia (South African rand)		
Lithuania	Guinea-Bissau	Nepal (Indian rupee)		Seychelles
Marshall Islands[11]	Mali			Slovak Republic[14]
Micronesia, Federated	Niger	San Marino[11] (Italian lira)		Tonga
States of[11]	Senegal	Swaziland (South African rand)		Vanuatu
Oman	Togo			
Palau[11]				
Panama[11]				
St. Kitts and Nevis				
St. Lucia				
St. Vincent and the				
Grenadines				
Syrian Arab Rep.[5]				

[1]The classification of members' exchange rate arrangements in this table reflect the official declaration of country authorities, as well as IMF staff views, and may not reflect the actual or de facto policies they may follow.

[2]In all countries listed in this column, the U.S. dollar was the currency against which exchange rates showed limited flexibility.

[3]This category consists of countries participating in the exchange rate mechanism (ERM) of the European Monetary System (EMS). In each case, the exchange rate is maintained within a margin of ±15 percent around the bilateral central rates against other participating currencies, with the exception of Germany and the Netherlands, in which case the exchange rate is maintained within a margin of ±2.25 percent.

[4]Exchange rates are determined on the basis of a fixed relationship to the SDR, within margins of up to ±7.25 percent. However, because of the maintenance of a relatively stable relationship with the U.S. dollar, these margins are not always observed.

[5]Member maintained exchange arrangement involving more than one market. The arrangement shown is that maintained in the major market.

[6]The exchange rate is maintained within margins of ±47 percent.

[7]The exchange rate is maintained within a band of R$1.1435–R$1.1495.

[8]The exchange rate, which is pegged to the ECU, is maintained within margins of ±2.25 percent.

[9]The exchange rate is maintained within a crawling band of ±12.5 percent on either side of a weighted composite of the currencies of the main trading areas. The exchange arrangement involves more than one market.

Flexibility Limited vis-à-vis a Single Currency or Group of Currencies		More Flexible		
Single currency[2]	Cooperative arrangements[3]	Other managed floating		Independently floating
Bahrain[4]	Austria	Algeria	Solomon Islands	Afghanistan, Islamic State of[5]
Qatar[4]	Belgium	Belarus	Sri Lanka	Albania
Saudi Arabia[4]	Denmark	Bolivia	Sudan[5]	Armenia
United Arab Emirates[4]	Finland	Brazil[5,7]	Suriname	Australia
	France	Cambodia[5]	Tajikistan[5]	Azerbaijan
	Germany	Chile[5,9]	Thailand	Canada
	Greece	China, People's Rep. of	Tunisia	Congo, Dem. Rep.[5]
	Ireland	Colombia[12]	Turkey	Eritrea
	Italy	Costa Rica	Turkmenistan[5]	Gambia, The
	Luxembourg	Croatia	Ukraine[13]	Ghana
	Netherlands	Czech Republic	Uruguay	Guatemala
	Portugal	Dominican Rep.[5]	Uzbekistan[5]	Guinea
	Spain	Ecuador[5,16]	Venezuela[15]	Guyana
		Egypt[5]	Vietnam[17]	Haiti
		El Salvador		India
		Ethiopia		Indonesia
		Georgia		Jamaica
		Honduras[5,18]		Japan
		Hungary[19]		Korea
		Iran, Islamic Rep. of[5]		Lebanon
		Israel[20]		Liberia
		Kazakhstan		Madagascar
		Kenya		Mexico
		Kyrgyz Republic		Moldova
		Lao P.D.R.[5]		Mongolia
		Macedonia, former Yugoslav Republic of		Mozambique
		Malawi		New Zealand
		Malaysia		Papua New Guinea
		Maldives		Paraguay
		Mauritania		Peru
		Mauritius		Philippines
		Nicaragua		Rwanda
		Nigeria[5]		São Tomé and Príncipe[5]
		Norway		Sierra Leone
		Pakistan[5]		Somalia
		Poland[21]		South Africa
		Romania		Sweden
		Russian Federation[22]		Switzerland
		Singapore		Tanzania
		Slovenia		Trinidad and Tobago
				Uganda
				United Kingdom
				United States
				Yemen, Republic of
				Zambia
				Zimbabwe

[10]The exchange rate is maintained within margins of ±6 percent.
[11]Country uses peg currency as legal tender.
[12]The exchange rate is maintained within a crawling band of ±7 percent.
[13]The exchange rate is maintained within a band of Hrv 1.80–2.25 per U.S. dollar.
[14]The exchange rate is maintained within margins of ±7 percent with regard to the currency basket.
[15]The exchange rate is maintained within a crawling band of ±7.5 percent.
[16]The exchange rate is maintained within a crawling band of ±10 percent.
[17]The exchange rate is maintained within margins of ±10 percent.
[18]The exchange rate is maintained within margins of ±7 percent.
[19]The exchange rate is maintained within a crawling band of ±2.25 percent with regard to the currency basket.
[20]The exchange rate is maintained within an asymmetric crawling band of width of 29 percent.
[21]The exchange rate is maintained within a crawling band of ±10 percent against a basket of currencies.
[22]The exchange rate is maintained within margins of ±15 percent.

Principal Policy Decisions of the Executive Board

A. Access Policy—Guidelines on Access Limits—Review

1. Pursuant to Decision No. 10181-(92/132),[1] adopted November 3, 1992, and Decision No. 10819-(94/95),[2] adopted October 24, 1994, as amended by Decision No. 11593-(97/106), adopted October 23, 1997, the Fund has reviewed the guidelines and the limits for access by members to the Fund's general resources under the credit tranches and the Extended Fund Facility, including the decision to raise the annual limit to 100 percent of quota, and decided that (i) the annual access limit of 100 percent of quota established by Decision No. 10819-(94/95), as amended, shall remain in effect through October 31, 1998, and (ii) the other provisions of Decision No. 10181-(92/132) and Decision No. 10819-(94/95) remain appropriate in the present circumstances.

2. The next of the annual reviews prescribed by Decision No. 10181-(92/132), adopted November 3, 1992, and by Decision No. 10819-(94/95), adopted October 24, 1994, as amended, shall be completed by October 31, 1998.

Decision No. 11608-(97/112)
November 13, 1997

B. IMF's Income Position

(a) Retroactive Reduction of Rate of Charge— Amendment of Decision No. 11482-(97/42);[3] ESAF Trust—Reserve Account—Transfer to the ESAF-HIPC Trust; and Supplemental Reserve Facility— Disposition of Net Operational Income

1. Retroactive Reduction of Rate of Charge—Amendment of Decision No. 11482-(97/42)

Paragraph 2 of Decision No. 11482-(97/42), adopted April 21, 1997, shall be amended by replacing "109.6 percent" with "107 percent."

2. ESAF Trust—Transfer to the ESAF-HIPC Trust

For financial year 1998, no reimbursement shall be made to the General Resources Account from the ESAF Trust Reserve Account for the cost of administering the ESAF Trust. An amount equivalent to such cost shall be transferred after the end of the financial year from the ESAF Trust

Reserve Account (through the Special Disbursement Account) to the ESAF-HIPC Trust.

3. Supplemental Reserve Facility—Disposition of Net Operational Income

For financial year 1998, after meeting the cost of administering the ESAF Trust, any remaining net operational income generated by the Supplemental Reserve Facility shall be transferred, after the end of the financial year, to the General Reserve.

Decision No. 11683-(98/27)
March 12, 1998

(b) Disposition of Net Income for FY 1998

SDR 98,483,336 of the Fund's net income for financial year 1998 shall be placed in the Fund's Special Reserve after the end of the financial year.

Decision No. 11710-(98/49)
April 28, 1998

(c) Rate of Charge on the Use of Fund Resources for FY 1999

1. Notwithstanding Rule I-6(4)(a), effective May 1, 1998, the proportion of the rate of charge referred to in Rule I-6(4) to the SDR interest rate under Rule T-1 shall be 107 percent.

2. Any net income for financial year 1999 in excess of an amount equivalent to 5 percent of the Fund's reserves at the beginning of that financial year shall be used to reduce retroactively the proportion of the rate of charge to the SDR interest rate for financial year 1999. If net income for financial year 1999 is below an amount equivalent to 5 percent of the Fund's reserves at the beginning of that financial year, the amount of projected net income for financial year 2000 shall be increased by the equivalent of that shortfall. For the purpose of this provision, net income shall be calculated without taking into account net operational income generated by the Supplemental Reserve Facility.

Decision No. 11711-(98/49)
April 28, 1998

C. Enhanced Structural Adjustment Facility (ESAF)

(a) Use of Resources for Commercial Debt- and Debt-Service-Reduction Operations—ESAF Trust Instrument—Amendment

1. The Instrument to Establish the Enhanced Structural Adjustment Facility Trust annexed to Decision No. 8759-

---

[1]See *Selected Decisions,* Twenty-Second Issue (June 30, 1997), pages 238–39.

[2]Ibid., page 239.

[3]Ibid., page 318.

(87/176) ESAF,[4] as amended, shall be further amended by adding the following subparagraph at the end of Section II, paragraph 3(b):

> Notwithstanding the previous subparagraph, if in the determination of access under a three-year arrangement or at the time of approval of an annual arrangement, resources are committed to help finance the cost of a debt- and debt-service-reduction operation with commercial banks, the resources so committed shall be disbursed only at the time the operation materializes, the program supported by the arrangement remains on track, and the Executive Board is satisfied that such use would be efficient and market based; provided, however, that the resources may be made available from the outset of an arrangement if the above conditions are met.

Decision No. 11533-(97/67) ESAF
July 2, 1997

(b) ESAF-HIPC Initiative—Status Report and Options for Financing

Special Disbursement Account—Transfer of Resources from Reserve Account of 1987 ESAF Trust and Use for Special ESAF Operations

The Executive Board has agreed to a transfer of SDR 70 million from the ESAF Trust Reserve Account to the Special Disbursement Account and use for special ESAF operations. The Executive Board agreed to return to consider the financing issues by mid-summer 1998.

The Executive Board has adopted the following decision to amend the Instrument to Establish the Enhanced Structural Adjustment Facility Trust:

> Section V, subparagraph 5(b) of the Instrument to Establish the Enhanced Structural Adjustment Facility Trust shall be amended by substituting "SDR 250 million" for "SDR 180 million."

Decision No. 11610-(97/113)
November 24, 1997

(c) ESAF Trust—Reserve Account—Review

Pursuant to Executive Board Decision No. 10286-(93/23) ESAF,[5] the Fund has reviewed the adequacy of the Reserve Account of the ESAF Trust, and determines that amounts held in the account are sufficient to meet all obligations which could give rise to a payment from the Reserve Account to lenders to the Loan Account of the ESAF Trust in the six months from January 1 to June 30, 1998.

Decision No. 11648-(98/1) ESAF
December 30, 1997

(d) ESAF Trust—Transfer to the ESAF-HIPC Trust

(See Section B(a) above, IMF's Income Position, for the full text of this Decision.)

Decision 11683-(98/27)
March 12, 1998

(e) ESAF Trust—Reserve Account—Transfer to the ESAF-HIPC Trust

For financial year 1999, no reimbursement shall be made to the General Resources Account from the ESAF Trust Reserve Account for the cost of administering the ESAF Trust. One-fourth of the estimated annual cost shall be transferred after the end of each financial quarter ended July 31 and October 31, 1998 and January 31 and April 30, 1999 from the ESAF Trust Reserve Account (through the Special Disbursement Account) to the ESAF-HIPC Trust.

Decision No. 11713-(98/49) ESAF
April 28, 1998

D. Supplemental Reserve Facility

(a) Establishment

1. (a) The Fund will be prepared to provide financial assistance in accordance with the terms of this Decision to a member that is experiencing exceptional balance of payments difficulties due to a large short-term financing need resulting from a sudden and disruptive loss of market confidence reflected in pressure on the capital account and the member's reserves, if there is a reasonable expectation that the implementation of strong adjustment policies and adequate financing will result, within a short period of time, in an early correction of such difficulties.

(b) This facility is likely to be utilized in cases where the magnitude of the outflows may create a risk of contagion that could pose a potential threat to the international monetary system.

(c) When approving a request for the use of its resources under this Decision, the Fund will take into account the financing provided by other creditors. In order to minimize moral hazard, a member using resources under this Decision will be encouraged to seek to maintain participation of creditors, both official and private, until the pressure on the balance of payments ceases. All options should be considered to ensure appropriate burden sharing.

(d) The Fund may make the use of its resources under this Decision conditional upon the adoption by the member of measures under Article VI, Section 1 of the Fund's Articles of Agreement.

2. Financing under this Decision will be available to members under a stand-by or extended arrangement in addition to resources in the credit tranches or under the extended Fund facility, in cases where (i) a member faces the type of balance of payments difficulties described in paragraph 1 above and (ii) the projected access in the credit tranches or under the extended Fund facility, taking into account outstanding purchases, would otherwise exceed either the annual or cumulative limit. In those cases, unless the member's medium-term financing needs require access in the credit tranches or under the extended Fund facility beyond the annual or cumulative limit, financing in the credit tranches or under the extended Fund facility will not be provided beyond the annual or cumulative limit, and financing beyond either limit will be provided only under this Decision.

3. Financing under this Decision will be determined by the Fund, taking into account the financing needs of the member, its capacity to repay, including in particular the strength of its program, its outstanding use of Fund credit,

---

[4]Ibid., pages 25–42.
[5]Ibid., pages 353–55.

and its record in using Fund resources in the past and in cooperating with the Fund in surveillance, as well as the Fund's liquidity.

4. Financing under this Decision will be committed for a period of up to one year, even if the corresponding arrangement is for a longer period, and will generally be available in two or more purchases. The first purchase will be available at the time of approval of financing under this Decision, which will normally coincide with the approval of the corresponding arrangement. The subsequent purchases will be available subject to the conditions of the corresponding arrangement.

5. The corresponding arrangement will identify the total amount and phasing of the financing provided under this Decision.

6. (a) A member making purchases under this Decision shall repurchase the outstanding amounts of its currency resulting from such purchases within two to two and a half years from the date of each purchase in two equal semiannual installments; the first installment shall become due two years and the second installment two and a half years from the date of each purchase.

(b) The member will be expected to repurchase those amounts one year before they become due, provided that the Fund may, upon request by the member, decide to extend each such repurchase expectation by up to one year. If a member fails to make a repurchase as expected, the Fund may require the member to make the repurchase in question within a specified period not to exceed the repurchase schedule under (a) above.

(c) The Fund shall not approve, and the Managing Director shall not recommend for approval, a request for the use of the general resources of the Fund by a member that is failing to meet a repurchase expectation under (b) above. Provision shall be made in each Stand-By and Extended Arrangement for the suspension of further purchases under the arrangement whenever a member fails to meet a repurchase expectation under (b) above.

7. Purchases under this Decision and holdings resulting from such purchases shall be excluded for the purposes of the definition of "reserve tranche purchase" pursuant to Article XXX(c).

8. During the first year from the date of approval of financing under this Decision, the rate of charge under Article V, Section 8(b) on holdings acquired as a result of purchases under this Decision shall be 300 basis points per annum above the rate of charge referred to in Rule I-6(4) as adjusted for purposes of burden sharing. Such rate shall be increased by 50 basis points at the end of that period and every six months thereafter, until the surcharge reaches 500 basis points, subject to the provisions of paragraph 9.

Pending a Decision on the use to be given to the income generated under this Decision, such income shall not be taken into account when determining the amount of net income in excess of the net income target for purposes of paragraph 3 of Decision No. 11482-(97/42), adopted April 21, 1997.

9. The provisions of Decision No. 8165-(85/189) G/TR,[6] December 30, 1985, except Section IV, shall apply

to overdue financial obligations arising under this Decision, subject to the following provision:

The rate of charge on overdue repurchases shall be determined by the Fund but shall not be less than the maximum rate of charge specified in paragraph 8.

10. Except for the purposes of determining the level of conditionality applied to purchases in the credit tranches, the Fund's holdings of a member's currency resulting from purchases under this Decision shall be considered separate from the Fund's holdings of the same currency resulting from purchases made under any other policy on the use of the Fund's general resources.

11. In order to carry out the purposes of this Decision, the Fund will be prepared to grant a waiver of the limitation of 200 percent of quota in Article V, Section 3(b) (iii), whenever necessary to permit purchases under this Decision or to permit other purchases that would raise the Fund's holdings of the purchasing member's currency above that limitation because of purchases outstanding under this Decision.

12. This Decision and its operation will be reviewed no later than December 31, 1998.

Decision No. 11627-(97/123) SRF
December 17, 1997

(b) Disposition of Net Operational Income

(See Section B(a) above, IMF's Income Position, for the full text of this Decision.)

Decision No. 11683-(98/27)
March 12, 1998

For financial year 1999, after meeting the cost of administering the ESAF Trust, any remaining net operational income generated by the Supplemental Reserve Facility shall be transferred, after the end of that financial year, to the General Reserve.

Decision No. 11716-(98/49)
April 28, 1998

E. General Arrangements to Borrow—Renewal

Executive Board Decision No. 1289-(62/1)[7] on the General Arrangements to Borrow, as amended, is hereby renewed for a period of five years from December 26, 1998.

Decision No. 11609-(97/112)
November 19, 1997

F. Increases in Quotas of Members

(a) Periods for Consent to and Payment for Increases in Quotas Under Ninth General Review—Extension

1. Pursuant to paragraph 4 of the Resolution of the Board of Governors No. 45-2, "Increases in Quotas of Members—Ninth General Review," the Executive Board decides that notices in accordance with paragraph 2 of that Resolution must be received in the Fund before 6:00 p.m., Washington time, on December 31, 1997.

2. Pursuant to paragraph 5 of the Board of Governors Resolution No. 45-2, the Executive Board decides that each

---

[6]Ibid., pages 279–81.

[7]Ibid., pages 358–69

member shall pay to the Fund the increase in its quota under the Ninth Review within 1,876 days after the later of (a) the date on which it notifies the Fund of its consent, or (b) November 11, 1992.

Decision No. 11517-(97/61)
June 17, 1997

1. Pursuant to paragraph 4 of the Resolution of the Board of Governors No. 45-2, "Increases in Quotas of Members—Ninth General Review," the Executive Board decides that notices in accordance with paragraph 2 of that Resolution must be received in the Fund before 6:00 p.m., Washington time, on June 30, 1998.

2. Pursuant to paragraph 5 of the Board of Governors Resolution No. 45-2, the Executive Board decides that each member shall pay to the Fund the increase in its quota under the Ninth Review within 2,057 days after the later of (a) the date on which it notifies the Fund of its consent, or (b) November 11, 1992.

Decision No. 11649-(98/1)
December 30, 1997

(b) Eleventh General Review of Quotas—Report to the Board of Governors and Proposed Resolution

I. The Executive Board approves the Report of the Executive Board to the Board of Governors, attached hereto, entitled "Increases in Quotas of Fund Members—Eleventh General Review," for transmission to the Board of Governors.

II. 1. The Board of Governors is requested to vote without meeting pursuant to Section 13 of the By-Laws upon the proposed Resolution entitled "Increases in Quotas of Fund Members—Eleventh General Review: Resolution of the Board of Governors."

2. The Secretary is directed to send the Report of the Executive Board and the proposed Resolution, both entitled "Increases in Quotas of Fund Members—Eleventh General Review," to each member of the Fund by rapid means of communication on or before December 23, 1997.

3. To be valid, votes must be cast by Governors or Alternate Governors and must be received at the seat of the Fund on or before 6:00 p.m., Washington time on January 30, 1998. Votes received after that time will not be counted.

4. The effective date of the Resolution of the Board of Governors shall be the last day for voting.

5. All votes cast pursuant to this decision shall be held in the custody of the Secretary until counted, and all proceedings with respect thereto shall be confidential until the Executive Board determines the result of the vote.

6. The Secretary is authorized to take such further action as he shall deem appropriate in order to carry out the purposes of this decision.

Decision No. 11644-(97/127)
December 22, 1997

Attachment
Report of the Executive Board to the Board of Governors: Increase in Quotas of Fund Members— Eleventh General Review

1. Article III, Section 2(*a*) of the Articles of Agreement provides that "The Board of Governors shall, at intervals of not more than five years, conduct a general review, and if it deems it appropriate, propose an adjustment of the quotas of the members. It may also, if it thinks fit, consider at any other time the adjustment of any particular quota at the request of the member concerned." This report and the attached Resolution on increases in quotas under the current, that is, Eleventh General Review, are submitted to the Board of Governors in accordance with Article III, Section 2.

2. The five-year period prescribed by Article III, Section 2(*a*) for the Eleventh General Review of Quotas ends on March 31, 1998, five years from the date on which the Tenth General Review of Quotas should have been concluded.[8] The Tenth General Review of Quotas was completed in early 1995 without recommending an increase in quotas to the Board of Governors. At that time, the Executive Board reported to the Board of Governors that:

> . . . the Fund is at present relatively well-positioned to meet a prospective substantial demand for its resources over the next three years. Nevertheless, the Fund's liquidity position is expected to decline over the next few years from its currently strong position. Furthermore, considerable uncertainties can be expected as regards the supply of usable resources, which depends on the continued relative strength in the balance of payments and reserve positions of mainly the industrial countries in the Fund. The continued adequacy of members' quotas, including the Fund's liquidity position, will be closely monitored by the Executive Board in the period ahead.

3. The conduct of the Eleventh General Review of Quotas has been guided by the views expressed by the Interim Committee since the Spring of 1995. At its meeting in April of that year, the Interim Committee requested the Executive Board "to continue to review the adequacy of the Fund's resources, and, in connection with its review of the role of the Fund, to carry forward its work on the Eleventh General Review of Quotas." At its meeting in October 1995, the Committee "welcomed the progress already made by the Executive Board on Fund quotas, and requested the Board to move forward with the Eleventh Quinquennial Review." The Committee's April 1996 Communiqué stated, with respect to the Fund's financial resources and assistance to members, that the Committee "notes the progress made by the Executive Board in preparatory work for the Eleventh General Review of Quotas and stresses the need to ensure the adequacy of the quotas for the Fund to continue to carry out its mandate, taking into account changes in the world economy since the last increase in quotas was agreed in 1990." In September 1996, the Committee reiterated its request to the Executive Board "to continue its work on the Review and to do its utmost to reach a conclusion as soon as possible." In April 1997, the Committee requested the Executive Board to complete its work on quotas as soon as possible and to report to it in time for the Hong Kong meeting of the Committee. The Committee also stated that "the proposed distribution should be predominantly equiproportional while contributing to a correction of the most impor-

---

[8]The five-year period prescribed by Article III, Section 2(*a*) for the Tenth General Review ended on March 31, 1993 (paragraph 2 of the "Report of the Executive Board to the Board of Governors" of December 12, 1994 on Increases in Quotas of Members—Tenth General Review).

tant anomalies in the present quota distribution. The Executive Board should also review the quota formulae promptly after the completion of the Eleventh Review of Quotas." The Executive Board reached agreement on the size and distribution of the increase in quotas, which was endorsed by the Interim Committee at its meeting on September 21, 1997, in Hong Kong, China.

4. The Interim Committee agreed that:

- the present total of Fund quotas would be increased by 45 percent;
- 75 percent of the overall increase would be distributed in proportion to present quotas;
- 15 percent of the overall increase would be distributed in proportion to members' shares in calculated quotas (based on 1994 data), so as to better reflect the relative economic positions of members; and
- the remaining 10 percent of the overall increase would be distributed among those members whose present quotas are out of line with their positions in the world economy (as measured by the excess of their share in calculated quotas over their share in actual quotas), of which 1 percent of the overall increase would be distributed among five members whose current quotas are far out of line with their relative economic positions, and which are in a position to contribute to the Fund's liquidity over the medium term.

The Committee requested the Executive Board to submit before the end of this year a proposed resolution for the approval of the Board of Governors to effect the agreed increases in quotas. The Committee reiterated its view that the formulas used to calculate quotas should be reviewed by the Board promptly after the completion of the Eleventh General Review.

5. In its discussions on the Eleventh General Review, the Executive Board has considered, inter alia (i) the size of the overall increase in quotas; (ii) the distribution of the overall increase; (iii) the procedures for consent and payment for the increase in quotas, including by members with overdue obligations in the General Resources Account; and (iv) the media for payment for the increase in quotas. In its preparatory work on the Review, the Executive Board also considered issues relating to the role of the Fund in providing balance of payments financing, the quota formulas used in making quota calculations, and the declining share in quotas of developing countries in the Fund.

6. In assessing the Fund's need for resources over the medium term in order to carry out its purposes, the Executive Board stressed that (i) the Fund is the central institution in the international monetary system and it must be adequately endowed with financial resources to enable it to act effectively when dealing with members' balance of payments difficulties; (ii) the Fund, in fulfilling its function at the center of the system, must ensure that its resources are fully safeguarded, including by the adoption and implementation of appropriate policies by members supported by use of the Fund's general resources, and that its resources are provided on a temporary basis, thereby ensuring that its resources revolve; and (iii) the Fund must hold a level of usable assets that are sufficient to protect the liquidity and immediate usability of members' claims on the Fund, so as to maintain members' confidence in and support of the institution.

7. In its consideration of the size of the increase in quotas, the Executive Board has taken into account a range of factors, including the growth of world trade and payments since 1990; the scale of potential payments imbalances, including imbalances that may stem from sharp changes in capital flows; the prospective demand for Fund resources, including the need for the Fund to support members' growth-oriented adjustment programs, which, in many cases, may involve far-reaching economic and structural reforms; and the rapid globalization and the associated liberalization of trade and payments, including on capital account, that has characterized the development of the world economy since the last increase in quotas was agreed in 1990. The Executive Board has also considered the Fund's current and prospective liquidity position, and has also taken into account the adequacy of the Fund's borrowing arrangements, in particular the General Arrangements to Borrow (GAB) and the prospective coming into effect of the New Arrangements to Borrow (NAB). These borrowing arrangements are an important buttress to the Fund's liquidity but are not a substitute for larger quotas. The Executive Board reiterated its view that the Fund should continue to rely on its quota resources as its principal form of financing and should resort to borrowing only in exceptional circumstances.

In its consideration of the prospective demand for the Fund's resources in the context of the globalized economy, the Executive Board stressed that members should approach the Fund at an early stage of their balance of payments difficulties, and take all appropriate steps to maintain the confidence of markets, not only through the pursuit of adequate and transparent policy actions but also through the timely and transparent provision of economic and financial information to the markets.

8. In the light of these considerations, and taking into account the agreement reached by the Executive Board at the Annual Meetings in Hong Kong, which was endorsed by the Interim Committee at its meeting on September 21, 1997 in Hong Kong, the Executive Board now proposes to the Board of Governors that the present total of Fund quotas be increased by 45 percent, from approximately SDR 146 billion to approximately SDR 212 billion.

9. As regards the distribution of the overall increase in quotas, the Executive Board has been guided by the views of the Interim Committee as expressed in its communiqués of April and September 1997, and summarized in paragraph 4 above.

10. In reaching the agreement on the size and distribution of the increase in quotas, Directors confirmed that there was no intention to re-open the issues of the size and composition of the Executive Board, and that the existing representation of developing countries should not be affected.

11. The Executive Board also proposes adjustments in the quotas of France, Germany, Italy, and the United Kingdom in a manner that would maintain unchanged the increases in quotas for all other members as determined under paragraph 4 above. The Executive Board notes that the United Kingdom and France have agreed to maintain the equal distribution of quotas between themselves under the Eleventh General Review as first agreed under the Ninth General Review.

12. The Executive Board proposes that the quotas determined in paragraph 4 above be rounded to the nearest multi-

ple of SDR 0.1 million. The quotas proposed under the Eleventh Review for those members that have not yet consented or paid for their proposed increase in quotas under the Ninth Review (Resolution No. 45-2 of the Board of Governors) have been calculated on the basis of their proposed Ninth Review quotas.

13. The list of proposed quotas for all members is to be found in the Annex to the draft Resolution proposed for adoption by the Board of Governors.

14. Under the proposed Resolution, a member that does not have overdue obligations with respect to purchases, charges, or assessments to the General Resources Account will be able to consent to the amount of quota proposed for it in the Annex to the proposed Resolution. The member will be able to consent to the increase in its quota at any time before 6:00 p.m., Washington time, January 29, 1999. In order to meet this deadline, the member will have to have completed before that date whatever action may be necessary under its laws to enable it to give its consent. The Executive Board is authorized by paragraph 4 of the proposed Resolution to extend the period of consent.

15. A member's quota cannot be increased until it has consented to the increase and paid the subscription. Under the proposed Resolution, the increase in a member's quota will take effect only after the Fund has received the member's consent to the increase in quota and the member has paid the increase in subscription, provided that the quota increase cannot become effective before the date on which the Fund determines that the participation requirement in paragraph 3 of the proposed Resolution has been satisfied. The participation requirement in paragraph 3 of the proposed Resolution will be reached when the Fund determines that members having not less than 85 percent of the total of quotas on December 23, 1997 have consented to the increases in their respective quotas as set out in the Annex.

16. Taking into consideration the situation of members that may still wish to consent to or pay for their quota increases under the Ninth Review, the Executive Board recommends that the periods for consent and payment for quota increases under the Ninth Review be extended until the date when the participation requirement in paragraph 3 of the proposed Resolution on the Eleventh Review has been reached. Such extension of the periods of consent and payment for quota increases under the Ninth Review is provided for in paragraph 7 of the proposed Resolution.

17. The proposed Resolution provides that a member must pay the increase in its subscription within 30 days after (a) the date on which the member notifies the Fund of its consent, or (b) the date on which the participation requirement is met, whichever is the later. A member may not make such a payment unless it is current in its obligations with respect to repurchases, charges, and assessments to the General Resources Account. The Executive Board is authorized in paragraph 5 of the proposed Resolution to extend the period for payment.

18. The Executive Board has agreed that, when considering any extension of the period for consent or payment, it shall give particular consideration to the situation of members that may still wish to consent to or pay for the increase in quota, including those members with protracted arrears to the General Resources Account, consisting of overdue repur-

chases, charges, or assessments to the General Resources Account, that are judged to be cooperating with the Fund toward the settlement of these obligations.

19. Article III, Section 3(a) provides that 25 percent of any increase in quota shall be paid in special drawing rights, but permits the Board of Governors to prescribe, inter alia, that this payment may be made on the same basis for all members, in whole or in part, in the currencies of other members specified by the Fund, subject to their concurrence. Paragraph 8 of the Resolution provides that 25 percent of the increase in quotas proposed as a result of the current review should be paid in SDRs or in currencies of other members selected by the Fund, subject to their concurrence, or in any combination of SDRs and such currencies. The balance of the increase shall be paid in a member's own currency. A reserve asset payment will help strengthen the liquidity of the Fund and will not impose an undue burden on members, because under the existing decisions of the Fund, a reserve asset payment will either enlarge or create a reserve tranche position of an equivalent amount. In addition, the Fund stands ready to assist members that do not hold sufficient reserves to make their reserve asset payments to the Fund to borrow SDRs from other members willing to cooperate; these loans would be made on the condition that such members would repay on the same day the loans from the SDR proceeds of drawings of reserve tranche positions which had been established by the payment of SDRs.

20. The Executive Board recommends that the Board of Governors adopt the attached Resolution that covers all the matters on which the Governors are requested to act. The adoption of the Resolution requires positive responses from Governors having an 85 percent majority of the total voting power.

Attachment
Proposed Resolution of the Board of Governors: Increase in Quotas of Fund Members— Eleventh General Review

WHEREAS the Executive Board has submitted to the Board of Governors a report entitled "Increases in Quotas of Fund Members—Eleventh General Review" containing recommendations on increases in the quotas of individual members of the Fund; and

WHEREAS the Executive Board has recommended the adoption of the following Resolution of the Board of Governors, which Resolution proposes increases in the quotas of members of the Fund as a result of the Eleventh General Review of Quotas and deals with certain related matters, by vote without meeting pursuant to Section 13 of the By-Laws of the Fund;

NOW, THEREFORE, the Board of Governors hereby RESOLVES that:

1. The International Monetary Fund proposes that, subject to the provisions of this Resolution, the quotas of members of the Fund shall be increased to the amounts shown against their names in the Annex to this Resolution.

2. A member's increase in quota as proposed by this Resolution shall not become effective unless the member has notified the Fund of its consent to the increase not later than the date prescribed by or under paragraph 4

below and has paid the increase in quota in full within the period prescribed by or under paragraph 5 below, provided that no member with overdue repurchases, charges, or assessments to the General Resources Account may consent to or pay for the increase in its quota until it becomes current in respect of these obligations.

3. No increase in quotas shall become effective before the date of the Fund's determination that members having not less than 85 percent of the total of quotas on December 23, 1997 have consented to the increases in their quotas.

4. Notices in accordance with paragraph 2 above shall be executed by a duly authorized official of the member and must be received in the Fund before 6:00 p.m., Washington time, January 29, 1999, provided that the Executive Board may extend this period as it may determine.

5. Each member shall pay to the Fund the increase in its quota within 30 days after the later of (a) the date on which it notifies the Fund of its consent, or (b) the date of the Fund's determination under paragraph 3 above, provided that the Executive Board may extend the payment period as it may determine.

6. When deciding on an extension of the period for consent to or payment for the increase in quotas, the Executive Board shall give particular consideration to the situation of members that may still wish to consent to or pay for the increase in quota, including members with protracted arrears to the General Resources Account, consisting of overdue repurchases, charges, or assessments to the General Resources Account, that, in its judgment, are cooperating with the Fund toward the settlement of these obligations.

7. For members that have not yet consented to their increases in quotas under the Ninth Review, the period for consent to such quota increases shall extend to the date determined under paragraph 3 above. For members that have not yet paid for their quota increases under the Ninth Review, the period for payment for such quota increases shall extend to 30 days after the date determined under paragraph 3 above.

8. Each member shall pay 25 percent of its increase either in special drawing rights or in the currencies of other members specified, with their concurrence, by the Fund, or in any combination of special drawing rights and such currencies. The balance of the increase shall be paid by the member in its own currency.

The Board of Governors adopted the foregoing Resolution, effective January 30, 1998, which was designated Resolution No. 53-2.

Annex to Resolution No. 53-2

	Proposed Quota		Proposed Quota
	(In millions of SDRs)		*(In millions of SDRs)*
1. Afghanistan, Islamic State of	161.9	34. Chile	856.1
2. Albania	48.7	35. China	4,687.2
3. Algeria	1,254.7	36. Colombia	774.0
4. Angola	286.3	37. Comoros	8.9
5. Antigua and Barbuda	13.5	38. Congo, Democratic Republic of the	533.0
6. Argentina	2,117.1	39. Congo, Republic of	84.6
7. Armenia	92.0	40. Costa Rica	164.1
8. Australia	3,236.4	41. Côte d'Ivoire	325.2
9. Austria	1,872.3	42. Croatia	365.1
10. Azerbaijan	160.9	43. Cyprus	139.6
11. Bahamas, The	130.3	44. Czech Republic	819.3
12. Bahrain	135.0	45. Denmark	1,642.8
13. Bangladesh	533.3	46. Djibouti	15.9
14. Barbados	67.5	47. Dominica	8.2
15. Belarus	386.4	48. Dominican Republic	218.9
16. Belgium	4,605.2	49. Ecuador	302.3
17. Belize	18.8	50. Egypt	943.7
18. Benin	61.9	51. El Salvador	171.3
19. Bhutan	6.3	52. Equatorial Guinea	32.6
20. Bolivia	171.5	53. Eritrea	15.9
21. Bosnia and Herzegovina	169.1	54. Estonia	65.2
22. Botswana	63.0	55. Ethiopia	133.7
23. Brazil	3,036.1	56. Fiji	70.3
24. Brunei Darussalam	215.2	57. Finland	1,263.8
25. Bulgaria	640.2	58. France	10,738.5
26. Burkina Faso	60.2	59. Federal Republic of Yugoslavia (Serbia/Montenegro)[1]	467.7
27. Burundi	77.0	60. Gabon	154.3
28. Cambodia	87.5	61. Gambia, The	31.1
29. Cameroon	185.7	62. Georgia	150.3
30. Canada	6,369.2	63. Germany	13,008.2
31. Cape Verde	9.6	64. Ghana	369.0
32. Central African Republic	55.7	65. Greece	823.0
33. Chad	56.0	66. Grenada	11.7

Annex to Resolution No. 53-2 *(concluded)*

	Proposed Quota *(In millions of SDRs)*		Proposed Quota *(In millions of SDRs)*
67. Guatemala	210.2	126. Palau, Republic of	3.1
68. Guinea	107.1	127. Panama	206.6
69. Guinea-Bissau	14.2	128. Papua New Guinea	131.6
70. Guyana	90.9	129. Paraguay	99.9
71. Haiti	81.9	130. Peru	638.4
72. Honduras	129.5	131. Philippines	879.9
73. Hungary	1,038.4	132. Poland	1,369.0
74. Iceland	117.6	133. Portugal	867.4
75. India	4,158.2	134. Qatar	263.8
76. Indonesia	2,079.3	135. Romania	1,030.2
77. Iran, Islamic Republic of	1,497.2	136. Russia	5,945.4
78. Iraq	1,188.4	137. Rwanda	80.1
79. Ireland	838.4	138. Samoa	11.6
80. Israel	928.2	139. San Marino	17.0
81. Italy	7,055.5	140. São Tomé and Príncipe	7.4
82. Jamaica	273.5	141. Saudi Arabia	6,985.5
83. Japan	13,312.8	142. Senegal	161.8
84. Jordan	170.5	143. Seychelles	8.8
85. Kazakhstan	365.7	144. Sierra Leone	103.7
86. Kenya	271.4	145. Singapore	862.5
87. Kiribati	5.6	146. Slovak Republic	357.5
88. Korea	1,633.6	147. Slovenia	231.7
89. Kuwait	1,381.1	148. Solomon Islands	10.4
90. Kyrgyz Republic	88.8	149. Somalia	81.7
91. Lao People's Democratic Republic	52.9	150. South Africa	1,868.5
92. Latvia	126.8	151. Spain	3,048.9
93. Lebanon	203.0	152. Sri Lanka	413.4
94. Lesotho	34.9	153. St. Kitts and Nevis	8.9
95. Liberia	129.2	154. St. Lucia	15.3
96. Libya	1,123.7	155. St. Vincent and the Grenadines	8.3
97. Lithuania	144.2	156. Sudan	315.1
98. Luxembourg	279.1	157. Suriname	92.1
99. Macedonia, former Yugoslav Republic of	68.9	158. Swaziland	50.7
100. Madagascar	122.2	159. Sweden	2,395.5
101. Malawi	69.4	160. Switzerland	3,458.5
102. Malaysia	1,486.6	161. Syrian Arab Republic	293.6
103. Maldives	8.2	162. Tajikistan	87.0
104. Mali	93.3	163. Tanzania	198.9
105. Malta	102.0	164. Thailand	1,081.9
106. Marshall Islands	3.5	165. Togo	73.4
107. Mauritania	64.4	166. Tonga	6.9
108. Mauritius	101.6	167. Trinidad and Tobago	335.6
109. Mexico	2,585.8	168. Tunisia	286.5
110. Micronesia, Federated States of	5.1	169. Turkey	964.0
111. Moldova	123.2	170. Turkmenistan	75.2
112. Mongolia	51.1	171. Uganda	180.5
113. Morocco	588.2	172. Ukraine	1,372.0
114. Mozambique	113.6	173. United Arab Emirates	611.7
115. Myanmar	258.4	174. United Kingdom	10,738.5
116. Namibia	136.5	175. United States	37,149.3
117. Nepal	71.3	176. Uruguay	306.5
118. Netherlands	5,162.4	177. Uzbekistan	275.6
119. New Zealand	894.6	178. Vanuatu	17.0
120. Nicaragua	130.0	179. Venezuela	2,659.1
121. Niger	65.8	180. Vietnam	329.1
122. Nigeria	1,753.2	181. Yemen, Republic of	243.5
123. Norway	1,671.7	182. Zambia	489.1
124. Oman	194.0	183. Zimbabwe	353.4
125. Pakistan	1,033.7		

[1]Under Executive Board Decision No. 10237-(92/150) adopted December 14, 1992, the Federal Republic of Yugoslavia (Serbia/Montenegro) may succeed to the membership of the former Socialist Federal Republic of Yugoslavia.

G. Special One-Time Allocation of SDRs—Report to Board of Governors on Proposed Fourth Amendment of Articles of Agreement

Pursuant to the request of the Interim Committee that an amendment of the Articles of Agreement be proposed providing for a special one-time allocation of SDRs, the Executive Board:

(a) adopts the Report of the Executive Board to the Board of Governors on the Proposed Fourth Amendment of the Articles of Agreement of the International Monetary Fund;

(b) proposes the introduction in the Articles of Agreement of the modifications included in the Proposed Fourth Amendment attached to the Resolution in Part IV of the Report;

(c) recommends the adoption by the Board of Governors of the Resolution in Part IV of the Report.

Decision No. 11578-(97/96)
September 19, 1997

Resolution No. 52-4
Special One-Time Allocation of SDRs
Proposed Fourth Amendment of the Articles of Agreement

WHEREAS the Interim Committee of the Board of Governors has invited the Executive Board to propose an amendment of the Articles of Agreement of the International Monetary Fund providing for a special one-time allocation of SDRs to allow all participants in the Special Drawing Rights Department to receive an equitable share of cumulative SDR allocations; and

WHEREAS the Executive Board has proposed such an amendment and prepared a report on the same;

NOW, THEREFORE, The Board of Governors, noting the said Report of the Executive Board, hereby RESOLVES that:

1. The proposals for modifications (Proposed Fourth Amendment) that are attached to this Resolution and are to be incorporated in the Articles of Agreement of the International Monetary Fund are approved.

2. The Secretary of the Fund is directed to ask, by circular letter, telegram, or other rapid means of communications, all members of the Fund whether they accept, in accordance with the provisions of Article XXVIII of the Articles, the Proposed Fourth Amendment.

3. The circular letter, telegram, or other communication to be sent to all members in accordance with 2 above shall specify that the Proposed Fourth Amendment shall enter into force for all members as of the date on which the Fund certifies, by formal communication addressed to all members, that three-fifths of the members, having eighty-five percent of the total voting power, have accepted the modifications.

Attachment to Resolution No. 52-4

Proposed Fourth Amendment of the Articles of Agreement of the International Monetary Fund

The Governments on whose behalf the present Agreement is signed agree as follows:

1. The text of Article XV, Section 1 shall be amended to read as follows:

(a) To meet the need, as and when it arises, for a supplement to existing reserve assets, the Fund is authorized to allo-

cate special drawing rights in accordance with the provisions of Article XVIII to members that are participants in the Special Drawing Rights Department.

(b) In addition, the Fund shall allocate special drawing rights to members that are participants in the Special Drawing Rights Department in accordance with the provisions of Schedule M.

2. A new Schedule M shall be added to the Articles, to read as follows:

"Schedule M
Special One-Time Allocation of Special Drawing Rights

1. Subject to 4 below, each member that, as of September 19, 1997, is a participant in the Special Drawing Rights Department shall, on the 30th day following the effective date of the fourth amendment of this Agreement, receive an allocation of special drawing rights in an amount that will result in its net cumulative allocation of special drawing rights being equal to 29.315788813 percent of its quota as of September 19, 1997, provided that, for participants whose quotas have not been adjusted as proposed in Resolution No. 45-2 of the Board of Governors, calculations shall be made on the basis of the quotas proposed in that resolution.

2. (a) Subject to 4 below, each country that becomes a participant in the Special Drawing Rights Department after September 19, 1997 but within three months of the date of its membership in the Fund shall receive an allocation of special drawing rights in an amount calculated in accordance with (b) and (c) below on the 30th day following the later of: (i) the date on which the new member becomes a participant in the Special Drawing Rights Department, or (ii) the effective date of the fourth amendment of this Agreement.

(b) For the purposes of (a) above, each participant shall receive an amount of special drawing rights that will result in such participant's net cumulative allocation being equal to 29.315788813 percent of its quota as of the date on which the member becomes a participant in the Special Drawing Rights Department, as adjusted:

(i) first, by multiplying 29.315788813 percent by the ratio of the total of quotas, as calculated under 1 above, of the participants described in (c) below to the total of quotas of such participants as of the date on which the member became a participant in the Special Drawing Rights Department, and

(ii) second, by multiplying the product of (i) above by the ratio of the total of the sum of the net cumulative allocations of special drawing rights received under Article XVIII of the participants described in (c) below as of the date on which the member became a participant in the Special Drawing Rights Department and the allocations received by such participants under 1 above to the total of the sum of the net cumulative allocations of special drawing rights received under Article XVIII of such participants as of September 19, 1997 and the allocations received by such participants under 1 above.

(c) For the purposes of the adjustments to be made under (b) above, the participants in the Special Drawing Rights Department shall be members that are participants as of September 19, 1997 and (i) continue to be participants in the Special Drawing Rights Department as of the date on which the member became a participant in the Special Drawing Rights Department, and (ii) have received all allocations made by the Fund after September 19, 1997.

3. (a) Subject to 4 below, if the Federal Republic of Yugoslavia (Serbia/Montenegro) succeeds to the membership in the Fund and the participation in the Special Drawing Rights Department of the former Socialist Federal Republic of Yugoslavia in accordance with the terms and conditions of Executive Board Decision No. 10237-(92/150), adopted December 14, 1992, it shall receive an allocation of special drawing rights in an amount calculated in accordance with (b) below on the 30th day following the later of: (i) the date on which the Federal Republic of Yugoslavia (Serbia/Montenegro) succeeds to membership in the Fund and participation in the Special Drawing Rights Department in accordance with the terms and conditions of Executive Board Decision No. 10237-(92/150), or (ii) the effective date of the fourth amendment of this Agreement.

(b) For the purposes of (a) above, the Federal Republic of Yugoslavia (Serbia/Montenegro) shall receive an amount of special drawing rights that will result in its net cumulative allocation being equal to 29.315788813 percent of the quota proposed to it under paragraph 3(c) of Executive Board Decision No. 10237-(92/150), as adjusted in accordance with 2(b)(ii) and (c) above as of the date on which the Federal Republic of Yugoslavia (Serbia/Montenegro) qualifies for an allocation under (a) above.

4. The Fund shall not allocate special drawing rights under this Schedule to those participants that have notified the Fund in writing prior to the date of the allocation of their desire not to receive the allocation.

5. (a) If, at the time an allocation is made to a participant under 1, 2, or 3 above, the participant has overdue obliga-tions to the Fund, the special drawing rights so allocated shall be deposited and held in an escrow account within the Special Drawing Rights Department and shall be released to the par-ticipant upon discharge of all its overdue obligations to the Fund.

(b) Special drawing rights being held in an escrow account shall not be available for any use and shall not be included in any calculations of allocations or holdings of spe-cial drawing rights for the purposes of the Articles, except for calculations under this Schedule. If special drawing rights allo-cated to a participant are held in an escrow account when the participant terminates its participation in the Special Drawing Rights Department or when it is decided to liquidate the Spe-cial Drawing Rights Department, such special drawing rights shall be canceled.

(c) For purposes of this paragraph, overdue obliga-tions to the Fund consist of overdue repurchases and charges in the General Resources Account, overdue principal and interest on loans in the Special Disbursement Account, overdue charges and assessments in the Special Drawing Rights Department, and overdue liabilities to the Fund as trustee.

(d) Except for the provisions of this paragraph, the principle of separation between the General Department and the Special Drawing Rights Department and the uncondi-tional character of special drawing rights as reserve assets shall be maintained."

The Board of Governors adopted the foregoing Resolution, effec-tive September 23, 1997.

IMF Relations with Other International Organizations

IMF cooperation with other international organizations that share common interests and goals, such as the World Bank, the United Nations, the World Trade Organization (WTO), and the International Labour Organization (ILO), continued to evolve in 1997/98 in response to the changing global economic environment and the emergence of new policy challenges.

Relations with the World Bank

Both the evaluations of the Enhanced Structural Adjustment Facility (ESAF) and the Asian financial crisis highlighted the importance of more effective IMF-World Bank collaboration in 1997/98, especially on financial sector, social, and debt issues.

• Building on the April 1997 Joint Statement by the Managing Director of the IMF and the President of the World Bank, an agreement on strengthening collaboration mechanisms for financial sector issues was discussed by the Executive Boards of both institutions and is being implemented. The agreement covers a wide range of activities in the financial sector, including diagnosis, policy advice, technical assistance, and training, as well as operational procedures in crisis situations. In particular, it clarifies the roles of the two institutions and defines and strengthens procedures for collaboration on financial sector issues. Accordingly, the Bank is concerned mainly with the sectoral and developmental aspects of financial systems in developing countries, while the IMF's involvement, including its surveillance, relates primarily to the macroeconomic aspects of financial systems and markets in all member countries.

• The broadening of the IMF's policy advice to include concern for the social impact of its policy advice—notably, to better protect vulnerable groups from the adverse effects of adjustment by ensuring well-designed and targeted social safety nets—has also called for closer collaboration with the World Bank, which undertakes much of the analysis and policy advice on social issues, along with the Food and Agriculture Organization (FAO), ILO, UN Development Programme (UNDP), and United Nations Children's Fund (UNICEF).

• During the financial year, the IMF continued to work closely with the Bank on the implementation of the HIPC Initiative for the heavily indebted poor countries (see Chapter IX). One of the guiding principles of the debt-relief Initiative is that assistance to eligible countries be coordinated among all creditors, with broad and equitable participation. IMF and World Bank staff initiate the consultation process with other creditors prior to the "decision point" to ensure that the

HIPC documents reflect the likely response of the international community. Immediately following the IMF and Bank Board meeting at the decision point and at the completion point, the IMF's Managing Director and the President of the World Bank send a joint letter to multilateral and bilateral creditors informing them of the decisions in principle by the IMF and World Bank.

Relations with the United Nations

Collaboration with the United Nations continued in 1997/98, both at the institution-wide and local levels. *Collaboration at the institution-wide level,* largely carried out and supported by the IMF's Office at the UN in New York, has entailed increased participation by IMF staff in meetings and initiatives organized by UN committees and commissions, exchange of information, and collaboration in the statistical area and postconflict situations. In addition, the IMF Office in Geneva works on trade-related issues with the UN Conference on Trade and Development (UNCTAD). In April 1998, the UN Economic and Social Council (ECOSOC) held a Special High-Level Meeting on "Global Financial Integration and Development and Recent Issues," which the IMF's Managing Director attended.

At *the country level,* IMF staff on missions continued to interact with the UN resident coordinators to exchange views on economic and other developments, and IMF resident representatives continued to stay in regular contact with UN resident coordinators, attend heads-of-agency meetings usually chaired by UN resident coordinators, and attend local aid coordination meetings. Collaboration with UN resident coordinators at the local level has been particularly intensive in those countries where the UN Development Programme and the IMF have been engaged in joint funding and implementation of technical assistance projects; the IMF's contribution has been sought in the preparation of Country Strategy Notes and in the United Nations Development Assistance Framework (UNDAF).

Relations with the World Trade Organization

The IMF Office in Geneva is responsible for monitoring and reporting on the activities of the Geneva-based World Trade Organization, and it represents the IMF at meetings of various WTO bodies, including the Balance of Payments Committee. Since a Cooperation Agreement between the IMF and the WTO came into effect in December 1996, implementation of its provisions—which cover institutional and staff consultations (such as the IMF's participation in the WTO Committee on Balance of Payments Restrictions), staff attendance at each other's meetings, and exchange of documents and information—has proceeded smoothly. Under the Agreement's provision on achieving greater coherence in global economic policymaking, a working group of senior staff from the IMF, the WTO, and the World Bank has been actively studying initiatives in that area. The Director-General of the WTO, in a November 1997 report to the General Council, noted that these working relationships had already been fruitful despite the Agreement's having been in effect for less than a year.

A further aspect of IMF-WTO cooperation is the IMF's participation in the Integrated Initiative for Least-Developed Countries' Trade Development, following a declaration at the 1996 Singapore Ministerial Conference of the WTO to promote "an integrated approach to assisting these countries in enhancing their trading opportunities." A subsequent meeting in October 1997, with the IMF among the participating organizations, endorsed guidelines on trade-related technical assistance under the initiative, including for human and institutional capacity-building. The IMF, as one of the six intergovernmental agencies involved in providing an "integrated response," had undertaken or given a commitment in principle to provide technical assistance to 27 countries by the end of the financial year. The IMF's advice on economic policies and technical assistance (particularly in fiscal and statistical areas) is recognized as supporting the establishment of more favorable macroeconomic conditions, thereby enabling these countries to participate more actively in the global trading system.

Relations with the International Labour Organization

Collaboration between the IMF and the ILO has been strengthened in recent years in recognition of the complementarity of the objectives of macroeconomic stability and higher levels of employment over the medium term. Such collaboration intensified in 1997/98 in the context of the Asian financial crisis. During the year, IMF staff attended the ILO-sponsored Asian Regional Conference, held in Bangkok on December 9–11, 1997; the conference dealt with labor market trends and poverty and human development issues in the region. IMF staff also attended the ILO High-Level Tripartite Meeting on the Social Responses to the Financial Crisis in East Asian Countries, in Bangkok on April 22–24, 1998. Contacts between IMF staff and management with ILO officials, as well as with those of labor union organizations, also increased substantially during the year.

Relations with Other Organizations

IMF collaboration with other international and regional organizations is carried out by the IMF's Office in Europe,

located in Paris, and the Regional Office for Asia and the Pacific, in Tokyo. The Office in Europe reports on the activities of the Europe-based international and regional institutions, including the Bank for International Settlements, the European Commission, and the Organization for Economic Cooperation and Development (OECD). The Paris Office monitors policies of the European Union, communicates with the OECD Secretariat, and participates in OECD committees. It provides continuing support to the work of the Group of Ten and is also the IMF's principal information office in Europe. The Regional Office for Asia and the Pacific facilitates the IMF's dialogue with regional policymakers by sponsoring various policy forums in the region.

Cooperation with Regional Development Banks

The IMF's close cooperation with such multilateral development banks as the African Development Bank (AfDB), the Asian Development Bank (ADB), the European Bank for Reconstruction and Development (EBRD), and the Inter-American Development Bank (IADB) intensified further in 1997/98, particularly in connection with the HIPC Initiative. Strengthening the institutional partnership with development banks, the IMF Executive Board approved on July 21, 1997, a proposal to allow representatives of multilateral creditors to attend country-specific Board discussions on HIPC Initiative matters. Collaboration with the multilateral development banks includes consultation on structural adjustment programs, including the financing of these programs, coordination of technical assistance, exchange of information, staff visits, and attendance at meetings. IMF staff members regularly attend meetings, seminars, and forums sponsored by other regional, economic, and financial organizations in Africa, Asia and the Pacific, Latin America and the Caribbean, and the Middle East.

Role of IMF Management

The IMF's close ties with other international organizations are enhanced by the Managing Director's attendance at conferences, meetings, and seminars sponsored by the UN, Bank for International Settlements, and other organizations. During the financial year, the Managing Director continued his regular exchanges with the UN Secretary-General, addressed and attended meetings of the UN ECOSOC, participated in meetings of the UN Administrative Committee on Coordination, and in October 1997 delivered an address on the Asian crisis to the Second Committee of the UN General Assembly. Consultations with the OECD in May were followed up by attendance at its Ministerial Meeting in November. And in May 1998 the Managing Director inaugurated the IMF-Singapore Regional Training Institute.

External Relations

The IMF has stepped up its external relations activities in recent years in a number of ways, including through more public appearances and interviews by its management and staff, by expanding its publications and information dissemination, and by encouraging its member countries to release more of their own documentation. The scale of the Asian financial crisis, its global reverberations, and the IMF's role at the center of efforts to manage and resolve the financial turbulence brought these activities into sharp relief in 1997/98. They stimulated unprecedented interest in what the IMF is and does and heightened the degree of scrutiny and debate over the policies advocated by the IMF, the magnitude of its lending, and its role in a globalized economy.

In response, the IMF expanded its media contacts; its management and staff delivered numerous speeches and offered official pronouncements in a wide range of forums; it disseminated more data and information, including through its publications and heavy recourse to the IMF's website, while actively encouraging member countries to do the same; and it engaged more intensively with representatives of the academic, corporate, and civil communities in its member countries.

Purposes

The IMF's external communications activities are aimed at contributing to the effectiveness of the institution's core work. Its external communications work serves three broad purposes:

- *promoting the understanding and pursuit of sound policies and best practices,* through the dissemination of staff analysis and research, advocacy, and consensus building;
- *contributing to public understanding and support for the institution,* by providing information on the IMF's work, policy positions, and processes and meeting a high standard of public accountability; and
- *helping influence economic policy in individual countries* through the communication of IMF views in the context of bilateral surveillance and the provision of financial assistance.

Audiences

The IMF's approach to external communications has evolved in recent years to target a variety of audiences, using a range of instruments. The main audiences are:

- *the public policy community,* which includes government and central bank officials who deal directly with the IMF, as well as parliamentarians who authorize the government's

participation in the IMF and are responsible for legislating economic policy, and influential public figures;
- *the media,* both print and broadcast, with the latter assuming a steadily more important role;
- *the academic community* and public policy institutes, which, through their publications and pronouncements, influence the media's and the public's understanding of economic issues and their perception of the work of the IMF;
- *financial markets and the business sector,* whose principal interest lies in information and data about member countries and in the types of policies being implemented with IMF advice and assistance;
- *civil society,* including in particular nongovernmental organizations, labor and religious groups, and women's groups. As civil society has come to acquire more influence in decision making nationally, the need has grown to ensure that these groups have access to reliable information and that there are adequate opportunities for interaction with them; and
- *kindred international organizations.*

Instruments

Each of the audiences is important in itself, but also—to varying degrees—as an intermediary between the IMF and the broader public. External communications initiatives have sought to convey the institution's messages in a number of ways, since audiences differ in the kinds of information they look to the IMF to provide, as well as in their attitudes toward the institution.

Publications and press releases have long been foremost among the IMF's established tools of communication. The IMF publishes reports, periodicals, statistical compilations, books, manuals, pamphlets, and working papers. Collectively, the various publications serve to disseminate information on sound economic policies, topical research, and national, regional, and world economic developments and prospects, thereby complementing the IMF's surveillance activities and fostering international economic cooperation. Publications also inform a broader audience of how the IMF works.

Press releases are the chief vehicle for informing the public in a timely fashion of Executive Board decisions on the use of IMF resources and on other issues of public interest. The Newsbrief series is used principally to make the public aware of management and senior staff views on topical matters. In 1997/98, written contributions to newspapers, for example, op-ed articles and letters to the editors, have allowed the IMF to state its case, and correct serious misconceptions, directly to the public.[1]

Speeches are also a key instrument. They allow management, and in particular the Managing Director as the IMF's principal spokesman, to set out the IMF's views on the major economic and financial issues of the day, to respond to the views of others, and to offer fresh ideas for public consideration.

Two other instruments have a similarly broad reach, yet with the capability of being focused on specific audiences and delivering specific messages: seminars and conferences, and management and staff contacts with nonofficials, including the media. Seminars and conferences provide a means of engaging and bringing the IMF's views to a wide range of interlocutors—professional peers, regional groups of journalists, policymakers, and representatives of civil society. Equally, they provide opportunities for the IMF to listen to and consider alternative views and perceptions. Management and staff contacts with the media range from one-on-one interviews and briefings for small groups to press conferences on events of major interest, such as the release of the *World Economic Outlook*. A feature of increasing importance in the institution's outreach to nonofficials has been the enhanced role of the IMF's resident representatives—and of staff in the IMF's overseas offices—in explaining the work of the institution. Also, heads of missions to member countries increasingly give press briefings at the conclusion of staff visits. IMF missions are also more routinely interacting with contacts in the academic community, the corporate sector, and civil society.

Finally, an innovation that has expanded the potential audience for the IMF has been the introduction, in 1996, of the IMF's external website at http://www.imf.org. "IMF Publications" has fairly consistently been the most frequently visited locale on the site, with much interest also in manage-

ment speeches and press conferences, transcripts of which are posted routinely. By the end of 1997/98, total visits to the site from outside the IMF averaged about one million a month, nearly five times the level a year earlier. In May 1998, 32 percent of visitors were identified as U.S.-based and 41 percent as outside the United States.

Initiatives in 1997/98

Building further on its expanded external communication efforts of recent years, the IMF responded to demands for greater openness in 1997/98 in the following ways:

- having its management and staff give an unprecedented number of speeches, press conferences, and on-the-record interviews to a broad spectrum of the media;
- conducting an extensive outreach effort—including public information visits and briefings for journalists—in Asia prior to the Hong Kong Annual Meetings;
- establishing an Office for Asia and the Pacific, in Tokyo, whose functions include external communications;
- expanding its program of issue-oriented and regional seminars (e.g., a seminar on Asia and the IMF in Hong Kong prior to the 1997 Annual Meetings) and introducing a program of seminars at the Joint Vienna Institute for parliamentarians from economies in transition;
- publishing the results of an external evaluation of the Enhanced Structural Adjustment Facility, launching a new IMF-sponsored *Finance & Development*, stepping up coverage of topical issues through its *Economic Issues* series, and introducing a new publication, *IMF Economic Reviews*, that is a collection of current Press (now "Public") Information Notices; and
- increasing substantially its recourse to the Internet to disseminate information and publications, which includes, for the first time, making available on line Letters of Intent and Memoranda of Economic and Financial Policies of member countries.

In recognition of the heightened importance of external communications in helping the IMF fulfill its role more effectively, the Executive Board called for a review and assessment of the IMF's communications strategy and performance, to be completed in 1998/99.

---

[1]In 1997/98, 58 press releases, 35 Newsbriefs, and 77 Press Information Notices were issued, and nearly a dozen letters to the editor and 10 articles by IMF management and senior staff appeared in major newspapers and journals.

Table V.1.

Publications Issued, Financial Year Ended April 30, 1998

Reports and Other Documents
Annual Report of the Executive Board for the Financial Year Ended April 30, 1997*
(English, French, German, and Spanish). Free.

Exchange Arrangements and Exchange Restrictions, Annual Report 1997
$76.00 ($38.00 to full-time university faculty members and students).

Summary Proceedings of the Fifty-Second Annual Meeting of the Board of Governors (1997). Free.
The IMF Committee on Balance of Payments Statistics, Annual Report, 1997. Free.

Periodic Publications
Balance of Payments Statistics Yearbook
Vol. 48, 1997. A two-part yearbook. $68.00 a year.

Direction of Trade Statistics
Quarterly, with yearbook. $110.00 a year. $55.00 to full-time university faculty members and students. $32.00 for yearbook only.

Government Finance Statistics Yearbook
Vol. 21, 1997 (introduction and titles of lines in English, French, and Spanish). $60.00.

International Financial Statistics
Monthly, with yearbook (English, French, and Spanish). $246.00 a year. $123.00 to full-time university faculty members and students. $65.00 for yearbook only. *International*

Financial Statistics is also available on CD-ROM. Price information is available on request.

Staff Papers

Four times a year. $56.00 a year. $28.00 to full-time university faculty members and students.

*Finance and Development**

Quarterly (English, Arabic, Chinese, French, and Spanish). Free. Airspeed delivery, $20.00.

*IMF Survey**

Twice monthly, but only once in December (English, French, and Spanish). Private firms and individuals are charged at an annual rate of $79.00.

Occasional Papers

No. 151. *Currency Board Arrangements: Issues and Experiences,* by Tómas J.T. Baliño and Charles Enoch.

No. 152. *Hong Kong, China: Growth, Structural Change, and Economic Stability During the Transition,* by John Dodsworth and Dubravko Mihaljek.

No. 153. *Pension Regimes and Saving,* by G.A. Mackenzie, Philip Gerson, and Alfredo Cuevas.

No. 154. *Credibility Without Rules,* by Carlo Cottarelli.

No. 155. *Fiscal Policy Issues During the Transition in Russia,* by Augusto Lopez-Claros and Sergei Alexashenko.

No. 156. *The ESAF at Ten Years: Economic Adjustment and Reform in Low-Income Countries,* by the Staff of the International Monetary Fund.

No. 157. *Central Bank Reforms in the Baltics, Russia, and the Other Countries of the Former Soviet Union,* by a Staff Team led by Malcolm Knight and comprising Susana Almuiña, John Dalton, Inci Otker, Ceyla Pazarbaşıoğlu, Arne B. Petersen, Peter Quirk, Nicholas M. Roberts, Gabriel Sensenbrenner, and Jan Willem van der Vossen.

No. 158. *Transparency in Government Operations,* by George Kopits and Jon Craig.

No. 159. *Hungary: Economic Policies for Sustainable Growth,* by Carlo Cottarelli, Thomas Krueger, Reza Moghadam, Perry Perone, Edgardo Ruggiero, and Rachel van Elkan.

No. 160. *Fiscal Reform in Low-Income Countries: Experience Under IMF-Supported Programs,* by George T. Abed, Liam Ebrill, Sanjeev Gupta, Benedict Clements, Ronald McMorran, Anthony Pellechio, Jerald Schiff, and Marijn Verhoeven.

No. 161. *The Nordic Banking Crises: Pitfalls in Financial Liberalization?* by Burkhard Drees and Ceyla Pazarbaşıoğlu.

Occasional Papers Nos. 151–53 are available for $15.00 each, with a special price of $12.00 each to full-time university faculty members and students; Occasional Papers No. 154–61 are available for $18.00 each, with a special price of $15.00 each to full-time university faculty and students.

World Economic and Financial Surveys

*World Economic Outlook: A Survey by the Staff of the International Monetary Fund**

Twice a year (May and October) (Arabic, English, French, and Spanish).

$36.00 ($25.00 to full-time university faculty and students).

*Staff Studies for the World Economic Outlook**

By the Research Department of the International Monetary Fund. $25.00 ($20.00 to full-time university faculty and students).

World Economic Outlook: Interim Assessment, December 1997*

A Survey by the Staff of the International Monetary Fund. $36.00 ($25.00 to full-time university faculty and students).

*International Capital Markets: Developments, Prospects, and Policy Issues**

By a Staff Team led by David Folkerts-Landau, with Donald J. Mathieson and Garry J. Schinasi

$20.00 ($12.00 to full-time university faculty and students).

Official Financing for Developing Countries

By a Staff Team in the Policy Development and Review Department led by Anthony R. Boote and Doris C. Ross. $25.00 ($20.00 to full-time university faculty and students).

Toward a Framework for Financial Stability

By a Staff Team led by David Folkerts-Landau and Carl-Johan Lindgren.

$25.00 ($20.00 to full-time university faculty and students).

Trade Liberalization in IMF-Supported Programs

By a Staff Team led by Robert Sharer. $25.00 ($20.00 to full-time university faculty and students).

Books and Seminar Volumes

A Global Integration Strategy for the Mediterranean Countries: Open Trade and Market Reform, by Oleh Havrylyshyn. $15.00

Banking Soundness and Monetary Policy: Issues and Experiences in the Global Economy, by Charles A. Enoch, John H. Green, and Manuel Guitián.
$29.50

Coordinating Public Debt and Monetary Management: Institutional and Operational Arrangements, by V. Sundararajan, Peter Dattels, and Hans J. Blommestein.
$27.00

Current Legal Issues Affecting Central Banks, Vol. V, edited by Robert Effros.
$65.00

Deepening Structural Reform in Africa: Lessons from East Asia, edited by Laura Wallace.
$20.00

EMU and the International Monetary System, by Paul R. Masson, Thomas H. Krueger, and Bart Turtelboom.
$35.00

External Finance for Low-Income Countries, by Zubair Iqbal and Ravi Kanbur.
$22.50

Financial Systems and Labor Markets in the Gulf Cooperation Council Countries, by Abdelali Jbili, Vicente Galbis, and Amer Bisat.
$15.00

Fiscal Federalism in Theory and Practice, edited by Teresa Ter-Minassian.
$35.00

Instruments of Monetary Management: Issues and Country Experiences, by Tómas T. Baliño and Lorena M. Zamalloa.
$22.50

Macroeconomic Accounting and Analysis in Transition Economies, by Abdessatar Ouanes and Subhash Thakur.
$19.00

Macroeconomic Issues Facing ASEAN Countries, by Anoop Singh, David Robinson, and John Hicklin.
$26.00

Payment Systems, Monetary Policy, and the Role of the Central Bank, by Omotunde E.G. Johnson with Richard K. Abrams, Jean-Marc Destresse, Tonny Lybek, Nicholas M. Roberts, and Mark Swinburne.
$25.00

Social Safety Nets: Issues and Recent Experiences, by Ke-Young Chu and Sanjeev Gupta.
$28.50

Systemic Bank Restructuring and Macroeconomic Policy, edited by Carl-Johan Lindgren, William E. Alexander, Liam Ebrill, and Jeffrey Davis.
$23.50

The Economy of the Middle East and North Africa in 1997, by Mohamed A. El-Erian and Susan Fennell.
$15.00

Economic Issues*

No. 8. *Why Is China Growing So Fast?*
By Zuliu Hu and Mohsin S. Khan
(Chinese).
Free.

No. 9. *Protecting Bank Deposits*
By Gillian G. Garcia
Free.

No. 10. *Deindustrialization—Its Causes and Implications*
By Robert Rowthorn and Ramana Ramaswamy
Free.

No. 11. *Does Globalization Lower Wages and Export Jobs?*
By Matthew J. Slaughter and Phillip Swagel
Free.

No. 12. *Roads to Nowhere: How Corruption in Public Investment Hurts Growth*
By Vito Tanzi and Hamid Davoodi
Free.

No. 13. *Fixed or Flexible? Getting the Exchange Rate Right in the 1990s*
By Francesco Caramazza and Jahangir Aziz
Free.

No. 14. *Lessons from Systemic Bank Restructuring*
By Claudia Dziobek and Ceyla Pazarbaşıoğlu
Free.

Pamphlets

No. 51. *Debt Relief for Low-Income Countries: The HIPC Initiative*
By Anthony R. Boote and Kamau Thugge
Free.

Booklets

The Challenges of Globalization in an Interdependent World Economy
Four Addresses by Michel Camdessus
Free.

Good Governance: The IMF's Role *
Free.

What Is the IMF? (revised edition)*
Free.

Working Papers and Papers on Policy Analysis and Assessment*

IMF Working Papers and *Papers on Policy Analysis and Assessment* are designed to make IMF staff research available to a broad audience. They represent works in progress and reflect the views of the individual authors rather than those of the IMF.

Working Papers 97/46–97/182 and 98/1–98/62 were issued in 1997/98.
$7.00 each; $210.00 for annual subscription.

Papers on Policy Analysis and Assessment 97/4–97/11 and 98/1–98/2 were issued in 1997/98.
$7.00 each; $80.00 for annual subscription.

Staff Country Reports*

IMF Staff Country Reports consist of comprehensive material on economic developments and trends in member countries. The reports are prepared by IMF staff missions as background information for the periodic consultations with members. They contain reports on recent economic developments, background papers, and statistical annexes and appendices.

Staff Country Reports 97/25–97/121 and 98/1–98/30 were issued in 1997/98.
$15.00 each.

Copies of IMF publications may be obtained from Publication Services, International Monetary Fund, 700 19th Street, N.W., Washington, D.C. 20431, U.S.A.:
Telephone: (202) 623-7430
Telefax: (202) 623-7201
E-mail: publications@imf.org
Internet: http://www.imf.org

Additional information about the IMF and its publications, including the current *Publications Catalog,* a searchable IMF Publications Database, and ordering information and forms, is available on the IMF's website (http://www.imf.org).
*Available in English in full text on the IMF's website (http://www.imf.org).

Press Communiqués of the Interim Committee and the Development Committee

Interim Committee of the Board of Governors of the International Monetary System
PRESS COMMUNIQUÉS

Forty-Ninth Meeting, Hong Kong, China, September 21, 1997

1. The Interim Committee held its forty-ninth meeting in Hong Kong, China on September 21, 1997 under the Chairmanship of Mr. Philippe Maystadt, Deputy Prime Minister and Minister of Finance and Foreign Trade of Belgium.

2. The Committee welcomed the generally favorable prospects for the continued expansion of world output and trade. There are, nevertheless, risks that confront individual countries and that could also affect the world economy, if not decisively addressed.

- In the advanced economies as a group, growth with low inflation is projected to continue. However, sustained fiscal consolidation remains a challenge for many countries, requiring resolute policies over the near and medium term. Exchange rates among the major currencies should reflect economic fundamentals bearing in mind the importance of avoiding large external imbalances. In countries that have reached high levels of resource use, including the United States, monetary policy will need to guard against the reemergence of inflation. In continental Europe, monetary policy should remain consistent with sustained expansion of domestic demand. The challenge for Japan is to achieve the objective of domestic demand-led growth with a supportive stance of monetary policy while proceeding vigorously with its structural reform program and further consolidating its fiscal position over the medium term. High levels of structural unemployment in several European countries point to the pressing need for more determined efforts to increase efficiency and adaptability in labor and product markets and to reform tax, social benefits, and other entitlement systems.
- The growth performance and prospects of developing countries as a group have strengthened in recent years. However, further improvements are needed in many cases to achieve significant reductions in poverty. This highlights the need to maintain macroeconomic discipline and accelerate structural reforms, including "second-generation" reforms aimed at strengthening public administration and financial sector management, developing human capital, promoting basic infrastructure, and fostering a conducive and transparent environment for private investment.
- In some emerging market economies, large external imbalances and fragile banking systems have adversely affected investor confidence and exacerbated the risks emanating from volatile capital movements.
- In the transition countries, growth has resumed following good progress, in most cases, with macroeconomic stabilization and structural reforms. Strengthening growth performance depends on speeding up legal, institutional, and other reforms that encourage private economic activity and investment. To safeguard and build upon the achievements thus far, inflation will in most cases need to be lowered further through disciplined macroeconomic policies.

3. The Committee welcomed progress made toward a successful European Economic and Monetary Union (EMU) that contributes to stability in the international monetary system. The economic convergence achieved in Europe and the strong commitment to start EMU on schedule constitute a sound basis for securing a smooth transition to the euro on January 1, 1999. The best way to ensure a solid and stable EMU will be for its participants to demonstrate not only their commitment to the fiscal requirements of the Stability and Growth Pact, but also their resolve to attack the root causes of Europe's high unemployment.

4. The Committee reaffirmed the vital contribution of globalization to economic growth worldwide. Adherence by all members to the policy guidelines set out in the Committee's "Declaration on Partnership for Sustainable Global Growth" is essential to ensuring that all share in the benefits of globalization. The Committee welcomed the recent adoption by the Fund of guidelines on governance issues as well as the ongoing efforts to enhance the soundness of financial systems, notably the establishment of the "Core Principles of Effective Banking Supervision" developed by the Basle Committee in conjunction with the supervisory authorities in a number of emerging market economies.

5. The Committee noted that recent disturbances in Asian financial markets have again underscored the importance for policymakers in all countries to ensure the internal consistency of macroeconomic policies, strengthen financial systems, and avoid excessive external deficits and reliance on short-term

foreign borrowing. Although the impact of recent financial market turmoil on some of the countries affected is expected to result in a slowdown of growth in the near term, the countries. economic fundamentals remain solid and their longer-term outlook is favorable, provided the required adjustment policies are sustained. The Committee also noted that the recent Asian experience has illustrated that rising capital flows may require some adaptation of exchange rate arrangements to changing circumstances. Regardless of a country's exchange rate arrangement, the maintenance of appropriate macroeconomic and structural policies consistent with the arrangement remains crucial.

6. The Committee commended the Fund for its prompt and effective response to the events in Asia, welcomed the support provided by the region, and invited the Executive Board to examine what further lessons could be drawn for the Fund's work and to report its findings to the next meeting of the Committee. In this context, the Committee recognized that the recent developments raised a number of analytical issues, including on the prevention of crises and contagion effects. The Committee stressed the importance of openness and accountability of economic policymaking, and of transparency, to achieving policy credibility and confidence building in a globalized environment. It would be useful for the Fund to work in this area, including the possibility of developing a code of good practices. Timely and accurate economic information is also needed to improve the functioning of markets. The Committee welcomed the Fund's Special Data Dissemination Standard and the recent voluntary release of Press Information Notices on the conclusions of Fund surveillance in individual members, making an important contribution to transparency. The Committee looked forward to the strengthening of the Fund's Special Data Dissemination Standard.

7. The Committee reiterated its view that an open and liberal system of capital movements, supported by sound macroeconomic policies and strong financial systems, enhances economic welfare and prosperity in the world economy. The Committee adopted the Statement on "The Liberalization of Capital Movements Under an Amendment of the Fund's Articles," and considered that an amendment of the Fund's Articles will provide the most effective means of promoting an orderly liberalization of capital movements consistent with the Fund's role in the international monetary system. The Committee requested the Executive Board to accord high priority to completing its work and submitting a report and a proposed draft amendment to the Board of Governors.

8. The Committee welcomed the agreement reached by the Executive Board on both the size of the increase in quotas under the Eleventh General Review and on the method to be used to distribute the overall increase in quotas. The Committee agreed that:
• The present total of Fund quotas would be increased by 45 percent;
• Seventy-five percent of the overall increase would be distributed in proportion to present quotas;
• Fifteen percent of the overall increase would be distributed in proportion to members' shares in calculated quotas (based on 1994 data), so as to better reflect the relative economic positions of members; and

• The remaining 10 percent of the overall increase would be distributed among those members whose present quotas are out of line with their positions in the world economy (as measured by the excess of their share in calculated quotas over their share in actual quotas), of which 1 percent of the overall increase would be distributed among five members whose current quotas are far out of line with their relative economic positions, and which are in a position to contribute to the Fund's liquidity over the medium term.

The Committee requested the Executive Board to submit before the end of this year a proposed resolution for the approval of the Board of Governors to effect the agreed increases in quotas. The Committee reiterated its view that the formulas used to calculate quotas should be reviewed by the Board promptly after the completion of the Eleventh General Review.

9. The Committee welcomed the agreement reached by the Executive Board on an amendment of the Articles to provide all members with an equitable share of cumulative SDR allocations through a special one-time SDR allocation amounting to SDR 21.4 billion, which will double the amount of SDRs already allocated. Accordingly, it recommends the adoption by the Board of Governors of the proposed Resolution.

10. The Committee welcomed the recent progress made in the implementation of the HIPC Initiative, including the decisions, in principle, of the Executive Boards of the Fund and Bank to provide assistance to Uganda, Bolivia, and Burkina Faso, and the preliminary discussions on Côte d'Ivoire, Guyana, and Mozambique. The Committee encouraged countries that could qualify under the Initiative to expeditiously take the necessary adjustment measures to benefit from this special assistance.

11. The Committee welcomed the continuing efforts to help secure the resources needed to complete the financing of the ESAF and HIPC initiatives. It noted that, in light of the bilateral pledges received or in prospect, and the need to continue making commitments under the HIPC Initiative, further steps to secure the timely funding of these initiatives would have to be considered soon.

The Committee will meet again in Washington, D.C., on April 16, 1998.

Statement of the Interim Committee on the Liberalization of Capital Movements Under an Amendment of the Articles

1. It is time to add a new chapter to the Bretton Woods agreement. Private capital flows have become much more important to the international monetary system, and an increasingly open and liberal system has proved to be highly beneficial to the world economy. By facilitating the flow of savings to their most productive uses, capital movements increase investment, growth, and prosperity. Provided it is introduced in an orderly manner, and backed both by adequate national policies and a solid multilateral system for surveillance and financial support, the liberalization of capital flows is an essential element of an efficient international monetary system in this age of globalization. The IMF's central role in the international monetary system, and its near universal membership, make it uniquely placed to help this process.

The Committee sees the Fund's proposed new mandate as bold in its vision, but cautious in implementation.

2. International capital flows are highly sensitive, inter alia, to the stability of the international monetary system, the quality of macroeconomic policies, and the soundness of domestic financial systems. The recent turmoil in financial markets has demonstrated again the importance of underpinning liberalization with a broad range of structural measures, especially in the monetary and financial sector, and within the framework of a solid mix of macroeconomic and exchange rate policies. Particular importance will need to be attached to establishing an environment conducive to the efficient utilization of capital and to building sound financial systems solid enough to cope with fluctuations in capital flows. This phased but comprehensive approach will tailor capital account liberalization to the circumstances of individual countries, thereby maximizing the chances of success, not only for each country but also for the international monetary system.

3. These efforts should lead to the establishment of a multilateral and nondiscriminatory system to promote the liberalization of capital movements. The Fund will have the task of assisting in the establishment of such a system and stands ready to support members' efforts in this regard. Its role is also key to the adoption of policies that would facilitate properly sequenced liberalization and reduce the likelihood of financial and balance of payments crises.

4. In light of the foregoing, the Committee invites the Executive Board to complete its work on a proposed amendment of the Fund's Articles that would make the liberalization of capital movements one of the purposes of the Fund, and extend, as needed, the Fund's jurisdiction through the establishment of carefully defined and consistently applied obligations regarding the liberalization of such movements. Safeguards and transitional arrangements are necessary for the success of this major endeavor. Flexible approval policies will have to be adopted. In both the preparation of an amendment to its Articles and in its implementation, the members' obligations under other international agreements will be respected. In pursuing this work, the Committee expects the IMF and other institutions to cooperate closely.

5. Sound liberalization and expanded access to capital markets should reduce the frequency of recourse to Fund resources and other exceptional financing. Nevertheless, the Committee recognizes that, in some circumstances, there could be a large need for financing from the Fund and other sources. The Fund will continue to play a critical role in helping to mobilize financial support for members' adjustment programs. In such endeavors, the Fund will continue its central catalytic role while minimizing moral hazard.

6. In view of the importance of moving decisively toward this new worldwide regime of liberalized capital movements, and welcoming the very broad consensus of the membership on these basic guidelines, the Committee invites the Executive Board to give a high priority to the completion of the required amendment of the Fund's Articles of Agreement.

Annex: Interim Committee Attendance
September 21, 1997

Chairman

Philippe Maystadt, Deputy Prime Minister, Minister of Finance and Minister of External Trade of Belgium

Managing Director

Michel Camdessus

Members or Alternates

Ahmad Mohd Don, Governor, Bank Negara Malaysia

Ibrahim A. Al-Assaf, Minister of Finance and National Economy, Saudi Arabia

Erik Åsbrink, Minister of Finance, Sweden

Gordon Brown, Chancellor of the Exchequer, United Kingdom

P. Chidambaram, Minister of Finance, India

Carlo Azeglio Ciampi, Minister of the Treasury, Italy

Peter Costello, Treasurer, Australia

Dai Xianglong, Governor, People's Bank of China

Rodrigo de Rato Figaredo, Second-Vice President and Minister of Economy and Finance, Spain

Marcel Doupamby Matoka, Minister of Finance, Economy, Budget, and Equity Financing, Gabon

Sergei Dubinin, Chairman, Central Bank of the Russian Federation

Roque B. Fernández, Minister of Economy and Public Works and Services, Argentina

Abdelouahab Keramane, Governor, Banque d'Algérie

Sultan Bin Nasser Al-Suwaidi, Governor, United Arab Emirates Central Bank (Alternate for Mohammed K. Khirbash, Minister of State for Finance and Industry, United Arab Emirates)

Pedro Sampaio Malan, Minister of Finance, Brazil

Justin C. Malewezi, Vice President and Minister of Finance, Malawi

Gordon Thiessen, Governor, Bank of Canada (a.m. session) and James A. Judd, Assistant Deputy Minister, International Trade and Finance, Department of Finance, Canada (p.m. session) (Alternate for Paul Martin, Minister of Finance, Canada)

Jean-Claude Juncker, Prime Minister and Minister of Finance, Luxembourg (a.m. session) and Wolfgang Ruttenstorfer, Secretary of State, Federal Ministry of Finance, Austria (p.m. session) (Alternate for Philippe Maystadt, Deputy Prime Minister, Minister of Finance and Minister of External Trade, Belgium)

Hiroshi Mitsuzuka, Minister of Finance, Japan

Robert E. Rubin, Secretary of the Treasury, United States

Dominique Strauss-Kahn, Minister of Economy, Finance and Industry, France

Kaspar Villiger, Minister of Finance, Switzerland

Theo Waigel, Federal Minister of Finance, Germany

Gerrit Zalm, Minister of Finance, Netherlands

Observers

Yilmar Akyuz, Chief, Macroeconomics and Development Policies Branch, UNCTAD

Andrew D. Crockett, General Manager, BIS

Yves-Thibault de Silguy, Commissioner for Economic, Monetary and Financial Affairs, EC

Driss Jettou, Chairman, Joint Development Committee

Donald J. Johnston, Secretary-General, OECD

Rilwanu Lukman, Secretary General, OPEC

Rubens Ricupero, UN

Jesús Seade, Deputy Director-General, WTO

James D. Wolfensohn, President, World Bank

Fiftieth Meeting, Washington, D.C., April 16, 1998

1. The Interim Committee held its fiftieth meeting in Washington, D.C. on April 16, 1998 under the Chairmanship of Mr. Philippe Maystadt, Deputy Prime Minister and Minister of Finance and Foreign Trade of Belgium.

The World Economic Outlook, Including the Causes and Effects of the Asian Crisis

2. The Committee agreed that, while the countries at the center of the crisis will suffer significantly from the recent financial turmoil in Asia, the global outlook for world economic growth can be regarded as cautiously optimistic. This assessment reflects the continued strong performance expected in most industrial countries, sustained corrective policies in emerging market countries that helped avert a wider crisis, and progress in much of the developing world and among the transition countries in improving medium-term fundamentals.

Notwithstanding these positive aspects, there are downside risks, calling for resolute action in a number of areas to support global noninflationary economic growth.

- Among the countries at the center of the crisis, determined implementation of agreed policy programs is essential to restore confidence and sustainable growth. This includes maintenance of appropriately firm monetary policies to underpin the recovery in exchange rates, fiscal discipline, and the implementation, without delay, of structural reforms, especially in the financial sector, which are essential to strengthen medium-term prospects. It is equally important for all countries to keep markets open.
- In Japan, both fiscal and structural measures, including comprehensive regulatory and financial sector reforms, are needed to secure an early and lasting recovery. The Committee welcomed the recent announcement of the economic policy package, as well as steps taken earlier to strengthen the financial system. It will be important now to implement effective fiscal measures and appropriate structural reforms promptly. Decisive and rapid action in the financial sector is important to restore public confidence. Any support to the banking system should be accompanied by appropriate action on closure or consolidation, and undertaken as part of a coherent medium-term policy framework. Such actions are particularly crucial at the current conjuncture, given the importance of the Japanese economy for the region and for the world.
- In those industrial countries operating near capacity, including the United States and the United Kingdom, the authorities need to remain vigilant as always to inflation risks. In the United States, prospective fiscal surpluses should help to address the issue of the low national savings rate.
- In continental Europe, the Committee welcomed the economic convergence of the countries aspiring to initial participation in EMU and looked forward to the historic decisions to be taken shortly. Further progress with fiscal consolidation is desirable in a number of countries, especially to provide for the needed scope for policy flexibility within the Stability and Growth Pact, and there continues to be a strong need for progress in implementing structural reforms, especially in labor markets, to help reduce unemployment and contribute in this regard to the success of EMU. Moreover, it will be important for balanced world growth that growth in continental Europe be led increasingly by domestic demand. The Committee requested the Executive Board to examine further the implications of EMU for Fund operations and for the conduct of Fund surveillance, and to report its findings in time for the next meeting of the Committee.
- For developing countries, the focus should remain on sound macroeconomic policies, open markets, and structural reforms—particularly building soundly managed and supervised market-oriented financial sectors. While those emerging market economies not at the center of the crisis have generally weathered the crisis well thus far, it remains prudent for them to continue to strengthen policies, particularly by containing external balances, avoiding overheating, strengthening the financial system, and enhancing data provision. In Africa, strong structural adjustment policies and continued support from the international community are needed to sustain the progress made by several countries in raising living standards. Although a number of developing countries would benefit, the recent sharp declines in oil and other commodity prices pose considerable challenges for a number of other developing countries, and could temporarily affect growth and investment and slow progress in reducing poverty, especially in some African countries.
- For the transition countries, the move to positive growth with lower inflation in 1997 represents an important achievement, but many countries still need to reduce fiscal deficits by strengthening revenue collection and improving the efficiency of social security and welfare systems and of governmental services more generally.

Strengthening the Architecture of the International Monetary System—Prevention, Management, and Resolution of Crises

3. The Committee discussed emerging lessons from the Asian crisis and steps required for strengthening the architecture of the international monetary system. Such a strengthening was regarded as needed, particularly in light of globalization, which has brought clear benefits, but at the same time has posed challenges. It has reinforced the importance of sound macroeconomic policies and strong financial systems to guard against vulnerability to shifts in market sentiment and to contagion effects from policy weaknesses in other countries. The Committee considered that action to help prevent financial crises, and resolve them when they occur, should center on the following pillars.

a. Strengthened International and Domestic Financial Systems
- Sound and stable macroeconomic policies are critical to financial stability.
- Action is also needed to strengthen domestic financial systems, by developing supervisory and regulatory frameworks consistent with internationally accepted practices and strengthened standards for bank and nonbank financial entities. Work in this area is already in progress in various forums, notably the Basle Committee's Core Principles for strengthening banking regulation and supervision. The Committee noted that such work should be further

advanced in the appropriate forums to cover other important areas, which could include accounting, auditing, disclosure, asset valuation, bankruptcy, and corporate governance. The Committee called on the Fund to work with other concerned institutions and organizations responsible for the development of standards and guidelines in these areas, and in the context of its surveillance activities, to consider how best the Fund could assist in the dissemination of such standards to the membership and to encourage members to adopt them. The Committee welcomes ongoing efforts to facilitate the exchange of information and greater coordination among financial supervisors, to help strengthen domestic financial systems.

b. Strengthened Fund Surveillance and Recommendations
• The Committee agreed that the Fund should intensify its surveillance of financial sector issues and capital flows, give particular attention to policy interdependence and risks of contagion, and ensure that it is fully aware of market views and perspectives.
• The Committee noted that the Fund's enhanced surveillance should include a focus on the risks posed by potentially abrupt reversals of capital flows, particularly those of a short-term nature. It requested the Executive Board to examine ways to strengthen the monitoring of capital flows.
• The Committee encouraged further efforts by the Fund and the Bank to find the most effective way—possibly through new forms of joint collaboration, and drawing on relevant outside expertise—to offer their members the best possible advice on strengthening the financial sector.
• It emphasized the need for the Fund's views to be communicated effectively to members and to be brought to bear in members' policy deliberations. In this context, it requested the Executive Board to develop a "tiered response," whereby countries that are believed to be seriously off course in their policies are given increasingly strong warnings.

c. Greater Availability and Transparency of Information Regarding Economic Data and Policies
• Noting that the effectiveness of surveillance depended critically on the timely availability of accurate information, the Committee underscored members' obligation to provide timely and accurate data to the Fund. If persistent deficiencies in disclosing relevant data to the Fund seriously impede surveillance, conclusion of Article IV consultations should be delayed.
• The Committee welcomed the progress made on implementation of the Special and General Data Dissemination Initiatives. It requested the Fund to expedite its efforts to broaden and strengthen the Special Data Dissemination Standard (SDDS) to cover additional financial data, including net reserves (reserve-related liabilities, central bank derivative transactions and positions); debt, particularly short-term debt; and indicators of the stability of the financial sector. The Committee recognized the importance of encouraging more members to subscribe to the SDDS and of supporting efforts by members to improve compilation and provision of data with technical assistance from the Fund and other agencies. The Committee also emphasized the importance of subscribers being in full observance of

the standard by the end of the transition period in December 1998. Consideration should be given to increase its usefulness, accessibility to the public and market participants, and publication of compliance.
• It further requested the Fund to continue its efforts to increase dissemination of information on its policy recommendations and encouraged member countries to increase the transparency of their policies.
• The Committee encouraged more members to release Press Information Notices on the conclusions of Article IV consultations, and it welcomed the upcoming review as a good occasion to take stock of the experience.

d. Central Role of the Fund in Crisis Management
• The Committee welcomed the timely response to the crisis by the international community, including from the Fund. It welcomed the establishment of the Supplemental Reserve Facility and the use of emergency procedures in the Fund's rapid response in support of the countries in crisis.
• The Fund's role in responding to members experiencing a large financing need should remain central, in particular because of the Fund's role, through its conditionality, in supporting the necessary reforms. The Fund cannot be expected to be able to finance whatever large balance of payments deficit. Its role is essential to catalyze other sources of financing and, when needed, to coordinate support from other sources.
• The Committee noted the sharp weakening of the Fund's liquidity position and stressed the need to ensure that the Fund has adequate resources. It called for the rapid implementation of the increase in quotas approved by the Board of Governors in January 1998 and of the New Arrangements to Borrow.

e. More Effective Procedures to Involve the Private Sector in Forestalling or Resolving Financial Crises
• The Committee observed that, while many in the private sector had incurred substantial losses in the recent crises, it was important that all creditors, including short-term creditors, more fully bear the consequences of their actions.
• It noted that, in the first instance, measures to discourage excessive reliance on short-term financing and strengthen countries' capacity to withstand sudden shifts in market sentiment are essential preventive elements.
• The Committee agreed that, when warranted by crisis situations, ways needed to be found to involve private creditors at an early stage, in order to achieve equitable burden sharing vis-à-vis the official sector and to limit moral hazard. While noting the difficult issues involved, the Committee requested the Executive Board to intensify its consideration of possible steps to strengthen private sector involvement.
• Efforts should also be devoted to strengthening incentives for creditors and investors to better use information to analyze risks appropriately and avoid excessive risk taking.
• The Committee suggested that different mechanisms for meeting this objective could be considered:
  • closer contacts with creditors for explaining Fund arrangements and catalyzing private sector financing;
  • studying further the possibility of introducing provisions in bond contracts for bondholders to be repre-

sented, in case of nonpayment, in negotiations on bond
contract restructuring;
- extending the Fund's policy of providing financing to
members in arrears on their debt payments to some private creditors under appropriate safeguards;
- encouraging the adoption of strong bankruptcy systems
for the operation of both domestic and international
capital markets;
- advising members to exercise caution with respect to
public guarantees to reduce the risk of a private debt
problem turning into a sovereign debt problem.

The Committee requested the Executive Board to report
on all aspects of its work in these areas at the next meeting of
the Committee.

Liberalization of Capital Movements Under an Amendment of the Articles

4. The financial crisis in Asia has given heightened attention to the role of capital flows in economic development.
The effects of the crisis have not negated the contribution
that capital movements have made to economic progress in
the Asian countries before the crisis erupted. Rather, the crisis
has underscored the importance of orderly and properly
sequenced liberalization of capital movements, the need for
appropriate macroeconomic and exchange rate policies, the
critical role of sound financial sectors, and effective prudential
and supervisory systems. The Committee reaffirmed its view,
expressed in the Hong Kong communiqué last September,
that it is now time to add a new chapter to the Bretton
Woods Agreement by making the liberalization of capital
movements one of the purposes of the Fund and extending,
as needed, the Fund's jurisdiction for this purpose. The Committee noted the progress made thus far and the provisional
agreement reached by the Executive Board on that part of the
amendment dealing with the Fund's purposes. It requested
the Executive Board to pursue with determination its work
on other aspects, including policy issues, with the aim of submitting an appropriate amendment of the Articles for the
Committee's consideration as soon as possible.

Code of Good Practices on Fiscal Transparency— Declaration on Principles

5. The Committee adopted the attached "Code of Good
Practices on Fiscal Transparency—Declaration on Principles"[1]
to serve as a guide for members to increase fiscal transparency, and thereby enhance the accountability and credibility of fiscal policy as a key feature of good governance. The
Committee encouraged member countries to adhere to the
principles and implement the practices of the Code, recognizing that implementation will be affected by diversity in fiscal
institutions, legal systems, and implementation capacity. The
Committee requested the IMF to monitor progress in implementing the Code in the context of its surveillance. The
Committee also encouraged the Executive Board to examine
the desirability of developing a code of good practices with
respect to financial and monetary policies, in cooperation
with the appropriate institutions.

[1]The Committee noted that a "Code of Good Practices" does not
imply a legal obligation on members.

ESAF and HIPC Initiatives—Implementation, Financing, and Evaluation

6. The Committee welcomed the progress made to date
in the implementation of the HIPC Initiative, including (i)
the release by the Executive Boards of the Fund and the Bank
of assistance for Uganda when it reached its completion point
in early April; (ii) the decisions, in principle, to provide assistance to Bolivia, Burkina Faso, Côte d'Ivoire, Guyana, and
Mozambique; and (iii) the preliminary discussions on Guinea-
Bissau and Mali. The Committee encouraged countries that
could qualify for assistance under the Initiative to take expeditiously the necessary adjustment measures to qualify for this
special assistance.

The Committee noted the need to reactivate the efforts by
the Fund to secure the full financing of the ESAF and the
HIPC Initiative. In view of the present and expected future
commitments under the HIPC Initiative and the significant
costs resulting from the delay in mobilizing the necessary
financial resources, the Committee urged all members to
move quickly to complete the financing of these initiatives as
soon as possible. The Committee requested that the Executive Board report back to the Interim Committee on this
issue at its next meeting.

The Committee expressed its appreciation for the work of
the external evaluators of the ESAF. Their report, which
complemented the earlier internal evaluation of the ESAF,
reaffirmed the view that the ESAF is a valuable instrument to
assist low-income countries. The Committee noted that,
together, the internal and external evaluations provided
important lessons and a useful basis for public debate. The
Committee welcomed the intention of the Executive Board
to draw operational conclusions from the issues raised by the
evaluations so as to strengthen the ability of the Fund to foster sustained growth and external viability in poor countries.

The next meeting of the Interim Committee will be held
in Washington, D.C. on October 4, 1998.

Attachment
Code of Good Practices on Fiscal Transparency— Declaration on Principles

The Interim Committee stressed the importance of good
governance when it adopted the Partnership for Sustainable
Global Growth in September 1996, and again at its September 1997 meeting in Hong Kong SAR. Fiscal transparency
would make a major contribution to the cause of good governance. It should lead to better-informed public debate about
the design and results of fiscal policy, make governments
more accountable for the implementation of fiscal policy, and
thereby strengthen credibility and public understanding of
macroeconomic policies and choices. In a globalized environment, fiscal transparency is of considerable importance to
achieving macroeconomic stability and high-quality growth.
However, it is only one aspect of good fiscal management,
and attention has to be paid also to increasing the efficiency
of government activity and establishing sound public
finances.

Because of its fiscal management expertise and universal
membership, the IMF is well placed to take the lead in promoting greater fiscal transparency. The Interim Committee is
therefore seeking to encourage IMF member countries to
implement the following Code of Good Practices on Fiscal

Transparency. The Code is based around the following key objectives: roles and responsibilities in government should be clear; information on government activities should be provided to the public; budget preparation, execution, and reporting should be undertaken in an open manner; and fiscal information should be subjected to independent assurances of integrity. The Code sets out what governments should do to meet these objectives in terms of principles and practices. These principles and practices are distilled from the IMF's knowledge of fiscal management practices in member countries. The Code will facilitate surveillance of economic policies by country authorities, financial markets, and international institutions.

Guidelines to the implementation of the Code are to be provided in a supporting manual, which is currently being developed. The Code acknowledges diversity across countries in fiscal management systems and in cultural, constitutional, and legal environments, as well as differences across countries in the technical and administrative capacity to improve transparency. While there is scope in all countries for improvement with respect to some aspects of fiscal transparency covered in the Code, diversity and differences across countries inevitably imply that many countries may not be able to move quickly to implement the Code. Moreover, it is recognized that there may be a need for technical assistance if existing fiscal management practices are to be changed, and the IMF must be prepared to provide technical assistance, in cooperation with other international organizations, to those countries that request it in connection with improving fiscal transparency. Modifications to the Code should be considered periodically, in light of the experience with its implementation.

I. Clarity of Roles and Responsibilities

1.1 *The government sector should be clearly distinguished from the rest of the economy, and policy and management roles within government should be well defined.*

1.1.1 The boundary between the government sector and the rest of the economy should be clearly defined and widely understood. The government sector should correspond to the general government, which comprises the central government and lower levels of government, including extrabudgetary operations.

1.1.2 Government involvement in the rest of the economy (e.g., through regulation and equity ownership) should be conducted in an open and public manner on the basis of clear rules and procedures, which are applied in a nondiscriminatory manner.

1.1.3 The allocation of responsibilities between different levels of government, and between the executive branch, the legislative branch, and the judiciary, should be clearly defined.

1.1.4 Clear mechanisms for the coordination and management of budgetary and extrabudgetary activities should be established, and well-defined arrangements vis-à-vis other government entities (e.g., the central bank, and state-controlled financial and nonfinancial enterprises) should be specified.

1.2 *There should be a clear legal and administrative framework for fiscal management.*

1.2.1 Fiscal management should be governed by comprehensive laws and administrative rules applying to budgetary and extrabudgetary activities. Any commitment or expenditure of government funds should have a legal authority.

1.2.2 Taxes, duties, fees, and charges should have an explicit legal basis. Tax laws and regulations should be easily accessible and understandable, and clear criteria should guide any administrative discretion in their application.

1.2.3 Ethical standards of behavior for public servants should be clear and well publicized.

II. Public Availability of Information

2.1 *The public should be provided with full information on the past, current, and projected fiscal activity of government.*

2.1.1 The annual budget should cover all central government operations in detail and should also provide information on central government extrabudgetary operations. In addition, sufficient information should be provided on the revenue and expenditure of lower levels of government to allow a consolidated financial position for the general government to be presented.

2.1.2 Information comparable to that in the annual budget should be provided for the outturns of the two preceding fiscal years, together with forecasts of key budget aggregates for the two years following the budget.

2.1.3 Statements should be published with the annual budget giving a description of the nature and fiscal significance of contingent liabilities, tax expenditures, and quasi-fiscal activities.

2.1.4 The central government should regularly publish information on the level and composition of its debt and financial assets.

2.2 *A public commitment should be made to the timely publication of fiscal information.*

2.2.1 Specific commitments should be made to the publication of fiscal information (e.g., in a budget law).

2.2.2 Advance release date calendars for fiscal reporting to the public should be announced.

III. Open Budget Preparation, Execution, and Reporting

3.1 *Budget documentation should specify fiscal policy objectives, the macroeconomic framework, the policy basis for the budget, and identifiable major fiscal risks.*

3.1.1 A statement of fiscal policy objectives and an assessment of sustainable fiscal policy should provide the framework for the annual budget.

3.1.2 Any fiscal rules that have been adopted (e.g., a balanced budget requirement and borrowing limits for lower levels of governments) should be clearly specified.

3.1.3 The annual budget should be presented within a comprehensive and consistent quantitative macroeconomic framework, and the economic assumptions and key parameters (e.g., effective tax rates) underlying budget estimates should be provided.

3.1.4 Existing commitments should be distinguished from new policies included in the annual budget.

3.1.5 Major risks to the annual budget should be identified and quantified where possible, including variations in economic assumptions and the uncertain costs of specific expenditure commitments (e.g., financial restructuring).

3.2 *Budget estimates should be classified and presented in a way that facilitates policy analysis and promotes accountability.*

3.2.1 Government transactions should be on a gross basis, distinguishing revenue, expenditure, and financing, and classifying expenditures on an economic and functional basis.

In addition, expenditure should be classified by administrative category. Data on extrabudgetary operations should be similarly classified. Budget data should be presented in a way that allows international comparisons.

3.2.2 A statement of objectives to be achieved by major budget programs (e.g., improvement in relevant social indicators) should be provided.

3.2.3 The overall balance of the general government should be a standard summary indicator of the government's financial position. It should be supplemented by other fiscal indicators (e.g., operational balance, structural balance, and primary balance) when economic circumstances make it inappropriate to base judgments about fiscal policy stance on the overall deficit alone.

3.2.4 The annual budget and final accounts should include a statement of the accounting basis (i.e., cash or accrual) and standards used in the preparation and presentation of budget data.

3.3 *Procedures for the execution and monitoring of approved expenditures should be clearly specified.*

3.3.1 A comprehensive, integrated accounting system should be established. It should provide a reliable basis for assessing payments arrears.

3.3.2 Procedures for procurement and employment should be standardized and accessible to all interested parties.

3.3.3 Budget execution should be internally audited, and audit procedures should be open to review.

3.4 *Fiscal reporting should be timely, comprehensive, reliable, and identify deviations from the budget.*

3.4.1 During the year, there should be regular, timely reporting of budget and extrabudgetary outturns, which should be compared with original estimates. In the absence of detailed information on lower levels of government, available indicators of their financial position (e.g., bank borrowing and bond issues) should be provided.

3.4.2 Timely, comprehensive, audited final accounts of budget operations, together with full information on extrabudgetary accounts, should be presented to the legislature.

3.4.3 Results achieved relative to the objectives of major budget programs should be reported to the legislature.

IV. Independent Assurances of Integrity

4.1 *The integrity of fiscal information should be subject to public and independent scrutiny.*

4.1.1 A national audit body, or equivalent organization, should be appointed by the legislature, with the responsibility to provide timely reports to the legislature and public on the financial integrity of government accounts.

4.1.2 Macroeconomic forecasts (including underlying assumptions) should be available for scrutiny by independent experts.

4.1.3 The integrity of fiscal statistics should be enhanced by providing the national statistics office with institutional independence.

Annex: Interim Committee Attendance
April 16, 1998

Chairman

Philippe Maystadt, Deputy Prime Minister, Minister of Finance and Minister of External Trade of Belgium

Managing Director

Michel Camdessus

Members or Alternates

Ibrahim A. Al-Assaf, Minister of Finance and National Economy, Saudi Arabia

Gordon Brown, Chancellor of the Exchequer, United Kingdom

Chaiyawat Wibulswasdi, Governor, Bank of Thailand

Cassim Chilumpha, Minister of Finance, Malawi

Carlo Azeglio Ciampi, Minister of the Treasury, Italy

Peter Costello, Treasurer, Australia

Liu Mingkang, Deputy Governor, People's Bank of China (Alternate for Dai Xianglong, Governor, People's Bank of China)

Marcel Doupamby Matoka, Minister of Finance, Economy, Budget, and Equity Financing, in charge of Privatization, Gabon

Sergei Dubinin, Chairman, Central Bank of the Russian Federation

Roque B. Fernández, Minister of Economy and Public Works and Services, Argentina

José Angel Gurria, Secretary of Finance and Public Credit, Mexico

Marianne Jelved, Minister of Economic Affairs, Denmark

Abdelouahab Keramane, Governor, Banque d'Algérie

Sultan Bin Nasser Al-Suwaidi, Governor, United Arab Emirates Central Bank (Alternate for Mohammed K. Khirbash, Minister of State for Finance and Industry, United Arab Emirates)

Pedro Sampaio Malan, Minister of Finance, Brazil

Paul Martin, Minister of Finance, Canada

Wolfgang Ruttenstorfer, Deputy Minister of Finance, Austria (Alternate for Philippe Maystadt, Deputy Prime Minister, Minister of Finance and Minister of External Trade, Belgium)

Shozaburo Nakamura, State Secretary for Finance, Ministry of Finance, Japan

Robert E. Rubin, Secretary of the Treasury, United States

Yashwant Sinha, Minister of Finance, India

Dominique Strauss-Kahn, Minister of Economy, Finance and Industry, France

Kaspar Villiger, Minister of Finance, Switzerland

Theo Waigel, Federal Minister of Finance, Germany

A.H.E.M. Wellink, President, De Nederlandsche Bank (Alternate for Gerrit Zalm, Minister of Finance, Netherlands)

Observers

Yilmar Akyuz, Chief, Macro-Economics and Development Policies Branch, UNCTAD

Anwar Ibrahim, Chairman, Joint Development Committee

Andrew D. Crockett, General Manager, BIS

Yves-Thibault de Silguy, Commissioner for Economic, Monetary and Financial Affairs, CEC

Donald J. Johnston, Secretary-General, OECD

Ian Kinniburgh, Director, Development Policy Analysis Division, Department of Economic and Social Affairs, UN

Renato Ruggiero, Director-General, WTO

James D. Wolfensohn, President, World Bank

Joint Ministerial Committee of the Boards of Governors of the Bank and the Fund on the Transfer of Real Resources to Developing Countries (Development Committee)

PRESS COMMUNIQUÉS

Fifty-Sixth Meeting, Hong Kong, China, September 22, 1997

1. The fifty-sixth meeting of the Development Committee was held in Hong Kong, China, on September 22, 1997 under the chairmanship of Mr. Driss Jettou, Minister of Finance, Commerce, Industry and Handicrafts of Morocco.[2]

2. *Helping Countries Combat Corruption and Improve Governance.* Ministers agreed that corruption and weak governance undermine macroeconomic stability, private sector activity and sustainable development objectives, and may erode international support for development cooperation. They emphasized that corruption is a global problem that requires complementary actions by all countries. While stressing that member governments have the primary responsibility for combating corruption and strengthening governance, they welcomed the more active involvement of the Bank and the Fund, each within their respective mandate, in responding to member governments requests to strengthen their institutions and performance in these areas, including the introduction of greater transparency in the public sector. They welcomed the relevant strategies and guidelines recently issued by the Bank and the Fund. The Committee stressed the importance of a consistent and evenhanded approach, as well as the need to take governance issues and corruption explicitly into account in lending and other decision making when they significantly affect project or macroeconomic and country performance. The Committee asked that the Bank and Fund report to the Committee in a year's time on the implementation of their respective strategies and guidelines.

3. Ministers invited other Multilateral Development Banks (MDBs) to develop similar strategies and guidelines. The MDBs were encouraged, as a matter of urgency, to establish procurement procedures and oversight mechanisms of the highest standard and as uniform as possible, including antibribery provisions. Ministers noted the ultimate responsibility of borrowers for ensuring fair and effective procurement, and stressed the importance of MDBs increasing their assistance to help build borrower capacity and accountability.

4. Ministers welcomed the efforts under way in other international and regional bodies to coordinate efforts to combat corruption. In particular, the Committee encouraged governments to criminalize international bribery, in an effective and coordinated way.

5. *Multilateral Investment Guarantee Agency (MIGA).* Ministers reiterated their support for MIGA's continued growth in response to the expanding demand for its services.

They welcomed the consensus on addressing MIGA's resource constraints by means of a three-part funding package comprising an IBRD grant of $150 million, paid-in capital of $150 million, plus $700 million of callable capital. Ministers urged the IBRD management and Board of Executive Directors to move swiftly to implement the $150 million grant. Ministers urged MIGA's Board to reach agreement on implementation of the remainder of the package. They also urged the MIGA Board to reach clear understandings on core policy issues as soon as possible. These measures would relieve MIGA's short-term financial constraints and provide it with a sustainable capital structure for the medium to long term. Ministers urged the MIGA Board and other relevant parties to come to closure on the capital increase by the time of the Committee's next meeting in April 1998.

6. *Private Involvement in Infrastructure.* Ministers welcomed the World Bank Group Action Program designed to strengthen the Group's ability to increase private participation in infrastructure in the context of its overall objectives to support poverty reduction and sustainable development. While ministers recognized that governments continue to play a significant role in infrastructure investment, they emphasized the important and increasing opportunities for more active private sector involvement. Ministers encouraged the Bank Group to strengthen its catalytic role through early and effective implementation of the Action Program's comprehensive range of assistance in the areas of finance, advisory services, risk mitigation, and knowledge and information. The Committee stressed the importance of coordination among the Bank Group based on agreed country frameworks and strategies.

7. *Implementation of the Debt Initiative for Heavily Indebted Poor Countries.* The Committee welcomed the further progress that had been made in implementing the Initiative to support governments that show strong commitment to reform. The Committee also encouraged eligible countries to undertake the policy actions necessary to put them on the path to securing debt relief. Decisions to provide assistance of about $0.9 billion (in present value terms), which will generate debt-service reduction of about $1.5 billion, have been made for Bolivia, Burkina Faso, and Uganda; decisions on Côte d'Ivoire, Guyana, and Mozambique are expected in the near future. Ministers stressed the importance of adequate interim financing by all creditors. The Committee expressed appreciation for the continuing close collaboration among creditors in implementing the Initiative, including understandings among them on the approach to burden sharing. Ministers also appreciated that bilateral contributions of about $100 million had already been made or pledged to the HIPC Trust Fund (administered by the World Bank), and urged other governments to contribute as well. They also encouraged international financial institutions that have not yet finalized mechanisms for participation in the Initiative to do so as soon as possible. Ministers noted that additional resources will be needed to help finance the African Development Bank's full participation in the Initiative. They also

---

[2]Mr. Zhu Rongji, Vice Premier of China, Mr. James D. Wolfensohn, President of the World Bank, Mr. Michel Camdessus, Managing Director of the International Monetary Fund, and Mr. Antonio Casas González, Governor of the Central Bank of Venezuela and Chairman of the Group of Twenty-Four, addressed the plenary session. Observers from a number of international and regional organizations also attended.

noted the need for additional resources to finance the Fund's contribution to the HIPC Initiative for countries beyond those noted above and, more generally, the need to complete the funding of ESAF.

8. *Strategic Compact.* The Committee welcomed the progress made in beginning to meet the Compact's ambitious objectives to strengthen the Bank's effectiveness, as reflected in Management's first semiannual progress report to the Executive Directors.

9. *Bank-Fund Collaboration on Strengthening Financial Sectors.* Ministers noted the importance for macroeconomic stability and growth of strengthening the financial systems of developing countries, as recent events have shown. They welcomed an increased emphasis on this area in Bank and Fund operations. Ministers viewed enhanced cooperation between the Bank and the Fund as an urgent priority and welcomed the recent agreement guiding increased collaboration to help member countries strengthen their financial systems.

10. *Note of Appreciation.* Ministers expressed their deep appreciation for the warm hospitality provided by the Chinese authorities and the Hong Kong Monetary Authority.

11. *Next Meeting.* The Committee's next meeting will be held on April 17, 1998 in Washington, D.C.

Fifty-Seventh Meeting, Washington, D.C., April 17, 1998

1. The fifty-seventh meeting of the Development Committee was held in Washington, D.C. on April 17, 1998 under the chairmanship of Dato' Seri Anwar Ibrahim, Deputy Prime Minister and Minister of Finance of Malaysia.[3]

2. *Implications of the Asian Financial Crisis.* The Committee reviewed, in the context of a globalized economy, the implications of the Asian financial crisis for the World Bank Group. In a wide-ranging discussion, ministers recognized that the crisis risks damaging the region's remarkable development achievements, particularly its especially effective antipoverty performance. Ministers expressed strong support for the active role played by the Bank Group and the International Monetary Fund, together with the Asian Development Bank, in the international effort to restore confidence and sustainable growth, and to help ensure stability in the international financial system. They especially appreciated their rapid and substantial response to the crisis, including significant financial assistance to underpin stabilization measures, programs of structural reform and technical assistance in key sectors in the most affected countries. Ministers also noted that while the region has vast potential for sustained high levels of economic growth through its own efforts, significant external support would still be required for a number of these countries over the foreseeable future.

3. Members welcome the efforts of the World Bank and the IMF to help governments address the social consequences of crises, including shielding targeted public expenditures,

improving labor standards, and strengthening social safety nets for the most vulnerable. They expressed strong support for the Bank's actions to help governments protect the poor, enhance the quality of social services, improve the design and financing of social funds, and promote sustainable environmental management. Ministers also welcomed the active support of the Bank and the Fund for design and implementation of financial and corporate restructuring and governance, and enhanced country capacity for better economic management and financial resiliency.

4. Ministers urged the Bank, in implementing the Strategic Compact and maintaining its support for all its members, to strengthen its ability to address rapidly situations of this kind and to help governments avoid such crises in the future. Thus, the Committee urged the Bank to assist countries in strengthening key institutions and structural policies, and to augment its skills and capacities in related areas, including particularly the financial sector, corporate restructuring and governance, and poverty reduction and social sustainability.

5. Given the breadth and depth of the issues involved in helping member governments confront such difficult situations, Ministers urged the Bank and the Fund, building on their long tradition of working together, to review and reinforce their partnership based on their respective mandates. This partnership has become even more important in light of the growing significance of structural factors in assisting member governments, and the increased demands on both institutions.

6. *Implementation of the Debt Initiative for Heavily Indebted Poor Countries (HIPC).* The Committee was pleased by the increasing momentum in the implementation of the HIPC Initiative. Ministers congratulated Uganda on its continued strong economic reform effort and on becoming the first country to reach its completion point under the HIPC Initiative, resulting in savings in nominal debt service of about $650 million (about $350 million in NPV terms). The Committee welcomed decisions made, since its last meeting, by the Executive Boards of the IMF and IDA/IBRD, to add Guyana, Côte d'Ivoire, and Mozambique to the group of countries for which debt-reduction packages have been agreed. In the case of Mozambique, this involved exceptional commitments by members of the Paris Club, and in particular Russia as Mozambique's largest creditor, as well as contributions from other countries and extraordinary assistance by IDA and the Fund to secure the large debt relief required. The six countries that have qualified for assistance under the Initiative would be eligible to receive estimated debt relief amounting to about $5.7 billion (the equivalent of $3 billion in NPV terms).

7. Ministers noted that Mali and Guinea-Bissau are expected to join this group shortly, and that the Boards' consideration of eligibility under the Initiative of other countries will occur as soon as their track records and progress in negotiation of Bank/Fund-supported programs warrant. Ministers encouraged potentially eligible countries to undertake such programs in a timely manner, so that by the year 2000 as many as possible could be included in the Initiative. Ministers welcomed the increasing number of countries that were contributing bilaterally to the HIPC Trust Fund. They also stressed the importance of additional contributions to the HIPC Initiative to assist all multilateral institutions to meet

[3]Mr. James D. Wolfensohn, President of the World Bank, Mr. Michel Camdessus, Managing Director of the International Monetary Fund, Mr. Abdelkrim Harchaoui, Minister of Finance of Algeria and Chairman of the Group of Twenty-Four, addressed the plenary session. Observers from a number of international and regional organizations also attended.

their share of the cost, including, in particular, the African Development Bank.

8. *Multilateral Investment Guarantee Agency (MIGA)*. Ministers welcomed the successful conclusion of deliberations by the MIGA Board of Directors on MIGA's $850 million general capital increase (including a $150 million paid-in portion), as well as the agreement by IBRD governors to transfer $150 million as a grant to MIGA. These measures, reflecting agreements reached by the Committee at its last meeting, will relieve MIGA's short term financial constraints and provide it with a sustainable capital structure for the medium to long term, thus enabling it to respond to continuing growth in demand for its services. The Committee also welcomed the progress achieved by the MIGA Board on core policy issues, and urged the Board to continue its discussions and to reach clear understandings on the remaining issues as soon as possible.

9. *Report of the Multilateral Development Banks (MDBs)*. Ministers expressed appreciation to the Presidents of the four regional development banks and the World Bank for their comprehensive report on MDB follow-up to the recommendations of the Committee's MDB Task Force. The Committee welcomed the progress made by the MDBs in implementing programs designed to strengthen the effectiveness of each institution. Ministers also welcomed the efforts made by the MDB Presidents to strengthen their collaboration on important areas—such as program evaluation and procurement rules—and their commitment to expand this cooperation, consistent with their respective mandates, in additional areas of high priority—such as governance, corruption, and capacity building; financial sector fundamentals and reform; and infra-structure financing. Members also agreed on the importance of MDBs addressing the considerable challenges that remain in further strengthening this cooperation and suggested in particular that practical objectives be established for the next few years in areas such as evaluation. They urged the MDBs to continue to work closely with member governments to implement practical measures designed to ensure more effective in-country coordination, based on a shared strategic view, and enhanced development impact.

10. Members requested that the World Bank President inform the Committee at the spring 1999 meeting of progress achieved in strengthening World Bank cooperation with the regional development banks.

11. Ministers also noted that the Committee had made notable progress over the last two years on a number of important issues with broad systemic significance for all MDBs and the IMF, such as the HIPC Initiative and governance. This meeting's discussion of the implications of the Asian financial crisis is a further example, and ministers agreed that the Committee should continue to develop this practice, as recommended in the MDB Task Force Report, drawing on contributions where appropriate from other MDBs.

12. *World Bank Net Income Dynamics*. Ministers considered issues raised by a decline in IBRD net income at the same time that potential demands on this income were increasing. They urged the Bank's Board of Directors to review, on an urgent basis, all available options and to make appropriate recommendations and decisions in the next three months.

13. *Next Meeting*. The Committee's next meeting will be held on October 5, 1998 in Washington, D.C.

Executive Directors and Voting Power
on April 30, 1998

Director *Alternate*	Casting Votes of	Votes by Country	Total Votes[1]	Percent of IMF Total[2]
Appointed				
Karin Lissakers *Barry S. Newman*	United States	265,518	265,518	17.78
Bernd Esdar *Wolf-Dieter Donecker*	Germany	82,665	82,665	5.53
Yukio Yoshimura *Hideaki Ono*	Japan	82,665	82,665	5.53
Jean-Claude Milleron *Ramon Fernandez*	France	74,396	74,396	4.98
Gus O'Donnell *Jon Shields*	United Kingdom	74,396	74,396	4.98
Elected				
Willy Kiekens (Belgium) *Johann Prader (Austria)*	Austria	12,133		
	Belarus	3,054		
	Belgium	31,273		
	Czech Republic	6,146		
	Hungary	7,798		
	Kazakhstan	2,725		
	Luxembourg	1,605		
	Slovak Republic	2,824		
	Slovenia	1,755		
	Turkey	6,670	75,983	5.09
J. de Beaufort Wijnholds (Netherlands) *Yuriy G. Yakusha (Ukraine)*	Armenia	925		
	Bosnia and Herzegovina	1,462		
	Bulgaria	4,899		
	Croatia	2,866		
	Cyprus	1,250		
	Georgia	1,360		
	Israel	6,912		
	Macedonia, former Yugoslav Republic of	746		
	Moldova	1,150		
	Netherlands	34,692		
	Romania	7,791		
	Ukraine	10,223	74,276	4.97
Juan José Toribio (Spain) *Javier Guzmán-Calafell (Mexico)*	Costa Rica	1,440		
	El Salvador	1,506		
	Guatemala	1,788		
	Honduras	1,200		
	Mexico	17,783		
	Nicaragua	1,211		
	Spain	19,604		
	Venezuela	19,763	64,295	4.30

Director *Alternate*	Casting Votes of	Votes by Country	Total Votes[1]	Percent of IMF Total[2]
Elected *(continued)*				
Enzo R. Grilli (Italy)	Albania	603		
John Spraos (Greece)	Greece	6,126		
	Italy	46,157		
	Malta	925		
	Portugal	5,826		
	San Marino	350	59,987	4.02
Thomas A. Bernes (Canada)	Antigua and Barbuda	335		
Charles X. O'Loghlin (Ireland)	Bahamas, The	1,199		
	Barbados	739		
	Belize	385		
	Canada	43,453		
	Dominica	310		
	Grenada	335		
	Ireland	5,500		
	Jamaica	2,259		
	St. Kitts and Nevis	315		
	St. Lucia	360		
	St. Vincent and the Grenadines	310	55,500	3.72
Kai Aaen Hansen (Denmark)	Denmark	10,949		
Olli-Pekka Lehmussaari (Finland)	Estonia	715		
	Finland	8,868		
	Iceland	1,103		
	Latvia	1,165		
	Lithuania	1,285		
	Norway	11,296		
	Sweden	16,390	51,771	3.47
Abdulrahman A. Al-Tuwaijri (Saudi Arabia)	Saudi Arabia	51,556	51,556	3.45
Sulaiman M. Al-Turki (Saudi Arabia)				
Dinah Z. Guti (Zimbabwe)	Angola	2,323		
José Pedro de Morais, Jr. (Angola)	Botswana	616		
	Burundi	822		
	Eritrea	365		
	Ethiopia	1,233		
	Gambia, The	479		
	Kenya	2,244		
	Lesotho	489		
	Liberia	963		
	Malawi	759		
	Mozambique	1,090		
	Namibia	1,246		
	Nigeria	13,066		
	Sierra Leone	1,022		
	South Africa	13,904		
	Swaziland	615		
	Tanzania	1,719		
	Uganda	1,589		
	Zambia	3,885		
	Zimbabwe	2,863	51,292	3.43
Gregory F. Taylor (Australia)	Australia	23,582		
Okyu Kwon (Korea)	Kiribati	290		
	Korea	8,246		
	Marshall Islands	275		
	Micronesia, Federated States of	285		
	Mongolia	621		
	New Zealand	6,751		
	Papua New Guinea	1,203		
	Philippines	6,584		
	Samoa	335		
	Seychelles	310		
	Solomon Islands	325		
	Vanuatu	375	49,182	3.29

Director *Alternate*	Casting Votes of	Votes by Country	Total Votes[1]	Percent of IMF Total[2]
Elected *(continued)*				
A. Shakour Shaalan (Egypt)	Bahrain	1,078		
Mohamad Hassan Elhage (Lebanon)	Egypt	7,034		
	Iraq	5,290		
	Jordan	1,467		
	Kuwait	10,202		
	Lebanon	1,710		
	Libya	8,426		
	Maldives	305		
	Oman	1,444		
	Qatar	2,155		
	Syrian Arab Republic	2,349		
	United Arab Emirates	4,171		
	Yemen, Republic of	2,015	47,646	3.19
ZAMANI Abdul Ghani (Malaysia)	Brunei Darussalam	1,750		
Cyrillus Harinowo (Indonesia)	Cambodia	900		
	Fiji	761		
	Indonesia	15,226		
	Lao People's Democratic Republic	641		
	Malaysia	8,577		
	Myanmar	2,099		
	Nepal	770		
	Singapore	3,826		
	Thailand	5,989		
	Tonga	300		
	Vietnam	2,666	43,505	2.91
Aleksei V. Mozhin (Russia)	Russia	43,381	43,381	2.90
Andrei Vernikov (Russia)				
Roberto F. Cippa (Switzerland)	Azerbaijan	1,420		
Wieslaw Szczuka (Poland)	Kyrgyz Republic	895		
	Poland	10,135		
	Switzerland	24,954		
	Tajikistan	850		
	Turkmenistan	730		
	Uzbekistan	2,245	41,229	2.76
Abbas Mirakhor	Afghanistan, Islamic State of	1,454		
(Islamic Republic of Iran)	Algeria	9,394		
Mohammed Daïri (Morocco)	Ghana	2,990		
	Iran, Islamic Republic of	11,035		
	Morocco	4,527		
	Pakistan	7,832		
	Tunisia	2,310	39,542	2.65
Alexandre Kafka (Brazil)	Brazil	21,958		
Hamid O'Brien (Trinidad and Tobago)	Colombia	5,863		
	Dominican Republic	1,838		
	Ecuador	2,442		
	Guyana	922		
	Haiti	857		
	Panama	1,746		
	Suriname	926		
	Trinidad and Tobago	2,718	39,270	2.63
M. R. Sivaraman (India)	Bangladesh	4,175		
A. G. Karunasena (Sri Lanka)	Bhutan	295		
	India	30,805		
	Sri Lanka	3,286	38,561	2.58
ZHANG Zhixiang (China)	China	34,102	34,102	2.28
HAN Mingzhi (China)				

Director *Alternate*	Casting Votes of	Votes by Country	Total Votes[1]	Percent of IMF Total[2]
Elected *(concluded)*				
A. Guillermo Zoccali (Argentina)	Argentina	15,621		
Nicolas Eyzaguirre (Chile)	Bolivia	1,512		
	Chile	6,467		
	Paraguay	971		
	Peru	4,911		
	Uruguay	2,503	31,985	2.14
Koffi Yao (Côte d'Ivoire)	Benin	703		
Alexandre Barro Chambrier	Burkina Faso	692		
(Gabon)	Cameroon	1,601		
	Cape Verde	320		
	Central African Republic	662		
	Chad	663		
	Comoros	315		
	Congo, Republic of	829		
	Côte d'Ivoire	2,632		
	Djibouti	365		
	Equatorial Guinea	493		
	Gabon	1,353		
	Guinea	1,037		
	Guinea-Bissau	355		
	Madagascar	1,154		
	Mali	939		
	Mauritania	725		
	Mauritius	983		
	Niger	733		
	Rwanda	845		
	São Tomé and Príncipe	305		
	Senegal	1,439		
	Togo	793	19,936	1.33
			1,0492,639[3]	99.93[4]

[1]Voting power varies on certain matters pertaining to the General Department with use of the IMF's resources in that department.

[2]Percentages of total votes (1,493,603) in the General Department and the SDR Department.

[3]This total does not include the votes of Palau and Somalia, which did not participate in the 1996 Regular Election of Executive Directors. The votes of these member are 964—0.07 percent of those in the General Department and SDR Department. Also, the total does not include the votes of the Democratic Republic of the Congo and Sudan, which were suspended effective June 2, 1994 and August 9, 1993, respectively, pursuant to Article XXVI, Section 2 *(b)* of the Articles of Agreement.

[4]This figure may differ from the sum of the percentages shown for individual Directors because of rounding.

Changes in Membership of the Executive Board

Changes in membershp of the Executive Board between May 1, 1997 and April 30, 1998 were as follows:

Hamid O'Brien (Trinidad and Tobago) was appointed Alternate Executive Director to Alexandre Kafka (Brazil), effective May 1, 1997.

Okyu Kwon (Korea) was appointed Alternate Executive Director to Ewen L. Waterman (Australia), effective May 1, 1997.

Ewen L. Waterman (Australia) resigned as Executive Director for Australia, Kiribati, Korea, Marshall Islands, Federated States of Micronesia, Mongolia, New Zealand, Papua New Guinea, Philippines, Samoa, Seychelles, Solomon Islands, and Vanuatu, effective May 9, 1997.

Gregory F. Taylor (Australia) was elected Executive Director for Australia, Kiribati, Korea, Marshall Islands, Federated States of Micronesia, Mongolia, New Zealand, Papua New Guinea, Philippines, Samoa, Seychelles, Solomon Islands, and Vanuatu, effective May 10, 1997.

Ambroise Fayolle (France) relinquished his duties as Alternate Executive Director to Marc-Antoine Autheman (France), effective August 29, 1997.

Ramon Fernandez (France) was appointed as Alternate Executive Director to Marc-Antoine Autheman (France), effective August 30, 1997.

Danuta Gotz-Kozierkiewicz (Poland) relinquished her duties as Alternate Executive Director to Daniel Kaeser (Switzerland), effective October 10, 1997.

Wieslaw Szczuka (Poland) was appointed as Alternate Executive Director to Daniel Kaeser (Switzerland), effective October 11, 1997.

Daniel Kaeser (Switzerland) resigned as Executive Director for Azerbaijan, Kyrgyz Republic, Poland, Switzerland, Tajikistan, Turkmenistan, and Uzbekistan, effective October 31, 1997.

Roberto F. Cippa (Switzerland), formerly Advisor to Executive Director Daniel Kaeser (Switzerland), was elected Executive Director for Azerbaijan, Kyrgyz Republic, Poland, Switzerland, Tajikistan, Turkmenistan, and Uzbekistan, effective November 1, 1997.

Yacoob Yousef Mohammed (Bahrain) relinquished his duties as Alternate Executive Director to A. Shakour Shaalan (Egypt), effective November 1, 1997.

Marc-Antoine Autheman (France) relinquished his duties as Executive Director for France, effective November 30, 1997.

Benny Andersen (Denmark) relinquished his duties as Alternate Executive Director to Eva Srejber (Sweden), effective December 31, 1997.

Eva Srejber (Sweden) resigned as Executive Director for Denmark, Estonia, Finland, Iceland, Latvia, Lithuania, Norway, and Sweden, effective December 31, 1997.

Kai Aaen Hansen (Denmark) was elected Executive Director for Denmark, Estonia, Finland, Iceland, Latvia, Lithuania, Norway, and Sweden, effective January 1, 1998.

Eva Srejber (Sweden), formerly Executive Director for Denmark, Estonia, Finland, Iceland, Latvia, Lithuania, Norway, and Sweden, was appointed as Alternate Executive Director to Kai Aaen Hansen (Denmark), effective January 1, 1998.

Nikolaos Coumbis (Greece) relinquished his duties as Alternate Executive Director to Enzo R. Grilli (Italy), effective February 5, 1998.

John Spraos (Greece) was appointed as Alternate Executive Director to Enzo R. Grilli (Italy), effective February 6, 1998.

Jean-Claude Milleron (France) was appointed as Executive Director for France, effective February 7, 1998.

H.B. Disanayaka (Sri Lanka) relinquished his duties as Alternate Executive Director to M.R. Sivaraman (India), effective March 31, 1998.

Eva Srejber (Sweden) relinquished her duties as Alternate Executive Director to Kai Aaen Hansen (Denmark), effective March 31, 1998.

A.G. Karunasena (Sri Lanka) was appointed as Alternate Executive Director to M.R. Sivaraman (India), effective April 1, 1998.

Olli-Pekka Lehmussaari (Finland) was appointed as Alternate Executive Director to Kai Aaen Hansen (Denmark), effective April 1, 1998.

Subarjo Joyosumarto (Indonesia) relinquished his duties as Alternate Executive Director to ZAMANI Abdul Ghani (Malaysia), effective April 19, 1998.

Cyrillus Harinowo (Indonesia) was appointed as Alternate Executive Director to ZAMANI Abdul Ghani (Malaysia), effective April 20, 1998.

Mohamad Hassan Elhage (Lebanon) was appointed as Alternate Executive Director to A. Shakour Shaalan (Eygpt), effective April 24, 1998.

The following served as Temporary Alternate Executive Directors to the Executive Directors indicated during 1997/98:

Temporary Alternate Executive Director	Executive Director for Whom Temporary Alternate Served
Wafa Fahmi Abdelati (*Egypt*)	A. Shakour Shaalan (*Egypt*)
Hj. Ibrahim Abdul Rahman (*Brunei Darussalam*)	ZAMANI Abdul Ghani (*Malaysia*)
Aidar Abdychev (*Kyrgyz Republic*)	Daniel Kaeser (*Switzerland*)
	Roberto F. Cippa (*Switzerland*)
Meekal A. Ahmed (*Pakistan*)	Abbas Mirakhor (*Iran, Islamic Republic of*)
Patrick A. Akatu (*Nigeria*)	Dinah Z. Guti (*Zimbabwe*)
Zhanat Akhmetova (*Kazakhstan*)	Willy Kiekens (*Belgium*)
Mario B. Alemán (*Nicaragua*)	Juan José Toribio (*Spain*)
Ahmed Saleh Alosaimi (*Saudi Arabia*)	Abdulrahman A. Al-Tuwaijri (*Saudi Arabia*)
Mostafa Askari-Rankouhi (*Canada*)	Thomas A. Bernes (*Canada*)
Christopher Austin (*United Kingdom*)	Gus O'Donnell (*United Kingdom*)
Taye Berrihun Belay (*Ethiopia*)	Dinah Z. Guti (*Zimbabwe*)
Olver Luis Bernal (*Colombia*)	Alexandre Kafka (*Brazil*)
Nicolas R. F.Blancher (*France*)	Marc-Antoine Autheman (*France*)
	Jean-Claude Milleron (*France*)
Jitendra G. Borpujari (*India*)	Abdulrahman A. Al-Tuwaijri (*Saudi Arabia*)
Peter I. Botoucharov (*Bulgaria*)	J. de Beaufort Wijnholds (*Netherlands*)
Olivier Bourges (*France*)	Jean-Claude Milleron (*France*)
Martha Brettschneider (*United States*)	Karin Lissakers (*United States*)
Tabeila Brizuela (*Venezuela*)	Juan José Toribio (*Spain*)
Martin Arnulf Brooke (*United Kingdom*)	Gus O'Donnell (*United Kingdom*)
Sarah Kate Brownlee (*United Kingdom*)	Gus O'Donnell (*United Kingdom*)
Michele Shannon Budington (*United States*)	Karin Lissakers (*United States*)
Erik Martin Carlens (*Sweden*)	Eva Srejber (*Sweden*)
	Kai Aaen Hansen (*Denmark*)
Jeffrey Allen Chelsky (*Canada*)	Thomas A. Bernes (*Canada*)
Denia Nery Chen Pineda (*Panama*)	Alexandre Kafka (*Brazil*)
In-Kang Cho (*Korea*)	Gregory F. Taylor (*Australia*)
Melinda Ann Cilento (*Australia*)	Ewen L. Waterman (*Australia*)
	Gregory F. Taylor (*Australia*)
Roberto F. Cippa (*Switzerland*)	Daniel Kaeser (*Switzerland*)
Henry William Cocker (*Tonga*)	ZAMANI Abdul Ghani (*Malaysia*)
Ana Lucia Coronel (*Ecuador*)	Alexandre Kafka (*Brazil*)
Jose Antonio Costa (*Argentina*)	A. Guillermo Zoccali (*Argentina*)
Daniel A.A. Daco (*Belgium*)	Willy Kiekens (*Belgium*)
Christoph Karl Ernst Duenwald (*Germany*)	Thomas A. Bernes (*Canada*)
Lodewyk J. F. Erasmus (*South Africa*)	Dinah Z. Guti (*Zimbabwe*)
Julio C. Estrella (*Dominican Republic*)	Alexandre Kafka (*Brazil*)
Samia S. Farid (*Egypt*)	A. Shakour Shaalan (*Egypt*)
Laurent Fontaine (*France*)	Marc-Antoine Autheman (*France*)
Pierre-Michel Fremann (*France*)	Marc-Antoine Autheman (*France*)
	Jean-Claude Milleron (*France*)
Daiho Fujii (*Japan*)	Yukio Yoshimura (*Japan*)
Shunichi Fukushima (*Japan*)	Yukio Yoshimura (*Japan*)
Jean-Daniel Gerber (*Switzerland*)	Daniel Kaeser (*Switzerland*)
Danute Giga (*Latvia*)	Eva Srejber (*Sweden*)
Alessandro Giustiniani (*Italy*)	Enzo R. Grilli (*Italy*)
Norbert Goffinet (*Luxembourg*)	Willy Kiekens (*Belgium*)
Celia M. Gonzalez (*Philippines*)	Ewen L. Waterman (*Australia*)
	Gregory F. Taylor (*Australia*)
Werner Gruber (*Switzerland*)	Daniel Kaeser (*Switzerland*)
	Roberto F. Cippa (*Switzerland*)
Andreas Guennewich (*Germany*)	Bernd Esdar (*Germany*)
Nikolay Kirov Gueorguiev (*Bulgaria*)	J. de Beaufort Wijnholds (*Netherlands*)
Harry Hagan (*United Kingdom*)	Gus O'Donnell (*United Kingdom*)
Mohamed Ali Hammoudi (*Algeria*)	Abbas Mirakhor (*Iran, Islamic Republic of*)
Robert Josef Heinbuecher (*Germany*)	Bernd Esdar (*Germany*)

Temporary Alternate Executive Director	Executive Director for Whom Temporary Alternate Served
Kerstin M. Heinonen *(Finland)*	Eva Srejber *(Sweden)*
	Kai Aaen Hansen *(Denmark)*
Oscar A. Hendrick Fong *(Peru)*	A. Guillermo Zoccali *(Argentina)*
Oussama A. Himani *(Lebanon)*	Abdulrahman A. Al-Tuwaijri *(Saudi Arabia)*
Johanna Kim Honeyfield *(New Zealand)*	Ewen L. Waterman *(Australia)*
	Gregory F. Taylor *(Australia)*
HUANG Xinghai *(China)*	ZHANG Zhixiang *(China)*
Garbis M. Iradian *(Canada)*	A. Shakour Shaalan *(Egypt)*
Abdel Rehman Ismael *(Mauritius)*	Koffi Yao *(Côte d'Ivoire)*
Ourkali Issaev *(Kyrgyz Republic)*	Daniel Kaeser *(Switzerland)*
Narendra Jadhav *(India)*	M.R. Sivaraman *(India)*
Hossein Javaheri *(Iran, Islamic Republic of)*	Abbas Mirakhor *(Iran, Islamic Republic of)*
Hervé Joly *(France)*	Jean-Claude Milleron *(France)*
Jiri Jonas *(Czech Republic)*	Willy Kiekens *(Belgium)*
J. Mills Jones *(Liberia)*	Dinah Z. Guti *(Zimbabwe)*
Eric Jourcin *(France)*	Marc-Antoine Autheman *(France)*
	Jean-Claude Milleron *(France)*
Ramalinga Kannan *(India)*	M.R. Sivaraman *(India)*
Katrin Kask *(Estonia)*	Eva Srejber *(Sweden)*
	Kai Aaen Hansen *(Denmark)*
Heinz Kaufmann *(Switzerland)*	Daniel Kaeser *(Switzerland)*
	Roberto F. Cippa *(Switzerland)*
Michael Stuart Kell *(United Kingdom)*	Gus O'Donnell *(United Kingdom)*
Subodh Kumar Keshava *(India)*	M.R. Sivaraman *(India)*
Brenda Killen *(United Kingdom)*	Gus O'Donnell *(United Kingdom)*
Bernard Konan *(Côte d'Ivoire)*	Koffi Yao *(Côte d'Ivoire)*
Ekaterina Kouprianova *(Russia)*	Aleksei V. Mozhin *(Russia)*
Kwassivi Kpetigo *(Togo)*	Koffi Yao *(Côte d'Ivoire)*
Tuseno-Minu Kudiwu *(Congo, Dem. Rep. of)*	Koffi Yao *(Côte d'Ivoire)*
Kitty Lai *(China)*	ZHANG Zhixiang *(China)*
Jurgen Pieter Leijdekker *(Netherlands)*	J. de Beaufort Wijnholds *(Netherlands)*
Azriel Levy *(Israel)*	J. de Beaufort Wijnholds *(Netherlands)*
James M. Lister *(United States)*	Karin Lissakers *(United States)*
David G. Loevinger *(United States)*	Karin Lissakers *(United States)*
Benoit Loutrel *(France)*	Marc-Antoine Autheman *(France)*
LU Ang *(China)*	ZHANG Zhixiang *(China)*
Cascone Angelo Lucenti *(Venezuela)*	Juan José Toribio *(Spain)*
Andrei Lushin *(Russia)*	Aleksei V. Mozhin *(Russia)*
Boris M. Lvin *(Russia)*	Aleksei V. Mozhin *(Russia)*
Mohd. Zubir bin Maatan *(Malaysia)*	ZAMANI Abdul Ghani *(Malaysia)*
John Mafararikwa *(Zimbabwe)*	Dinah Z. Guti *(Zimbabwe)*
Mohammad-Hadi Mahdavian *(Iran, Islamic Republic of)*	Abbas Mirakhor *(Iran, Islamic Republic of)*
Scott Daniel Melese-d'Hospital *(United States)*	Karin Lissakers *(United States)*
Melhem F. Melhem *(Lebanon)*	Abdulrahman A. Al-Tuwaijri *(Saudi Arabia)*
Francesca Mercusa *(Italy)*	Enzo R. Grilli *(Italy)*
Daniel Merino *(Argentina)*	A. Guillermo Zoccali *(Argentina)*
Wolfgang Merz *(Germany)*	Bernd Esdar *(Germany)*
Iljae Moon *(Korea)*	Ewen L. Waterman *(Australia)*
Helio Mori *(Brazil)*	Alexandre Kafka *(Brazil)*
James A. K. Munthali *(Malawi)*	Dinah Z. Guti *(Zimbabwe)*
Simon N'guiamba *(Cameroon)*	Koffi Yao *(Côte d'Ivoire)*
Melih Nemli *(Turkey)*	Willy Kiekens *(Belgium)*
Mikhail Nikitenko *(Belarus)*	Willy Kiekens *(Belgium)*
Jean-Christian Obame *(Gabon)*	Koffi Yao *(Côte d'Ivoire)*
Ricardo Ochoa *(Mexico)*	Juan José Toribio *(Spain)*
Hiroshi Ogushi *(Japan)*	Yukio Yoshimura *(Japan)*
Ovidio Otazú *(Paraguay)*	A. Guillermo Zoccali *(Argentina)*
Lev Valentinovich Palei *(Russia)*	Aleksei V. Mozhin *(Russia)*

Temporary Alternate Executive Director	Executive Director for Whom Temporary Alternate Served
Axel R. Palmason *(Iceland)*	Eva Srejber *(Sweden)*
	Kai Aaen Hansen *(Denmark)*
Hélène Paris *(France)*	Marc-Antoine Autheman *(France)*
	Jean-Claude Milleron *(France)*
José Luis Pascual Pascual *(Spain)*	Juan José Toribio *(Spain)*
Yasmin Patel *(Mozambique)*	Dinah Z. Guti *(Zimbabwe)*
Manh Hung Phan *(Vietnam)*	ZAMANI Abdul Ghani *(Malaysia)*
Laura Pinzani *(Italy)*	Enzo R. Grilli *(Italy)*
Tomislav Presecan *(Croatia)*	J. de Beaufort Wijnholds *(Netherlands)*
QI Jianming *(China)*	ZHANG Zhixiang *(China)*
Eugen T. Radulescu *(Romania)*	J. de Beaufort Wijnholds *(Netherlands)*
Ganga P. Ramdas *(United States)*	Alexandre Kafka *(Brazil)*
Borut Repansek *(Slovenia)*	Willy Kiekens *(Belgium)*
Vladimir Rigász *(Slovak Republic)*	Willy Kiekens *(Belgium)*
Eddy Rodríguez *(Costa Rica)*	Juan José Toribio *(Spain)*
James Roaf *(United Kingdom)*	Gus O'Donnell *(United Kingdom)*
Sadok Rouai *(Tunisia)*	Abbas Mirakhor *(Iran, Islamic Republic of)*
Daniel Saha *(Cameroon)*	Koffi Yao *(Côte d'Ivoire)*
Joao Santos *(Portugal)*	Enzo R. Grilli *(Italy)*
Felix Jakob Dominik Schaad *(Switzerland)*	Roberto F. Cippa *(Switzerland)*
Oliver Schmalzriedt *(Germany)*	Bernd Esdar *(Germany)*
Todd Turner Schneider *(United States)*	Karin Lissakers *(United States)*
Ann W. Scoffier *(France)*	Marc-Antoine Autheman *(France)*
	Jean-Claude Milleron *(France)*
Ommar Sein *(Myanmar)*	ZAMANI Abdul Ghani *(Malaysia)*
Sigurd Simonsen *(Norway)*	Eva Srejber *(Sweden)*
	Kai Aaen Hansen *(Denmark)*
Raju Jan Singh *(Switzerland)*	Roberto F. Cippa *(Switzerland)*
Mark Sobel *(United States)*	Karin Lissakers *(United States)*
SONG Jianqi *(China)*	ZHANG Zhixiang *(China)*
David L. Stanton *(United Kingdom)*	Gus O'Donnell *(United Kingdom)*
Yoshiyuki Tahara *(Japan)*	Yukio Yoshimura *(Japan)*
Ulugbek Y. Tilyayev *(Uzbekistan)*	Daniel Kaeser *(Switzerland)*
	Roberto F. Cippa *(Switzerland)*
Vishwapati Trivedi *(India)*	M.R. Sivaraman *(India)*
Therese Turner-Huggins *(The Bahamas)*	Thomas A. Bernes *(Canada)*
Laura van Geest *(Netherlands)*	J. de Beaufort Wijnholds *(Netherlands)*
Marius Vismantas *(Lithuania)*	Eva Srejber *(Sweden)*
	Kai Aaen Hansen *(Denmark)*
WANG Xiaolei *(China)*	ZHANG Zhixiang *(China)*
Ratan Prakash Watal *(India)*	M.R. Sivaraman *(India)*
Myles Wickstead *(United Kingdom)*	Gus O'Donnell *(United Kingdom)*
Paul Winje *(Norway)*	Kai Aaen Hansen *(Denmark)*
Abdul-Gafoor Yakub *(Seychelles)*	Ewen L. Waterman *(Australia)*
	Gregory F. Taylor *(Australia)*
Matthew Yiu *(Hong Kong)*	Gus O'Donnell *(United Kingdom)*
Szilvia Zádor *(Hungary)*	Willy Kiekens *(Belgium)*
Igor Zakharchenkov *(Russia)*	Aleksei V. Mozhin *(Russia)*
Edgar Zamalloa *(Peru)*	A. Guillermo Zoccali *(Argentina)*
ZHANG Fengming *(China)*	ZHANG Zhixiang *(China)*
ZHENG Hong *(China)*	ZHANG Zhixiang *(China)*
Zubir bin Abdullah *(Singapore)*	ZAMANI Abdul Ghani *(Malaysia)*

Financial Statements

Report of the External Audit Committee

Washington, D.C.
June 18, 1998

Authority and Scope of the Audit

In accordance with Section 20(b) of the By-Laws of the International Monetary Fund we have audited the financial statements of the International Monetary Fund covering the:

- General Department for the year ended April 30, 1998,
- SDR Department for the year ended April 30, 1998, and
- Accounts Administered by the International Monetary Fund for the year ended April 30, 1998, which consist of the:
    1. Enhanced Structural Adjustment Facility Trust,
    2. Enhanced Structural Adjustment Facility Administered Accounts:
        - Austria,
        - Belgium,
        - Botswana,
        - Chile,
        - Greece,
        - Indonesia,
        - Islamic Republic of Iran,
        - Portugal,
        - Saudi Fund for Development Special Account,
    3. ESAF-HIPC Trust, including the Umbrella Account for HIPC Operations,
    4. Administered Accounts Established at the Request of Members:
        - Administered Account Japan,
        - Administered Account for Selected Fund Activities—Japan,
        - Framework Administered Account for Technical Assistance Activities,
        - Administered Account for Rwanda,
    5. Trust Fund,
    6. Supplementary Financing Facility Subsidy Account,
    7. Retired Staff Benefits Investment Account.

Our audit was conducted in accordance with generally accepted auditing standards and included reviews of accounting and internal control systems and tests of the accounting records. We evaluated the extent and results of the work of the outside accounting firm as well as that of the Office of Internal Audit and Inspection of the International Monetary Fund and also used other audit procedures as deemed necessary.

Audit Opinion

In our opinion, the financial statements of the General Department, the SDR Department, and the Accounts Administered by the International Monetary Fund have been prepared in accordance with generally accepted accounting principles applied on a basis consistent with that of the preceding year and give a true and fair view of the respective financial positions and the allocations and holdings of SDRs as at April 30, 1998, and of the financial results of operations and transactions during the period then ended.

EXTERNAL AUDIT COMMITTEE:

/s/ Amaffe Roger Ako, Chairman (Côte d'Ivoire)

/s/ José Nicolás Agudin (Argentina)

/s/ Stephen Park (United Kingdom)

General Department

Balance Sheets
as at April 30, 1998 and 1997

(In thousands of SDRs)
(Note 1)

	1998	1997
Assets		
General Resources Account		
Currencies and securities (Notes 2 and 5)	144,638,372	143,698,359
SDR holdings (Note 3)	764,424	1,494,149
Gold holdings (Note 4)	3,624,797	3,624,797
Charges, interest, and other receivables (Notes 2 and 5)	1,586,322	1,321,781
Other assets (Note 6)	263,920	227,754
Total General Resources Account	150,877,835	150,366,840
Special Disbursement Account		
Structural Adjustment Facility loans	921,793	1,219,681
Interest receivable	6,454	6,196
Total Special Disbursement Account	928,247	1,225,877
Total Assets	151,806,082	151,592,717
Quotas, Reserves, Liabilities, and Resources		
General Resources Account		
Quotas (Note 2)	145,321,050	145,318,800
Reserves (Note 7)	2,133,515	1,969,667
Special Contingent Accounts (Note 5)	1,883,888	1,785,404
Liabilities		
Remuneration payable (Note 5)	433,730	273,495
Other liabilities	188,016	144,909
	621,746	418,404
Deferred income (Note 5)	917,636	874,565
Total General Resources Account	150,877,835	150,366,840
Special Disbursement Account		
Accumulated resources	923,107	1,221,497
Deferred income (Note 5)	5,140	4,380
Total Special Disbursement Account	928,247	1,225,877
Total Quotas, Reserves, Liabilities, and Resources	151,806,082	151,592,717

The accompanying notes and schedules are an integral part of the financial statements.

/s/ David Williams
Treasurer

/s/ M. Camdessus
Managing Director

General Department

Income Statements
for the Years Ended April 30, 1998 and 1997

(In thousands of SDRs)
(Note 1)

	1998	1997
General Resources Account		
Operational Income (Note 5)		
Periodic charges	1,852,807	1,525,109
Interest on SDR holdings	37,426	57,593
Other charges and income	99,650	38,880
Burden-sharing contributions, net of refunds (Note 5)		
Additional charges	73,961	81,812
Reduction of remuneration	72,928	116,960
Deferred income, net of settlements	(43,071)	(39,874)
	2,093,701	1,780,480
Operational Expenses		
Remuneration (Note 5)	1,462,905	1,217,948
Allocation to the Special Contingent Accounts (Note 5)	98,483	151,944
	1,561,388	1,369,892
Net Operational Income	532,313	410,588
Administrative Expenses (Notes 1 and 8)	368,465	316,794
Net Income of the General Resources Account	163,848	93,794
Special Disbursement Account		
Interest and special charges	4,531	6,079
	4,531	6,079
Administrative expenses (Note 8)	—	30,700
Net Income (Loss) of the Special Disbursement Account	4,531	(24,621)

The accompanying notes and schedules are an integral part of the financial statements.

General Department
Statements of Changes in Reserves and Resources
for the Years Ended April 30, 1998 and 1997

(In thousands of SDRs)
(Note 1)

	1998	1997
Reserves—General Resources Account		
Special Reserve (Note 7)		
Balance, beginning of the year	1,604,087	1,510,293
Net income transferred to the Special Reserve	98,483	93,794
Balance, end of the year	1,702,570	1,604,087
General Reserve (Note 7)		
Balance, beginning of the year	365,580	365,580
Net income transferred to the General Reserve	65,365	—
Balance, end of the year	430,945	365,580
Total Reserves of the General Resources Account	2,133,515	1,969,667
Resources—Special Disbursement Account		
Balance, beginning of the year	1,221,497	1,547,179
Transfers from the Trust Fund	660	4,860
Transfers from the Supplementary Financing Facility Subsidy Account	—	179
Net transfers to the ESAF Trust (Note 8)	(242,592)	(306,100)
Transfers to the ESAF-HIPC Trust (Note 8)	(60,989)	—
	918,576	1,246,118
Net income (loss)	4,531	(24,621)
Total Resources of the Special Disbursement Account	923,107	1,221,497

The accompanying notes and schedules are an integral part of the financial statements.

General Department
Notes to the Financial Statements
as at April 30, 1998 and 1997

General Department

The General Department consists of the General Resources Account, the Special Disbursement Account, and the Investment Account, which had not been activated at April 30, 1998.

General Resources Account

The General Resources Account reflects the receipt of quota subscriptions, purchases and repurchases, collection of charges on members' use of IMF credit, and payment of remuneration on members' creditor positions in the IMF. Assets held in the General Resources Account include currencies of the IMF's member countries, SDR holdings, and gold.

The IMF makes its resources available to its members in accordance with established policies by selling to members, in exchange for their own currencies, SDRs or currencies of other members. When members make purchases they incur an obligation to repurchase, within specified periods, the IMF's holdings of their currencies by payments in SDRs or other currencies determined by the IMF. The IMF's policies on the use of its general resources are intended to ensure that their use is temporary and will be reversed within the agreed repurchase periods.

The composition of the IMF's holdings of currencies changes as a result of the IMF's transactions, including purchases and repurchases. Currencies consist of currency holdings and notes payable on demand, which substitute for the members' currencies.

A member has a reserve tranche in the IMF to the extent that the IMF's holdings of its currency, excluding holdings that reflect the member's use of IMF credit, are less than the member's quota. A member's reserve tranche is considered a part of the member's external reserves, and it may draw on the reserve tranche at any time when it represents that it has a need. Reserve tranche purchases are not considered a use of IMF credit and are not subject to repurchase obligations or charges.

A member is entitled to repurchase at any time the IMF's holdings of its currency on which the IMF levies charges and is expected to make repurchases as and when its balance of payments and reserve position improve.

Special Disbursement Account

The Special Disbursement Account was activated on June 30, 1981 to receive transfers from the Trust Fund, which is being wound up. The Structural Adjustment Facility (SAF) was established in March 1986 within the Special Disbursement Account to provide balance of payments assistance on concessional terms to qualifying low-income developing country members.

The Special Disbursement Account is a part of the General Department of the IMF. The assets of the account are held separate from resources of other accounts of the General Department. Assets that exceed the needs of the account are transferred to the Reserve Account of the Enhanced Structural Adjustment Facility Trust (ESAF Trust), which is separately administered by the IMF as Trustee. Resources of the ESAF Trust Reserve Account that are determined to be in excess of its estimated needs are to be transferred back to the Special Disbursement Account. Upon liquidation of the ESAF Trust, the amounts remaining in the ESAF Trust Reserve Account after the discharge of all liabilities shall be transferred to the Special Disbursement Account. The IMF has also transferred certain resources derived from the termination of the 1976 Trust Fund to the ESAF Trust Subsidy Account. Upon liquidation of the ESAF Trust, any resources remaining in the ESAF Trust Subsidy Account will be returned to the Special Disbursement Account and the contributors of the ESAF Trust Subsidy Account.

1. Summary of Significant Accounting Practices

Unit of Account

The accounts of the General Department are expressed in terms of the SDR. The currency value of the SDR is determined by the IMF each day by summing the values in U.S. dollars, based on market exchange rates, of a basket of five currencies. The IMF reviews the SDR valuation basket every five years. The SDR valuation basket was last reviewed in financial year 1996. The currencies in the basket and their amounts are as follows:

Currency	Amount
U.S. dollar	0.582
Deutsche mark	0.446
Japanese yen	27.2
French franc	0.813
Pound sterling	0.105

Valuation of Currencies

Currencies are valued in terms of the SDR on the basis of the representative exchange rate determined for each currency. Each member is obligated to maintain the value of the balances of its currency held by the IMF in the General Resources Account in terms of the SDR. Whenever the IMF revalues its holdings of a member's currency, a receivable or a payable is established for the amount of currency payable by or to the member in order to maintain the SDR value of the IMF's holdings of the currency. The balances of the receivables or payables are included in the IMF's total currency holdings.

Income Recognition

The IMF maintains its accounts on the accrual basis; accordingly, income is recognized as it is earned, and expenses are recorded as they are incurred, except that income from charges from members that are overdue in settling their obligations to the IMF by six months or more is deferred and is recognized as income only when paid unless the member has remained current in settling charges when due. The IMF generates compensating income for the amount of charges being deferred through the burden sharing mechanism (for a more detailed description of this mechanism, see Note 5).

Capital Assets

Land, buildings, and equipment are capitalized at cost and depreciated using the straight-line method over the estimated useful lives of the assets. The IMF capitalizes assets with a cost in excess of $100,000.

2. Quotas, Currencies, and Securities

Each member is required to pay to the IMF the amount of its initial quota and subsequent increases partly in the member's own currency and the remainder in the form of reserve assets, except that in 1978 members were permitted to pay the entire increase in their own currencies. A member's quota is not increased until the member consents to the increase and pays the subscription. Each member has the option to substitute nonnegotiable and non-interest-bearing securities for the amount of its currency held by the IMF in the General Resources Account that is in excess of ¼ of 1 percent of the member's quota. These securities, which are part of the IMF's currency holdings, are encashable by the IMF on demand.

Changes in the IMF's holdings of members' currencies for the years ended April 30, 1998 and 1997 were as follows:

	April 30, 1996	Net Change	April 30, 1997	Net Change	April 30, 1998
	In millions of SDRs				
Members' quotas	145,319	—	145,319	2	145,321
Quota subscription receivable	—	—	—	(2)	(2)
Members' outstanding use of IMF credit in the GRA	36,268	(1,729)	34,539	15,162	49,701
Members' outstanding reserve tranche positions in the GRA	(37,352)	1,249	(36,103)	(14,221)	(50,324)
Other receivables	(56)	—	(56)	—	(56)
Administrative currency balances	2	(3)	(1)	(1)	(2)
Currencies and securities	144,181	(483)	143,698	940	144,638

On Decexmber 14, 1992, the Federal Republic of Yugoslavia (Serbia/Montenegro) agreed, as a successor state, to share in the assets and liabilities of the former Socialist Federal Republic of Yugoslavia. As of April 30, 1998, this state had not succeeded to IMF membership. IMF credit outstanding with respect to the Federal Republic of Yugoslavia (Serbia/Montenegro) amounted to SDR 56.1 million at April 30, 1998 and 1997. This amount is included in charges, interest, and other receivables in the balance sheet.

Receivables and payables arising from valuation adjustments at April 30, 1998, when all holdings of currencies of members were last revalued, amounted to SDR 11,249.8 million and SDR 1,139.2 million, respectively (SDR 7,970.0 million and SDR 4,055.9 million, respectively, at April 30, 1997). At June 11, 1998, the amounts receivable were SDR 9,471.0 million, and the amounts payable were SDR 1,155.7 million.

The IMF's holdings of members' currencies at April 30, 1998 are shown in Schedule 1.

3. SDR Holdings

SDRs are reserve assets created by the IMF and allocated to members participating in the SDR Department. Although SDRs are not allocated to the IMF, the IMF may acquire, hold, and dispose of SDRs through the General Resources Account. The IMF receives SDRs from members in the settlement of their financial obligations to the IMF and uses SDRs in transactions and operations between the IMF and its members. The IMF earns interest on its SDR holdings at the same rate as all other holders of SDRs.

4. Gold Holdings

The Articles of Agreement limit the use of gold in the IMF's operations and transactions. Any use provided for in the Articles requires the approval by 85 percent majority of the total voting power of the Executive Board. In accordance with provisions of the Articles, proceeds from the sale of gold in excess of the stipulated valuation, as described below, are to be transferred to the Special Disbursement Account, to the Investment Account, or to members that were members on August 31, 1975.

At April 30, 1998 and 1997, the IMF held 3,217,341 kilograms equal to 103,439,916 fine ounces of gold at designated depositories. In accordance with the IMF's Articles of Agreement, gold is valued on the basis of 0.888671 gram of fine gold per SDR, which is equivalent to SDR 35 per fine ounce, except for 21,396 fine ounces of gold that were acquired at a market value equivalent to SDR 5.1 million. This valuation is equal to the original cost at which the gold was acquired. As of April 30, 1998, the value of the IMF's holdings of gold calculated at the market price was SDR 23.9 billion (SDR 25.8 billion at April 30, 1997).

5. IMF Operations

The IMF's financial resources are made available to members under a number of policies and facilities that differ in the type of balance of payments need they seek to address, in the length of repurchase period, and in the degree of conditionality attached to them. Changes in the outstanding use of IMF credit under various facilities during the years ended April 30, 1998 and 1997 were as follows:

	April 30, 1996	Pur-chases	Repur-chases	April 30, 1997	Pur-chases	Repur-chases	April 30, 1998
			In millions of SDRs				
Regular facilities	18,623	1,837	3,923	16,537	9,027	1,104	24,460
Extended Fund Facility	7,435	2,821	793	9,463	2,824	948	11,339
Supplemental Reserve Facility	—	—	—	—	7,100	—	7,100
Systemic Transfor-mation Facility	3,984	—	—	3,984	—	115	3,869
Enlarged Access	4,436	—	1,390	3,046	—	957	2,089
Compensatory and Contin-gency Financ-ing Facility	1,602	282	549	1,335	—	650	685
Supplementary Financing Facility	188	—	14	174	—	15	159
Total	36,268	4,940	6,669	34,539	18,951	3,789	49,701

The Supplemental Reserve Facility (SRF) was established on December 17, 1997 to provide financial assistance to members experiencing exceptional balance of payments difficulties owing to a short-term financing need resulting from a sudden and disruptive loss of market confidence reflected in pressure on the capital account and the member's reserves. Financing under the SRF is made available in the form of additional resources under a Stand-By or Extended Arrangement.

Members' use of IMF resources is shown in Schedule 1; scheduled repurchases in the General Resources Account and repayments of loans to the Special Disbursement Account are shown in Schedule 2. As of April 30, 1998 and 1997, use of credit in the General Resources Account by the largest users was as follows:

	1998		1997	
	In millions of SDRs and percent of total GRA credit			
Largest user of credit	11,200.0	22.5%	9,075.5	26.3%
Three largest users of credit	28,151.3	56.6%	20,566.4	59.5%
Five largest users of credit	34,510.4	69.4%	23,783.2	68.9%

Arrangements in the General Department

At April 30, 1998, 27 arrangements were in effect, and undrawn balances under these arrangements amounted to SDR 19,196.7 million (SDR 9,055.6 million under 25 arrangements at April 30, 1997). These arrangements are listed in Schedule 3.

Charges

The IMF levies periodic charges on its holdings of members' currencies that derive from their use of IMF credit. The rate of charge is set as a proportion of the SDR interest rate. This rate is adjusted periodically to offset the effect on the IMF's income of the deferral of unpaid charges and to finance the additions to the first Special Contingent Account during the year ended April 30, 1998 (the first and second Special Contingent Accounts during the year ended April 30, 1997), as discussed below. A surcharge progressing from 300 basis points above the rate of charge up to 500 basis points applies to use of credit under the SRF. Special charges are levied on holdings that are not repurchased when due, and on overdue charges that are not settled when due. Special charges do not apply to members that are six months or more overdue to the IMF. A service charge is levied by the IMF on each purchase, except on a reserve tranche purchase; a stand-by fee is charged on Stand-By and Extended Arrangements and is refunded in proportion to purchases made under the arrangement.

At April 30, 1998, the total holdings on which the IMF levied charges amounted to SDR 49,701.2 million (SDR 34,539.2 million at April 30, 1997).

Remuneration

The IMF pays remuneration on a member's remunerated reserve tranche position. A remunerated reserve tranche position is the amount by which the IMF's holdings of a member's currency (excluding holdings that derive from the use of IMF credit) is below the member's norm. The norm varies for each member and, on average, amounted to 94.5 percent of quota at April 30, 1998 and 1997. The rate of remuneration is equal to the SDR interest rate and is adjusted, subject to a specific floor, to offset the effect of the deferral of charges on income and to finance the additions to the first Special Contingent Account during the year ended April 30,

1998 (the first and second Special Contingent Accounts during the year ended April 30, 1997), as discussed below.

At April 30, 1998, total creditor positions on which the IMF paid remuneration amounted to SDR 44,010.6 million (SDR 29,676.1 million at April 30, 1997).

Borrowing Arrangements

Under the General Arrangements to Borrow (GAB), the IMF may borrow up to SDR 18.5 billion when supplementary resources are needed, in particular, to forestall or to cope with an impairment of the international monetary system. The GAB became effective on October 24, 1962, and has been extended through December 25, 1998. At April 30, 1998, the GAB had not been activated. On January 27, 1997, the IMF adopted the New Arrangements to Borrow (NAB), under which the IMF may borrow up to SDR 34 billion of supplementary resources. The NAB will enter into force when adopted by participants with credit arrangements totaling no less than SDR 28.9 billion, including the five participants with the largest credit arrangements. While the NAB will be the facility of first and principal recourse, it does not replace the GAB which will remain in force. Outstanding drawings and commitments under these two borrowing arrangements are limited to a combined total of SDR 34 billion.

Overdue Obligations

At April 30, 1998 and 1997, six members were six months or more overdue in settling their financial obligations to the IMF and four of these members were overdue to the General Department. In addition, the Federal Republic of Yugoslavia (Serbia/Montenegro) was also six months or more overdue in meeting its financial obligations to the IMF. Credit extended to these members and the Federal Republic of Yugoslavia (Serbia/Montenegro) through the General Resources Account and the Special Disbursement Account, including SAF loans, amounted to SDR 1,182.0 million as of April 30, 1998 (SDR 1,215.0 million at April 30, 1997).

Repurchases and SAF loan repayments and charges and SAF interest that are six months or more overdue to the General Department were as follows:

	Repurchases and SAF Loans		Charges and SAF Interest	
	1998	1997	1998	1997
	In millions of SDRs			
Total overdue	1,156	1,165	911	867
Overdue for six months or more	1,147	1,147	885	842
Overdue for three years or more	1,064	1,043	768	719

The type and duration of these arrears as of April 30, 1998, were as follows:

	Repurchases and SAF Loans	Charges and SAF Interest	Total Obligation	Longest Overdue Obligation
	In millions of SDRs			
Congo, Democratic Republic of	275.0	53.5	328.5	May 1991
Liberia	201.5	206.0	407.5	April 1985
Somalia	105.5	74.8	180.3	July 1987
Sudan	517.7	561.3	1,079.0	July 1985
Yugoslavia, Federal Republic of (Serbia/ Montenegro)	56.1	15.0	71.1	September 1992
Total	1,155.8	910.6	2,066.4	

Strengthened Cooperative Strategy

The IMF follows a cooperative strategy aimed at resolving the issue of overdue obligations to the IMF. Three major elements form the basis of the cooperative strategy: (1) preventive measures, (2) remedial and deterrent measures, and (3) intensified collaboration and the rights approach. Under the intensified collaborative approach, the IMF has developed IMF-monitored programs and rights accumulation programs, which permit a member with protracted arrears to the IMF to establish a track record of performance related to policy implementation and payments. A rights accumulation program allows the member to earn rights toward future financing through the implementation of a comprehensive economic program. Rights would be encashed under a successor arrangement after clearance of arrears and when all the requirements for that successor arrangement are met.

Deferred Income and Special Contingent Accounts

It is the policy of the IMF to exclude from current income charges due by members that are six months or more overdue in meeting payments to the IMF unless the member is current in the payment of charges. Charges excluded from income are recorded as deferred income. Charges due and accrued by members that are six months or more overdue and that have been deferred amounted to SDR 917.6 million at April 30, 1998 (SDR 874.6 million at April 30, 1997).

Since May 1, 1986, the IMF has adopted decisions whereby debtor and creditor members share equally the financial consequences of overdue obligations. An amount equal to deferred charges (excluding special charges) is generated and included in the IMF's income each quarter by an adjustment of the rate of charge and the rate of remuneration. However, the average rate of remuneration is not to be reduced below 85 percent of the SDR interest rate for the financing of deferred charges and the first Special Contingent Account (see following paragraphs). The proceeds from the subsequent settlement of overdue charges are distributed to members that paid additional charges or received reduced remuneration, when and to the extent that deferred charges that gave rise to adjustments are paid.

In view of the existence of protracted overdue obligations, the IMF accumulates precautionary balances, inter alia, in the Special Contingent Accounts. At April 30, 1998, SDR 1,883.9 million was held in the first and second Special Contingent Accounts (SCA-1 and SCA-2). SDR 883.9 million was held in the SCA-1 and SDR 1,000.0 million was held in the SCA-2 at April 30, 1998 (SDR 785.4 million and SDR 1,000.0 million, respectively, at April 30, 1997). The Special Contingent Accounts are financed by quarterly adjustments to the rate of charge and the rate of remuneration. Balances in the SCA-1 are to be distributed to the members that share the cost of financing it when there are no outstanding overdue charges and repurchases, or at such earlier time as the IMF may decide.

The SCA-2 was established on July 1, 1990 as part of the strengthened cooperative strategy to accumulate SDR 1.0 billion over a period of approximately five years through a further adjustment to the rate of charge and the rate of remuneration. Financing of the SCA-2 was completed during financial year 1997. The resources accumulated in the SCA-2 safeguard against potential losses arising from purchases made under a successor arrangement after a rights accumulation program has been successfully completed by members with protracted arrears to the IMF at the end of 1989, while at the same time providing additional liquidity to assist in financing such purchases. Refunds of contributions are to be made after all repurchases under the rights approach have been made, or at such earlier date as the IMF may determine. Outstanding credit in the General Resources Account following the completion and encashment of rights accumulation programs amounted to SDR 514.1 million at April 30, 1998 (SDR 621.3 million at April 30, 1997).

The adjustments to charges and remuneration in respect of the Special Contingent Accounts and the costs of deferred charges during the years ended April 30, 1998 and 1997 were as follows:

| | Adjustments to | | Total | |
	Charges	Remuneration	1998	1997
	In millions of SDRs			
Deferred charges	24.9	23.8	48.7	47.5
SCA-1	49.7	49.7	99.4	94.8
SCA-2	—	—	—	58.6
Refunds of deferred charges settled	(0.6)	(0.6)	(1.2)	(2.1)
Burden-sharing contributions, net of refunds	74.0	72.9	146.9	198.8

The cumulative charges, net of settlements, that have been deferred since May 1, 1986 and have resulted in adjustments to charges and remuneration amounted to SDR 729.2 million at April 30, 1998 (SDR 680.8 million at April 30, 1997). The cumulative refunds for the same period, resulting from the settlements of deferred charges for which burden sharing adjustments have been made, amounted to SDR 961.9 million (SDR 960.7 million at April 30, 1997).

6. Other Assets

Other assets include capital assets which at April 30, 1998 and 1997 amounted to SDR 216.3 million and SDR 194.0 million, respectively, and consisted of:

	1998	1997
	In millions of SDRs	
Land and buildings	274.7	246.3
Equipment	29.6	24.1
	304.3	270.4
Less accumulated depreciation	88.0	76.4
	216.3	194.0

7. Reserves

The IMF determines annually what part of its net income shall be placed to the General Reserve or to the Special Reserve, and what part, if any, shall be distributed. The Articles of Agreement permit the IMF to use the Special Reserve for any purpose for which it may use the General Reserve, except distribution. An administrative deficit for any financial year must be charged first against the Special Reserve.

8. Administrative Expenses

The administrative expenses for the years ended April 30, 1998 and 1997 were as follows:

	1998	1997
	In millions of SDRs	
General Resources Account		
Personnel	243.5	246.9
Travel	54.6	46.6
Other	74.8	58.2
Less reimbursements for the administration of:		
The SDR Department	(4.4)	(4.2)
The ESAF Trust and the Special Disbursement Account	—	(30.7)
Total administrative expenses, net of reimbursements	368.5	316.8
Special Disbursement Account		
Reimbursement to the GRA for the administration of the ESAF Trust and the Special Disbursement Account	—	30.7

The General Resources Account is to be reimbursed annually for expenses incurred in administering the Special Disbursement Account and the ESAF Trust; however, following the establishment of the SRF and the consequent increase in net operational income, the Board decided to forgo such reimbursement for financial years 1998 and 1999 and to transfer the amount that would otherwise have been reimbursed to the GRA, SDR 40.7 million for financial year 1998, from the ESAF Trust Reserve Account, through the Special Disbursement Account, to the ESAF-HIPC Trust. This amount has been included under Transfers to ESAF-HIPC Trust in the Statements of Changes in Reserves and Resources.

The IMF has a funded defined-benefit Staff Retirement Plan and a funded defined-benefit Supplemental Retirement Benefits Plan ("the Plans") covering nearly all staff. Contributions to the Plans and all other assets, liabilities, and income of the Plans are administered separately from the General Department and can be used only for the benefit of the participants in the Plans and their beneficiaries. Participants contribute a fixed percentage of their pensionable remuneration. The IMF contributes the remainder of the cost of funding the Plans and pays certain administrative costs of the Plans. The IMF uses the aggregate cost method for determining its pension cost. Under this method, the IMF's contributions, including those for cost of living adjustments and for experience gains and losses, are spread over the expected future working lifetimes of the participants in the Plans. The funding and cost of the Plans for the year ended April 30, 1998, are based on an actuarial valuation at April 30, 1997. The actuarial assumptions are included in the notes to the financial statements of the Plans.

During the year ended April 30, 1998 the IMF contributed SDR 13.7 million to the Plans (SDR 23.5 million during the year ended April 30, 1997). The present value of the benefits payable under the Plans at April 30, 1998 amounted to SDR 1,998.3 million in comparison to assets, which, for actuarial purposes, are valued at SDR 1,894.5 million (SDR 1,875.4 million and SDR 1,691.7 million, respectively, at April 30, 1997).

The IMF provides certain health care benefits to retirees that elect to continue participation in its medical benefits and group life insurance plans through retirement. Participants and the IMF contribute toward meeting the costs of these benefits. The IMF's cost, which includes a current-year cost and a past-service obligation, is determined actuarially using the projected unit credit method and the funding and cost for the year ended April 30, 1998 are based on an actuarial valuation at May 1, 1997. The cumulative cost was estimated at SDR 136.0 million at April 30, 1998 (SDR 131.9 million at April 30, 1997). The IMF has established a Retired Staff Benefits Investment Account to hold and invest the resources contributed by the IMF toward the payment of postretirement medical and life insurance benefits. At April 30, 1998, an amount of SDR 130.3 million was held by that account (SDR 108.7 million at April 30, 1997).

Schedule 1

General Department

Quotas, Fund's Holdings of Currencies, Members' Use of Fund Resources, and Reserve Tranche Positions as at April 30, 1998

(In thousands of SDRs)

| Member | | General Resources Account | | | Use of Fund Resources | | | | |
| | | Fund's holdings of currencies[1] | | Reserve tranche position | GRA[2] | | SDA[3] | ESAF Trust[4] | Total[5] |
	Quota	Total	Percent of quota		Amount (A)	Percent	+ (B)	+ (C)	= (D)
Afghanistan, Islamic State of	120,400	115,488	95.9	4,928	—	—	—	—	—
Albania	35,300	44,125	125.0	5	8,825	0.02	—	31,060	39,885
Algeria	914,400	2,505,273	274.0	7	1,590,875	3.20	—	—	1,590,875
Angola	207,300	207,445	100.1	—	—	—	—	—	—
Antigua and Barbuda	8,500	8,499	100.0	1	—	—	—	—	—
Argentina	1,537,100	5,694,740	370.5	—	4,157,615	8.37	—	—	4,157,615
Armenia, Republic of	67,500	114,750	170.0	5	47,250	0.10	—	67,500	114,750
Australia	2,333,200	1,692,226	72.5	641,035	—	—	—	—	—
Austria	1,188,300	295,980	24.9	892,306	—	—	—	—	—
Azerbaijan	117,000	266,170	227.5	10	149,170	0.30	—	55,580	204,750
Bahamas, The	94,900	88,665	93.4	6,239	—	—	—	—	—
Bahrain	82,800	35,653	43.1	47,156	—	—	—	—	—
Bangladesh	392,500	392,364	100.0	139	—	—	13,369	248,250	261,619
Barbados	48,900	48,879	100.0	25	—	—	—	—	—
Belarus, Republic of	280,400	464,758	165.7	20	184,358	0.37	—	—	184,358
Belgium	3,102,300	2,106,516	67.9	995,804	—	—	—	—	—
Belize	13,500	10,587	78.4	2,914	—	—	—	—	—
Benin	45,300	43,129	95.2	2,176	—	—	15,451	53,950	69,401
Bhutan	4,500	3,930	87.3	570	—	—	—	—	—
Bolivia	126,200	117,338	93.0	8,875	—	—	12,244	178,055	190,299
Bosnia and Herzegovina	121,200	151,505	125.0	—	30,300	0.06	—	—	30,300
Botswana	36,600	11,473	31.3	25,129	—	—	—	—	—
Brazil	2,170,800	2,187,142	100.8	—	15,539	0.03	—	—	15,539
Brunei Darussalam	150,000	114,750	76.5	35,255	—	—	—	—	—
Bulgaria	464,900	1,101,230	236.9	32,635	668,959	1.35	—	—	668,959
Burkina Faso	44,200	36,992	83.7	7,221	—	—	19,592	48,290	67,882
Burundi	57,200	51,342	89.8	5,860	—	—	3,843	15,702	19,545
Cambodia	65,000	70,730	108.8	—	5,729	0.01	—	42,000	47,729
Cameroon	135,100	173,866	128.7	410	39,155	0.08	—	54,040	93,195
Canada	4,320,300	3,153,200	73.0	1,167,169	—	—	—	—	—
Cape Verde	7,000	6,999	100.0	1	—	—	—	—	—
Central African Republic	41,200	46,461	112.8	96	5,355	0.01	4,864	—	10,219
Chad	41,300	46,184	111.8	280	5,163	0.01	5,814	33,040	44,017
Chile	621,700	339,675	54.6	282,026	—	—	—	—	—
China	3,385,200	1,329,508	39.3	2,055,694	—	—	—	—	—
Colombia	561,300	241,892	43.1	319,414	—	—	—	—	—
Comoros	6,500	5,962	91.7	540	—	—	1,980	—	1,980
Congo, Democratic Republic of	291,000	449,180	154.4	—	158,180	0.32	143,083	—	301,263
Congo, Republic of	57,900	65,195	112.6	536	7,813	0.02	—	13,896	21,709
Costa Rica	119,000	110,288	92.7	8,725	—	—	—	—	—
Côte d'Ivoire	238,200	238,032	99.9	178	—	—	—	416,850	416,850
Croatia, Republic of	261,600	430,904	164.7	92	169,390	0.34	—	—	169,390
Cyprus	100,000	74,553	74.6	25,453	—	—	—	—	—
Czech Republic	589,600	589,600	100.0	3	—	—	—	—	—
Denmark	1,069,900	349,904	32.7	719,999	—	—	—	—	—

Schedule 1 (*continued*)

Member	Quota	General Resources Account Fund's holdings of currencies[1] Total	Percent of quota	Reserve tranche position	Use of Fund Resources GRA[2] Amount (A)	Percent +	SDA[3] (B) +	ESAF Trust[4] (C) =	Total[5] (D)
Djibouti	11,500	15,475	134.6	—	3,975	0.01	—	—	3,975
Dominica	6,000	5,992	99.9	9	—	—	106	—	106
Dominican Republic	158,800	168,474	106.1	3	9,675	0.02	—	—	9,675
Ecuador	219,200	288,587	131.7	17,153	86,538	0.17	—	—	86,538
Egypt	678,400	624,673	92.1	53,750	—	—	—	—	—
El Salvador	125,600	125,603	100.0	—	—	—	—	—	—
Equatorial Guinea	24,300	24,309	100.0	—	—	—	8,069	1,650	9,719
Eritrea	11,500	11,500	100.0	5	—	—	—	—	—
Estonia, Republic of	46,500	81,564	175.4	6	35,069	0.07	—	—	35,069
Ethiopia	98,300	91,211	92.8	7,099	—	—	48,008	14,745	62,753
Fiji	51,100	41,016	80.3	10,087	—	—	—	—	—
Finland	861,800	405,492	47.1	456,320	—	—	—	—	—
France	7,414,600	5,126,398	69.1	2,288,331	—	—	—	—	—
Gabon	110,300	202,343	183.4	66	92,102	0.19	—	—	92,102
Gambia, The	22,900	21,418	93.5	1,485	—	—	911	6,573	7,484
Georgia	111,000	188,700	170.0	10	77,700	0.16	—	111,000	188,700
Germany	8,241,500	3,303,249	40.1	4,938,279	—	—	—	—	—
Ghana	274,000	266,666	97.3	17,380	10,042	0.02	33,742	232,927	276,711
Greece	587,600	473,913	80.7	113,687	—	—	—	—	—
Grenada	8,500	8,501	100.0	—	—	—	—	—	—
Guatemala	153,800	153,806	100.0	—	—	—	—	—	—
Guinea	78,700	78,628	99.9	75	—	—	3,474	79,983	83,457
Guinea-Bissau	10,500	10,500	100.0	*6	—	—	675	10,500	11,175
Guyana	67,200	68,292	101.6	—	1,090	—	27,798	82,665	111,553
Haiti	60,700	77,056	126.9	45	16,400	0.03	—	15,175	31,575
Honduras	95,000	95,000	100.0	—	—	—	—	33,222	33,222
Hungary	754,800	698,706	92.6	56,097	—	—	—	—	—
Iceland	85,300	74,811	87.7	10,489	—	—	—	—	—
India	3,055,500	3,340,186	109.3	212,793	497,375	1.00	—	—	497,375
Indonesia	1,497,600	3,699,073	247.0	—	2,201,472	4.43	—	—	2,201,472
Iran, Islamic Republic of	1,078,500	1,078,502	100.0	—	—	—	—	—	—
Iraq	504,000	504,013	100.0	—	—	—	—	—	—
Ireland	525,000	170,865	32.5	354,145	—	—	—	—	—
Israel	666,200	666,195	100.0	11	—	—	—	—	—
Italy	4,590,700	2,354,017	51.3	2,236,687	—	—	—	—	—
Jamaica	200,900	285,619	142.2	—	84,669	0.17	—	—	84,669
Japan	8,241,500	1,163,787	14.1	7,077,818	—	—	—	—	—
Jordan	121,700	448,258	368.3	2	326,560	0.66	—	—	326,560
Kazakhstan, Republic of	247,500	610,475	246.7	5	362,975	0.73	—	—	362,975
Kenya	199,400	187,023	93.8	12,405	—	—	30,530	148,708	179,238
Kiribati	4,000	4,001	100.0	—	—	—	—	—	—
Korea	799,600	11,999,570	1,500.7	33	11,200,000	22.53	—	—	11,200,000
Kuwait	995,200	827,656	83.2	167,546	—	—	—	—	—
Kyrgyz Republic	64,500	95,756	148.5	5	31,256	0.06	—	88,150	119,406
Lao People's Democratic Republic	39,100	39,100	100.0	—	—	—	12,306	35,190	47,496
Latvia, Republic of	91,500	146,686	160.3	5	55,186	0.11	—	—	55,186
Lebanon	146,000	127,168	87.1	18,833	—	—	—	—	—
Lesotho	23,900	20,382	85.3	3,523	—	—	3,171	16,686	19,857
Liberia	71,300	272,738	382.5	28	201,457	0.41	—	—	225,550[5]
Libya	817,600	498,628	61.0	318,980	—	—	—	—	—

Schedule 1 *(continued)*

Member	Quota	General Resources Account			Use of Fund Resources				
		Fund's holdings of currencies[1]		Reserve tranche position	GRA[2]		SDA[3]	ESAF Trust[4]	Total[5]
		Total	Percent of quota		Amount (A)	Percent	+ (B) +	(C) =	(D)
Lithuania, Republic of	103,500	293,884	283.9	16	190,397	0.38	—	—	190,397
Luxembourg	135,500	102,744	75.8	32,760	—	—	—	—	—
Macedonia, former Yugoslav Republic of	49,600	96,702	195.0	—	47,100	0.09	—	18,188	65,288
Madagascar	90,400	90,373	100.0	27	—	—	14,276	35,914	50,190
Malawi	50,900	59,805	117.5	2,230	11,134	0.02	9,114	50,442	70,690
Malaysia	832,700	388,025	46.6	444,681	—	—	—	—	—
Maldives	5,500	4,621	84.0	879	—	—	—	—	—
Mali	68,900	60,140	87.3	8,761	—	—	16,764	109,907	126,671
Malta	67,500	35,880	53.2	31,636	—	—	—	—	—
Marshall Islands	2,500	2,500	100.0	1	—	—	—	—	—
Mauritania	47,500	47,506	100.0	—	—	—	4,427	78,155	82,582
Mauritius	73,300	65,934	90.0	7,368	—	—	—	—	—
Mexico	1,753,300	8,488,385	484.1	173	6,735,240	13.55	—	—	6,735,240
Micronesia	3,500	3,500	100.0	1	—	—	—	—	—
Moldova, Republic of	90,000	252,419	280.5	5	162,419	0.33	—	—	162,419
Mongolia	37,100	37,100	100.0	5	—	—	—	35,245	35,245
Morocco	427,700	397,387	92.9	30,316	—	—	—	—	—
Mozambique	84,000	84,000	100.0	7	—	—	2,208	147,450	149,658
Myanmar	184,900	184,902	100.0	—	—	—	—	—	—
Namibia	99,600	99,571	100.0	32	—	—	—	—	—
Nepal	52,000	46,277	89.0	5,730	—	—	5,222	16,225	21,447
Netherlands	3,444,200	1,794,917	52.1	1,649,297	—	—	—	—	—
New Zealand	650,100	443,310	68.2	206,792	—	—	—	—	—
Nicaragua	96,100	96,110	100.0	—	—	—	—	36,838	36,838
Niger	48,300	45,295	93.8	8,561	5,555	0.01	1,795	44,428	51,778
Nigeria	1,281,600	1,281,575	100.0	68	—	—	—	—	—
Norway	1,104,600	283,111	25.6	821,521	—	—	—	—	—
Oman	119,400	88,336	74.0	31,146	—	—	—	—	—
Pakistan	758,200	1,254,889	165.5	61	496,750	1.00	174,816	399,660	1,071,226
Palau	2,250	—	—	—	—	—	—	—	—
Panama	149,600	240,680	160.9	11,860	102,929	0.21	—	—	102,929
Papua New Guinea	95,300	130,603	137.0	53	35,340	0.07	—	—	35,340
Paraguay	72,100	57,578	79.9	14,525	—	—	—	—	—
Peru	466,100	1,162,205	249.3	—	696,072	1.40	—	—	696,072
Philippines	633,400	1,410,251	222.6	87,104	863,942	1.74	—	—	863,942
Poland, Republic of	988,500	911,369	92.2	77,131	—	—	—	—	—
Portugal	557,600	131,236	23.5	426,381	—	—	—	—	—
Qatar	190,500	164,100	86.1	26,401	—	—	—	—	—
Romania	754,100	1,217,659	161.5	—	463,554	0.93	—	—	463,554
Russian Federation	4,313,100	14,528,375	336.8	926	10,216,058	20.56	—	—	10,216,058
Rwanda	59,500	83,318	140.0	—	23,800	0.05	5,256	—	29,056
St. Kitts and Nevis	6,500	6,488	99.8	15	—	—	—	—	—
St. Lucia	11,000	11,000	100.0	1	—	—	—	—	—
St. Vincent and the Grenadines	6,000	5,500	91.7	500	—	—	—	—	—
Samoa	8,500	7,824	92.0	683	—	—	—	—	—
San Marino, Republic of	10,000	7,649	76.5	2,352	—	—	—	—	—
São Tomé and Príncipe	5,500	5,503	100.1	—	—	—	240	—	240
Saudi Arabia	5,130,600	4,601,963	89.7	528,641	—	—	—	—	—
Senegal	118,900	133,031	111.9	1,328	15,457	0.03	6,446	203,451	225,354
Seychelles	6,000	5,196	86.6	804	—	—	—	—	—

Member	Quota	General Resources Account		Reserve tranche position	Use of Fund Resources				
		Fund's holdings of currencies[1]			GRA[2]		SDA[3]	ESAF Trust[4]	Total[5]
		Total	Percent of quota		Amount (A)	Percent	+ (B)	+ (C)	= (D)
Sierra Leone	77,200	77,185	100.0	24	—	—	27,020	96,848	123,868
Singapore	357,600	109,185	30.5	248,423	—	—	—	—	—
Slovak Republic	257,400	420,147	163.2	—	162,742	0.33	—	—	162,742
Slovenia, Republic of	150,500	137,631	91.4	12,875	—	—	—	—	—
Solomon Islands	7,500	6,967	92.9	538	—	—	—	—	—
Somalia	44,200	140,907	318.8	—	96,701	0.19	8,840	—	112,004[5]
South Africa	1,365,400	1,595,722	116.9	95	230,411	0.46	—	—	230,411
Spain	1,935,400	487,448	25.2	1,447,956	—	—	—	—	—
Sri Lanka	303,600	283,378	93.3	20,250	—	—	42,389	252,000	294,389
Sudan	169,700	687,443	405.1	11	517,722	1.04	—	—	576,950[5]
Suriname	67,600	67,601	100.0	—	—	—	—	—	—
Swaziland	36,500	33,504	91.8	3,002	—	—	—	—	—
Sweden	1,614,000	972,907	60.3	641,101	—	—	—	—	—
Switzerland	2,470,400	794,897	32.2	1,675,512	—	—	—	—	—
Syrian Arab Republic	209,900	209,903	100.0	5	—	—	—	—	—
Tajikistan, Republic of	60,000	90,000	150.0	2	30,000	0.06	—	—	30,000
Tanzania	146,900	136,932	93.2	9,975	—	—	14,980	163,093	178,073
Thailand	573,900	2,573,897	448.5	20	2,000,000	4.02	—	—	2,000,000
Togo	54,300	54,046	99.5	254	—	—	8,256	66,780	75,036
Tonga	5,000	3,795	75.9	1,210	—	—	—	—	—
Trinidad and Tobago	246,800	246,786	100.0	15	—	—	—	—	—
Tunisia	206,000	329,002	159.7	42	123,038	0.25	—	—	123,038
Turkey	642,000	1,000,666	155.9	32,275	390,938	0.79	—	—	390,938
Turkmenistan, Republic of	48,000	48,000	100.0	5	—	—	—	—	—
Uganda	133,900	133,907	100.0	—	—	—	8,964	285,927	294,891
Ukraine	997,300	2,814,127	282.2	8	1,816,828	3.66	—	—	1,816,828
United Arab Emirates	392,100	172,729	44.1	219,372	—	—	—	—	—
United Kingdom	7,414,600	5,217,884	70.4	2,196,750	—	—	—	—	—
United States	26,526,800	12,994,063	49.0	13,528,378	—	—	—	—	—
Uruguay	225,300	209,932	93.2	15,375	—	—	—	—	—
Uzbekistan, Republic of	199,500	364,700	182.8	5	165,200	0.33	—	—	165,200
Vanuatu	12,500	10,006	80.0	2,496	—	—	—	—	—
Venezuela	1,951,300	2,976,956	152.6	144,950	1,170,604	2.36	—	—	1,170,604
Vietnam	241,600	313,133	129.6	5	71,533	0.14	—	241,600	313,133
Yemen, Republic of	176,500	317,865	180.1	13	141,375	0.28	—	44,000	185,375
Yugoslavia, Federal Republic of (Serbia/Montenegro)	—	—	—	—	56,056	0.11	—	—	56,056
Zambia	363,500	363,501	100.0	18	—	—	181,750	661,682	843,432
Zimbabwe	261,300	386,229	147.8	164	125,092	0.25	—	146,430	271,522
Total	145,321,050	144,638,372		50,324,030	49,701,200	100.00	921,793	5,269,650	55,982,431

[1]Includes nonnegotiable, non-interest-bearing notes that members are entitled to issue in substitution for currencies, and outstanding currency valuation adjustments.

[2]Includes the share of the Federal Republic of Yugoslavia (Serbia/Montenegro) in the liabilities of the former Socialist Federal Republic of Yugoslavia, although this state has not succeeded to Fund membership.

[3]The Special Disbursement Account (SDA) of the General Department provides financing under Structural Adjustment Facility (SAF) and Enhanced Structural Adjustment Facility (ESAF) arrangements.

[4]For information purposes only. The ESAF Trust provides financing under ESAF arrangements and is not a part of the General Department.

[5]Includes outstanding Trust Fund loans to Liberia (SDR 24.1 million), Somalia (SDR 6.5 million), and Sudan (SDR 59.2 million).

[6]Less than SDR 500.

General Department
Schedule of Repurchases and Repayments of Loans
as at April 30, 1998

(In thousands of SDRs)

Financial Year Ending April 30	General Resources Account[1]	Special Disbursement Account
Overdue	1,030,116	125,733
1999	9,446,675	261,658
2000	13,804,740	175,076
2001	6,820,322	79,024
2002	7,302,323	90,679
2003	5,544,501	61,864
2004	1,937,681	50,823
2005	1,519,936	40,270
2006	1,169,964	36,666
2007	807,110	—
2008	317,832	—
Total	49,701,200	921,793

[1]A member is entitled to repurchase at any time the IMF's holdings of its currency subject to charges and is expected to make repurchases as and when its balance of payments and reserve position improve.

General Department
Status of Arrangements
as at April 30, 1998
(In thousands of SDRs)

Member	Date of Arrangement	Expiration	Total Amount Agreed	Undrawn Balance
General Resources Account				
Stand-By Arrangements				
Bulgaria	April 11, 1997	June 10, 1998	371,900	124,300
Cape Verde	February 20, 1998	April 19, 1999	2,100	2,100
Djibouti	April 15, 1996	June 30, 1998	6,600	2,625
Egypt	October 11, 1996	September 30, 1998	271,400	271,400
El Salvador	February 28, 1997	May 30, 1998	37,680	37,680
Estonia, Republic of	December 17, 1997	March 16, 1999	16,100	16,100
Indonesia	November 5, 1997	November 4, 2000	7,338,240	5,136,768
Korea	December 4, 1997	December 3, 2000	15,500,000[1]	4,300,000
Latvia, Republic of	October 10, 1997	April 9, 1999	33,000	33,000
Philippines	April 1, 1998	March 31, 2000	1,020,790	1,020,790
Romania	April 22, 1997	May 21, 1998	301,500	180,900
Thailand	August 20, 1997	June 19, 2000	2,900,000	900,000
Ukraine	August 25, 1997	August 24, 1998	398,920	217,593
Uruguay	June 20, 1997	March 19, 1999	125,000	125,000
Total Stand-By Arrangements			28,323,230	12,368,256
Extended Arrangements				
Algeria	May 22, 1995	May 21, 1998	1,169,280	84,480
Argentina	February 4, 1998	February 3, 2001	2,080,000	2,080,000
Azerbaijan	December 20, 1996	December 19, 1999	58,500	26,330
Croatia, Republic of	March 12, 1997	March 11, 2000	353,160	324,380
Gabon	November 8, 1995	November 7, 1998	110,300	49,630
Jordan	February 9, 1996	February 8, 1999	238,040	47,350
Kazakhstan, Republic of	July 17, 1996	July 16, 1999	309,400	309,400
Moldova, Republic of	May 20, 1996	May 19, 1999	135,000	97,500
Pakistan	October 20, 1997	October 19, 2000	454,920	398,060
Panama	December 10, 1997	December 9, 2000	120,000	110,000
Peru	July 1, 1996	March 31, 1999	300,200	139,700
Russian Federation	March 26, 1996	March 25, 1999	6,901,000	3,064,736
Yemen, Republic of	October 29, 1997	October 28, 2000	105,900	96,900
Total Extended Arrangements			12,335,700	6,828,466
Total General Resources Account			40,658,930	19,196,722

[1] Includes SDR 9.95 billion available until December 17, 1998 under the Supplemental Reserve Facility.

SDR Department
Statements of Allocations and Holdings
as at April 30, 1998 and 1997
(In thousands of SDRs)
(Note 1)

	1998	1997
Allocations		
Net cumulative allocations of SDRs	21,433,330	21,433,330
Overdue charges (Note 2)	78,666	64,611
Total Allocations	21,511,996	21,497,941
Holdings		
Participants with holdings above allocations		
Allocations	10,457,271	10,399,818
Net receipts of SDRs	6,731,164	5,162,821
	17,188,435	15,562,639
Participants with holdings below allocations		
Allocations	10,976,059	11,033,512
Net uses of SDRs	7,802,687	7,899,301
	3,173,372	3,134,211
Total holdings of participants	20,361,807	18,696,850
General Resources Account	764,424	1,494,149
Holdings of SDRs by prescribed holders	385,765	1,306,942
Total Holdings	21,511,996	21,497,941

The accompanying notes are an integral part of the financial statements.

/s/ David Williams
Treasurer

/s/ M. Camdessus
Managing Director

SDR Department

Statements of Receipt and Use
for the Year Ended April 30, 1998
with Comparative Totals for the Year Ended April 30, 1997

(In thousands of SDRs)
(Note 1)

	Participants	General Resources Account	Prescribed Holders	Total 1998	Total 1997
Total holdings, beginning of the year	18,696,850	1,494,149	1,306,942	21,497,941	21,486,742
Receipt of SDRs					
Transfers among participants and prescribed holders					
Transactions by agreement	8,539,330		27,561	8,566,891	7,410,518
Operations					
Forward operations	—			—	27,400
Settlement of financial obligations	52,234		34,176	86,410	60,144
Fund-related operations					
SAF/ESAF loans	351,745			351,745	165,127
SAF repayments and interest			107,672	107,672	130,079
Special charges on SAF, ESAF, and Trust Fund			6	6	1
ESAF contributions and payments	33,310		95,934	129,244	84,369
ESAF repayments and interest			311,285	311,285	225,936
HIPC contributions and payments			1,000	1,000	—
Net interest on SDRs (Note 2)	242,541		41,715	284,256	268,156
Transfers from participants to General Resources Account					
Repurchases		2,917,685		2,917,685	4,364,074
Charges		1,877,315		1,877,315	1,615,675
Interest on SDRs (Note 2)		44,431		44,431	51,346
Assessment on SDR allocation (Note 2)		4,350		4,350	4,138
Transfers from General Resources Account to participants					
Purchases	4,243,310			4,243,310	4,060,395
In exchange for currencies of members					
Acquisitions to pay charges	19,952			19,952	223,774
Remuneration	1,220,129			1,220,129	1,054,830
Other					
Refunds and adjustments	90,115			90,115	26,813
Total receipts	14,792,666	4,843,781	619,349	20,255,796	19,772,775

SDR Department

Statements of Receipt and Use *(concluded)*
for the Year Ended April 30, 1998
with Comparative Totals for the Year Ended April 30, 1997

(In thousands of SDRs)
(Note 1)

	Participants	General Resources Account	Prescribed Holders	Total 1998	1997
Use of SDRs					
Transfers among participants and prescribed holders					
Transactions by agreement	7,463,648		1,103,243	8,566,891	7,410,518
Operations					
Forward operations			—	—	27,400
Settlement of financial obligations	34,182		52,228	86,410	60,144
Fund-related operations					
SAF/ESAF loans			351,745	351,745	165,127
SAF repayments and interest	107,672			107,672	130,079
Special charges on SAF, ESAF, and Trust Fund	6			6	1
ESAF contributions and payments	95,934		33,310	129,244	84,369
ESAF repayments and interest	311,285			311,285	225,936
HIPC contributions and payments	1,000			1,000	—
Transfers from participants to General Resources Account					
Repurchases	2,917,685			2,917,685	4,364,074
Charges	1,877,315			1,877,315	1,615,675
Assessment on SDR allocation (Note 2)	4,350			4,350	4,138
Transfers from General Resources Account to participants					
Purchases		4,243,310		4,243,310	4,060,395
In exchange for currencies of members					
Acquisitions to pay charges		19,952		19,952	223,774
Remuneration		1,220,129		1,220,129	1,054,830
Other					
Refunds and adjustments		90,115		90,115	26,813
Charges paid in the SDR Department (Note 2)					
Net charges due	328,687			328,687	319,502
Charges not paid when due	(18,335)			(18,335)	(15,689)
Settlement of unpaid charges	4,280			4,280	4,490
Total uses	13,127,709	5,573,506	1,540,526	20,241,741	19,761,576
Total holdings, end of the year	20,361,807	764,424	385,765	21,511,996	21,497,941

The accompanying notes are an integral part of the financial statements.

SDR Department
Notes to the Financial Statements
as at April 30, 1998 and 1997

SDR Department

All transactions and operations involving SDRs are conducted through the SDR Department. At April 30, 1998, all members of the IMF were participants in the SDR Department. SDRs are reserve assets allocated by the IMF to members that are participants in the SDR Department in proportion to their quotas in the IMF. Six allocations have been made (in 1970, 1971, 1972, 1979, 1980, and 1981) for a total of SDR 21.4 billion. A proposed amendment of the IMF's Articles of Agreement has been approved to allow for a special one-time allocation of SDRs equal to SDR 21.4 billion. The amendment will enter into force after three-fifths of the members, having 85 percent of the total voting power, have accepted it. Upon termination of participation or liquidation of the SDR Department, the IMF will provide to holders the currencies received from the participants in settlement of their obligations. The IMF is empowered to prescribe certain official entities as holders of SDRs, and, at April 30, 1998, 15 institutions have been prescribed as holders. These prescribed holders do not receive allocations.

Uses of SDRs

Participants and prescribed holders can use and receive SDRs in transactions and operations by agreement among themselves. Participants can also use SDRs in operations and transactions involving the General Resources Account, such as the payment of charges and repurchases. The IMF ensures, by designating participants to provide freely usable currency in exchange for SDRs, that a participant can use its SDRs to obtain an equivalent amount of currency if it has a need because of its balance of payments or its reserve position or developments in its reserves.

1. Unit of Account

The accounts of the SDR Department are expressed in terms of the SDR. The currency value of the SDR is determined by the IMF each day by summing the values in U.S. dollars, based on market exchange rates, of a basket of five currencies. The IMF reviews the SDR valuation basket every five years. The SDR valuation basket was last revised in financial year 1996. The currencies comprising the basket and their amounts in the basket are as follows:

Currency	Amount
U.S. dollar	0.582
Deutsche mark	0.446
Japanese yen	27.2
French franc	0.813
Pound sterling	0.105

2. Interest, Charges, and Assessment

Interest is paid on holdings of SDRs. Charges are levied on each participant's net cumulative allocation plus any negative balance of the participant or unpaid charges. Interest on SDR holdings is paid, and charges on net cumulative allocations are collected, on a quarterly basis. Interest and charges are levied at the same rate and are settled by crediting and debit-ing individual holdings accounts on the first day of the subsequent quarter. The SDR Department is required to pay interest to each holder, whether or not sufficient SDRs are received to meet the payment of interest. If sufficient SDRs are not received, because charges are overdue, additional SDRs are temporarily created.

At April 30, 1998, charges amounting to SDR 78.7 million were overdue to the SDR Department (SDR 64.6 million at April 30, 1997). At April 30, 1998 and 1997, six members were six months or more overdue in meeting their financial obligations to the IMF, and five of these members were six months or more overdue to the SDR Department at April 30, 1998 (four members at April 30, 1997). In addition, the Federal Republic of Yugoslavia (Serbia/Montenegro) was also six months or more overdue in meeting its financial obligations. While the Federal Republic of Yugoslavia (Serbia/Montenegro) agreed to its share in the assets and liabilities of the former Socialist Federal Republic of Yugoslavia in the IMF, it had not succeeded to membership in the IMF as of April 30, 1998, and consequently, it is not a participant in the SDR Department.

Charges due from members (including Serbia/Montenegro) that are six months or more overdue were as follows:

	1998	1997
	In millions of SDRs	
Total overdue charges	78.7	62.9
Overdue for six months or more	71.3	58.1
Overdue for three years or more	43.8	35.1

The duration and amount of arrears were as follows:

	Total	Longest Overdue Obligation
	In millions of SDRs	
Afghanistan	2.5	February 1996
Congo, Democratic Republic of	5.4	November 1996
Iraq	32.9	November 1990
Liberia	16.4	August 1988
Somalia	6.1	February 1991
Yugoslavia, Federal Republic of (Serbia/Montenegro)	15.4	November 1992
Total	78.7	

The rate of interest on the SDR is determined by reference to a combined market interest rate, which is a weighted average of yields or rates on short-term instruments in the capital markets of France, Germany, Japan, the United Kingdom, and the United States. The combined market interest rate used to determine the SDR interest rate is calculated each Friday, using the yields or rates of that day. The SDR interest rate, which is set equal to the combined market interest rate, enters into effect on the following Monday and applies until the end of the following Sunday.

The expenses of conducting the business of the SDR Department are paid by the IMF from the General Resources Account, which is reimbursed in SDRs by the SDR Department at the end of each financial year. For this purpose, the SDR Department levies an assessment on all participants in proportion to their net cumulative allocation.

Enhanced Structural Adjustment Facility Trust
Combined Balance Sheets
as at April 30, 1998
with Comparative Totals as at April 30, 1997

(In thousands of SDRs)
(Note 1)

	Loan Account	Reserve Account	Subsidy Account	Combined 1998	Combined 1997
Assets					
Loans receivable	5,269,650	—	—	5,269,650	4,590,574
Investments (Notes 2 and 4)	233,787	2,022,703	1,827,572	4,084,062	3,648,538
Interest receivable	11,371	40,851	27,178	79,400	47,507
Currencies	—	—	—	—	2
Accrued account transfers	(15,059)	66,960	(51,901)	—	—
Total Assets	5,499,749	2,130,514	1,802,849	9,433,112	8,286,621
Resources and Liabilities					
Resources	—	2,089,814	1,623,882	3,713,696	3,332,746
Borrowing (Note 4)	5,436,635	—	176,816	5,613,451	4,900,730
Interest payable	63,114	—	2,151	65,265	53,145
Transfer payable (Note 6)	—	40,700	—	40,700	—
Total Resources and Liabilities	5,499,749	2,130,514	1,802,849	9,433,112	8,286,621

The accompanying notes and schedules are an integral part of the financial statements.

/s/ David Williams
Treasurer

/s/ M. Camdessus
Managing Director

Enhanced Structural Adjustment Facility Trust
Combined Income Statements
for the Year Ended April 30, 1998
with Comparative Totals for the Year Ended April 30, 1997

(In thousands of SDRs)
(Note 1)

	Loan Account	Reserve Account	Subsidy Account	Combined 1998	Combined 1997
Income					
Investment income	89	80,095	77,012	157,196	130,173
Interest on loans	24,124	—	—	24,124	21,726
Exchange valuation gain	10	38	—	48	74
	24,223	80,133	77,012	181,368	151,973
Expense					
Interest expense	183,002	—	3,663	186,665	158,597
Other expenses	38	—	—	38	87
	183,040	—	3,663	186,703	158,684
Net Income (Loss)	(158,817)	80,133	73,349	(5,335)	(6,711)

The accompanying notes and schedules are an integral part of the financial statements.

Enhanced Structural Adjustment Facility Trust
Combined Statements of Changes in Resources
for the Year Ended April 30, 1998
with Comparative Totals for the Year Ended April 30, 1997

(In thousands of SDRs)
(Note 1)

	Loan Account	Reserve Account	Subsidy Account	Combined 1998	Combined 1997
Balance, beginning of the year	—	1,773,448	1,559,298	3,332,746	2,830,999
Contributions (Note 3)	—	—	143,693	143,693	202,358
Transfers from the Special					
Disbursement Account	—	303,581	—	303,581	306,100
Transfers through the Special					
Disbursement Account to the					
ESAF-HIPC Trust (Note 6)	—	(60,989)	—	(60,989)	—
Net transfers between:					
Loan and Reserve Accounts	6,359	(6,359)	—	—	—
Loan and Subsidy Accounts	152,458	—	(152,458)	—	—
Net income (loss)	(158,817)	80,133	73,349	(5,335)	(6,711)
Balance, end of the year	—	2,089,814	1,623,882	3,713,696	3,332,746

The accompanying notes and schedules are an integral part of the financial statements.

Enhanced Structural Adjustment Facility Trust

Notes to the Financial Statements
as at April 30, 1998 and 1997

Purpose

The Enhanced Structural Adjustment Facility Trust ("the Trust"), for which the IMF is Trustee, was established in December 1987 and was extended and enlarged in February 1994 to provide loans on concessional terms to qualifying low-income developing country members. The resources of the Trust are separate from the assets of all other accounts of, or administered by, the IMF and may not be used to discharge liabilities or to meet losses incurred in the administration of other accounts.

The operations of the Trust are conducted through a Loan Account, a Reserve Account, and a Subsidy Account.

Loan Account

The resources of the Loan Account consist of the proceeds from borrowing and principal and interest payments on loans extended by the Trust. Resources of the Loan Account are committed to qualifying members for a three-year period, upon approval by the Trustee, in support of the member's macroeconomic and structural adjustment programs. Interest on the outstanding loan balances is currently set at the rate of ½ of 1 percent a year. At April 30, 1998, loans totaling SDR 5,269.6 million were outstanding (SDR 4,590.6 million at April 30, 1997). Members' outstanding loans are presented in Schedule 1.

Reserve Account

The resources of the Reserve Account consist of amounts transferred by the IMF from the Special Disbursement Account and net earnings from investment of resources held in the Reserve Account and in the Loan Account.

The resources held in the Reserve Account are to be used by the Trustee to pay loan principal and interest on borrowing of the Loan Account in the event that amounts payable from borrowers' principal repayments and interest together with the authorized interest subsidy are insufficient.

Subsidy Account

The resources held in the Subsidy Account consist of donations to the Trust, including transfers of net earnings from ESAF Administered Accounts and SDR 400 million transferred by the IMF from the Special Disbursement Account, of net earnings on loans made to the Trust for the Subsidy Account, and the net earnings from investment of Subsidy Account resources.

The resources available in the Subsidy Account are drawn by the Trustee to pay the difference, with respect to each interest period, between the interest due from the borrowers under the Trust and the interest due on resources borrowed for Loan Account loans.

1. Accounting Practices

The accounts of the Trust are expressed in terms of the SDR. SDRs are reserve assets allocated to participants in the IMF's SDR Department. The currency value of the SDR is determined by the IMF each day by summing the values in U.S. dollars, based on market exchange rates, of a basket of five currencies. The IMF reviews the SDR valuation basket every five years. The SDR valuation basket was last reviewed in financial year 1996. The currencies in the basket and their amounts are as follows:

Currency	Amount
U.S. dollar	0.582
Deutsche mark	0.446
Japanese yen	27.2
French franc	0.813
Pound sterling	0.105

Members are not obligated to maintain the SDR value of their currencies held in the accounts of the Trust.

The accounts of the Trust are maintained on the accrual basis; accordingly, income is recognized as it is earned, and expenses are recorded as they are incurred.

2. Investments

The resources of the Trust are invested pending their use. Investments are denominated in SDRs or in currency and are carried at cost, which does not exceed net realizable value. Pending their investment, resources may be temporarily held in currency, which also may give rise to valuation gains and losses.

3. Contributions

The Trustee accepts contributions of resources for the Subsidy Account on such terms and conditions as agreed between the Trust and the contributor. At April 30, 1998, cumulative contributions received, including transfers from the Special Disbursement Account, amounted to SDR 1,866.7 million (SDR 1,723.0 million at April 30, 1997). Cumulative contributions are listed in Schedule 2.

4. Borrowing

The Trust borrows resources for the Loan Account and for the Subsidy Account on such terms and conditions as agreed between the Trust and the lenders.

Schedules 3 and 4, respectively, present lenders' borrowing agreements and scheduled repayments of outstanding borrowing. The following summarizes the borrowing agreements concluded as at April 30, 1998:

	Amount Agreed	Amount Undrawn
	In thousands of SDRs	
Loan Account	9,288,529	3,379,332
Subsidy Account	243,481	6,665

The Trustee has agreed to hold and invest, on behalf of a lender, principal repayments of Trust borrowing in a suspense account within the Loan Account. Principal repayments will be accumulated until the final maturity of the borrowing, when the full proceeds are to be transferred to the lender. Amounts deposited in this account are invested by the Trustee, and payments of interest to the lender are to be made exclusively from the earnings on the amounts invested.

5. Commitments Under Loan Arrangements

At April 30, 1998, undrawn balances under 33 loan arrangements amounted to SDR 2,164.5 million (SDR 1,675.7 million under 35 arrangements at April 30, 1997). Loan arrangements are listed in Schedule 5. Scheduled repayments of outstanding loans receivable are shown in Schedule 6.

6. Transfers Through the Special Disbursement Account

The expenses of conducting the business of the Trust are paid by the General Resources Account of the IMF and reimbursed through the Special Disbursement Account; corresponding transfers are made from the Reserve Account to the Special Disbursement Account when and to the extent needed. For financial year 1998, the Executive Board decided to forgo such reimbursement and to transfer an amount of SDR 40.7 million from the Reserve Account, through the Special Disbursement Account, to the ESAF-HIPC Trust.

Resources of up to SDR 250 million may be transferred, as needed, from the Reserve Account through the Special Disbursement Account to the ESAF-HIPC Trust to be used to provide grant or loans to eligible members under the HIPC initiative. At April 30, 1998, SDR 20.3 million had been transferred for this purpose.

Enhanced Structural Adjustment Facility Trust

Schedule of Outstanding Loans
as at April 30, 1998

(In thousands of SDRs)

Member	ESAF Loan Account		Structural Adjustment Facility[1]	
	Balance	Percent	Balance	Percent
Albania	31,060	0.59	—	—
Armenia, Republic of	67,500	1.28	—	—
Azerbaijan	55,580	1.05	—	—
Bangladesh	248,250	4.71	13,369	1.45
Benin	53,950	1.02	15,451	1.68
Bolivia	178,055	3.38	12,244	1.33
Burkina Faso	48,290	0.92	19,592	2.13
Burundi	15,702	0.30	3,843	0.42
Cambodia	42,000	0.80	—	—
Cameroon	54,040	1.03	—	—
Central African Republic	—	—	4,864	0.53
Chad	33,040	0.63	5,814	0.63
Comoros	—	—	1,980	0.21
Congo, Democratic Republic of	—	—	143,083	15.51
Congo, Republic of	13,896	0.26	—	—
Côte d'Ivoire	416,850	7.91	—	—
Dominica	—	—	106	0.01
Equatorial Guinea	1,650	0.03	8,069	0.88
Ethiopia	14,745	0.28	48,008	5.21
Gambia, The	6,573	0.12	911	0.10
Georgia	111,000	2.11	—	—
Ghana	232,927	4.42	33,742	3.66
Guinea	79,983	1.52	3,474	0.38
Guinea-Bissau	10,500	0.20	675	0.07
Guyana	82,665	1.57	27,798	3.02
Haiti	15,175	0.29	—	—
Honduras	33,222	0.63	—	—
Kenya	148,708	2.82	30,530	3.31
Kyrgyz Republic	88,150	1.67	—	—
Lao People's Democratic Republic	35,190	0.67	12,306	1.34
Lesotho	16,686	0.32	3,171	0.34
Macedonia, former Yugoslav Republic of	18,188	0.35	—	—
Madagascar	35,914	0.68	14,276	1.55
Malawi	50,442	0.96	9,114	0.99
Mali	109,907	2.10	16,764	1.82
Mauritania	78,155	1.48	4,427	0.48
Mongolia	35,245	0.67	—	—
Mozambique	147,450	2.80	2,208	0.24
Nepal	16,225	0.31	5,222	0.57
Nicaragua	36,838	0.70	—	—
Niger	44,428	0.84	1,795	0.19
Pakistan	399,660	7.58	174,816	18.95
Rwanda	—	—	5,256	0.57
São Tomé and Príncipe	—	—	240	0.03
Senegal	203,451	3.86	6,446	0.70
Sierra Leone	96,848	1.84	27,020	2.93
Somalia	—	—	8,840	0.96
Sri Lanka	252,000	4.78	42,389	4.60
Tanzania	163,093	3.09	14,980	1.63
Togo	66,780	1.27	8,256	0.90
Uganda	285,927	5.43	8,964	0.97
Vietnam	241,600	4.58	—	—
Yemen, Republic of	44,000	0.83	—	—
Zambia	661,682	12.54	181,750	19.71
Zimbabwe	146,430	2.78	—	—
Total loans outstanding	5,269,650	100.00	921,793	100.00

[1]Since Structural Adjustment Facility (SAF) loans have been disbursed in connection with ESAF arrangements, the above list includes these loans, as well as loans disbursed to members under SAF arrangements. These loans are held by the Special Disbursement Account, and repayments of all loans are transferred to the ESAF Reserve Account when received.

Enhanced Structural Adjustment Facility Trust

Contributions to and Resources of the Subsidy Account as at April 30, 1998

(In thousands of SDRs)

Contributor[1]	Amount
Direct Contributions to the Subsidy Account	
Argentina	9,067
Bangladesh	186
Canada	79,298
China	4,000
Czech Republic	4,000
Denmark	41,044
Egypt	4,000
Finland	22,684
Germany	107,967
Iceland	2,200
India	2,706
Italy	122,574
Japan	392,999
Korea	28,826
Luxembourg	3,744
Morocco	2,759
Netherlands	68,740
Norway	25,239
Sweden	103,338
Switzerland	12,360
United Kingdom	242,898
United States	72,128
Total direct contributions to the Subsidy Account	1,352,757
Net Income Transferred from Administered Accounts	
Austria	29,438
Belgium	60,089
Botswana	629
Chile	1,589
Greece	19,420
Indonesia	1,647
Iran, Islamic Republic of	328
Portugal	811
Total net income transferred from Administered Accounts	113,951
Total contributions received	1,466,708
Transfers from Special Disbursement Account	400,000
Total contributions received and transfers from Special Disbursement Account	1,866,708
Cumulative net income of the Subsidy Account	448,579
Resources disbursed to subsidize Trust lending	(691,405)
Total resources of the Subsidy Account	1,623,882

[1]In addition to direct contributions, a number of members also make loans available to the Loan Account on concessional terms. See Schedule 3.

Enhanced Structural Adjustment Facility Trust

Schedule of Borrowing Agreements
as at April 30, 1998

(In thousands of SDRs)

Member	Interest Rate (in percent)	Amount of Agreement	Amount Drawn	Outstanding Balance
Loan Account				
Prior to enlargement of ESAF				
Canada	Fixed[1]	300,000	300,000	273,094
France	0.50[2]	800,000	800,000	644,069
Germany	Variable[3]	700,000	700,000	627,730
Italy	Variable[3]	370,000	370,000	349,480
Japan	Variable[3]	2,200,000	2,200,000	1,966,213
Korea	Variable[3]	65,000	65,000	59,058
Norway	Variable[3]	90,000	90,000	80,940
Spain	Variable[3]	220,000	216,429[4]	181,861
Switzerland	—	200,000	200,000	56,205
Total prior to enlargement of ESAF		4,945,000	4,941,429	4,238,650
For enlargement of ESAF				
Canada	Variable[3]	200,000	81,046	81,046
China	Variable[3]	100,000	42,320	42,320
Egypt	Variable[3]	100,000	49,348	49,348
France	0.50[2]	750,000	213,165	213,165
Germany	Variable[3]	700,000	189,677	189,677
Japan	Variable[3]	2,150,000	243,510	243,510
Korea	Variable[3]	27,700	9,094	9,094
Norway	Variable[3]	60,000	24,060	24,060
OPEC Fund for International Development	Variable[3]	37,129[5]	—	—
Spain	0.50	67,000	14,620	14,620
Switzerland	Variable[3]	151,700	97,358	97,358
Total for enlargement of ESAF		4,343,529	964,198	964,198
Resources held pending repayment	—	—	—	233,787[6]
Total—Loan Account		9,288,529	5,905,627	5,436,635
Subsidy Account				
Malaysia (1988 and 1989 loans)	0.50	40,000	40,000	40,000
Malaysia (1994 loan)	2.00	40,000	40,000	40,000
Malta	0.50	2,730	2,730	2,730
Pakistan	0.50	10,000	3,335	3,335
Singapore	2.00	80,000	80,000	80,000
Thailand	2.00[7]	60,000	60,000	—
Tunisia	0.50	3,551	3,551	3,551
Uruguay	Variable[8]	7,200	7,200	7,200
Total—Subsidy Account		243,481	236,816	176,816

[1]The loans under this agreement are made at market-related rates of interest fixed at the time the loan was disbursed.

[2]The agreement with France made before the enlargement of ESAF (SDR 800 million) provides that the interest rate shall be 0.5 percent on the first SDR 700 million drawn, and for variable, market-related rates of interest thereafter. The agreement with France made for the enlargement of the ESAF (SDR 750 million) provides that the interest rate shall be 0.5 percent until the cumulative implicit interest subsidy reaches SDR 250 million, and at variable, market-related rates of interest thereafter.

[3]The loans under these agreements are made at variable, market-related rates of interest.

[4]The agreement expired with an undrawn balance of SDR 3.6 million.

[5]The agreement with the OPEC Fund for International Development is for an amount of $50 million.

[6]This amount represents principal repayments held and invested on behalf of a lender.

[7]In accordance with the agreement with Thailand, outstanding borrowings were repaid at the request of Thailand on January 30, 1998.

[8]The interest rate payable on the borrowing from Uruguay is equal to the rate on SDR-denominated deposits less 2.6 percent a year.

Schedule 4

Enhanced Structural Adjustment Facility Trust
Schedule of Repayments of Borrowing
as at April 30, 1998

(In thousands of SDRs)

Periods of Repayment, Financial Year Ending April 30[1]	Loan Account[1]	Subsidy Account
1999	310,313	40,000
2000	393,078	20,000
2001	466,532	10,000
2002	494,968	10,000
2003	520,222	1,365
2004	624,369	—
2005	601,542	90,751
2006	1,158,857	—
2007	502,744	—
2008	364,010	1,365
2010	—	2,668
2014	—	667
Total	5,436,635	176,816

[1]Repayment periods are as provided in the borrowing agreements between the Trustee and lenders, including maximum periods for those repayments which are to be held in suspense, as agreed with the lender. See Note 4.

Enhanced Structural Adjustment Facility Trust

Status of Loan Arrangements[1]
as at April 30, 1998

(In thousands of SDRs)

Member	Date of Arrangement	Expiration	Amount Agreed	Undrawn Balance
Armenia, Republic of	Feb. 14, 1996	Feb. 13, 1999	101,250	33,750
Azerbaijan	Dec. 20, 1996	Dec. 19, 1999	93,600	38,020
Benin	Aug. 28, 1996	Aug. 27, 1999	27,180	18,120
Bolivia	Dec. 19, 1994	Sep. 9, 1998	100,960	—
Burkina Faso	June 14, 1996	June 13, 1999	39,780	19,890
Cameroon	Aug. 20, 1997	Aug. 19, 2000	162,120	108,080
Chad	Sep. 1, 1995	Aug. 31, 1998	49,560	16,520
Congo, Republic of	June 28, 1996	June 27, 1999	69,480	55,584
Côte d'Ivoire	Mar. 17, 1998	Mar. 16, 2001	285,840	202,470
Ethiopia	Oct. 11, 1996	Oct. 10, 1999	88,470	73,725
Georgia	Feb. 28, 1996	Feb. 27, 1999	166,500	55,500
Ghana	June 30, 1995	June 29, 1999	164,400	68,500
Guinea	Jan. 13, 1997	Jan. 12, 2000	70,800	35,400
Guinea-Bissau	Jan. 18, 1995	July 24, 1998	10,500	—
Haiti	Oct. 18, 1996	Oct. 17, 1999	91,050	75,875
Kenya	Apr. 26, 1996	Apr. 25, 1999	149,550	124,625
Macedonia, former Yugoslav Republic of	Apr. 11, 1997	Apr. 10, 2000	54,560	36,372
Madagascar	Nov. 27, 1996	Nov. 26, 1999	81,360	54,240
Malawi	Oct. 18, 1995	Oct. 17, 1998	45,810	15,270
Mali	Apr. 10, 1996	Apr. 9, 1999	62,010	20,670
Mauritania	Jan. 25, 1995	July 13, 1998	42,750	—
Mongolia	July 30, 1997	July 29, 2000	33,390	27,825
Mozambique	June 21, 1996	June 20, 1999	75,600	25,200
Nicaragua	Mar. 18, 1998	Mar. 17, 2001	100,905	84,088
Niger	June 12, 1996	June 11, 1999	57,960	19,320
Pakistan	Oct. 20, 1997	Oct. 19, 2000	682,380	454,920
Senegal	Apr. 20, 1998	Apr. 19, 2001	107,010	89,175
Sierra Leone	Mar. 28, 1994	May 4, 1998	101,904	5,056
Tanzania	Nov. 8, 1996	Nov. 7, 1999	161,590	74,468
Togo	Sep. 16, 1994	June 29, 1998	65,160	10,860
Uganda	Nov. 10, 1997	Nov. 9, 2000	100,425	60,255
Yemen	Oct. 29, 1997	Oct. 28, 2000	264,750	220,750
Zambia	Dec. 6, 1995	Dec. 5, 1998	701,682	40,000
			4,410,286	2,164,528

[1]The Saudi Fund for Development may also provide resources to support arrangements under the ESAF through loans to qualifying members in association with loans under the ESAF. As at April 30, 1998, SDR 49.5 million of such associated loans had been disbursed.

Enhanced Structural Adjustment Facility Trust
Schedule of Repayments of Loans Receivable
as at April 30, 1998

(In thousands of SDRs)

Periods of Repayment, Financial Year Ending April 30	Loan Account
1999	375,767
2000	463,331
2001	511,686
2002	680,726
2003	722,241
2004	803,893
2005	677,260
2006	565,749
2007	303,663
2008	165,334
Total	5,269,650

Enhanced Structural Adjustment Facility Administered Accounts

Balance Sheets
as at April 30, 1998 and 1997

(In thousands of SDRs)
(Note 1)

	Austria		Belgium		Botswana		Chile	
	1998	1997	1998	1997	1998	1997	1998	1997
Assets								
Investments (Note 2)	62,000	74,000	180,000	180,000	6,894	6,894	15,000	15,000
Interest receivable	1,736	740	1,521	872	71	66	557	370
Advance payments to the								
ESAF Subsidy Account	—	—	—	—	44	49	—	—
Total Assets	63,736	74,740	181,521	180,872	7,009	7,009	15,557	15,370
Resources and Liabilities								
Resources	1,496	491	1,365	717	—	—	514	327
Deposits (Note 3)	62,000	74,000	180,000	180,000	6,894	6,894	15,000	15,000
Interest payable	240	249	156	155	115	115	43	43
Total Resources and Liabilities	63,736	74,740	181,521	180,872	7,009	7,009	15,557	15,370

	Greece		Indonesia		Iran, I. R. of		Portugal	
	1998	1997	1998	1997	1998	1997	1998	1997
Assets								
Investments (Note 2)	42,000	49,000	25,000	25,000	4,000	3,000	8,764	6,573
Interest receivable	1,334	551	764	281	41	29	40	29
Advance payments to the								
ESAF Subsidy Account	—	—	—	139	—	—	2	2
Total Assets	43,334	49,551	25,764	25,420	4,041	3,029	8,806	6,604
Resources and Liabilities								
Resources	1,295	498	286	—	23	15	—	—
Deposits (Note 3)	42,000	49,000	25,000	25,000	4,000	3,000	8,764	6,573
Interest payable	39	53	478	420	18	14	42	31
Total Resources and Liabilities	43,334	49,551	25,764	25,420	4,041	3,029	8,806	6,604

The accompanying notes are an integral part of the financial statements.

/s/ David Williams
Treasurer

/s/ M. Camdessus
Managing Director

Enhanced Structural Adjustment Facility Administered Accounts

Income Statements
for the Years Ended April 30, 1998 and 1997

(In thousands of SDRs)
(Note 1)

	Austria		Belgium		Botswana		Chile	
	1998	1997	1998	1997	1998	1997	1998	1997
Investment income	2,808	3,080	7,869	7,235	287	269	636	594
Interest expense on deposits	335	395	900	900	138	138	75	75
Net Income	2,473	2,685	6,969	6,335	149	131	561	519

	Greece		Indonesia		Iran, I. R. of		Portugal	
	1998	1997	1998	1997	1998	1997	1998	1997
Investment income	1,886	2,050	1,059	989	163	113	374	259
Interest expense on deposits	223	258	558	503	20	14	43	32
Net Income	1,663	1,792	501	486	143	99	331	227

The accompanying notes are an integral part of the financial statements.

Enhanced Structural Adjustment Facility Administered Accounts

Statements of Changes in Resources
for the Years Ended April 30, 1998 and 1997

(In thousands of SDRs)
(Note 1)

	Austria		Belgium		Botswana		Chile	
	1998	1997	1998	1997	1998	1997	1998	1997
Balance, beginning of the year	491	232	717	378	—	—	327	—
Net income	2,473	2,685	6,969	6,335	149	131	561	519
Transfers to the ESAF Trust Subsidy Account	(1,468)	(2,426)	(6,321)	(5,996)	(149)	(131)	(374)	(192)
Balance, end of the year	1,496	491	1,365	717	—	—	514	327

	Greece		Indonesia		Iran, I. R. of		Portugal	
	1998	1997	1998	1997	1998	1997	1998	1997
Balance, beginning of the year	498	5	—	—	15	10	—	—
Net income	1,663	1,792	501	486	143	99	331	227
Transfers to the ESAF Trust Subsidy Account	(866)	(1,299)	(215)	(486)	(135)	(94)	(331)	(227)
Balance, end of the year	1,295	498	286	—	23	15	—	—

The accompanying notes are an integral part of the financial statements.

Enhanced Structural Adjustment Facility Administered Accounts
Saudi Fund for Development Special Account

Statements of Receipts and Uses of Resources
as at April 30, 1998 and 1997

(In thousands of SDRs)
(Note 1)

	1998	1997
Receipts of Resources		
Cumulative transfers from the Saudi Fund for Development	49,500	49,500
Cumulative repayments of associated loans	5,450	1,750
Cumulative receipts of interest on associated loans	1,082	843
Accrued interest on associated loans	75	81
	56,107	52,174
Uses of Resources		
Associated loans (Note 4)	49,500	49,500
Cumulative repayments to the Saudi Fund for Development	5,450	1,750
Cumulative payments of interest on transfers......................................	1,082	843
Accrued interest on transfers	75	81
	56,107	52,174

The accompanying notes are an integral part of the financial statements.

Enhanced Structural Adjustment Facility Administered Accounts

Notes to the Financial Statements
as at April 30, 1998 and 1997

Purpose

At the request of certain member countries, the IMF has established administered accounts for the benefit of the Subsidy Account of the Enhanced Structural Adjustment Facility Trust (the ESAF Trust) for the administration of resources deposited therein. The difference between interest earned by the administered accounts and the interest payable on deposits is transferred to the Subsidy Account of the ESAF Trust.

The Saudi Fund for Development (SFD) Special Account was established at the request of the SFD for the disbursement of amounts under loans made in association with loans under the Enhanced Structural Adjustment Facility (ESAF) by the SFD to recipient countries (associated loans). Disbursements were made simultaneously with ESAF disbursements, and payments of interest and repayments of principal due to the SFD under associated loans are to be transferred to the SFD. The IMF acts as agent of the SFD in that respect.

The resources of each administered account are separate from the assets of all other accounts of, or administered by, the IMF and may not be used to discharge liabilities or to meet losses incurred in the administration of other accounts.

1. Accounting Practices

The administered accounts are expressed in terms of the SDR. SDRs are reserve assets allocated to participants in the IMF's SDR Department. The currency value of the SDR is determined by the IMF each day by summing the values in U.S.

dollars, based on market exchange rates, of a basket of five currencies. The IMF reviews the SDR valuation basket every five years. The SDR valuation basket was last reviewed in financial year 1996. The currencies in the basket and their amounts are as follows:

Currency	Amount
U.S. dollar	0.582
Deutsche mark	0.446
Japanese yen	27.2
French franc	0.813
Pound sterling	0.105

The administered accounts are maintained on the accrual basis; accordingly, income is recognized as it is earned, and expenses are recorded as they are incurred.

2. Investments

The resources of each administered account are invested in SDR-denominated deposits and valued at cost, which approximates market value.

3. Deposits

The Administered Account Austria was established on December 27, 1988 for the administration of resources deposited in the account by the Austrian National Bank. Two deposits (one of SDR 60.0 million made on December 30, 1988, and one of SDR 50.0 million made on August 10,

1995) are to be repaid in ten equal semiannual installments beginning 5½ years after the date of each deposit and ending at the end of the tenth year after the date of each deposit. The deposits bear interest at a rate of ½ of 1 percent a year.

The Administered Account Belgium was established on July 27, 1988 for the administration of resources deposited in the account by the National Bank of Belgium. Four deposits (one of SDR 30.0 million made on July 29, 1988; one of SDR 35.0 million made on December 30, 1988; one of SDR 35.0 million made on June 30, 1989; and one of SDR 80.0 million made on April 29, 1994) have an initial maturity of six months and are renewable, at the option of the IMF, on the same basis. The final maturity of each deposit, including renewals, will be ten years from the initial date of the individual deposits. The deposits bear interest at a rate of ½ of 1 percent a year.

The Administered Account Botswana was established on July 1, 1994 for the administration of resources deposited in the account by the Bank of Botswana. The deposit, totaling SDR 6.9 million, is to be repaid in one installment ten years after the date of deposit. The deposit bears interest at a rate of 2 percent a year.

The Administered Account Chile was established on October 4, 1994 for the administration of resources deposited in the account by the Banco Central de Chile. The deposit, totaling SDR 15.0 million, is to be repaid in one installment ten years after the date of deposit. The deposit bears interest at a rate of ½ of 1 percent a year.

The Administered Account Greece was established on November 30, 1988 for the administration of resources deposited in the account by the Bank of Greece. Two deposits, of SDR 35.0 million each (December 15, 1988 and April 29, 1994), are to be repaid in ten equal semiannual installments beginning 5½ years after the date of deposit and will be completed at the end of the tenth year after the date of the deposits. The deposits bear interest at a rate of ½ of 1 percent a year.

The Administered Account Indonesia was established on June 30, 1994 for the administration of resources deposited in the account by the Bank Indonesia. The deposit, totaling SDR 25.0 million, is to be repaid in one installment ten years after the date the deposit was made. The interest payable on the deposit is equivalent to that obtained for the investment of the deposit less 2 percent a year.

The Administered Account Islamic Republic of Iran was established on June 6, 1994 for the administration of resources deposited in the account by the Central Bank of the Islamic Republic of Iran (CBIRI). The CBIRI has agreed to make five annual deposits, each of SDR 1.0 million. All of the deposits will be repaid at the end of ten years after the date of the first deposit. Each deposit bears interest at a rate of ½ of 1 percent a year.

The Administered Account Portugal was established on May 16, 1994 for the administration of resources deposited in the account by the Banco de Portugal (BdP). The BdP has agreed to make six annual deposits, each of SDR 2.2 million. Each deposit is to be repaid in five equal annual installments beginning six years after the date of the deposit and will be completed at the end of the tenth year after the date of the deposit. Each deposit bears interest at a rate of ½ of 1 percent a year.

4. Associated Loans

The SFD agreed to provide resources up to the equivalent of SDR 200.0 million to support arrangements under the ESAF through loans in association with loans under the ESAF. Funds become available under an associated loan after a bilateral agreement between the SFD and the recipient country has been effected. Amounts denominated in SDRs, for disbursement to a recipient country under an associated loan, are placed by the SFD in the Special Account for disbursement by the IMF simultaneously with disbursements under an ESAF arrangement. These loans are repayable in ten equal semiannual installments commencing not later than the end of the first six months of the sixth year, and are to be completed at the end of the tenth year after the date of disbursement. Interest on the outstanding balance is currently set at the rate of ½ of 1 percent a year.

ESAF-HIPC Trust

Balance Sheets
as at April 30, 1998 and 1997

(In thousands of SDRs)
(Note 1)

	ESAF-HIPC Trust Account 1998	1997	Umbrella Account for HIPC Operations for the Period April 1, 1998 to April 30, 1998
Assets			
Investments (Note 2)	19,236	16,884	51,514
Transfer receivable (Note 3)	40,700	—	—
Interest receivable	50	—	99
	59,986	16,884	51,613
Resources and Liabilities			
Resources	44,374	2,277	51,613
Deposits (Note 4)	15,607	14,607	—
Interest payable	5	—	—
	59,986	16,884	51,613

The accompanying notes are an integral part of the financial statements.

/s/ David Williams
Treasurer

/s/ M. Camdessus
Managing Director

ESAF-HIPC Trust

Income Statements and Changes in Resources
for the Years Ended April 30, 1998 and 1997

(In thousands of SDRs)
(Note 1)

	ESAF-HIPC Trust Account 1998	1997	Umbrella Account for HIPC Operations for the Period April 1, 1998 to April 30, 1998
Balance, beginning of the year	2,277	—	—
Transfers through the Special Disbursement Account from the ESAF Trust Reserve Account (Note 3)	60,989	—	—
Contributions received (Note 3)	31,928	2,261	—
Income earned on investments (Note 2)	991	16	99
HIPC grants (Note 5)	(51,514)	—	51,514
Interest expense on deposits (Note 4)	(297)	—	—
Net changes in resources	42,097	2,277	51,613
Balance, end of the year	44,374	2,277	51,613

The accompanying notes are an integral part of the financial statements.

ESAF-HIPC Trust
Notes to the Financial Statements
as at April 30, 1998 and 1997

Purpose

The Trust for Special ESAF Operations for the Heavily Indebted Poor Countries and for Interim ESAF Subsidy Operations ("the ESAF-HIPC Trust"), for which the IMF is Trustee, was established on February 4, 1997 to provide balance of payments assistance to low-income developing members by making grants and loans to eligible members for the purpose of reducing their external debt burden and for interim ESAF subsidy purposes. The resources of the Trust are separate from the assets of all other accounts of, or administered by, the IMF and may not be used to discharge liabilities or to meet losses incurred in the administration of other accounts.

The operations of the Trust are conducted through the ESAF-HIPC Trust Account and the Umbrella Account for HIPC Operations.

ESAF-HIPC Trust Account

The resources of the ESAF-HIPC Trust Account consist of grant contributions, deposits, loans, and other types of investments made by contributors; amounts transferred by the IMF from the Special Disbursement Account; and net earnings from investment of resources held in the ESAF-HIPC Trust Account.

The resources held in the ESAF-HIPC Trust Account are to be used by the Trustee to make grants or loans to eligible members that qualify for assistance under the HIPC Initiative and for subsidizing the interest rate on interim ESAF operations to ESAF-eligible members.

Umbrella Account for HIPC Operations

The Umbrella Account for HIPC Operations ("Umbrella Account") receives and administers the proceeds of grants or loans made to eligible members that qualify for assistance under the terms of the ESAF-HIPC Trust. Within the Umbrella Account, resources received are administered through the establishment of subaccounts for each eligible member upon the approval of a disbursement under the ESAF-HIPC Trust.

The resources of a subaccount of the Umbrella Account consist of (i) amounts disbursed from the ESAF-HIPC Trust Account as grants or loans for the benefit of a member, and (ii) net earnings from investment of the resources held in the subaccount.

The resources held in a subaccount of the Umbrella Account are to be used to meet the member's debt obligations to the IMF in accordance with the schedule agreed upon by the Trustee and the member for the use of the proceeds of ESAF-HIPC disbursements.

1. Accounting Practices

The accounts of the Trust are expressed in terms of the SDR. SDRs are reserve assets allocated to participants in the IMF's SDR Department. The currency value of the SDR is determined by the IMF each day by summing the values in U.S. dollars, based on market exchange rates, of a basket of five

currencies. The IMF reviews the SDR valuation basket every five years. The SDR valuation basket was last reviewed in financial year 1996. The currencies in the basket and their amounts are as follows:

Currency	Amount
U.S. dollar	0.582
Deutsche mark	0.446
Japanese yen	27.2
French franc	0.813
Pound sterling	0.105

Members are not obligated to maintain the SDR value of their currencies held in the accounts of the Trust.

The accounts of the Trust are maintained on the accrual basis; accordingly, income is recognized as it is earned, and expenses are recorded as they are incurred.

2. Investments

The resources of the ESAF-HIPC Trust are invested pending their use. Investments are denominated in SDRs or in currency and are carried at cost, which does not exceed net realizable value. Pending their investment, resources may be temporarily held in currency, which also may give rise to valuation gains and losses.

3. Contributions and Transfers

ESAF-HIPC Trust Account

The Trustee accepts contributions of resources on such terms and conditions as agreed between the Trust and the contributor. At April 30, 1998, four contributions amounting to SDR 34.2 million had been received: SDR 2.3 million from Finland; SDR 1.1 million from Nigeria; SDR 27.2 million from Japan; and SDR 3.6 million from the Netherlands. The contribution from the Netherlands is earmarked for interim ESAF subsidy operations. At April 30, 1997, one contribution amounting to SDR 2.3 million had been received from Finland. This amount was transferred to the Trust from the Temporary Administered Account for ESAF-HIPC Operations, which was terminated on February 12, 1997.

Total transfers from the ESAF Trust Reserve Account through the Special Disbursement Account amount to SDR 61.0 million. Of this amount, SDR 20.3 million has been transferred to the Trust from the ESAF Trust Reserve Account, through the Special Disbursement Account to provide grants or loans to eligible members. In addition, the Executive Board decided to transfer an amount of SDR 40.7 million from the ESAF Trust Reserve Account, through the Special Disbursement Account, to the ESAF-HIPC Trust.

Umbrella Account

The Umbrella Account receives the proceeds of grants or loans disbursed by the ESAF-HIPC Trust on behalf of an eligible member. At April 30, 1998 a grant amounting to SDR 51.5 million had been received on behalf of Uganda.

4. Deposits

ESAF-HIPC Trust Account

The Trustee accepts deposits, loans, and other types of investments made by contributors to the Trust on such terms and conditions as agreed between the Trust and the Contributor. At April 30, 1998, two deposits amounting to SDR 15.6 million had been received by the ESAF-HIPC Trust Account. The first deposit of SDR 14.6 million bears interest at a rate of 2 percent a year and is to be repaid in one installment five years after the date of deposit, made on April 30, 1997. The second deposit of SDR 1 million bears interest at a rate of ½ of 1 percent a year and is to be repaid in one installment ten years after the date of the deposit, made on May 30, 1997.

5. Disbursements

ESAF-HIPC Trust Account

The proceeds of grants or loans made on behalf of an eligible member are paid in a single disbursement to the Umbrella Account for the benefit of that member. Resources needed for interim ESAF subsidy operations will be drawn by the Trustee on an as-needed basis. At April 30, 1998, a single disbursement of SDR 51.5 million had been made to the Umbrella Account for the benefit of Uganda.

Umbrella Account

The resources of a subaccount within the Umbrella Account, including any income from investment, shall be used to meet the member's debt service payments on its existing debt to the IMF as they fall due in accordance with the schedule agreed upon by the Trustee and the member. At April 30, 1998, no disbursements had been made from a subaccount within the Umbrella Account.

Administered Accounts
Established at the Request of Members
Balance Sheets
as at April 30, 1998 and 1997
(Note 1)

	Administered Account Japan		Administered Account for Selected Fund Activities—Japan		Framework Administered Account for Technical Assistance Activities		Administered Account for Rwanda	
	1998	1997	1998	1997	1998	1997	1998	1997
	(In thousands of U.S. dollars)						*(In thousands of SDRs)*	
Assets								
Investments (Note 2)	96,700	91,500	20,634	14,996	3,389	3,029	788	1,118
Currency deposit	83	61	—	—	—	—	—	—
Interest receivable	—	—	—	—	—	—	8	11
Total Assets	96,783	91,561	20,634	14,996	3,389	3,029	796	1,129
Resources								
Total Resources	96,783	91,561	20,634	14,996	3,389	3,029	796	1,129

The accompanying notes are an integral part of the financial statements.

/s/ David Williams
Treasurer

/s/ M. Camdessus
Managing Director

Administered Accounts
Established at the Request of Members
Income Statements and Changes in Resources
for the Years Ended April 30, 1998 and 1997
(Note 1)

	Administered Account Japan		Administered Account for Selected Fund Activities—Japan		Framework Administered Account for Technical Assistance Activities		Administered Account for Rwanda	
	1998	1997	1998	1997	1998	1997	1998	1997
	(In thousands of U.S. dollars)						*(In thousands of SDRs)*	
Balance, beginning of the year	91,561	71,102	14,996	11,742	3,029	970	1,129	1,432
Contributions	—	16,495	18,868	20,950	2,961	2,985	—	—
Income earned on investments (Note 2)	5,222	3,964	1,073	788	177	97	38	49
	96,783	91,561	34,937	33,480	6,167	4,052	1,167	1,481
Payments to beneficiaries ..	—	—	14,303	18,484	2,778	1,023	371	352
Balance, end of the year	96,783	91,561	20,634	14,996	3,389	3,029	796	1,129

The accompanying notes are an integral part of the financial statements.

Administered Accounts Established at the Request of Members

Notes to the Financial Statements
as at April 30, 1998 and 1997

Purpose

At the request of members, the IMF has established special purpose accounts to administer contributed resources and to perform financial and technical services consistent with the purposes of the IMF. The assets of each account and each subaccount are separate from the assets of all other accounts of, or administered by, the IMF and are not to be used to discharge liabilities or to meet losses incurred in the administration of other accounts.

Administered Account Japan

At the request of Japan, the IMF established an account on March 3, 1989 to administer resources, made available by Japan or other countries with Japan's concurrence, that are to be used to assist certain members with overdue obligations to the IMF. The resources of the account are to be disbursed in amounts specified by Japan and to members designated by Japan. At April 30, 1998 and 1997, cumulative resources received amounted to $135.2 million, of which $72.5 million had been disbursed.

Administered Account for Selected Fund Activities—Japan

At the request of Japan, the IMF established the Administered Technical Assistance Account—Japan on March 19, 1990 to administer resources contributed by Japan that are used to finance technical assistance to member countries. On July 21, 1997 the account was renamed the Administered Account for Selected Fund Activities—Japan and amended to include the administration of resources contributed by Japan in support of the IMF's Regional Office for Asia and the Pacific (OAP). The resources of the account designated for technical assistance activities are used with the approval of Japan and include the provision of scholarships; the resources designated for the OAP are used as agreed between Japan and the IMF for certain activities of the IMF with respect to Asia and the Pacific through the OAP. Disbursements can also be made from the account to the General Resources Account to reimburse the IMF for qualifying technical assistance projects and OAP expenses. At April 30, 1998, cumulative contributions received by the account designated for technical assistance amounted to $98.2 million, of which $81.3 million had been disbursed ($80.6 million and $68.0 million, respectively, at April 30, 1997). Cumulative contributions include $4.7 million earmarked for scholarships, of which $4.4 million had been disbursed at April 30, 1998 ($3.5 million and $3.3 million, respectively, at April 30, 1997). At April 30, 1998, contributions designated for the OAP amounted to $1.2 million, of which $1.0 million had been disbursed.

Framework Administered Account for Technical Assistance Activities

The Framework Administered Account for Technical Assistance Activities ("the Framework Account") was established by the IMF on April 3, 1995 to receive and administer contributed resources that are to be used to finance technical assistance consistent with the purposes of the IMF. The financing of technical assistance activities is implemented through the establishment and operation of subaccounts within the Framework Account. The establishment of a subaccount requires the approval of the Executive Board.

Resources are to be used in accordance with the written understandings between the contributor and the Managing Director. Disbursements can also be made from the Framework Account to the General Resources Account to reimburse the IMF for its costs incurred on behalf of technical assistance activities financed by resources from the Framework Account. At April 30, 1998, cumulative contributions received by the account amounted to $7.1 million, of which $4.0 million had been disbursed ($4.1 million and $1.2 million, respectively, at April 30, 1997).

Subaccount for Japan Advanced Scholarship Program

At the request of Japan, this subaccount was established on June 6, 1995 to finance the cost of studies and training of nationals of member countries in macroeconomics and related subjects at selected universities and institutions. The scholarship program focuses primarily on the training of nationals of Asian member countries, including Japan. At April 30, 1998, cumulative contributions received amounted to $2.9 million, of which $1.3 million had been disbursed ($1.4 million and $0.3 million, respectively, at April 30, 1997).

Rwanda—Macroeconomic Management Capacity Subaccount

At the request of Rwanda, this subaccount was established on December 20, 1995 to finance technical assistance to rehabilitate and strengthen Rwanda's macroeconomic management capacity. At April 30, 1998, cumulative contributions received amounted to $1.5 million, of which $1.3 million had been disbursed ($1.5 million and $0.6 million, respectively, at April 30, 1997).

Australia—IMF Scholarship Program for Asia Subaccount

At the request of Australia, this subaccount was established on June 5, 1996 to finance the cost of studies and training of government and central bank officials in macroeconomic management so as to enable them to contribute to their countries' achievement of sustainable economic growth and development. The program focuses primarily on the training of nationals of Asian countries. At April 30, 1998, cumulative contributions received amounted to $0.5 million, of which $0.3 million had been disbursed ($0.5 million and $0.07 million, respectively, at April 30, 1997).

Switzerland Technical Assistance Subaccount

At the request of Switzerland, this subaccount was established on August 27, 1996 to finance the costs of technical assistance activities of the IMF that consist of policy advice and training in macroeconomic management. At April 30, 1998, cumulative contributions received amounted to $2.0 million, of which $0.9 million had been disbursed ($0.6 million and $0.08 million, respectively, at April 30, 1997).

French Technical Assistance Subaccount

At the request of France, this subaccount was established on September 30, 1996 to cofinance the costs of training in economic fields for nationals of certain member countries. At April 30, 1998, cumulative contributions received amounted to $0.26 million, of which $0.13 million had been disbursed ($0.09 million, all of which had been disbursed at April 30, 1997).

Administered Account for Rwanda

At the request of the Netherlands, Sweden, and the United States ("the donor countries"), the IMF established an account on October 27, 1995 to administer resources contributed by the donor countries to provide grants to Rwanda. These grants are to be used for reimbursing the service charge and reducing, to the equivalent of a rate of 0.5 percent a year, the rate of the quarterly charges payable by Rwanda on its use of the IMF's financial resources under the Compensatory and Contingency Financing Facility (CCFF). At April 30, 1998, cumulative contributions received by the account amounted to SDR 1.54 million, of which SDR 0.86 million had been disbursed (SDR 1.54 million and SDR 0.49 million, respectively, at April 30, 1997).

1. Accounting Practices

The accounts are maintained on the accrual basis; accordingly, income is recognized as it is earned, and expenses are recorded as they are incurred.

Administered Account Japan, Administered Account for Selected Fund Activities—Japan, and Framework Administered Account for Technical Assistance Activities

The accounts are expressed in U.S. dollars. All transactions and operations of these accounts, including the transfers to and from the accounts, are denominated in U.S. dollars, except for transactions and operations in respect of the OAP, which are denominated in Japanese yen, or in other currencies as agreed between Japan and the IMF. Contributions denominated in other currencies are converted into U.S. dollars upon receipt of the funds.

Administered Account for Rwanda

The accounts are expressed in SDRs. The currency value of the SDR is determined by the IMF each day by summing the values in U.S. dollars, based on market exchange rates, of a basket of five currencies. The IMF reviews the SDR valuation basket every five years. The SDR valuation basket was last reviewed in financial year 1996. The currencies in the basket and their amounts are as follows:

Currency	Amount
U.S. dollar	0.582
Deutsche mark	0.446
Japanese yen	27.2
French franc	0.813
Pound sterling	0.105

Transfers to and disbursements from the accounts are made in U.S. dollars or in other freely usable currencies. Transactions and operations of the accounts shall be denominated in SDRs. Contributions denominated in other currencies are converted into SDRs upon receipt of the funds.

2. Investments

The assets of the accounts are invested pending their disbursement and are valued at cost, which approximates market value. Interest received on these assets varies and is market related.

3. Accounts Termination

Administered Account Japan

The account can be terminated by the IMF or by Japan. Any remaining resources in the account at termination are to be returned promptly to Japan.

Administered Account for Selected Fund Activities—Japan

The account can be terminated by the IMF or by Japan. Any resources that may remain in the account at termination, net of accrued liabilities under technical assistance projects or in respect of the OAP, are to be returned promptly to Japan.

Framework Administered Account for Technical Assistance Activities

The Framework Account or any subaccount thereof may be terminated by the IMF at any time. The termination of the Framework Account shall terminate each subaccount thereof. A subaccount may also be terminated by the contributor of the resources to the subaccount. Termination shall be effective on the date that the IMF or the contributor, as the case may be, receives notice of termination. Any balances, net of the continuing liabilities and commitments under the activities financed, that may remain in a subaccount upon its termination are to be returned promptly to the contributor.

Administered Account for Rwanda

The account can be terminated at any time by the IMF or by unanimous agreement of the donor countries. The account shall, in any case, be terminated by the IMF when Rwanda's financial obligations to the IMF under the CCFF have been fully discharged or when the resources of the account have been exhausted, whichever is earlier. Any balance in the account at termination shall be transferred promptly to the donor countries, in proportion to their contribution, or to Rwanda, if so instructed.

Trust Fund

Balance Sheets
as at April 30, 1998 and 1997

(In thousands of SDRs)
(Note 1)

	1998	1997
Assets		
Loans receivable (Note 2)	89,784	90,444
Interest and charges receivable and accrued (Note 3)	25,952	25,501
Total Assets	115,736	115,945
Resources and Deferred Income		
Trust resources	89,784	90,444
Deferred income (Note 3)	25,952	25,501
Total Resources and Deferred Income	115,736	115,945

The accompanying notes are an integral part of the financial statements.

/s/ David Williams
Treasurer

/s/ M. Camdessus
Managing Director

Trust Fund

Income Statements
for the Years Ended April 30, 1998 and 1997

(In thousands of SDRs)
(Note 1)

	1998	1997
Income		
Interest and charges on loans (Note 2)	450	469
Deferred income, net of settlements (Note 3)	(450)	(300)
Net Income	—	169

The accompanying notes are an integral part of the financial statements.

Trust Fund

Statements of Changes in Resources
for the Years Ended April 30, 1998 and 1997

(In thousands of SDRs)
(Note 1)

	1998	1997
Balance, beginning of the year	90,444	95,135
Net Income	—	169
Balance before transfers to the Special Disbursement Account	90,444	95,304
Transfers to the Special Disbursement Account (Note 4)	(660)	(4,860)
Balance, end of the year	89,784	90,444

The accompanying notes are an integral part of the financial statements.

Trust Fund

Notes to the Financial Statements
as at April 30, 1998 and 1997

Purpose

The Trust Fund, for which the IMF is Trustee, was established in 1976 to provide balance of payments assistance on concessional terms to eligible members that qualify for assistance.

In 1980, the IMF, as Trustee, decided that, upon the completion of the final loan disbursements, the Trust Fund would be terminated as of April 30, 1981, and after that date the activities of the Trust Fund have been confined to the conclusion of its affairs. The resources of the Trust Fund are separate from the assets of all other accounts of, or administered by, the IMF and cannot be used to discharge liabilities or to meet losses incurred in the administration of other IMF accounts.

1. Accounting Practices

The accounts of the Trust Fund are expressed in terms of the SDR. SDRs are reserve assets allocated to participants in the IMF's SDR Department. The currency value of the SDR is determined by the IMF each day by summing the values in U.S. dollars, based on market exchange rates, of a basket of five currencies. The IMF reviews the SDR valuation basket every five years. The SDR valuation basket was last reviewed in financial year 1996. The currencies in the basket and their amounts are as follows:

Currency	Amount
U.S. dollar	0.582
Deutsche mark	0.446
Japanese yen	27.2
French franc	0.813
Pound sterling	0.105

The accounts are maintained on the accrual basis; accordingly, income is recognized as it is earned, and expenses are recorded as they are incurred, except that interest income from members that are overdue in settling their obligations to the Trust Fund by six months or more is deferred and is recognized as income only when paid, unless the member has remained current in settling charges when due (see Note 3). Following the termination of the Trust Fund as of April 30, 1981, residual administrative costs have been absorbed by the General Resources Account of the IMF.

2. Loans

Loans were made from the Trust Fund to those eligible members that qualified for assistance in accordance with the provisions of the Trust Fund instrument. The final Trust Fund loan installment was due on March 31, 1991. Interest on the outstanding loan balances is charged at the rate of ½ of 1 percent a year, although special charges have been levied on overdue payments of interest and principal since February 1986. Beginning May 1, 1993, special charges on overdue obligations to the Trust Fund have been suspended for members who are more than six months overdue.

3. Overdue Obligations

At April 30, 1998 and 1997, three members with obligations to the Trust Fund were six months or more overdue in discharging their obligations to the Trust Fund. The recognition of interest income on the loans outstanding to these members and of special charges due from them is being deferred. At April 30, 1998, total deferred income amounted to SDR 26.0 million (SDR 25.5 million at April 30, 1997). Overdue loan repayments and interest and special charges due from these members were as follows:

	Loans		Interest and Special Charges	
	1998	1997	1998	1997
	In millions of SDRs			
Total overdue	89.8	90.4	25.8	25.4
Overdue six months or more	89.8	90.4	25.6	25.1
Overdue three years or more	89.8	90.4	24.4	23.9

The type and duration of the arrears of these members at April 30, 1998 were as follows:

Member	Loans	Interest and Special Charges	Total	Longest Overdue Obligation
	In millions of SDRs			
Liberia	24.1	6.7	30.8	January 1985
Somalia	6.5	1.3	7.8	July 1987
Sudan	59.2	17.8	77.0	June 1985
Total	89.8	25.8	115.6	

4. Transfer of Resources

The resources of the Trust Fund held on April 30, 1981 or received thereafter have been used to pay interest and principal when due on loan obligations and to make transfers to the Special Disbursement Account.

Supplementary Financing Facility Subsidy Account

Balance Sheets
as at April 30, 1998 and 1997

(In thousands of SDRs)
(Note 1)

	1998	1997
Assets		
Deposits (Note 2)	2,381	2,286
Interest receivable	25	22
Total Assets	2,406	2,308
Resources		
Total Resources	2,406	2,308

The accompanying notes are an integral part of the financial statements.

/s/ David Williams
Treasurer

/s/ M. Camdessus
Managing Director

Supplementary Financing Facility Subsidy Account

Income Statements and Changes in Resources
for the Years Ended April 30, 1998 and 1997

(In thousands of SDRs)
(Note 1)

	1998	1997
Balance, beginning of the year	2,308	2,395
Investment income	98	92
Balance before transfers	2,406	2,487
Transfers to the Special Disbursement Account (Note 3)	—	(179)
Balance, end of the year	2,406	2,308

The accompanying notes are an integral part of the financial statements.

Supplementary Financing Facility Subsidy Account
Notes to the Financial Statements
as at April 30, 1998 and 1997

Purpose

The Supplementary Financing Facility Subsidy Account ("the Subsidy Account"), which is administered by the IMF, was established in December 1980 to assist low-income developing country members to meet the cost of using resources made available through the IMF's Supplementary Financing Facility and under the policy on exceptional use. All repurchases due under these policies were scheduled for completion by January 31, 1991, and the final subsidy payments were approved in July 1991. However, two members (Liberia and Sudan), overdue in the payment of charges, remain ineligible to receive previously approved subsidy payments until their overdue charges are settled. Accordingly, the account remains in operation and has retained amounts for payment to these members after the overdue charges are paid.

The resources of the Subsidy Account are separate from the assets of all other accounts of, or administered by, the IMF and cannot be used to discharge liabilities or to meet losses incurred in the administration of other IMF accounts.

1. Accounting Practices

The accounts of the Subsidy Account are expressed in terms of the SDR. SDRs are reserve assets allocated to participants in the IMF's SDR Department. The currency value of the SDR is determined by the IMF each day by summing the values in U.S. dollars, based on market exchange rates, of a basket of five currencies. The IMF reviews the SDR valuation basket every five years. The SDR valuation basket was last reviewed in financial year 1996. The currencies in the basket and their amounts are as follows:

Currency	Amount
U.S. dollar	0.582
Deutsche mark	0.446
Japanese yen	27.2
French franc	0.813
Pound sterling	0.105

The accounts are maintained on the accrual basis; accordingly, income is recognized as it is earned, and expenses are recorded as they are incurred.

2. Deposits

The assets of the Subsidy Account, pending their disbursement, are held in the form of interest-earning time deposits denominated in SDRs.

3. Transfer of Resources

Resources in excess of the remaining subsidy payments are to be transferred to the Special Disbursement Account. At April 30, 1998 and 1997, subsidy payments totaling SDR 2.2 million had not been made to Liberia and Sudan and were being held pending the payment of overdue charges by these members.

Retired Staff Benefits Investment Account
Balance Sheets
as at April 30, 1998 and 1997

(In thousands of U.S. dollars)
(Note 1)

	1998	1997
Assets		
Investments (Note 2)		
Cash equivalents	29,495	32,010
Other	144,878	115,239
	174,373	147,249
Interest and other receivables	1,931	1,171
Total Assets	176,304	148,420
Liabilities and Resources		
Accounts payable	—	3,572
Total Liabilities	—	3,572
Total Resources	176,304	144,848
Total Resources and Liabilities	176,304	148,420

The accompanying notes are an integral part of the financial statements.

/s/ David Williams
Treasurer

/s/ M. Camdessus
Managing Director

Retired Staff Benefits Investment Account
Income Statements and Changes in Resources
for the Years Ended April 30, 1998 and 1997

(In thousands of U.S. dollars)
(Note 1)

	1998	1997
Balance, beginning of the year	144,848	122,310
Contributions received	12,600	12,100
Income earned on investments (Note 2)	7,189	6,547
Net gain in current value of investments (Note 2)	11,667	3,891
Total income	18,856	10,438
Balance, end of the year	176,304	144,848

The accompanying notes are an integral part of the financial statements.

Retired Staff Benefits Investment Account

Notes to the Financial Statements
as at April 30, 1998 and 1997

Purpose

The Retired Staff Benefits Investment Account ("the RSBIA") was established to hold, administer, and invest resources contributed by the IMF for meeting postretirement medical and life insurance benefits to eligible retirees of the IMF and other beneficiaries. The RSBIA accumulates resources to finance benefits to current and future retirees.

The assets of the RSBIA consist of the IMF's contributions and the income earned thereon. Assets are within the sole ownership of the IMF and are to be used to meet the claims of retirees and the administrative costs of the RSBIA. Contributions are made periodically from the General Resources Account to the RSBIA, taking into consideration the actuarial valuation of the IMF's cumulative cost of these benefits. Cumulative contributions received by the RSBIA amounted to $140.1 million at April 30, 1998 ($127.5 million at April 30, 1997).

The portion of the cumulative past-service cost that has been charged to income in the General Resources Account is fully funded.

The assets of the RSBIA are kept separate from the assets of all other accounts of, or administered by, the IMF and are not to be used to discharge liabilities or to meet losses incurred in the administration of other accounts.

1. Accounting Practices

Unit of Account

The RSBIA is expressed in U.S. dollars. All transactions and operations of the RSBIA, including the transfers to and by the RSBIA, are denominated in U.S. dollars. The cost of transactions in other currencies—for example, the payment of future benefits—will be paid by the RSBIA.

The RSBIA is maintained on the accrual basis; accordingly, income is recognized as it is earned, and expenses are recorded as they are incurred.

2. Investments

Resources placed to the RSBIA have been invested by the IMF. In accordance with its investment policy, the RSBIA invests in equity securities, debt securities, short-term investments, and real estate. Investments in securities listed on stock exchanges are valued at the last reported market sales price on the last business day of the accounting period. Over-the-counter securities are valued at their bid price on the last business day of the accounting period. The valuation of purchases and sales is made on the trade date basis.

The net gain in the current value of investments represents the gains and losses realized during the year from the sale of investments, the unrealized appreciation and depreciation of the market value of investments, and, for investments denominated in currencies other than the U.S. dollar, valuation differences arising from exchange rate changes of other currencies against the dollar market value.

A summary of the RSBIA's investments at market values is as follows:

Investments	1998	1997
	In millions of U.S. dollars	
Equity securities	63.3	52.4
Debt securities	62.0	62.7
Short-term investments	29.6	32.2
Real estate	20.6	1.1
	175.5	148.4

In addition to these investments, the RSBIA held commitments in fixed income futures contracts to minimize interest rate risk. At April 30, 1998 the notional value of these derivatives amounted to $11.1 million and the unrealized gain was less than $0.1 million.

3. Actuarial Valuation

Eligible retirees can elect to continue their life insurance coverage and medical coverage. The cost of these benefits is actuarially determined, based on the data in effect at the beginning of the year. The IMF's actuarially determined cost amounted to $183.2 million at April 30, 1998 ($180.1 million at April 30, 1997). Each year the IMF amortizes a portion of the past-service cost and recognizes the increase in the liability during the year as an expense in the General Resources Account. These amounts, less the return on investments, are transferred to the RSBIA to be held and invested pending their use by the IMF. During the year ended April 30, 1998, an amount of $12.6 million has been transferred to the RSBIA ($12.1 million during the year ended April 30, 1997).

It is expected that the RSBIA will be a net recipient of resources until the unfunded cost is fully amortized and its assets meet the cost of benefits to retirees.

4. Account Termination

The RSBIA can be terminated by the IMF at any time. After meeting any existing obligations, the resources remaining in the RSBIA are to be transferred to the General Resources Account of the IMF.

Report of the External Audit Committee
Staff Retirement Plan

Washington, D.C.
June 18, 1998

Authority and Scope of Audit

In accordance with Section 20(b) of the By-Laws of the International Monetary Fund, we have audited the financial statements of the Staff Retirement Plan for the year ended April 30, 1998.

Our audit was conducted in accordance with generally accepted auditing standards and included reviews of the accounting and internal control systems and tests of the accounting records. We evaluated the extent and results of the work of the outside accounting firm as well as that of the Office of Internal Audit and Inspection of the International Monetary Fund and also used other audit procedures as deemed necessary.

Audit Opinion

In our opinion, the financial statements of the Staff Retirement Plan have been prepared in accordance with generally accepted accounting principles applied on a basis consistent with that of the preceding year and give a true and fair view of the financial status of the Staff Retirement Plan as at April 30, 1998 and of the changes in financial status for the year then ended.

EXTERNAL AUDIT COMMITTEE:

/s/ Amaffe Roger Ako, Chairman (Côte d'Ivoire)

/s/ José Nicolás Agudin (Argentina)

/s/ Stephen Park (United Kingdom)

Staff Retirement Plan

Statements of Accumulated Plan Benefits and Net Assets Available for Benefits as at April 30, 1998 and 1997

(In thousands of U.S. dollars)
(Note 1)

	1998	1997
Accumulated Plan Benefits		
Actuarial present value of accumulated Plan benefits		
Vested benefits		
Retired participants	635,000	597,400
Active participants	595,800	516,800
Nonvested benefits	694,700	651,400
Total actuarial present value of accumulated Plan benefits	1,925,500	1,765,600
Assets Available for Benefits		
Investments (Note 3)	3,075,069	2,613,477
Receivables		
Accrued interest and dividends	13,303	12,894
Contributions	1,501	1,862
Other	36	66
	14,840	14,822
Total assets	3,089,909	2,628,299
Liabilities		
Accounts payable	5,428	4,278
Deferred contributions (Note 2)	14,729	—
Total liabilities	20,157	4,278
Net assets available for benefits	3,069,752	2,624,021
Excess of net assets available for benefits over actuarial present value of accumulated Plan benefits (Note 2)	1,144,252	858,421

The accompanying notes are an integral part of the financial statements.

/s/ David Williams
Treasurer

/s/ M. Camdessus
Managing Director

Staff Retirement Plan

Statements of Changes in Accumulated Plan Benefits for the Years Ended April 30, 1998 and 1997

(In thousands of U.S. dollars)
(Note 1)

	1998	1997
Actuarial present value of accumulated Plan benefits, beginning of the year	1,765,600	1,644,400
Increase (decrease) during the year attributable to		
Benefits accumulated (Note 1)	67,300	36,838
Interest accrued	147,800	137,600
Benefits paid	(55,200)	(53,238)
Net increase	159,900	121,200
Actuarial present value of accumulated Plan benefits, end of the year	1,925,500	1,765,600

The accompanying notes are an integral part of the financial statements.

Staff Retirement Plan

Statements of Changes
in Net Assets Available for Benefits
for the Years Ended April 30, 1998 and 1997

(In thousands of U.S. dollars)
(Note 1)

	1998	1997
Investment Income		
Net realized/unrealized gain on investments (Note 3)	404,944	129,507
Interest and dividends	87,296	84,769
	492,240	214,276
Contributions (Note 2)		
International Monetary Fund	151	29,548
Participants	20,970	19,759
Participants restored to service	133	275
Net transfers (to) from retirement plans of other international organizations	(209)	343
	21,045	49,925
Total additions	513,285	264,201
Benefits		
Pension	44,543	41,399
Commutation	5,045	8,183
Withdrawal	3,859	3,383
Death	406	273
	53,853	53,238
Investment Fees	13,701	12,617
Total payments	67,554	65,855
Net additions	445,731	198,346
Net Assets Available for Benefits		
Beginning of the year	2,624,021	2,425,675
End of the year	3,069,752	2,624,021

The accompanying notes are an integral part of the financial statements.

Staff Retirement Plan
Notes to the Financial Statements
as at April 30, 1998 and 1997

Description of the Plan

General

The Staff Retirement Plan ("the Plan") is a defined-benefit pension plan covering nearly all staff members of the International Monetary Fund ("the Employer"). All assets and income of the Plan are the property of the Employer and are held and administered by it separately from all its other property and assets and are to be used solely for the benefit of participants, retired participants, and their beneficiaries.

Benefits
Annual Pension

Participants are entitled to an unreduced pension beginning at normal retirement age of 62. The amount of the pension is based on the number of years of service, age at retirement, and highest average gross remuneration. The provisions for determining gross remuneration are different for benefits earned before and after May 1, 1990. The gross remuneration on which pensions from the Plan are based is limited to a predetermined amount, which is periodically adjusted. Pension benefits attributable to gross remuneration in excess of this amount are paid from the Supplemental Retirement Benefit Plan ("the SRBP").

The accrual rate of benefits earned before May 1, 1990 was 2 percent of gross remuneration for each year of service, while the accrual rate of benefits earned after May 1, 1990 is 2.2 percent for the first 25 years of service and 1.8 percent for the next 10 years of service. The pensions of participants hired before May 1, 1990 are based on a prorated combination of the old and new accrual rates, using the time period of service before and after May 1, 1990.

Participants between the ages of 50 and 55 may retire with a reduced pension if their age and years of service total at least 75. Participants aged 55 and older may retire with an unreduced pension if the sum of their age and years of service equals 85 or more.

Cost of Living Adjustment

Whenever the cost of living increases during a financial year, pensions shall be augmented by a pension supplement that, expressed in percentage terms, shall be equal to the increase in the cost of living for the financial year of the country of permanent residence. If the cost of living increase for a financial year exceeds 3 percent, the Employer has the right, for good cause, to reduce prospectively the additional supplement to not less than 3 percent. Deferred pensions become subject to cost of living adjustments when the sum of a former participant's age and years of service is at least 50.

Withdrawal Benefit

Upon withdrawal from the Plan, a participant with at least three years of eligible service may elect to receive either a withdrawal benefit or a deferred pension to commence after the participant has reached the age of 55 or age 50 if age and years of service add to at least 75. The withdrawal benefit is a percentage of the participant's highest average gross remuneration.

Commutation

A pensioner entitled to receive a normal, early retirement, or deferred pension may elect to commute up to one-third of his or her pension, and receive a lump-sum amount at retirement in lieu of the amount of pension commuted. A participant entitled to receive a disability pension may elect to commute one-third of the early retirement pension that would otherwise have been applicable.

Disability Pensions, Death Benefits, and Survivor Benefits

The Plan also provides for disability pensions, death benefits, and benefits to surviving spouses and children of deceased participants.

Currency of Pension Payments

A participant may elect to have his or her pension paid in the currency of the country in which he or she has established permanent residence or in a combination of two currencies—the U.S. dollar and the currency of the country in which the participant is a permanent resident.

Contributions
Participants

As a condition of employment, regular staff members are required to participate in, and to contribute to, the Plan. The contribution rate is presently 7 percent of the participant's gross remuneration. Certain other categories of staff members may elect to participate in the Plan.

Employer

The Employer meets certain administrative costs of the Plan, such as the actuary's fees, and contributes any additional amount not provided by the contribution of participants to pay costs and expenses of the Plan not otherwise covered. In financial year 1998, the administrative costs met by the Employer were approximately $0.09 million ($0.12 million in 1997).

Plan Termination

In the event of the termination of the Plan by the Employer, the assets of the Plan shall be used to satisfy all liabilities to participants, retired participants and their beneficiaries, and all other liabilities of the Plan. Any remaining balance of the assets shall be returned to the Employer.

1. Accounting Practices

The financial statements of the Plan are prepared on the accrual basis; accordingly, income is recognized as it is earned, and expenses are recorded as they are incurred.

Accumulated Plan Benefits

The actuarial value of vested benefits is presented for two categories. For retired participants, the amount presented equals the present value of the benefits expected to be paid over the future lifetime of the pensioner and, if applicable, the surviving spouse of the pensioner. For active participants, the amount presented equals the present value of the deferred pension earned to the valuation date for a participant, or, if greater, the value of the withdrawal benefit for that participant, summed over all participants. For the purpose of determining the actuarial value of the vested benefits at the end of the Plan year, it is assumed that the Plan will continue to exist and that salaries will continue to rise, but that participants will not earn pension benefits beyond the date of the calculation.

The amount of nonvested benefits represents the total of the withdrawal benefits of all participants with less than three years of eligible service together with the estimated effect of projected salary increases on benefits expected to be paid.

In contrast to the actuarial valuation for funding purposes, the actuarial valuation used for the financial statements represents the portion of the benefit obligation that had been accumulated by April 30, 1998. It reflects only the service to that date and does not take into account the fact that the value of accumulated benefits, which are the Plan's liabilities, is expected to increase each year. Nor does it take into account the fact that the market value of investments may fluctuate from year to year, which is significant because the Employer's liability is the excess of the present value of accumulated benefits over the value of the assets. Accordingly, the financial statements do not measure the amount that the Employer will be required to fund in the future.

Valuation of Investments

Investments are recorded at market value. For investments in securities listed on stock exchanges, market value is the last reported market sales price on the last business day of the accounting period. For over-the-counter securities, market value is the bid price on the last business day of the accounting period. For investments in real estate, market value is the last reported appraised value. Derivatives are valued at fair value, which is equivalent to the unrealized gain or loss.

Trading Instruments

The net gain in the market value of investments represents the gains and losses realized during the accounting period from the sale of investments, the unrealized appreciation and depreciation of the market value of investments, and, for investments denominated in currencies other than the U.S. dollar, valuation differences arising from exchange rate changes of other currencies against the dollar.

Risk-Management Instruments

The net fair value of forward contracts, futures contracts, swaps, and options is included in the net assets available for Plan benefits, and the changes in value of such contracts are recognized currently in the financial statements. For swap derivatives, options, and forward and futures contracts, the contract or notional amounts do not represent exposure to credit loss. The potential credit loss on these instruments, if any, approximates the unrealized gain on the open contract.

2. *Actuarial Valuation and Funding Policy*

Under the actuarial valuation used for funding purposes, it is assumed that the Plan will continue to exist and that active participants will continue to earn pension benefits beyond the date of the valuation until the date of withdrawal, disability, death, or retirement, but that no new participant will join the Plan (the "closed method").

Funding by the Employer is based on a valuation method, known as the "aggregate cost method," that expresses liabilities and contribution requirements as single consolidated figures that include provision for experience gains and losses and cost of living increases. Required Employer contributions are expressed as a percentage to be applied to the gross remuneration of participants and are based on the valuation completed 12 months previously. For the financial year that began on May 1, 1995, this rate was 14.25 percent and was 10.56 percent for the year that began on May 1, 1996. The rate for the year beginning May 1, 1997 for the Employer has been set at 5 percent of pensionable gross remuneration. Of this amount, 0.05 percent represents a current contribution (equal to $0.15 million) and 4.95 percent represents a deferred contribution (equal to $14.7 million). The deferred contribution represents the Employer's prepayment of future contributions.

The actuarial assumptions used in the valuation to determine the Employer's contributions include: (1) life expectancy based on the 1984 and 1982 United Nations mortality tables for men and women, respectively; (2) withdrawal or retirement of a certain percentage of staff at each age, differentiated by gender; (3) an average rate of return on investments of 8.5 percent a year; (4) a discount rate of 8.5 percent; (5) an average inflation rate of 5 percent a year; (6) salary increase percentages that vary with age; and (7) valuation of assets using a five-year moving-average method.

The results of the April 30, 1997 and 1996 valuations were:

	1997	1996
	In millions of U.S. dollars	
Present value of benefits payable	2,699	2,540
Less: Assets for valuation purposes	2,580	2,310
Required future funding	119	230
Less: Present value of prospective contributions from participants (7 percent of gross remuneration)	211	203
Present value of future funding required from the Employer	(92)	27

3. *Investments*

In accordance with its investment policy, the Plan invests in equity securities, debt securities, short-term investments, real estate investments, and other financial instruments for risk management including futures, forward currency contracts, options, and swaps.

A summary of the Plan's investments, valued at market value or fair value, is as follows:

	1998	1997
	In millions of U.S. dollars	
Equity securities	2,181	1,726
Debt securities	463	453
Real estate	259	251
Short-term investments	172	183
	3,075	2,613

In addition to the above investments, the Plan holds investments in derivatives, which are aimed at optimizing investment positions, given levels of market, credit, counterparty, and foreign currency risk. These derivative investments are recorded at fair value.

At April 30, 1998 and 1997, the notional value of the Plan's risk management investments was as follows:

	1998	1997
	In millions of U.S. dollars	
Futures		
Long positions	116	156
Short positions	25	69
Forwards		
Purchases	831	604
Sales	831	604
Swaps	2	2

Futures Contracts

Futures contracts are commitments to either purchase or sell a financial instrument at a future date for a specified price and may be settled in cash or through delivery of the underlying financial instrument. The credit risk of futures contracts is limited because of daily cash settlement of the net change in the value of open contracts; therefore, there were no unrealized gains or losses at April 30, 1998 or 1997.

The Plan enters into financial futures contracts to protect the Plan against market price risks and to take investment positions. Contracts generally have terms of less than one year.

Forward Contracts

Forward contracts are similar in character to futures contracts. However, they have a greater degree of credit risk, depending on the counterparties involved, because daily cash settlements are not required. To manage this exposure, the Plan deals with counterparties of good credit standing and enters into master netting agreements whenever possible.

The Plan's principal objective in entering into forward foreign currency exchange contracts is to manage foreign currency fluctuations relative to investments in its international portfolio. These contracts generally have terms of no more than three months. At April 30, 1998, the unrealized gain totaled $1.7 million ($1.8 million unrealized loss at April 30, 1997).

Options

Options can be either exchange traded or directly negotiated. They provide a right to buy or sell a security or an agreed amount of currency at a specified rate within a stated period. These contracts generally have terms of less than one year. At April 30, 1998, there were no options outstanding. (At April 30, 1997 the cost of these options totaled $0.3 million and the unrealized loss totaled $0.2 million.)

Swaps

Equity swaps are commitments to exchange the returns arising from one equity portfolio with the returns of another equity portfolio for a specified time period on a notional amount invested. Credit risk on an equity swap contract varies according to the terms of the agreement and the counterparties involved, which are only those of good credit standing.

The Plan's principal objective in entering into equity swap agreements is to facilitate a market-neutral strategy in the United Kingdom. At April 30, 1998, the unrealized loss totaled $1.6 million ($0.6 million at April 30, 1997).

Report of the External Audit Committee
Supplemental Retirement Benefit Plan

Washington, D.C.
June 18, 1998

Authority and Scope of Audit

In accordance with Section 20(b) of the By-Laws of the International Monetary Fund, we have audited the financial statements of the Supplemental Retirement Benefit Plan for the year ended April 30, 1998.

Our audit was conducted in accordance with generally accepted auditing standards and included reviews of the accounting and internal control systems and tests of the accounting records. We evaluated the extent and results of the work of the outside accounting firm as well as that of the Office of Internal Audit and Inspection and also used other audit procedures as deemed necessary.

Audit Opinion

In our opinion, the financial statements of the Supplemental Retirement Benefit Plan have been prepared in accordance with generally accepted accounting principles applied on a basis consistent with that of the preceding year and give a true and fair view of the financial status of the Supplemental Retirement Benefit Plan as at April 30, 1998 and of the changes in financial status for the year then ended.

EXTERNAL AUDIT COMMITTEE:

/s/ Amaffe Roger Ako, Chairman (Côte d'Ivoire)

/s/ José Nicolás Agudin (Argentina)

/s/ Stephen Park (United Kingdom)

Supplemental Retirement Benefit Plan

Statements of Accumulated Plan Benefits and Assets Available for Benefits as at April 30, 1998 and 1997

(In thousands of U.S. dollars)
(Note 1)

	1998	1997
Accumulated Plan Benefits		
Actuarial present value of accumulated Plan benefits		
Vested benefits	23,300	20,800
Nonvested benefits	100	100
Total actuarial present value of accumulated Plan benefits	23,400	20,900
Assets Available for Benefits		
Cash at bank	195	72
Contributions receivable	7	4
Total assets	202	76
Liabilities		
Deferred contributions (Note 2)	56	—
Net assets available for benefits	146	76
Excess of actuarial present value of accumulated Plan benefits over assets available for benefits	23,254	20,824

The accompanying notes are an integral part of the financial statements.

/s/ David Williams
Treasurer

/s/ M. Camdessus
Managing Director

Supplemental Retirement Benefit Plan

Statements of Changes in Accumulated Plan Benefits for the Years Ended April 30, 1998 and 1997

(In thousands of U.S. dollars)
(Note 1)

	1998	1997
Actuarial present value of accumulated		
Plan benefits, beginning of the year	20,900	16,000
Increase (decrease) during the period attributable to		
Benefits accumulated	2,300	4,832
Interest accrued	1,700	1,300
Benefits paid	(1,500)	(1,232)
Net increase	2,500	4,900
Actuarial present value of accumulated		
Plan benefits, end of the year	23,400	20,900

The accompanying notes are an integral part of the financial statements.

Supplemental Retirement Benefit Plan

Statements of Changes
in Assets Available for Benefits
for the Years Ended April 30, 1998 and 1997

(In thousands of U.S. dollars)
(Note 1)

	1998	1997
Investment Income		
Interest	5	—
	5	—
Contributions (Note 2)		
International Monetary Fund	1,513	1,277
Participants	75	30
Net transfers to retirement plans of other international organizations	(8)	—
	1,580	1,307
Total additions	1,585	1,307
Benefits		
Pension	1,515	1,232
Total payments	1,515	1,232
Net additions	70	75
Net Assets Available for Benefits		
Beginning of the year	76	1
End of the year	146	76

The accompanying notes are an integral part of the financial statements.

Supplemental Retirement Benefit Plan

Notes to the Financial Statements
as at April 30, 1998 and 1997

Description of the Plan

General

The Supplemental Retirement Benefit Plan ("the SRBP") is a defined-benefit pension plan covering all participants of the Staff Retirement Plan of the International Monetary Fund ("the Employer") and operates as an adjunct to that Plan. All assets and income of the SRBP are the property of the Employer and are held and administered by it separately from all its other property and assets and are to be used solely for the benefit of participants and retired participants and their beneficiaries.

Benefits

The Staff Retirement Plan has adopted limits to pensions payable from that Plan. The SRBP provides for the payment of any benefit that would otherwise have been payable if these limits had not been adopted.

In financial year 1998, 56 pensioners received benefits from the SRBP (52 in financial year 1997).

Contributions

Before retirement, the Employer partially prefunds the SRBP for non-U.S. citizens who plan to retire in the United States, so that the taxable income of the participant is approximately equal to, but not more than, such income that would have accrued if the entire benefit had been payable from any of the prefunded assets of the Staff Retirement Plan. The prefunded amounts are used to pay any of the benefits payable, whether for U.S. or non-U.S. staff. Should the assets of the SRBP be exhausted, benefits will be paid from current contributions by the Employer.

SRBP Termination

In the event of the termination of the SRBP by the Employer, the assets of the SRBP shall be used to satisfy all liabilities to participants, retired participants and their beneficiaries, and all other liabilities of the SRBP.

1. Accounting Practices

Accumulated SRBP Benefits

The actuarial present value of accumulated SRBP benefits is stated as at the date of the most recent actuarial valuation, which was April 30, 1998. The actuarial value of benefits is presented for two categories. The vested benefits relate to retired participants, and the amount presented equals the present value of the benefits expected to be paid over the future lifetime of the pensioner and, if applicable, of the surviving spouse of the pensioner.

The nonvested benefits relate to active participants, and the amount presented equals the present value of the supplemental deferred pension earned to the valuation date for a participant, taking into account the estimated effect of projected salary increases. For the purpose of determining the actuarial value of the benefits at the end of the period, it is assumed that the SRBP will continue to exist, but that participants will not accumulate further contributory service beyond the date of the calculation.

Income Recognition

The SRBP maintains its accounts on the accrual basis; accordingly, income is recognized as it is earned, and expenses are recorded as they are incurred.

2. Actuarial Valuation and Funding Policy

Under the actuarial valuation used for funding purposes, it is assumed that the Plan will continue to exist and that active participants will continue to earn pension benefits beyond the date of the valuation until the date of withdrawal, disability, death, or retirement, but that no new participant will join the Plan (the "closed method").

Funding by the Employer is based on a valuation method, known as the "aggregate cost method," that expresses liabilities and contribution requirements as single consolidated figures that include provision for experience gains and losses and cost of living increases. Required Employer contributions are expressed as a percentage to be applied to the gross remuneration of participants and are based on the valuation completed 12 months previously. For the financial year that began on May 1, 1995, this rate was 14.25 percent and was 10.56 percent for the year that began on May 1, 1996. The rate for the year beginning May 1, 1997 for the Employer has been set at 5 percent of pensionable gross remuneration. Of this amount, 0.05 percent represents a current contribution and 4.95 percent represents a deferred contribution (equal to $0.06 million). The deferred contribution represents the Employer's prepayment of future contributions.

The actuarial assumptions used in the valuation to determine the Employer's contributions include: (1) life expectancy based on the 1984 and 1982 United Nations mortality tables for men and women, respectively; (2) withdrawal or retirement of a certain percentage of staff at each age, differentiated by gender; (3) an average rate of return on investments of 8.5 percent a year; (4) a discount rate of 8.5 percent; (5) an average inflation rate of 5 percent a year; (6) salary increase percentages that vary with age; and (7) valuation of assets using a five-year moving-average method.